USING THE MMPI
WITH ADOLESCENTS

PERSONALITY ASSESSMENT

A series of volumes edited by
Charles D. Spielberger and James N. Butcher

USING THE MMPI
WITH ADOLESCENTS

Robert P. Archer
Eastern Virginia Medical School

LEA LAWRENCE ERLBAUM ASSOCIATES, PUBLISHERS
1987   Hillsdale, New Jersey   London

Lawrence Erlbaum Associates, Inc., Publishers
365 Broadway
Hillsdale, New Jersey 07642

Cover design by Beth-Ann Schmalz

Library of Congress Cataloging-in-Publication Data

Archer, Robert P.
  Using the MMPI with adolescents.

  (Personality assessmeent)
  Bibliography: p.
  Includes index.
  1. Minnesota Multiphasic Personality Inventory.
2. Adolescent psychology.   I. Title.   II. Series.
[DNLM: 1. MMPI. WM 145 A672u]
BF698.8.M5A73   155.5   86-30933
ISBN 0-89859-939-3

Printed in the United States of America
10   9   8   7   6   5   4   3   2   1

To Charles Spielberger and Robert Vidaver

The largest part of helping
is to give courage

—IRISH PROVERB

CONTENTS

PREFACE

The purpose of this volume is to provide an overview of the literature and to offer practical recommendations on the use of the MMPI with adolescent respondents. The motivations for undertaking this book stem from my MMPI assessment experiences in adolescent clinical settings over the past 10 years. For much of this period, I utilized the MMPI with adolescents but maintained many reservations concerning my assessment techniques. I often felt I had insufficient information to understand the implications of norm conversions or to most effectively employ particular interpretation strategies. Many assessment questions occurred to me, for which I often had inadequate answers. For example, how were the adolescent norms developed? What differences occurred when one used adolescent versus adult norms in profiling adolescent response patterns? Should one interpret adolescent responses using information from adult clinical corrrelate sources such as Lachar (1974) and Graham (1977), or from the actuarial data derived from adolescents by Marks, Seeman, and Haller (1974)? I was implicitly convinced that "somewhere" in the MMPI literature there were undoubtedly collections of solid empirical studies with well-reasoned suggestions to guide my assessment procedures, but it was clear that I had not successfully located these sources of information. Failing in this regard, I proceeded as those around me appeared to proceed, i.e., based on the subjective opinions and clinical lore that have developed concerning the use of the MMPI with adolescents. Although I was uncomfortably aware that such an approach stood in marked contrast to the very reason I was attracted to the MMPI, i.e., that the MMPI was an empirically based assessment instrument, I promised myself that I would eventually "do my homework" by carefully reviewing the literature on the use of the MMPI with adolescents. Such a review, I felt sure, would allow me to base my adolescent MMPI assessment practices on hard "scientific" data.

I finally began a comprehensive review of this literature in 1980, starting with the early works by Hathaway and Monachesi and proceeding to the more recent contributions of individuals including Phil Marks and David Lachar. The results of this literature review led me to the startling conclusion that my implicit assumptions regarding the nature of this research area had been in error. While individual contributions were often brilliant, the overall literature did not directly lead to a "road map" upon which to base assessment procedures with adolescents. In fact, the literature was often confusing and unclear, many basic issues were not addressed, and clear research summaries with concise recommendations concerning assessment practices were largely nonexistent. These observations directly led to my efforts over the past several years to create a source of information that would assist both the researcher and clinician.

The objective of this volume is to provide a clear and comprehensive review of the literature in the area of adolescents and the MMPI based on the research studies that have occurred over the past 40 years. It is written to provide the reader with an appreciation and understanding of the research that has occurred, including the outstanding contributions of Hathaway and Monachesi (1963), and Marks et al. (1974), as well as to highlight areas in which crucial research has essentially *not* occurred, such as systematic and ongoing investigations of the accuracy of clinical descriptive statements for adolescents based on adolescent and adult correlate data. The volume also attempts to provide a developmental perspective through which to understand adolescent response patterns as well as a clear discussion of the empirical implications of using adult and adolescent norm conversions for adolescent respondents. A series of direct, concrete recommendations are offered for the scoring and interpretation of adolescent response patterns, along with the empirical foundations on which these suggestions are based. Finally, this book provides a description of current norm development projects and future research directions. In summary, this text is written for those individuals who, like the author, want to approach the use of the MMPI with adolescent respondents based on a comprehensive understanding of the decades of clinical research that has been undertaken in this area. Clearly, the application of MMPI assessment procedures with adolescents will always involve some degree of the clinician's "art," but the Scientist-Practitioner model also implies that this clinical activity be based on sound scientific underpinnings.

This volume also represents the summation of a series of research projects centered on gaining a better understanding of the characteristics of the MMPI with adolescents. This work was begun at the Medical University of South Carolina where the author had the opportunity and the privilege to learn about adolescent psychiatry under the direction of Dr. George Orvin, and to gain an appreciation for MMPI research through the guidance of Dr. Patricia Sutker. The more recent work in this area has been done at Eastern Virginia Medical School and made possible through the support and encouragement of Dr. Robert Vidaver, Chair of the Department of Psychiatry and Behavioral Sciences, and funded, in part, through grants from the Charles G. Brown Trust and Norfolk Foundation.

The data involved in this series of research projects have included roughly 1,000 adolescents and several hundred parents of these teenagers, predominantly in clinical treatment settings in inpatient and outpatient programs. It has both amazed and encouraged us that so many adolescents and their families, intensely involved in their own psychological distress and pain, were willing to voluntarily donate time and effort to aid us in these investigations. A standard part of our consent forms has contained the following clause: "I understand that no benefit can be guaranteed or assured from my child's participation in this study except for the satisfaction of knowing that subjects and their families are potentially helping adolescents who may experience psychiatric problems in the future." Apparently, the vast majority of adolescents and their parents whom we have contacted have found the prospect of helping others sufficient to generously give of their time despite their own, often very serious, life problems. We would be remiss if we did not explicitly acknowledge the importance of their contributions to this work.

Finally, the author would like to mention several individuals who are centrally responsible for the creation of this volume. Mr. Raymont A. Gordon, research associate at Eastern Virginia Medical School, has invested countless hours of dedicated effort into all of the projects involving the MMPI and adolescents, and his intelligence, energies, and outstanding level of commitment have very tangibly facilitated these studies. Additionally, I would like to express my appreciation to Dr. Charles D. Spielberger, Professor of Psychology at the University of South Florida, for his continuing encouragement and guidance. The concepts and ideas for this volume were developed in conversations with Dr. Spielberger at the Twentieth Annual MMPI Symposium in Hawaii, and through his continued help and guidance I have been able to translate these concepts into a tangible product. I would also like to thank Dr. Dennis Jones, Director of Adolescent Inpatient Services at Coliseum Hospital in Macon, Georgia; Dr. Linda Archer, Department of Family and Community Medicine, Eastern Virginia Medical School; and Mr. Phillip Murphy, Department of Psychology, Texas Tech University, for their invaluable advice and assistance in the creation of this volume. They have read drafts of this manuscript with patience, encouragement, and kindness, and their feedback and suggestions have always been appreciated and have served to improve the overall quality of the work. I would also like to thank Ms. Janis Stewart for her long months of work in typing and revising this manuscript.

Dr. Irving Gottesman and his colleagues, and Dr. Robert Colligan and his associates have greatly assisted this work by providing very important appendices. Their willingness to share the benefits of their labors in this manner has enhanced the comprehensiveness of this volume.

Finally, I would like to thank Jack Graham and Roger Greene for their support and assistance. Dr. Graham offered very useful advice and counsel on this project across various stages of development. Dr. Greene has spent many hours of his time reviewing this manuscript in detail and greatly improving the presentation and discussion of numerous aspects of this work. I have come to sincerely appreciate Dr. Greene's expertise and his generosity.

ACKNOWLEDGMENTS

The author wishes to thank the organizations and individuals listed below for permission to use materials in this volume:

Archives of the Diseases in Childhood for permission to reproduce the 1965 selection from J. M. Tanner, R. H. Whitehouse, and M. Takaiski appearing in Chapter 1.

The American Psychological Association for permission to reproduce the 1976 selection from the Journal of Personality and Social Psychology by R. H. Dworkin, B. W. Burke, B. A. Maher, and I. I. Gottesman appearing in Chapter 3.

Blackwell Scientific Publications for permission to reproduce the 1962 selections from J. M. Tanner appearing in Chapter 1.

Clinical Psychology Review for permission to reproduce the 1984 selections by R. P. Archer appearing in Chapter 2.

Irving I. Gottesman for permission to reproduce the authored selections by I. I. Gottesman, D. R. Hanson, P. E. Briggs, and T. A. Kroeker appearing in Appendix C.

John Wiley & Sons Inc. for permission to reproduce the 1978 selections by J. E. Exner appearing in Chapter 1.

The Journal of Abnormal Child Psychology for permission to reproduce the 1986 selections by R. P. Archer, A. L. Stolberg, R. A. Gordon, and W. R. Goldman appearing in Chapters 3 and 7.

The Journal of Clinical Psychology for their permission to reproduce the 1979 selections by R. P. Archer, J. L. White, and G. H. Orvin appearing in Chapter 2.

The Journal of Personality Assessment for permission to reproduce the 1985 selection by R. P. Archer, J. D. Ball, and J. A. Hunter appearing in Chapter 3.

The Mayo Foundation for permission to reproduce the authored selections by R. C. Colligan and K. P. Offord appearing in Chapter 8 and Appendix B.

Philip A. Marks for his permission to reproduce the 1974 selections by P. A. Marks, W. Seeman, and D. L. Haller, appearing in Appendix A.

Williams & Wilkins Co. for permission to reproduce the 1974 selection by P. A. Marks, W. Seeman, and D. L. Haller, appearing in Chapter 2 and Appendix A.

The University of Minnesota Press for permission to reproduce the selections from the following:

Adolescent Personality and Behavior, 1963 by S. R. Hathaway and E. D. Monachesi appearing in Chapter 5.

An MMPI Handbook: Vol. 1, 1966, 1972, by W. G. Dahlstrom, G. S. Welsh, and L. E. Dahlstrom appearing in Appendices A and D.

FOREWORD

The pioneering work of Hathaway and Monachesi nearly a quarter-century ago provides the foundation for all subsequent research and clinical applications of the MMPI with adolescents. The book by Marks et al. on the actuarial use of the MMPI with adolescents also provides normative and codetype information of great value for researchers and clinicians, but this contribution was published more than a decade ago.

Over the past 25 years, numerous studies have been published on the use of the MMPI with adolescents, but as yet relatively little attention has been directed toward integrating the findings from an expanding research literature, and even less effort to drawing meaningful implications for clinical practice. This volume provides a comprehensive review of research findings on the use of the MMPI in the assessment of adolescent personality. It is designed as a primary resource for researchers and as an interpretive manual for clinicians who work with adolescent populations.

The book contains practical guidelines which clinicians will find indispensable in developing interpretive narratives for commonly occurring adolescent codetypes, and cogent examples of adolescent profiles produced under various response sets. The detailed descriptions of clinical codetype correlates for adolescents provide an authoritative basis for strategies of clinical interpretation. Both researchers and clinicians will find the discussion of profile validity and response set issues especially enlightening.

In reviewing the research literature, Dr. Archer creatively links the assessment of adolescent personality to genetic and environmental theories of childhood and human development. He also discusses up-to-the-minute information derived from recent normative research findings, and describes characteristic responses that are given in normal and clinical settings. In essence, this volume bridges the gap between historical developments, the current research literature, and clinical applications of the MMPI with adolescent clients.

In the preparation of this volume, Dr. Archer draws on more than a decade of MMPI assessment experience with adolescents in clinical and research settings. He has also conducted extensive reviews of the research literature, published a number of studies of the MMPI characteristics of adolescents and their families, and examined the salient clinical and research issues in the use of the MMPI with adolescents. On the basis of his research findings and clinical experience, and his critical evaluation of the major issues, he provides specific and detailed recommendations for the interpretation of adolescent MMPI response patterns. Most important, he documents the empirical foundations on which these recommendations are based.

As an editor of the LEA Monograph Series on Personality Assessment, I consider this volume an important milestone in the use of the MMPI in research and clinical practice. The book provides essential information for researchers who work in this important and expanding field and will serve to define the relevant issues for future investigators. It will also be of immediate and lasting value to clinicians who are called upon to evaluate adolescents for diagnosis, forensic decisions, and treatment planning. Along with the works of Hathaway and Monachesi, and Marks et al., it will assume a valued position in the libraries of clinical practitioners who use the MMPI with adolescents.

Charles D. Spielberger

1

INTRODUCTION:
A BRIEF OVERVIEW OF
ADOLESCENT DEVELOPMENT

To discuss meaningfully the use of the MMPI with adolescents it is beneficial to first briefly review our understanding of adolescence as a developmental period. As we shall see, much of the confusion and controversy
surrounding the use of the MMPI with adolescent respondents has resulted from inadequate or insufficient understanding of the unique characteristics of adolescent development. Indeed, many individuals have attempted to score and interpret adolescent responses in a manner identical
to procedures used with adults. Although there are a number of areas in
which adolescent response patterns may be seen as equivalent to adult
features on the MMPI, there are also a number of crucial areas in which
the use of adult-based practices or procedures will result in substantial interpretive errors for adolescents. Thus, the purpose of this chapter is to
provide an overall perspective on adolescent development including
both the areas of controversy and the areas of consistency.

Stone and Church (1957b) discussed the concept of adolescence as a
"cultural invention," which may be defined within the context of societal
responses and expectations regarding adolescent development. They
note that a variety of customs, norms, and laws have come to define and
describe the period of adolescence with wide cultural variations, often
with very marked areas of ambiguity. In regard to this point, Stone and
Church have stated, "In sum, adult ambiguity about the adolescent rein-
forces his own ambiguity about himself" (p. 8). Indeed, this ambiguity
can be seen in reference to controversy regarding such basic issues as the
age periods implied in the concept of adolescence (Kimmel & Weiner,
1985). Although there are many areas of ambiguity and confusion regarding adolescent development, there does appear to be a consensus regarding at least three important developmental areas that may occur relatively

1

independently during adolescence and which serve to define some of the basic developmental tasks during this period. Each of these three developmental areas is discussed below.

CHANGES AND CHALLENGES IN ADOLESCENCE

First, it is clear that fundamental physical changes occur during adolescence in terms of endocrinological, biochemical, and physiological processes. For example, Stone and Church (1957a) note that the adolescent may be expected to increase 25% in height and 100% in weight during adolescence. Additionally, there is a marked increase in pituitary activity leading to increased production of hormones by the thyroid, adrenal, and other glands that are centrally involved in sexual maturation. Often the clearer signs of adolescent development are physical changes associated with the onset of puberty. These physical changes are typically manifested in the growth of pubic hair, the growth of the testes and penis in boys, and the first menstruation and breast development in girls. The adolescent growth spurt typically begins approximately two to three years earlier for females than for males, although there are very wide individual variations in biological growth and sexual maturation for both sexes. Figures 1.1 and 1.2 show the velocity of growth in height and degrees of pubertal development for boys and girls at given ages (sources: J. M. Tanner, R. H. Whitehouse, & M. Takaishi, 1965, and J. M. Tanner, 1962, respectively, as reproduced in Kimmel & Weiner, 1985). The table of pubertal development demonstrates both the earlier maturation of females in relation to males and the wide differences in pubertal development within sexes at identical chronological ages.

Second, adolescence can be saliently defined in terms of changes in cognitive processes. The work of Piaget and his colleagues offers us an approach for understanding these cognitive changes in relation to age, physiological development, and environment. Specifically, Piaget (1969) noted that during early adolescence the youngster typically makes the transition from the stage of Concrete Operations to the Formal Operations stage, the latter characterized by the capacity to manipulate ideas and concepts. Piaget (1969) stated, "In a word, the adolescent is an individual who is capable of building and understanding ideas or abstract theories and concepts. The child does not build theories" (p. 105). Thus, the adolescent is capable of discerning the real from the ideal and of becoming passionately engaged by abstract concepts and notions. They begin to think of their worlds in new ways, including the ability to "think about thinking."

Finally, a host of psychological and emotional tasks including the processes of individualization and the formation of ego identity are accomplished during adolescence. Peter Blos (1967) discussed individualization

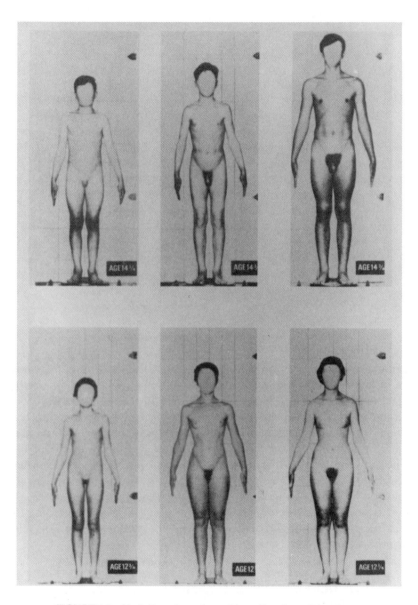

FIGURE 1.1   Variations in male and female pubertal development.

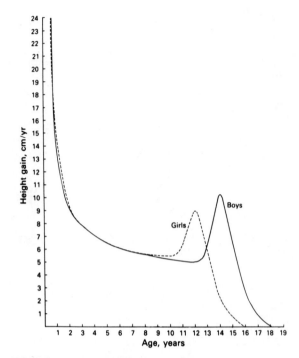

FIGURE 1.2   Velocity of growth in height at various ages.

during adolescence as a process involved with the development of relative independence from family relationships, the weakening of infantile object ties, and an increased capacity to assume a functional role as a member of adult society. Blos defined and described this task as similar to the more primitive struggle for individualization and the attainment of object constancy that occurs toward the end of the third year of life. Erikson (1956) described in detail the concept of the formation of ego identity during adolescence as the assembly of converging identity elements that occurs at the end of childhood, achieved through a process of "normative crises." Ego identity was viewed by Erikson as including the conscious sense of individual identity as well as unconscious strivings for a continuity of personal character.

IMPACT OF DEVELOPMENTAL TASKS
ON ADJUSTMENT

An interesting source of support for the impact of these forces on the development of the individual during early adolescence is provided in volume 2 of John Exner's series, *The Rorschach: A Comprehensive System*. In this volume (1978), Exner presents the research data supporting the interpretation of fundamental Rorschach indices in the Comprehensive System, including data related to the *EA:ep* relationship. Within the Comprehensive System, *EA* (Experience Actual) represents the sum of resources available to the individual to form and direct behaviors. Concretely, *EA* represents the summation of human movement responses (*M*) and color responses (*C, CF,* and *FC* in a weighted formula) produced by the subject in response to the stimulus plates. In contrast, *ep* (Experience Potential) represents a summation of factors operating on the individual, i.e., resources not under the control of the individual, and involves the summation of the shading features (sum *C*), animal movement responses (*FM*), and inanimate movement responses (*m*). The *EA:ep* relationship conceptually represents the individual's relative balance of resources available to form and direct his behavior versus the degree to which forces are impacting upon him in a manner that is unorganized. The larger, therefore, the sum of *EA* in relationship to *ep*, the greater the ability of that individual to form and direct his behavior in a competent, controlled, and nonimpulsive manner.

In Figure 1.3, Exner (1978) has provided data on the growth curve for the *EA:ep* relationship in reference to normative data derived from three normative samples of children: nonpatients; children diagnosed as evi-

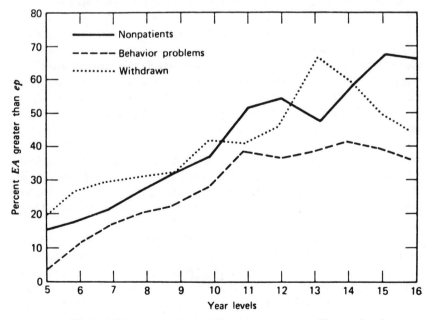

Percent *EA* greater than *ep* for three groups at 12 year levels.

FIGURE 1.3 Percent *EA* greater than *ep* for three groups at 12 year levels.

dencing behavioral problems, and children displaying behavioral problems labeled "withdrawn."

Of particular interest to our discussion of adolescent development is the growth curve found for the nonpatient sample. Table 3 clearly displays a continuing increase in the percentage of children who display an *EA* value that is greater than *ep*, with one notable exception. At age 13, or at the initiation of adolescence, there is a marked regression in the growth curve for this normal group. By age 14, however, a steady increase is resumed in the percentage of adolescents who demonstrate internal, organized resources that exceed the degree of unorganized factors impacting upon them. These data clearly imply that during the course of normal development some factor or set of factors are typically occurring that significantly impact the behavioral control and stress tolerance manifested by children during their early adolescent period. For children who will resume a normal course of development, a psychological "adjustment" appears to occur that allows for the resumption of growth and maturity. For children who develop behavioral problems or are labeled withdrawn, a leveling off or reduction in stress tolerance, impulse control, and the ability to competently organize and direct behaviors appears to occur during the remainder of adolescence. Inspection of normative data for these reference groups would indicate that the leveling off that occurs for the behavior problem group, and the decrease that occurs for the withdrawn group, are the results of significant increases during the adolescent years in the mean number of shading and achromatic responses, indices of painful affective processes. In contrast, for the normal group the number of shading and achromatic responses remains relatively constant during adolescence, but there is a steady increase in the number of human movement and color responses, indices of cognitive and emotional resources available to the individual.

Overall, the data presented by Exner strongly indicate that highly significant factors are occurring in the child's development during the early adolescent period that have marked implications for later development. We have discussed at least three factors that may be responsible for this affect, i.e., fundamental physical and cognitive changes, combined with unique psychological tasks imposed by adolescence.

Given a consensus regarding at least three areas of adolescent development (i.e., physical, cognitive, and psychological), a fundamental question remains concerning the typical processes through which the developmental tasks of adolescence are mastered. How did the "normal" children in Exner's study adjust to these forces and challenges? At the risk of oversimplification, it is suggested that there have been two contrasting views of adolescent development, one stemming from theoretical writings and case study observations and the other developed from more empirically based research investigations and surveys focused on adolescent development. These contrasting views and concepts of adolescent development have affected MMPI practices with adolescents. The most striking of these effects has been seen in relation to conflicts involving appropriate norm conversions with adolescent respondents.

CONTRASTING VIEWS OF ADOLESCENT DEVELOPMENT

The Storm and Stress Model

Historical perspectives on adolescent development have emphasized a "Sturm and Drang" or Storm and Stress model. This view, first expressed by G. Stanley Hall (1904), postulates that adolescence is a period of turbulent development marked by extreme variability in behavioral and emotional functioning. Hall's conception of adolescence has been influential in later theorists' attempts to conceptualize the adolescent developmental process.

Anna Freud (1958) stated that the typical adolescent developmental process was accomplished through a series of emotional upheavals reflected in behavioral disturbances, and that adolescents who did not demonstrate turbulent features of adjustment were at risk for the development of serious psychopathological symptoms in adulthood. Freud's well-known formulation of this view was represented in her statement that "the upholding of a steady equilibrium during the process (of adolescence) is, in itself, abnormal" (p. 275). Clarifying this point, Freud indicated,

> I take it that it is normal for the adolescent to behave for a considerable length of time in an inconsistent and unpredictable manner; to fight his impulses and to accept them; to ward them off successfully and to be overrun by them; to love his parents and hate them; to rebel against them and to be dependent on them; to be deeply ashamed to acknowledge his mother before others and, unexpectedly, to desire heart-to-heart talks with her; to thrive on imitation or identification with others while searching unceasingly for his own identity; to be more idealistic, artistic, generous, unselfish than he would ever be again, but also the opposite—self-centered, egotistic, calculating. Such fluctuations between extreme opposites would be deemed highly abnormal at any other point in life. At this time they may signify no more than that an adult structure of personality takes a long time to emerge, that the ego of the individual in question does not cease to experiment and is in no hurry to close down on possibilities. (p. 276)

Peter Blos (1962) has also taken the position that adolescents often exhibit varying degrees and types of symptomatology that resemble, but do not signify, true emotional illnesses. The psychiatric symptoms presented during adolescence were viewed by Blos as typically ill defined, unstable, and transitory in nature. Blos postulated that a profound reorganization of the emotional life takes place during adolescence, which results in chaotic and poorly controlled attempts at adaptation. Erikson (1956) also suggested that the adolescent's need to achieve psychosocial self-definition frequently results in deviations from normal behavior and development, which he has termed "identity diffusion" or "identity confusion."

James Masterson (1968) postulated that the upsurge of instinctual drives that occurs during the onset of puberty exacerbates any previously unresolved conflicts as well as initiates a variety of new developmental tasks. He perceives adolescent turmoil as an emotional process resulting from the stress of accommodating these internal forces in the presence of a relatively weak ego structure. A similar view has been presented by Sharp (1980), who believes that following the relative quietude of latency, instinctual forces, and developmental issues from prior psychosexual periods reemerge and are reactivated and reexperienced in the adolescent's feelings, thoughts, and behaviors. Incorporating these largely psychoanalytic views of adolescent development, the Group for the Advancement of Psychiatry (1968) stated, "One of the unique characteristics of adolescents . . . is the recurrent alternation of episodes of disturbed behavior with periods of quiescence" (p. 61).

Challenges to the Storm and Stress Model

Over the past two decades, a collection of writers have challenged the idea that storm and stress is an essential or inevitable part of adolescent development. Balswick and Macrides (1975) interpreted the anthropological findings of Margaret Mead (1928, 1930) as offering no support for the notion that adolescent turmoil is a universal characteristic. These authors viewed Mead's data as indicating cultural conditions rather than psychodynamic forces were responsible for the production of conflict during adolescence. Douvan and Adelson (1966) surveyed more than 3,000 adolescents and found little evidence of the maladaptive behaviors or emotional turmoil predicted by the Storm and Stress hypothesis. They reported that, except for infrequent problems in emotional adaptation that appeared to be a continuation of prepubertal disturbances, there was little evidence of significant distress among the majority of their sample.

The work of Bandura (1964) also failed to support the concept of a stormy developmental process during adolescence. His interview data indicated relationships between parents and children became more trusting and relaxed, rather than more conflictual, as youngsters moved from childhood to adolescence. In addition, peer group membership was not found to generate family conflict, nor were peer group values necessarily found to exist in opposition to family values. Bandura concluded that responses to stress during adolescence bore a greater relationship to the individual's past learning and behaviors than to age or developmental period per se.

Offer and Offer (1975) investigated male, suburban adolescents and found that although transient episodes of nondisabling depression and anxiety were common, only 20% of adolescents demonstrated moderate to severe symptomatology. In contrast, 20% of their sample did not appear to experience any significant turmoil during this developmental stage and appeared to be able to cope well with a variety of problems and challenges. The authors suggested that the notion of adolescent rebellion and turbulence appears to be more descriptive of the period of early adolescence when it may be manifested in arguments with parents concerning topics such as choice of music and clothing, and performance of household chores. Other research findings by Coleman (1978), Eme, Maisiak, and Goodale (1979), Looney and Gunderson (1978), Monge (1973), and Offer (1969) have challenged the idea that turmoil is the central characteristic of adolescent development.

Weiner and Del Gaudio (1976) reviewed the empirical literature relative to adolescent development and drew three main conclusions. First, with the exception of fleeting episodes of anxiety or depression, psychological distress that results in psychiatric symptoms is not a normative feature of adolescent development. Second, boundaries between normal and abnormal behaviors during adolescence can be drawn despite difficulties in differential diagnosis among closely related disturbance patterns. Finally, they concluded that it is unlikely that psychological disturbance during adolescence would remit without treatment and argued against the assumption that psychiatric disturbance was transient during this developmental period. The apparent contradiction between "storm and stress" views of adolescence based on clinically derived theoretical models and findings from research-based investigations that have often challenged the notion that turmoil is a typical characteristic of adolescent development has been discussed by Blotcky and Looney (1980) and by Archer (1984).

MMPI IMPLICATIONS

This brief review of adolescent development was presented to serve as a foundation for our discussions of the MMPI as an assessment instrument with adolescents. Our views of adolescents carry many implications for our assessment practices with respondents in this age group. The recognition that adolescence is a period of marked and dramatic physiological, cognitive, and psychological changes leads directly to the expectation that adolescents may interpret and respond to numerous MMPI items in a manner that is significantly different from that of adults. As we discuss more fully in later chapters, this expectation has been supported by empirical studies conducted by Hathaway and Monachesi (e.g., 1963) on the MMPI response patterns of thousands of normal adolescents. In response to the rapid physical changes that occur during this transitional stage, for example, adolescents respond very differently from adults to items such as "I am neither gaining nor losing weight." The vast majority of adult males, for example, endorse this item as true, and a false response for adult men could serve as a marker for serious psychopathology including depression. In contrast, only one out of four teenage boys endorsed this item as true in the Hathaway and Monachesi sample, and endorsements in the false direction for teenagers would not necessarily carry significance in terms of psychiatric symptomatology. Many additional items in the Hathaway and Monachesi investigation produced much higher true endorsement frequencies for adults than for adolescents, including such items as:

My relatives are nearly all in sympathy with me.
I am quite independent from family rules.
I am entirely self-confident.
I never worry about my looks.
It doesn't bother me that I am not better looking.

These differences in item endorsement patterns between adults and adolescents may be meaningfully viewed in reference to the adolescent's struggles with individualization from the family and the task of identity formation, including the development of the physical concept of self. Although these points may appear obvious, salient differences in the perceptions in life experiences of adolescents and adults have frequently been overlooked in research and clinical applications of the MMPI with adolescents.

A second important area with direct implication for MMPI practices with adolescents relates to our views of the typical or normative processes involved in adolescent development. If one assumes a continuous and similar developmental process encompassing both adolescence and adulthood and that the meaning of adolescent symptomatology is best examined against a backdrop of adult expectations and behaviors, then the use of adult norms with adolescent respondents could follow as a logical and rational practice. Further, this practice would also be reinforced by the perception that symptomatology expressed during adolescence is relatively permanent in nature rather than transient or diffuse in character. Arguing for marked consistency across these developmental stages, for example, Kimmel and Weiner (1985) have stated that "people remain basically the same in how they think, handle interpersonal relationships, and are perceived by others (across adolescence and adulthood). For better or worse, adults tend to display many of the same general personality characteristics and the same relative level of adjustment they did as adolescents" (p. 449). In contrast, the assumption that adolescence is a developmental stage with unique features during which a high base rate of aberrant and transient behaviors is likely to occur supports the use of adolescent or age-appropriate norms in describing and identifying adolescent MMPI features. From this perspective, use of adolescent norms would underscore the belief that pathological signs and syndromes might be identified and interpreted differently in adolescent populations in contrast to adult expectations. Ultimately, our views of adolescent development and our attempts to define normal and abnormal behaviors for adolescents are directly involved in the decisions we make concerning the norms by which we evaluate adolescents' MMPI response patterns.

Although resolving the conflicting views of adolescent development is clearly beyond the scope of this book, a careful review of differences in the normative data for adolescent and adult populations does shed significant light on the issue of the nature and characteristics of adolescent development. The next chapter of this book examines these normative issues in detail. As we shall see, findings of very marked differences in expected response patterns for adults and adolescents on specific MMPI scales provides evidence that adolescent development, at least in reference to symptomatology measured by the MMPI, is a period of substantial turbulence. This "turmoil" is manifested in the tendencies of adolescents to endorse a greater number of pathological symptoms, in contrast to adults, suggestive of serious psychopathology and deviant experiences, greater impulsivity and rebelliousness, and a greater sense of social isolation and alienation. Normalcy, as defined by the use of MMPI norms, appears to require substantially different reference points for adolescents and adults, and the use of adult norms with adolescent respondents tends to result in the over-identification or over-interpretation of pathological signs and symptoms. In a broader context, a major focus of this book is to provide the clinician with an understanding of those areas in which adolescents may be meaningfully evaluated in a manner consistent with adult respondents and those areas in which adolescents should be treated in a manner that significantly differs from current practices for adult respondents.

2

DEVELOPMENT OF THE MMPI
WITH ADOLESCENTS

OVERVIEW

This chapter reviews the development of the MMPI as an assessment instrument with adolescents with particular emphasis on the effects of use of adolescent and adult norms with adolescent respondents. As we shall discuss, the issue of norms is only one of the many fundamental issues that have remained unresolved over the 40-year period that the MMPI has been utilized for research and clinical purposes with adolescents. This observation may surprise many individuals who are aware of the enormous literature on the use of the MMPI with adult respondents and who may have assumed that similar levels of development have occurred for adolescent populations. Illustrating this contrast, Buros (1974) has reported that between 1963 and 1972 a study on the MMPI was published almost daily, and Butcher (1985a) has stated that over 8,000 books and articles have been published on the MMPI. A review of the available literature from 1945 thorugh 1985, however, resulted in identification of only approximately 100 publications that presented MMPI findings based on adolescent respondents.

This paucity of literature concerning the MMPI and adolescents may be productively framed in reference to two related perspectives. First, our current lack of research data concerning this topic may represent the failure of MMPI researchers to pursue systematically some excellent "beginnings." For example, in the late 1940s Hathaway and Monachesi (1963) undertook a landmark study of adolescent characteristics on the MMPI that involved 15,000 respondents from the Minnesota Public School system, thousands of hours of effort, and funding from both the National Institute of Mental Health and the University of Minnesota. This work continues to provide the foundations for our understanding of differences between adolescent and adult MMPI response patterns. Further, Marks et al. (1974) investigated the MMPI characteristics of 1,806 normal adolescents and 1,252 adolescents who were receiving psychological services at the time of assessment. The Marks et al. findings continue to serve as the primary source of normative and clinical correlate information concerning adolescent codetype data. A remarkable feature of the MMPI literature on adolescents concerns the degree to which these very substantial undertakings have not been systematically followed and built upon in subsequent research efforts.

Second, the relative lack of research concerning the use of the MMPI with adolescents may be seen within a broader context of the general scarcity of data-based research in adolescent development and adolescent psychiatry. As we have seen in the previous chapter, most of the writings on adolescence have been theoretically based rather than empirically grounded. A recent report of the Committee on Research of the American Society for Adolescent Psychiatry (Looney, 1985) clearly noted that little systematic research effort has been invested in the empirical study of adolescence and that much greater efforts are needed in this area. Similarly, Anthony (1975) commented on the marked discrepancy between the large amount of clinical services concentrated in the area of adolescent psychiatry and the relatively small amount of research focused on this patient group. He concluded that the limited research that has been accomplished has had little impact on clinical practices. This point is also underscored by Blotcky and Looney (1980) who observed,

> One is struck by the relative paucity of research data available on adolescents compared to the massive clinical efforts directed toward them, the latter being commonly reported in our literature. As clinicians, we do all kinds of things to help troubled youngsters, but, as noted, we infrequently involve ourselves in research-based efforts to understand the nature of normal adolescent growth and why some teenagers deviate from that progression, or to document the effectiveness of our clinical efforts. Our science is secondary to our art, and it behooves established clinicians to become involved in research to establish more solid scientific underpinnings of knowledge. (p. 198)

Thus, the relative lack of empirical investigation of the MMPI with adolescent samples may be seen as reflective of a more general trend of inadequate investigation of the psychological aspects of adolescence.

Recent developments have occurred of sufficient importance to modify and encourage clinical use of the MMPI with adolescents and to spur research interest in this field. For example, a number of recent reviews such as those provided by Archer (1984; in press), Greene (1980), and

Williams (1985) suggest that greater clarity has been developing concerning basic administration and scoring practices with adolescents. Longstanding issues such as the impact of the use of adult norms on adolescent respondents are beginning to gain sufficient definition to allow for meaningful resolutions. Further, independent efforts are currently ongoing at several institutions to provide new sets of adolescent norms for the MMPI, including a major restandardization project at the University of Minnesota described later in this book. Thus, a resurgence of interest in adolescent norms is creating a foundation for much future research on the effects of these norms in understanding and treating clinical populations. Finally, although the MMPI has undoubtedly suffered from relative neglect in terms of its research base with adolescent populations, it appears reasonable to assert that the MMPI is probably the most widely used objective measure in clinical adolescent settings. Indeed, in addition to the MMPI there are only two other major objective tests that are widely used in the clinical assessment of adolescents. These instruments are the Millon Adolescent Personality Inventory (Millon, Green, & Meagher, 1977) and the Personality Inventory for Children (Wirt, Lachar, Klinedinst, Seat, & Broen, 1982). Although both instruments have areas of strengths, they also contain substantial limitations or weaknesses that have tended to restrict their usefulness to clinicians. The Millon Adolescent Personality Inventory constitutes a theoretically promising instrument that has thus far received little empirical evaluation. The Personality Inventory for Children does not directly assess the adolescent's perceptions or responses but rather depends on the information provided by an adult, typically the child's mother, in describing the child's or adolescent's functioning and characteristics. The available evidence supports the view that the MMPI will continue to maintain a dominant status in the assessment of adolescents in the foreseeable future. Thus, the investment of time and energy into research with the MMPI and adolescents will undoubtedly prove worthwhile in terms of providing a broader empirical foundation for the widespread use of this instrument.

MAJOR CONTRIBUTIONS

The application of the MMPI to adolescent populations for both clinical and research purposes occurred early in the development of this instrument. The continued use of the MMPI with adolescents has frequently been based on the belief that "by the time a child has reached adolescence he has accumulated the effects of so wide and extensive an array of experiences that his behavior is already shaped and predictable to an important degree in many different situations" (Hathaway & Dahlstrom, 1974,

p. ix). Dahlstrom, Welsh, and Dahlstrom (1972) further noted that although the MMPI was originally intended for administration to individuals who were 16 years of age or older, the MMPI could be used successfully "with bright children" as young as 12. In addition, they indicated the determining conditions involved in the decision to administer this test to younger adolescents related to the respondents' ability to accurately read items, their willingness to stay with the task of answering the lengthy item pool, and their accumulation of a sufficiently broad range of experience through which to semantically and psychologically interpret MMPI items. The initial selection of age 12 as the lower limit for administration of the MMPI was probably related to the assumption of a sixth-grade reading level as a prerequisite for undertaking the MMPI.

The first application of the MMPI to adolescents appears to have been made by Dora Capwell in a 1945 study reported in Hathaway and Monachesi's (1953) book, *Analyzing and Predicting Juvenile Delinquency with the MMPI.* This study demonstrated the ability of the MMPI to discriminate between delinquent and nondelinquent adolescent girls based upon *Pd* scale elevations. Following this initial study, the MMPI was used with adolescents in various attempts to predict, diagnose, and plan programs of rehabilitation for delinquent youth (Hathaway & Dahlstrom, 1974). In this regard, Hathaway and Monachesi (1963) collected the largest data set ever obtained on adolescents in a study of the relationships of MMPI data to delinquency outcomes.

Hathaway and Monachesi administered the MMPI to 3,971 Minnesota ninth graders during the 1947–48 school year in a study that served as a prelude to the collection of a larger sample, termed the "statewide sample." The statewide sample was collected during the spring of 1954, when Hathaway and Monachesi tested over 11,000 more ninth graders in 92 public schools in 86 communities in Minnesota. Their combined sample, involving approximately 15,000 adolescents, included a wide selection of Minnesota children from both urban and rural settings. In addition to MMPI administrations, school records of the subjects were photographed and teachers were asked to indicate which students they felt were most likely either to have difficulty in terms of delinquency or to manifest psychiatric problems. Hathaway and Monachesi also gathered information concerning test scores on such instruments as intelligence tests and the Strong Vocational Interest Blank. The MMPI was then repeated on a sample of 3,976 of these children when they reached the 12th grade (i.e., during 1957).

Follow-up data were also obtained by field workers in the children's residence area, who searched files of public agencies including police and court records. The authors continued to acquire biographical information on members of this sample from the late 1940s to 1965 and a considerable subsample has been followed into adulthood. A summary of the earlier findings from this research has been published in a 1963 book by Hathaway and Monachesi entitled *Adolescent Personality and Behavior*. This information concerning characteristics of adolescents' responses to the MMPI continues to serve as the single best source for understanding adolescent item response patterns. This very extensive adolescent data sample has been examined by a number of other researchers in addition to Hathaway and Monachesi and is currently being evaluated and updated by Gottesman at the University of Virginia (personal communication, March, 1985).

Hathaway and Monachesi (1953, 1961, 1963) undertook collection of this large data set in order to design a prospective study that would identify personality variables related to the onset of delinquency. Rather than retroactively identifying a deviate sample of adolescents based upon psychosocial histories, they chose to follow adolescents longitudinally to predict involvement in antisocial or delinquent behaviors. Thus, Hathaway and Monachesi hoped to identify MMPI predictor variables that could serve as indicators of risk factors associated with later development of delinquent behaviors. Their data, as analyzed by Hathaway and Monachesi (1963) as well as by other researchers including Rempel (1958), Wirt and Briggs (1959), and Briggs, Wirt, and Johnson (1961), have demonstrated the ability of the MMPI to successfully predict delinquent behaviors based on the MMPI scores assessed prior to the onset of such antisocial actions. In particular, MMPI scales *F, Pd, Sc,* and *Ma* have been found most useful in these predictive efforts. Further, it has been noted that when these MMPI scales are combined with psychosocial and educational records such as absence from school (Rempel, 1958) or incidents of severe disease or death among family members (Briggs et al., 1961), prediction accuracy was substantially improved. These data are reviewed in more detail in chapter 5.

The Hathaway and Monachesi sample established that the MMPI could usefully predict at least one broad category of adolescent behavior, i.e., delinquency. The results of these investigations also provided a body of crucial information concerning differences in item endorsement patterns for adults and adolescents and for male and female adolescents, and identified important longitudinal test-retest differences in item endorsement patterns occurring between mid-to late adolescence. Finally, a subsample of this data set has provided a major portion of the current adolescent norms as developed by Marks et al. (1974).

Correlates for adolescent profile high points (the scale or scales most elevated in a profile) encountered by Hathaway and Monachesi were frequently similar to those found for adults. Elevations on the *Pd* scale, for example, were commonly found among adolescents and related to higher rates of delinquent behaviors. However, much of the data produced by adolescents also appeared to involve scale correlates uniquely characteristic of this developmental stage (Hathaway & Dahlstrom, 1974). For example, elevations on the *Sc* scale were frequently found in adolescents who produced no evidence of schizophrenic symptomatology or history, but were of lower intelligence (boys) and had a higher rate of parental separations and divorce (girls).

The recognition that adolescents produce MMPI profile features that may contain clinical correlates unique to adolescents prompted Marks et al. (1974) to undertake a major effort to clarify our understanding of the characteristics of MMPI profiles produced by normal adolescents and adolescents receiving psychiatric services. Their 1974 text, entitled *The Actuarial Use of the MMPI with Adolescents and Adults*, continues to provide the only source of actuarial-based personality descriptors based upon the response patterns of disturbed adolescents and is the most widely used source of adolescent norms.

The adolescent norms developed by Marks and his colleagues were based on the responses of approximately 1,800 normal adolescents and reported separately for males and females at age groupings of 17, 16, 15, and a category of 14 and below. The sample sizes used to create these norm groups ranged from 166 males and 139 females at age 17, to 271 males and 280 females at the grouping of 14 and below. The adolescent norms created by Marks et al. consisted of roughly 800 adolescents selected from data reported by Hathaway and Monachesi (1963) for the Minnesota Statewide Sample, combined with roughly 1,000 additional cases collected in 1964 and 1965 from white adolescent samples in rural and urban settings in Alabama, California, Kansas, Missouri, North Carolina, and Ohio. Marks et al. reported that this latter sample consisted entirely of white adolescents who were not receiving treatment for emotional disturbance at the time of MMPI testing. The norms developed by Marks, Seeman, and Haller have been reprinted in Dahlstrom et al. (1972), Lachar (1974), and Greene (1980).

The subject pool utilized by Marks et al. (1974) in deriving codetype descriptors involved 834 adolescents between the ages of 12 and 18 who had undertaken at least 10 hours of psychotherapy between the years of 1965 and 1970 and 419 adolescents who received psychiatric services during 1970–1973. In addition to the MMPI, adolescents in the Marks et al. sample completed a personal data sheet and Adjective Checklist Form. The study employed 172 psychotherapists to provide descriptive ratings on each adolescent without knowledge of the adolescents' MMPI responses. Clinician ratings involved multiple instruments including a data schedule, an adjective checklist, and a personality descriptor Q-sort. Data from adolescents were grouped into descriptive categories related to 29

MMPI high-point codetypes. The average sample size was 13.4 respondents per codetype. Descriptions were then developed that differentiated between "high" and "low" profiles (i.e., profiles markedly elevated for a given codetype and profiles that showed more moderate elevation for a particular two-scale combination) as well as between two-point code reversals (e.g., 2–4 as opposed to 4–2), so that a total of 61 separate descriptive narratives could potentially be generated from the information contained in the Marks, Seeman, and Haller text. A detailed discussion of the codetype procedure used in the Marks et al. study is presented later in this text in the discussion of adolescent codetype correlates.

The efforts of Marks and his colleagues served as a very important "first step" in developing a clinical data base for interpreting adolescent profiles. In addition to the unique value of this effort in providing the first source of adolescent norms for the MMPI, they also provided the exclusive source of descriptive data for adolescent MMPI profiles. In this regard, Marks et al's. practice of providing both low and high point profile data has resulted in a system that is capable of classifying a large proportion of the adolescent profiles typically obtained in clinical settings.

The works of Hathaway and Monachesi and Marks, Seeman, and Haller, although making landmark contributions to the understanding of adolescents and the MMPI, have also left a legacy of confusion and controversy surrounding some of the most basic aspects of adolescent MMPI interpretation. This lack of clarity is most obvious in relation to the selection of appropriate norm conversions for adolescents.

THE CONTINUED CONTROVERSY AND CONFUSION REGARDING NORM SELECTION

As the use of the MMPI was extended beyond the adult inpatient psychiatric populations for which it was originally intended, crucial questions have been raised concerning the utility of applying the original adult norms to groups of individuals that significantly varied in terms of important variables such as age or ethnic background from this normative sample. Bloom (1977) stated this general concern as follows: "The relevance of the traditional MMPI norms to select populations has become an issue of increasing importance. T scores could be grossly distorted or even meaningless when they are based on population samples with whom it is not sensible to compare the individuals one is assessing" (p. 505). In particular, many researchers, theorists, and practitioners have often been troubled by the application of adult norms to adolescent respondents. Data available from Hathaway and Monachesi (1963) clearly indicated significant differences in response patterns that occurred across adolescent age groupings. Other investigations by Colligan, Osborne, Swenson, and Offord (1984), Gynther and Shimkunas (1966), and Schenkenberg, Gottfredson, and Christensen (1984) have demonstrated significant age effects across adult populations involving MMPI scales Pd, Pa, Sc, and Ma. Collectively, these studies have shown that raw score values on several scales tend to decrease as a function of respondent age. Despite this evidence of significant age effects, conversion to adult norms continues to be a widespread practice with adolescent responses. The reasons for this phenomenon are complex and varied.

The advice of highly respected researchers concerning conversion of adolescent raw scores has often been consistent with use of the adult norms. In their work on MMPI response patterns of adolescents, Hathaway and Monachesi (1963) clearly recommended that adolescent responses be converted to adult norms despite their own data that indicated adolescent response patterns were often quite different from those derived from typical adult respondents. Specifically, they found that mean values on scales Pd, Sc, and Ma were well above the normal values produced by adults. In conceptualizing these findings, Hathaway and Monachesi (1963) stated:

> It may be assumed that youth not observed to be delinquent are, as a descriptive group characteristic, more prone to behavioral difficulties of the types found among the delinquent than would be true with adults. In tendencies toward exuberant vandalism and sexual promiscuity, youth is insurgent and held under control by the culture morals and institutions with special difficulty. (p. 43)

In response to the option of viewing adolescents against adolescent norms, Hathaway and Monachesi explicitly stated, "We do not advocate the use of special juvenile norms with the MMPI since to do so would arbitrarily erase much of the contrast between adolescents and adults" (p. 39). Similarly, Dahlstrom and Welsh (1960) stated there would be a strong risk of obscuring significant clinical material for adolescent respondents if adolescent norms were used. Specifically, they felt that adolescent psychopathological symptoms were of clinical significance even when they occurred with a high frequency or base rate in this population.

Even Marks et al. (1974) who developed an actuarial system for adolescents, as well as the first and most widely used age-appropriate adolescent norms, wrote in a footnote in their text, "We are in basic agreement with the recommendations of Hathaway and Monachesi that one shall view adolescent MMPI scores against an adult norm background" (p. 137). Marks et al. further proposed, however, that conversion to both adult and adolescent norms for adolescent respondents might serve as the most useful practice. This recommendation has served as the basic approach to norm conversions for adolescent MMPI profiles from 1974 until recently. Specifically, as noted by Archer (1984), the most common clinical recommendation concerning the interpretation of adolescent MMPI profiles rested upon a "compromise" of converting responses to both adolescent *and* adult norms, subsequently selecting for interpretation the profile that appears to provide the "best fit" to clinician's impressions and perceptions of the adolescent's clinical characteristics. As discussed later, the data currently available indicate that profiles generated from both adolescent and adult norms are likely to be markedly dissimilar, thus producing very different diagnostic and clinical features for the same respondent. The degree of interpretation bias that enters into the subjective selection of descriptors from such widely diverse profiles has served to reduce substantially the utility of the MMPI in the generation of actuarial statements for adolescents.

Most recently, published reviews by Archer (1984), Greene (1980), and Williams (1985) appear to be stabilizing on the recommendation that adolescent response pattern be evaluated with reference to adolescent norms. Archer (1984), for example, stated, "Current findings, although sparse, seem to suggest that the most appropriate conversion of adolescent raw scores would be to adolescent-based normative data" (p. 25). Similarly, Williams has stated, "The research literature on the MMPI and adolescents is not as extensive as what is available for adults. However, the majority of studies indicate that adolescent norms are more appropriate for this population" (p. 38). There are a variety of empirical grounds for these recent recommendations.

THE EFFECT OF ADULT AND ADOLESCENT NORMS

In general, when researchers have converted adolescent MMPI responses to adult norms, typically with K-correction, the resulting mean profiles have shown consistent patterns of MMPI elevations. Marks et al. (1974) reported mean profiles for groups of 952 male and 854 female adolescents from normal samples examined against adult norms. Their data, shown in Figs. 2.1 and 2.2, as well as related investigations of normal adolescents by Ball (1960), Baughman and Dahlstrom (1968), and Hathaway and Monachesi (1961), have shown notable subclinical elevations of profiles involving scales *F, Pd, Pt, Sc* and *Ma*.

Within clinical settings, a mean profile was reported in research by Archer, White, and Orvin (1979) for a sample of 64 male and female adolescent inpatients who were evaluated within 7 days of admission to an intensive psychiatric unit. This profile, shown in Fig. 2.3, reveals marked elevations on scales *F, Pd,* and *Sc.*

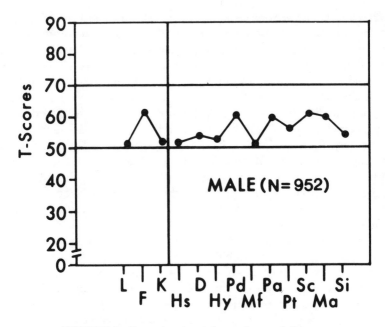

FIGURE 2.1   Normal male adolescents on adult norms.

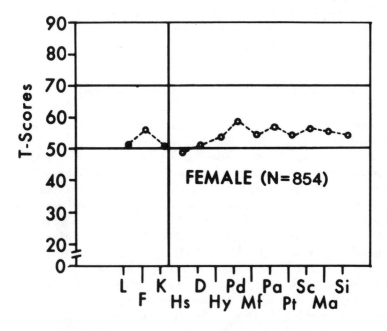

FIGURE 2.2   Normal female adolescents on adult norms.

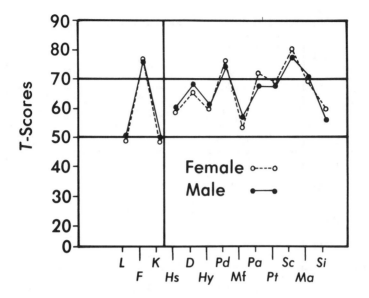

FIGURE 2.3   Adolescent inpatients on adult norms.

Highly similar MMPI profile patterns, with clinical range spikes on *F*, *Pd*, and *Sc*, have also been reported for samples of male and female adolescent inpatients by Mlott (1972) and Dudley, Mason, and Hughes (1972), and for inpatient and outpatient psychiatric samples by Burke and Eichberg (1972). Although these profile patterns were initially interpreted by researchers as an accurate reflection of adolescent inpatients (i.e., antisocial, impulsive, and thought-disordered features), more recent research has provided evidence that questions the accuracy of this modal profile in describing adolescent clinical features.

Several researchers have examined the effects of using both adolescent and adult norms in terms of profile elevation and configuration. Specifically, a series of studies by Klinge, Lachar, Grissell, and Berman (1978), Klinge and Strauss (1976), Archer (1984), and Ehrenworth and Archer (1985) have examined the effects of using adult and adolescent norms in profiling responses for groups of male and female adolescents admitted to adolescent inpatient psychiatric services. These studies have consistently shown that the degree of psychopathology displayed by adolescent respondents tends to be more pronounced when profiles are based on adult norms. Further, findings consistently indicate these differences tend to occur most markedly in relationship to scales *F*, *Pd*, and *Sc*. A typical finding from this research is presented in Figs. 2.4 and 2.5, which show the mean MMPI profiles for 34 male and 42 female inpatients converted to both adolescent and adult *K*-corrected norms (Archer, 1984).

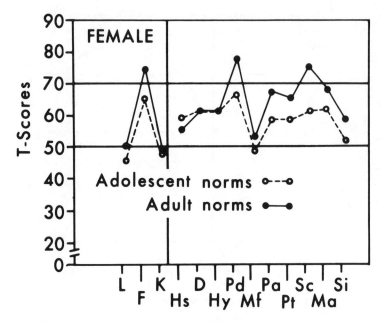

FIGURE 2.4   Female inpatients on adolescent and adult norms.

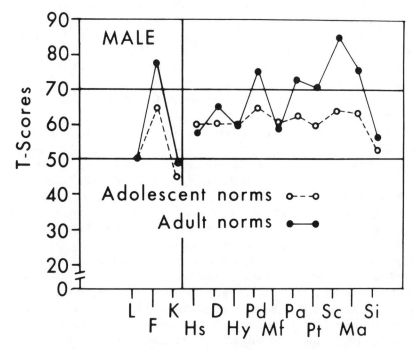

FIGURE 2.5   Male inpatients on adolescent and adult norms.

These mean profiles, contrasting the effects of adolescent and adult norms, differ significantly not only in terms of elevation (or the degree to which scale scores deviated from expected values in the pathological direction) but also in basic configuration (or the MMPI profile pattern created by differences in elevations across scales). Recent research by Ehrenworth and Archer (1985) has demonstrated that only 25% of adolescent inpatient profiles produce the same codetype high points on both adolescent and adult norms, with the remaining 75% resulting in significantly different two-point codetype classifications. In addition to these findings related to the effects on profile elevation and configuration, additional literature provides direct evidence concerning diagnostic accuracy of clinical descriptors from adolescent and adult scoring procedures.

A number of studies have indicated that the use of adult norms in samples of adolescent respondents tends to result in production of very high rates of false positive errors for psychotic diagnoses. Chase, Chaffin, and Morrison (1975), in a study of 100 consecutive admissions to an inpatient adolescent unit, found false positive schizophrenic profiles were produced from adult norms for 32.5% of this sample. Research by Ehrenworth (1984) examined the MMPI responses of inpatient adolescents scored on both adult and adolescent norms. The resulting profiles were placed into diagnostic categories based upon Lachar's (1974) classification system for MMPI profiles. The results of this procedure produced nearly twice as many adolescent profiles classified as psychotic using adult norms ($N = 25$) than were diagnosed psychotic utilizing adolescent norms ($N = 13$). The majority of profiles in which lack of classification agreement occurred were found to be classified as neurotic based on adolescent norm conversions and psychotic based on adult norms. Given the pattern of treatment team diagnoses in the Ehrenworth sample, it was concluded that adolescent norms produced a significantly lower false positive rate for psychotic diagnoses.

Hathaway, Monachesi, and Salasin (1970) followed a large sample of adolescent males and females who were tested in the original Minnesota ninth-grade sample and produced high Sc and high $Pa-Sc$ profiles on adult norms. Specifically, 254 boys and 231 girls with higher Sc and $Pa-Sc$ profiles were compared to a group of over 5,000 adolescents who produced normal range MMPI profiles. Groups were compared on such variables as socioeconomic status, school performance, and psychological adjustment in follow-up procedures that continued until subjects were age 25. Despite relatively unfavorable social outcomes associated with high Sc profiles, particularly when such profiles were coupled with low intelligence scores at original testing, the authors reported, "If higher 8 is indicative of a premorbid state, it appears that the rate of clinical schizophrenia as an adult outcome can not be greater than about 20% at most" (p. 185). Using data derived from a study of biological twins, Gottesman and

Fishman (1961) examined MMPI responses of 46 male and 87 female normal adolescents. Objective configural rules for discriminating psychotic from neurotic profiles (Meehl & Dahlstrom, 1960) were applied to these adolescent MMPI responses scored on adult norms. Gottesman and Fishman (1961) reported that 63.5% of their total sample of valid MMPI profiles were classified as psychotic based on adult norm patterns. The authors noted that this high rate of misidentification could be reduced by requiring both high *Sc* scores and low values on the MMPI *Es* (Ego Strength) special scale for application of diagnoses of schizophrenia.

Further distortions created by the use of adult norms have also been found. For example, Moore and Handal (1980) examined the MMPI responses of 16- and 17-year-old volunteers from high school settings in the St. Louis area and reported that although mean Affect Checklist scores for these respondents tended to occur within normal limits, many adolescents produced clinical range elevations on MMPIs scored on adult norms. When the authors reexamined their findings using adolescent norms, MMPI profiles generally fell within normal ranges. Additionally, findings by Newmark, Gentry, and Whitt (1983) have indicated that adolescent MMPI profiles scored using adult norms may be of limited utility in accurately identifying schizophrenia in adolescents when such diagnoses were established through the use of standardized structured interviews. The MMPI was administered to 30 males and 26 females who were admitted to an inpatient facility with an established diagnosis of schizophrenia. Of these subjects, only 6 males and 7 females obtained a profile using adult norms that fit objective MMPI criteria for a schizophrenic diagnosis. The authors concluded, "Quite possibly the diagnosis of schizophrenia for adolescents on the MMPI will require the use of non-*K*-corrected T-scores" (p. 171). These findings, which show the limitations of adult norms in the identification of psychiatric conditions among adolescents, may be compared with recent results by Archer, Ball, and Hunter (1985), which demonstrated that adolescent response patterns scored on adolescent norms were capable of accurately identifying borderline personality disorder in an adolescent inpatient setting. The results of this study indicated that the optimal combinations of MMPI validity scales with several clinical scales were able to accurately classify 82.1% of all borderline patients and 78.0% of non-borderline patients.

Other sources of investigation have supported the use of adolescent norms with adolescent respondents. Two of these studies have investigated the effects of the selection of adolescent versus adult norms on the accuracy of computerized descriptive statements generated for adolescent psychiatric patients. Lachar, Klinge, and Grissell (1976) examined the relative accuracy of computer-generated codetype narratives based exclusively on statements from adult correlate data, for adolescent responses scored on both adolescent and K-corrected adult norms. Subjects were 100 male and female adolescent psychiatric inpatients with their primary therapists serving as blind raters of narrative accuracy. The computer interpretations based on responses converted to adolescent norms were judged by clinicians as significantly more accurate than profile descriptors based on the application of adult T-scores, particularly for younger adolescents and for females.

More recently, Wimbish (1984) examined the accuracy of interpretations of adolescent MMPI profiles in a sample of 30 male adolescents (ages 15 to 18) participating in a residential substance abuse treatment program. Four narrative reports were generated for each patient based on (1) adolescent norms with narratives taken verbatim from Marks et al.'s (1974) adolescent sources; (2) adult norms with verbatim reproductions of interpretive statements contained in Lachar's (1974) automated interpretation system for adults; (3) adult norms with narratives generated by commercially available computer services for adults; and (4) a narrative report that contained randomly selected "bogus" statements unrelated to the MMPI response patterns of the subjects. These sets of four narrative reports were given to the primary therapists, who rated each in terms of accuracy of personality description, degree of psychopathology, interpersonal relationships, and overall accuracy. Wimbish (1984) found reports generated from adolescent norms were judged as significantly more accurate across rating dimensions than reports generated from adult norms and bogus reports. She concluded, "Results of this study indicate that the computerized interpretation services would do well to consider the incorporation of adolescent norms in their programs" (p. 81).

Finally, Archer (1984) submitted the MMPI scale scores of 156 male and female adolescents, using adolescent norm-based T-score conversions, to a principal components factor analysis. The respondents were 80 female and 76 male adolescents (mean age = 14.97 years) from residential inpatient settings assessed within 14 days of hospital admission. Table 2.1 shows the factor loading patterns for the four factors that accounted for a cumulative total of 69% of MMPI scale variance. The first factor, labeled Psychoticism, was characterized by high positive loadings on scales measuring psychotic symptomatology, with more moderate loadings on neurotic measures, and a negative loading on validity scale K. The second factor was characterized by high positive loadings on the neurotic triad (Hs, D, Hy) and on the Pd scale, and was defined as Neurotic-Characterological symptomatology. The third factor, with positive loadings on validity scales L and K and a negative loading on the Pd scale was labeled Overcontrol or Defensiveness. The fourth factor was identified with high

TABLE 2.1
Factor Pattern Loading of 13 MMPI Scales on Adolescent Norms
for 156 Male and Female Adolescents

| MMPI Scales | Factors | | | |
	1	2	3	4
L	−.06	.07	.82*	.26
F	.74*	.23	.04	.10
K	−.53*	.25	.56	−.21
Hs	.56*	.62*	.07	.13
D	.17	.74*	−.03	.38
Hy	.08	.87*	−.01	−.07
Pd	.24	.52*	−.56*	.22
Mf	.03	.00	−.03	.64*
Pa	.69*	.28	−.18	.10
Pt	.60*	.38	−.47	.14
Sc	.77*	.22	−.32	.22
Ma	.72*	−.10	−.15	−.41
Si	.29	.19	−.44	.65*
Sum of Variance	38%	14%	9%	8%
Cumulative Sum of Variance	38%	52%	61%	69%

*Factor loading ≥ .50.

positive loadings on the two "nonclinical" scales of *Mf* and *Si* and may be viewed as Nonclinical dimension.

Archer (1984) interpreted these findings in relationship to results from other factor analytic studies. This loading pattern was highly similar to typical findings for adult respondents employing adult norms as reported by Block (1965) and in cross-cultural studies by Butcher and Pancheri (1976). Thus, if we assume that the broad dimensions of psychopathology represented in the MMPI item pool should demonstrate a consistency between adolescent and adult respondents in a manner similar to the cross-cultural consistency found for adults by Butcher and Pancheri, then the Archer findings suggest that the application of adolescent norms to adolescent response patterns produces results that most closely match the underlying dimensions of MMPI psychopathology. Second, the Archer (1984) findings were substantially different from the three-factor pattern reported by Archer et al. (1979) for adolescent inpatients when responses were scored on adult *K*-corrected norms. Findings unique to the 1979 study, including a third factor labeled Sociopathy, may have been more reflective of the effects of scoring adolescent profiles on adult norms than of the broad dimensions in adolescents' self-reported psychopathology.

IMPLICATION OF FINDINGS REGARDING
ADOLESCENT AND ADULT NORMS

The findings regarding the use of the adolescent and adult norms for adolescent response patterns have two major implications. First, the consistent finding that adolescents tend to score significantly higher than adult counterparts on MMPI scales F, Pd, and Sc has direct relevance to theoretical perspectives concerning adolescent psychological development. Adolescents, in contrast to adults, tend to report more unusual symptoms suggestive of serious psychopathology and deviate social views (scale F), greater impulsivity, and antisocial attitudes and beliefs (scale Pd), and a greater sense of alienation and isolation from their social environments (scale Sc). These composite features of adolescent MMPI responses are consistent with analytic theorists' postulations of this developmental period as a stage marked by turbulence and emotional lability (e.g., Blos, 1962; Erikson, 1956; Freud, 1958; Hall, 1904; Masterson, 1968). Norm conversion differences can range as large as 20 T-score points or greater on scales F, Pd, and Sc when the same raw score values are plotted against the adolescent norms developed by Marks et al. and adult norms (Archer, 1984). Further, these differences do not appear to be simple artifacts of K-correction procedures, but rather appear to represent differences in relative frequency of item endorsement patterns between adults and adolescents (Archer, 1984).

These findings suggest, for example, that response patterns that indicate the occurrence of a schizophrenic process among adults may have a substantially different meaning for adolescents based on their tendency to critically endorse many more Sc scale items. Thus, viewing adolescent response patterns against adult norms may lead to significant diagnostic errors, with consequent negative effects for treatment planning and treatment evaluation. Archer (1984) has noted that in the absence of empirical evidence that the item endorsement patterns on scales F, Pd, and Sc have the same clinical correlates for adolescents that have been established for adult respondents, the use of adolescent norms appears to reduce the very marked possibility of "over-interpreting" pathological features of adolescent MMPI responses. Gottesman and Fishman (1961) have speculated that adolescents tend to score in elevated ranges on the MMPI in response to the "normative crises of adolescence" that may bear a misleading resemblance to the "crisis of psychosis" manifested by adults. Gottesman and Fishman observed that "The layman characterizes adolescent behavior with such adjectives as crazy, nutty, flighty, bewildered, giddy, frenzied, queer, odd and mixed up. Almost all of these words may be found in the Thesaurus under the word insanity" (p. 2). Findings from the MMPI serve, then, as a major source of empirical support for the Storm and Stress model of adolescent development.

The second major conclusion from findings regarding the effects of adult versus adolescent norms on adolescent response features is that sufficient evidence has been obtained to indicate that use of adult norms with adolescent respondents is an inappropriate and potentially dangerous practice. The literature clearly shows that the selection of adult or adolescent norms in profiling adolescent response patterns has significant implications in terms of profile elevation and configuration. Differences have also been shown in relation to diagnostic impressions based upon MMPI profile types, accuracy ratings of narrative statements, and factor analytic dimensions of psychopathology. This literature is consistent in indicating that the use of adolescent norms offers the most appropriate method for interpreting adolescent response patterns. Such a conclusion in no ways suggests that the use of adolescent norms is a panacea that will render the interpretation of adolescent response patterns to be a simple or "straightforward" process. Rather, this conclusion is meant to bring closure to one specific area of controversy concerning the use of the MMPI with adolescents that has been ambiguous and unclear for the past four decades. Stated most simply, the continued use of adult norms in research and clinical applications of the MMPI with adolescent respondents is unsupported by the available empirical data.

The long-standing ambivalence and confusion concerning the use of adolescent norms are reflected by several factors. First, it is notable that adolescent norm profiling sheets have not been available from the University of Minnesota Press, the Psychological Corporation, or the National Computer Systems Corporation. Profile sheets for adolescents using the Marks et al. (1974) norms may be currently obtained only through Psychological Assessment Resources, Inc., and these forms are included in Appendix E of this book. This tendency to avoid the adolescent area is also seen in a recent review by Butcher and Tellegen (1978) in which common methodological problems found in MMPI research were delineated. Despite having stressed the importance of viewing raw score data against the most appropriate T-score conversions, they did not directly discuss conversion of adolescent raw score responses to T-score values, nor did they review the use of the MMPI with adolescent respondents. The continued confusion regarding the use of appropriate norms with adolescents was most recently reflected in presentations at the 20th Annual Symposium of Recent Developments in the Use of the MMPI, held in 1985. Although this program contained a significant number of papers devoted to the use of the MMPI with adolescent respondents, roughly half of these involved investigations that converted adolescent raw scores to adult K-corrected T-score values. Thus, even current

MMPI investigators often emply adult norms as a standard procedure for evaluating adolescent response patterns.

In summary, these examples are cited to suggest that the use of adult norms has served to produce confused research findings for MMPI investigators and has contributed to significant and substantial difficulties in psychological evaluation, treatment planning, and treatment evaluation for adolescents in clinical settings. Therefore, the most productive and best supported recommendation concerning the use of the MMPI with adolescent respondents is that the raw score values be exclusively converted against adolescent norms. Clinicians and researchers may continue to employ the original form of the MMPI with adolescent norms as contained in Marks et al. (1974) or there may be a rapid and widespread adaptation of the revised adolescent MMPI form utilizing age-appropriate norms derived at the University of Minnesota. This issue will eventually be determined by the quality and speed of current restandardization and revision efforts. In either case, the recommendation that adolescent responses be converted to adolescent rather than adult norms will continue to be valid whether using the original or revised MMPI item pool with adolescent respondents.

THE INTERPRETATION
OF ADOLESCENT PROFILES

GENERAL ADMINISTRATIVE GUIDELINES

General administrative guidelines for the use of the MMPI with adolescents have been provided by Dahlstrom et al. (1972) and more recently by Williams (1985). We consider and discuss these criteria in reference to a variety of specific points.

Dahlstrom et al. (1972) stated that the MMPI may be administered to "bright subjects" as young as 12, and Williams (1985) had suggested that with younger subjects (i.e., ages 12 and 13) the MMPI should be selectively used based on the nature of the presenting complaints of the respondent. Both Dahlstrom et al. and Williams indicated that a minimum reading level of fifth to sixth grade is required in order to respond meaningfully to the MMPI. Williams also noted that although reading level may be evaluated by the use of such instruments as the reading component of the Wide Range Achievement Test (WRAT), a reasonably accurate screening can also be accomplished by requesting that the respondent read several items aloud from the MMPI item pool. If a respondent demonstrates reading difficulty, the administration may still be accomplished using the standardized audiotape version of the MMPI, available through National Computer Systems, if the problem appears to be specifically related to reading ability in contrast to limitations in comprehension ability or overall intelligence. Williams suggests that if an adolescent scores below 65 on a standardized IQ assessment or has less than a third-grade reading level, the MMPI should not be administered in any form. Related to this point, Ball and Carroll (1960) investigated the characteristics of Cannot Say (?) scores in a sample of 262 adolescents in Kentucky public schools. The authors found no evidence that failure to respond to items was differentially related to history of delinquent behaviors. In general, however, adolescents with low IQs and below average academic records tended to produce higher Cannot Say scores, perhaps indicating that failure to respond to the MMPI items typically reflects difficulty in item comprehension.

The second area of consideration in determining whether to administer the MMPI to adolescents concerns their ability and capacity to "stick to the task" of answering the lengthy MMPI item pool. This criterion relates to issues of both subject motivation and capability. For the acutely psychotic adolescent, or adolescents with severely limited reading ability, the MMPI can become an ordeal that resembles an endurance test. For the oppositional and angry adolescent, the MMPI may present a welcomed opportunity to display noncooperation by responding in the slowest and most inappropriate fashion to each item. As noted by Newmark and Thibodeau (1979), the administration of the MMPI to adolescents, particularly in psychiatric inpatient settings,

> tends to provoke and irritate restless adolescents, who then express their anger and defiance by seizing on the legitimate option of omitting items or failing to complete the test. This submarginal compliance with routine procedures tends to vitiate the results. Occasionally, staff assistance will lead to a completed MMPI but only after the adolescent has grudgingly completed a few items at a time over a period of several days. (p. 248)

It is also important that adolescents be given a reasonable environment in which to complete the MMPI. Thus, privacy and supervision are of central importance, and it is poor clinical practice to allow an adolescent to fill out the MMPI in an unsupervised setting in which privacy cannot be assured (e.g., at home or on the ward). Further, it is also important that adolescents be provided with the optimal vehicle to respond to the MMPI item pool. Williams notes that the card format of the MMPI, in which the respondent sorts items into true and false stacks, may elicit accurate responses from patients who could not or would not otherwise complete the MMPI. Current developments in computer administration of the MMPI item pool may also be found to hold special utility for reluctant adolescents. If the original Form R is used with adolescent respondents, the need for careful, individual administration and supervision is particularly important. The mechanical and structural problems with this MMPI administration vehicle often introduce substantial degrees of error into response patterns when test booklet pages are not correctly aligned with the answer sheet. This problem tends to be particularly marked for adolescents who may not employ the necessary time and concentration required to ensure proper alignment as they respond to the item pool.

A final criterion noted by both Williams (1985) and Dahlstrom et al. (1972) relates to the requirement that younger adolescents must bring to the testing situation a sufficiently wide range of experience to make the content of the items "psychologically and semantically" meaningful. Thus, it should be remembered that developmental maturity may often be as crucial a factor as chronological age in making the decision to administer, or not administer, the MMPI to adolescents. Williams (1985) noted, "In deciding to administer the MMPI to an adolescent, the examiner must consider his or her developmental level and if the task is appropriate to his or her cognitive, social, and emotional stages of development" (p. 38). Gynther (1972) has suggested semantic confusion may be a particular problem for adolescents in that numerous MMPI items employ terms or concepts typically unfamiliar to younger respondents. Similarly, Ball and Carroll (1960) have raised concerns that adolescents may frequently lack the necessary life experience prerequisites to fully understand the content of questions. In illustrating this point, one might note that the meaning of such questions as "My sex life is satisfactory" may be fundamentally and significantly different for younger adolescents than for an adult respondent. This difference in semantic meaning and interpretation of items renders the use of "critical item" analysis substantially more problematic with adolescent respondents. Further, as noted by Dahlstrom et al. (1972), many MMPI statements are worded in the past tense (e.g., "I liked school") in a manner that does not denote continuation into the present and that may serve to confuse younger respondents. A major outcome of the current efforts to revise and update responses will consist of the rewording of many items in a manner that will render the MMPI more relevant, and consequently more interpretable, for adolescents.

SHORT FORM ISSUES

In response to the problems created by the lengthy MMPI item pool, Newmark and Thibodeau (1979) recommended the use of "short" forms of the MMPI with hospitalized adolescents. Investigations of the characteristics of the MMPI-168 in adolescent samples have been provided by Macbeth and Cadow (1984) and Rathus (1978), and Mlott (1973) reported findings for the 71-item "mini-mult" with adolescent inpatients.

Butcher (1985b) has made a distinction between short forms of the MMPI, such as the mini-mult and the MMPI-168, and the abbreviated form or version of the MMPI, which involves administration of the first 399 items as they appear on Form R. In the abbreviated form the subject is not requested to respond to items at the back of the MMPI booklet and all basic validity and clinical scales may be scored. Special scales, however, cannot be produced from an abbreviated administration. Butcher noted that although the abbreviated form may be validly administered to subjects for whom special scale information may not be necessary or crucial, short forms of the MMPI may constitute an inappropriate attempt to "cut corners" in MMPI administration. The reduction in the number of items within particular scales entailed in short-form versions of the MMPI, for example, reduces the overall reliability of the measurement of scale constructs. Additionally, Butcher has noted that the shortened versions of the MMPI have been insufficiently validated against external criteria and that short form profiles and codetypes are frequently different from the results that would have been achieved for an individual based on standard MMPI item pool administration. For example, research by Hoffman and Butcher (1975) has shown that the mini-mult and full item pool administrations of the MMPI tend to produce the same MMPI codetype in only 33% of cases, and that the full MMPI and the MMPI-168 produce similar codetypes in only 40% of adult cases. Consistent with these findings, Lueger (1983) has reported that two-point codetypes derived from standard and MMPI-168 forms were different in over 50% of their sample of male adolescents.

These problems in MMPI short forms, although certainly important in the adult literature, appear to be of even greater importance when the MMPI is used for research or clinical purposes with adolescents. Stated most concisely, there is typically substantial "noise" in the MMPI profiles of adolescents, which renders the interpretation process difficult, and the inclusion of a short form administration procedure with adolescents is unwarranted. The use of a short form procedure, while perhaps saving time with adolescent respondents, is too likely to introduce more than an acceptable range of confusion into the meaning of the adolescent profile. Therefore, it is suggested that short forms, in contrast to abbreviated forms, not be used in adolescent populations. On the other hand, the abbreviated form of the MMPI as defined by Butcher may often serve as a reasonable resource in coping with administration problems with angry or poorly motivated adolescents.

PROFILING ADOLESCENTS' RESPONSE PATTERNS

A number of simple administration and scoring procedures are specifically noted that are preparatory to codetype interpretation, and that may serve to substantially strengthen the ability to meaningfully understand and describe patient functioning based upon profile features.

If significant errors are made in the administration or scoring of the MMPI, then the resulting codetype may appear to offer valuable information but will in fact be based upon crucial errors. In these cases then, the interpretation of resulting MMPI profiles will provide unreliable and potentially dangerous data. Thus, substantial care must be taken in eliminating as many sources of error as possible in deriving the MMPI profile for adolescents. Roger Greene (personal communication, May, 1986) has observed that roughly 25% of graduate students at Texas Tech commit major errors in scoring or profiling adolescent MMPIs, even following specific instructions for such procedures that emphasize potential problem areas.

Scoring procedures might start by carefully examining the actual response sheet for the adolescent to search for the presence of such factors as multiple items that are endorsed in both the true and false direction, evidence of test-taking response patterns that might suggest random markings or largely all true or all false response sets. Additionally, one might review the actual MMPI answer sheet to ascertain the number of items that were left unanswered by the respondent. If these features have been assessed, one can tabulate the raw score values for individual MMPI scales with greater confidence.

The actual summation of raw score values for adolescents is identical to the process utilized with adult respondents. The conversion of raw scores to T-score values for adolescents, however, is obviously *not* the same for adolescents and adults when adolescent norms are employed. This factor has been the largest single source of error in profiling adolescent response patterns by novice MMPI users. Because of the scarcity of adolescent profile sheets, the majority of psychologists have continued to employ adult MMPI profile sheets to plot adolescent response patterns. This procedure, however, requires that the clinician ignore the K-corrected T-score values placed on the adult form and plot the adolescent's actual T-score conversion values as found in adolescent norm tables provided by Marks et al. (1974), Dahlstrom et al. (1972), Lachar (1974), and others. Errors are frequently made in attempting to convert raw scores to appropriate T-scores in the adolescent norm tables because either the sex or the age of the adolescent was not correctly identified. Thus, rechecking one's procedure in converting raw scores to T-score values from normative data tables is advised. Once confirmed, T-score values can be accurately profiled on the adult form by carefully locating the correct T-score elevation for a particular scale based on the adolescent values. K correction is *not* used for adolescent profiling, and the raw score conversion guides printed on the adult form are *not* to be used with adolescents for either the validity or the clinical scales. The T-score plottings should be carefully checked to make certain that the elevations actually entered onto the profile sheet correspond to the T-score conversions in adolescent norms. Once these procedures have been followed, the resulting MMPI profile may be examined with the confidence that "careless" errors have not resulted in crucial distortions of profile features.

The procedures for scoring and profiling adolescent responses may be summarized as follows:

1. Carefully examine response sheet for unanswered items and evidence of response sets.
2. Perform a summation of raw score values for each scale using standard procedures.
3. Convert raw score totals to T-score values for each scale using adolescent norm tables, with particular attention to the age and sex of respondent.
4. If values are placed on adult profile sheets, ignore K-correction procedures and the T-score value conversions designed for adult respondents.

ISSUES OF PROFILE VALIDITY

Validity Scales

The task of evaluating the MMPI validity scale characteristics of adolescents is markedly complex, but such validity scale data appear to be related to important treatment variables for these respondents. Archer et al. (1979), for example, examined the utility of MMPI scale data in predicting 64 adolescents' length of stay in an inpatient psychiatric setting. Results of discriminative function analyses indicated that a linear combination of validity scale T-score data resulted in 68.80% overall accuracy in classifying adolescent patients into short-term and long-term treatment groups. Longer hospital stays (i.e., greater than 137) days were related to elevated L, F and K scores for this sample.

The Cannot Say (?) scale consists of the total number of items that the respondent fails to answer or answers in both the true and false directions. Thus, the Cannot Say scale is not a formal MMPI scale in the sense of having a consistent item pool or set number of items. Although several studies have examined characteristics of the Cannot Say scale in adult populations (Greene, 1980), very little research attention has been focused on this issue among adolescent respondents.

Ball and Carroll (1960) examined correlates of Cannot Say scores among 262 ninth-grade public school students in Kentucky. They reported that male respondents had a higher mean number of Cannot Say responses than females, and that items omitted by adolescents generally tended to fall into broad categories, including items not applicable to adolescents, religious items, items related to sexuality and bodily functions, and items that required adolescents to make a personal decision concerning characteristics about which they were ambivalent. Similarly, Hathaway and Monachesi (1963) found 23 items that were left unanswered by 2% of the male or female respondents in their statewide adolescent sample. They noted that items related to religion and sex appear to be the content areas that produce the most frequent omissions for both boys and girls, and that girls tended to leave a significantly larger number of sex-related items unanswered.

In general, adolescents in the Ball and Carroll study who tended to leave greater numbers of items unanswered also had lower IQ scores and below average academic grades. The authors found no evidence of a relationship between Cannot Say scores and delinquent behaviors in this sample. Thus, their findings suggest that adolescents' failure to complete items may be more closely associated with intellectual and reading limitations than with oppositional and defiant characteristics among adolescents.

Table 3.1 provides interpretative suggestions for varying levels of omitted items for adolescents. T-score conversions for the Cannot Say scale are not currently available for adolescents.

TABLE 3.1
Interpretations of Cannot Say (?) Scale Elevations[a]

Raw Score	Interpretation
0	1. Low. These adolescents are willing and capable of responding to the item pool and were not evasive of item content.
1–10	2. Normal. These adolescents have omitted a few items in a selective manner. Their omissions may be the result of limitations in life experiences which rendered some items unanswerable. There is little probability of profile distortions unless all omissions occurred from a single scale.
11–30	3. Moderate. These adolescents are omitting more items than expected and may be very indecisive. Their omissions may have distorted their profile elevations. Check the scale membership of missing items to evaluate profile validity.
31 and above	4. Marked. Adolescents in this range have left many items unanswered possibly as a result of a defiant or uncooperative stance or serious reading difficulties. The profile is probably invalid. If possible, the adolescent should complete unanswered items or retake the entire test.

[a]T-score conversions for the ? scale are not available from Marks, Seeman and Haller (1974).

The Lie Scale includes 15 items that were originally selected to identify individuals who were deliberately attempting to lie or to avoid answering the item pool in an open and honest manner. The scale is keyed in the false direction for all items, and was created based on a rational/intuitive identification of items. The scale covers a variety of content areas such as the denial of aggressive or dishonest impulses that constitute areas of common human failings for the majority of individuals. The Lie Scale appears to be one of the few MMPI indices that are relatively unaffected by the use of adolescent versus adult norms. A comparison of 15-year-old male and female mean values on the Lie Scale from Marks et al. (1974) with mean expectations from the adult normative sample indicates little difference in mean expectations across these age groups on this measure. In general, although little research has been done on this topic, the clinical correlates of Lie Scale elevations for adolescents also appear similar to the meaning of these elevations for adult respondents. Thus, moderate elevations in the range of *T*-score values of 61 to 70 are related to tendencies towards conformity and the use of denial among adolescent respondents, and marked elevations in excess of *T*-score values of 70 raise questions concerning an "all false" response set or unsophisticated attempts by the respondent to present himself in a favorable light and in a "saintly" manner. Table 3.2 provides interpretive suggestions for four levels of *L* scale elevations.

TABLE 3.2
Interpretations of L Scale Elevations for Adolescents

Raw Score	T-score[a]	Interpretation
0–3	46 and below	1. Low. "All true" or "fake bad" response sets are possible in this range. May reflect an open, confident stance among normal adolescents.
4–6	47–60	2. Normal. Scores in this range reflect an appropriate balance between the admission and denial of common social facults. These adolescents tend to be flexible and non-rigid.
7–9	61–70	3. Moderate. May reflect an emphasis on conformity and conventional behaviors among adolescents. Adolescents in psychiatric settings tend to employ denial as a central defense mechanism.
10 and above	71 and above	4. Marked. Scores in this range reflect extreme use of denial, poor insight, and lack of sophistication. Treatment efforts are likely to be longer and associated with guarded prognosis. An "all false" or "fake good" response set may have occurred.

[a]T-score ranges are approximate with actual values varying by sex and age.

TABLE 3.3
Interpretations of F Scale Elevations for Adolescents

Raw Score	T-score[a]	Interpretation
0–4	45 and below	1. Low. Scores in this range may reflect very conventional life experiences among normal adolescents, and possible "fake bad" attempts among disturbed adolescents.
5–11	boys: 46 to 55 girls: 46 to 60	2. Normal. Adollescents in this range have endorsed unusual experiences to a degree which is common during adolescence.
12–15	boys: 56 to 64 girls: 61 to 69	4. Marked. Validity indicators should be checked carefully for adolescents in this range. Valid profiles most likely reflect serious psychopathology including psychotic features and severe behavioral problems.
16–25	boys: 65 to 85 girls: 70 to 95	4. Marked. Validity indicators should be checked carefully for adolescents in this range. Valid profiles most likely reflect serious psychopathology including psychotic features and severe behavioral problems.
26 and above	boys: 86 and above girls: 96 and above	5. Extreme. Protocols with F scores in this range are likely to be invalid. If "fake-bad" and other response set issues are ruled out, may reflect severely disorganized or psychotic adolescents.

[a]T-score ranges are approximate with actual values varying by sex and age.

Scale *F* consists of 64 items selected on the basis that no more than 10% of the Minnesota Normative Sample answered these items in a deviant direction. The *F* scale is often referred to as the frequency or infrequency scale and it includes a wide variety of obvious items involving bizarre, strange or unusual experiences, thoughts and sensations. Thirty-five of the *F* scale items appear only on this MMPI dimension, with the majority of the overlapping items also appearing on scales *Pa, Pt, Sc,* or *Ma* (Greene, 1980). As we have noted, the *F* scale is particularly affected by the use of adolescent versus adult norms, and a review of expected mean values for 15-year-old males and females from Marks et al. (1974) in contrast with adult norm expected values reveals very marked differences of 4 raw score points or greater in expected response frequency. Table 3.3 presents a summary of interpretations for five levels of *F* scale elevations for adolescent respondents. A separate discussion of *F* scale validity criteria issues is presented in the following section based on the unique response patterns of adolescents on this MMPI scale.

The *K* scale consists of 30 items that were empirically selected to identify individuals who display significant degrees of psychopathology but tend to produce profiles that are within normal limits. Item content on the

TABLE 3.4
Interpretations of K Scale Elevations for Adolescents

Raw Score	T-score[a]	Interpretation
0–10	44 and below	1. Low. These adolescents may have poor self-concepts and limited resources for coping with stress. Scores in this range may be related to a "fake bad" attempt among normals or acute distress for adolescents in psychiatric settings.
11–13	45–55	2. Normal. Scores in this range reflect an appropriate balance between self-disclosure and guardedness. Prognosis for psychotherapy is often good.
16–20	56–65	3. Moderate. May reflect a self-reliant stance and reluctance to seek help from others. Among normal adolescents suggests defensiveness, and unwillingness to admit psychological problems for adolescents in psychiatric settings.
21 and above	66 and above	4. Marked. Scores in this range reflect extreme defensiveness related to a poor treatment prognosis and longer treatment duration. The possibility of a "fake good" response set should be considered.

[a]T-score ranges are approximate with actual values varying by sex and age.

K scale is quite diverse and covers issues including self-control, family relationships, and interpersonal relationships (Greene, 1980). Although the K-correction procedure has become a standard practice with adult respondents, the adolescent norms developed by Marks et al. (1974) do not employ K-correction in the derivation of adolescent T-score values. In general, the expected mean raw score values for adolescents and adults do not vary greatly on this MMPI measure, and comparison of mean values from Marks et al. (1974) with the mean values for the adult normative sample indicates relatively minor differences typically involving less than 1 raw score point. Although little research has been devoted to this issue, the available data would suggest that K scale elevations in adolescents may be related to the same clinical correlates as have been established for adult respondents. Thus, markedly low elevations on the K scale tend to be produced by adolescents who may be exaggerating their degree of symptomatology in an attempt to "fake bad" or as a cry for help in response to acute distress. Conversely, marked elevations on the K scale are often produced by individuals who are defensive and who are not open to psychological interventions. Further, these adolescents often are attempting to deny psychological problems and present a facade of adequate coping and adjustment. In adult and adolescent literature, high K scale profiles have been linked to a poor prognosis for psychological intervention because of the respondent's inability or refusal to cooperate with treatment efforts (e.g., Archer et al. 1979). Table 3.4 offers interpretive guides for four levels of K scale elevation produced by adolescent respondents.

F Scale and Related Validity Criteria

Certain types of "invalid" profiles tend to occur with a higher frequency in adolescent samples than in typical adult populations, particularly high F profiles. For example, in reviewing MMPI records of 188 young adults (mean age = 21.27 years) entering inpatient psychiatric treatment, in comparison with the response patterns of 219 adolescents (mean age = 14.67 years) entering inpatient services and 85 adolescents in outpatient treatment (mean age = 15.21 years), Archer (in press) found the rate of high F profiles ($F \geq 16$) for inpatient adolescents (46.3%) was substantially higher than for the adult inpatient sample (33.9%). Further, the frequency of high F profiles for the sample of outpatient adolescents (29.2%) was found to be consistent with that of adult inpatients. The frequencies of F raw scores in excess of 25 for adult inpatients, and for adolescent outpatients and inpatients, were 9.6%, 7.8%, and 17.3%, respectively.

Significant differences in F scale patterns between adolescents and adults have also been established through incidental or serendipitous findings from a number of studies. For example, Archer et al. (1979) and Dudley et al. (1972) examined the MMPI profiles of adolescents in residential treatment. They noted that high F scale values found for these groups raised significant issues regarding the use of F scale validity criteria employed to evaluate profile validity or interpretability. Both investigations found mean F scale raw score values of approximately 14 points for male and female respondents. Application of Meehl's (1956a) validity criterion of $F \geq 16$ in the Archer et al. (1979) study resulted in 43.8% of all adolescent profiles judged as invalid. Archer et al. expressed reservations concerning the potential loss of useful clinical data by employing conservative F scale validity criteria in adolescent samples. Identical findings have been more recently reported by Ehrenworth and Archer (1985) who found that 43.3% of their adolescent inpatient respondents obtained raw score F scale values of 16 or more. The distribution of clinical diagnoses for this high F group was found to be similar to the distribution of treatment team diagnoses for the total sample population in this study. Archer (1984) has suggested that

> The most prudent recommendation would appear to rest on employing flexible F scale validity criterion values based upon the degree of true and false negatives and positives that a researcher or a clinician is prepared to tolerate

within a particular reference group of respondents. F scale validity criteria may be lowered or raised for samples depending upon the purpose of the MMPI administration within a given clinical or normal population (e.g., screening, treatment planning, etc.). (p. 243)

Clearly, given the typical high F scale values found for adolescent populations, the use of conservative F scale validity criteria for all adolescents appears unwarranted. In contrast to the conservative F scale validity criterion recommended by Meehl (1956a) for adult respondents, higher F scale cutoffs have been suggested by other researchers ranging up to an F scale raw score value of 26 utilized by Marks et al. (1974). In utilizing F scale validity criteria with adolescents, it is important to remember Dahlstrom et al's. (1972) suggestion that profiles containing even very high F values may prove to be clinically useful and interpretable. In support of this point, Dahlstrom et al. (1972) cited the findings of Kanun and Monachesi (1960) that examined the characteristics of ninth-grade adolescent subjects who produced MMPI profiles with F scale values equal to or greater than a raw score of 16. Kanun and Monachesi reported meaningful correlates related to the occurrence of delinquent behavior for the high F group, which suggested that such profiles were neither random nor uninterpretable. Studies in adult population by Gynther (1961), Gynther, Altman, and Warbin (1972), Gynther and Shimkunas (1966), Post and Gasparikova-Krasnec (1979), and Rice (1968) have shown that high F scale values may reliably reflect psychopathological processes permitting for valid interpretation of the MMPI protocol. Major findings from these studies indicate that high F scale values are typically obtained for patients with substantial levels of psychotic symptomatology as well as for patients with high potentials for "acting out" aggressive impulses.

Both F scale validity criteria and F-K index criterion should be employed with substantial caution for adolescent respondents. Additionally, findings from the F scale may have implications for the use of critical item analysis in adolescent samples.

CRITICAL ITEMS

Sets of "critical" items, or items indicative of severe psychopathology, have been developed by Grayson (1951), Caldwell (1969), Lachar and Wrobel (1979), and others. Endorsement of such items in the pathological direction has been related to a variety of symptom content areas and a review of this literature is provided by Greene (1980). Recent data from adult populations (Evans, 1984; Fox, Sunlight, & Permanente, 1985) have raised substantial questions regarding the usefulness of critical item endorsement patterns. Further, Greene (1980) has shown that normal college students endorse a substantial number of critical items in the manner similar to both medical patients and college students receiving counseling services. These findings, coupled with the established tendency for adolescent respondents to endorse a higher frequency of Scale F and Scale Sc items than adult respondents, suggest substantial caution should be employed in attempts to interpret critical item endorsement patterns for adolescent respondents. Until such time as empirical investigations have established clinical correlates of critical item endorsements for adolescents, it would appear most appropriate to assume that endorsement of critical items on the MMPI lacks a clear or unambiguous meaning for adolescent respondents.

RESPONSE SET ISSUES

Characteristics of MMPI profiles that are generated based on systematic response sets such as "all true," "all false," and random patterns have been provided for adult respondents by Graham (1977) and Lachar (1974). Unfortunately, similar information has not been published for these response set patterns for adolescents scored on adolescent norms. Such data, however, have recently been evaluated (Archer, in press). If an adolescent answers all items in the true direction and standard scale responses are scored on adolescent norms, the resulting profile appears similar to the one presented in Fig. 3.1. The salient features of the profile for both male and female respondents include an extremely elevated F score with markedly low scale score values on L and K. Since scale L, and the majority of scale K, are keyed in the false direction for critical endorsements, both scales must yield raw score values of zero or near zero when items are endorsed in the all true response set. This feature, then, becomes a very important clue in detecting an all true endorsement pattern. Additionally, there is a very marked positive or psychotic slope on the clinical scale profile with spikes on scales Pa, Pt, Sc, and Ma. If the MMPI special scales are scored for the all true pattern, the A scale and the MAC scale will be elevated in high clinical ranges whereas the R and Es scales will have markedly low values. The characteristics of an all true response pattern for adolescents are very similar to the all true response pattern reported by Graham (1977) for adult respondents. To summarize, the characteristics of the all true profile may be stated as follows:

1. Extreme F scale elevation.
2. Markedly low score on scales L and K.
3. Psychotic slope on clinical profile.

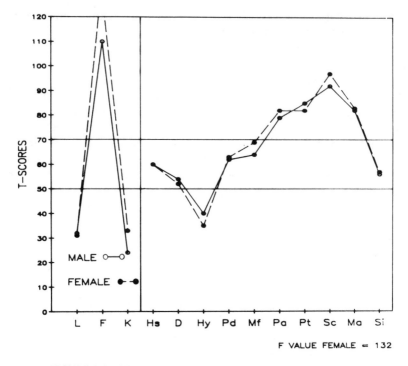

FIGURE 3.1   All true response pattern on adolescent norms.

4. If special scales are scored, *A* and *MAC* elevated in high clinical ranges and *R* and *ES* have very low values.

If a male or female adolescent responds false to all items, this response set will produce the profile shown in Fig. 3.2 when scored on adolescent norms for standard scales. The all false profile is characterized by extreme elevation on all validity scales and on the first three scales of the MMPI frequently referred to as the neurotic triad (i.e., *Hs*, *D* and *Hy*). Because scales *L* and *K* are predominantly keyed in the false direction, values on these scales must be extremely elevated under an all false endorsement set. If special scales are scored, extreme values will be found for the MMPI *R* scale. The standard scale all false pattern for adolescents on adolescent norms is also very similar to that produced by adult respondents as reported by Graham (1977) and Lachar (1974). The characteristics of the all false adolescent profile can be summarized as follows:

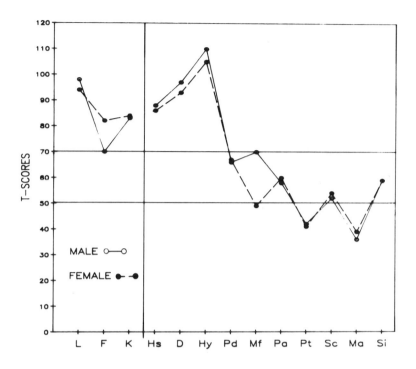

FIGURE 3.2   All false response pattern on adolescent norms.

1. Clinical level elevations on all validity scales.
2. Marked elevations on the neurotic triad (*Hs, D, Hy*).
3. If special scales are scored, extreme elevation on scale *R*.

Both the all true and all false patterns are easily discerned as invalid profiles by the typical MMPI interpreter. In addition to these response sets, however, adolescents may employ a deviant response set to the MMPI that involves random or "random-like" responses to the item pool. The profile configuration resulting from a random response set is shown in Fig. 3.3. This profile was produced by randomized responses generated by use of a table of random numbers. In the random response set the MMPI validity scale configuration is characterized by moderate to marked elevations on scale *F*, with moderate clinical scale elevations demonstrated for the neurotic triad and for the *Sc* scale. Random response sets must be considered whenever adolescents complete an

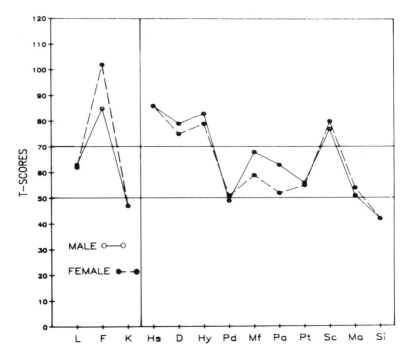

FIGURE 3.3   Random response pattern on adolescent norms.

MMPI "too quickly." Although somewhat similar to the random response set found for adult respondents as reported by Graham (1977), the random response pattern produced for adolescents scored on adolescent norms is much less elevated. Thus, random adolescent profiles are more difficult to detect as an invalid response pattern. Although the F scale score is high for these adolescents, it does not appear substantially different from F values frequently found for adolescents in inpatient psychiatric treatment. Further, the profile configuration, while unusual for adolescent respondents, does not appear so striking as to immediately indicate that an invalid response set was in operation. The implications of these series of simulated profiles for adolescents scored on adolescent norms are that although the all true and all false patterns are easily identifiable in adolescent populations, random response patterns are likely to be much more difficult to detect and particular caution and care should be applied in attempting to identify the latter set. The characteristics of the random response pattern may be summarized as follows:

1. Very short test completion time for respondent.
2. Moderate to marked elevation on Scale *F*.
3. Clinical elevations on the neurotic triad (*Hs, D,* and *Hy*) and scale *Sc*.

Another response set issue concerns the characteristics of profiles from adolescents who "fake good" or consciously seek to deny or underreport problems on the MMPI and those who "fake bad" or complete the MMPI with a desire to present a picture of their psychological functioning as involving a greater degree of symptomatology than they actually experience. Until very recently, there have been no experimental data that would allow us to characterize the MMPI profiles of adolescents who have been specifically instructed to respond to the MMPI in a "fake good" or "fake bad" set. Some conceptually based guidelines may be suggested, however, in attempting to evaluate adolescent profiles for these characteristics.

A "fake bad" response set should be considered whenever the raw score *F* values for adolescents exceed 25. As previously noted, Archer (in press) has found roughly 10% of adolescent outpatients and 17% of adolescent inpatients produce *F* scale values above 25. This does not imply that such a profile should be automatically rejected as invalid, but rather that this profile should be screened with particular care in relationship to the respondent's reading level, motivation, and ability. An MMPI profile should also be carefully evaluated for a "fake bad" response set whenever the MMPI profile produced by the respondent results in nine or more clinical scales elevated above a *T*-score value of 69. This "floating" profile characterized by all or nearly all clinical scales within clinical ranges is frequently associated with a response set to endorse items in the pathological direction without selectivity or specificity on the part of the respondent. Stated differently, the respondent has endorsed items in the pathological direction across the entirety of the MMPI item pool in a manner that typically does not realistically or accurately represent his or her degree of psychopathology. Floating profiles are found in roughly 1% of adolescent inpatients and outpatients (Archer, in press). In contrast, floating profile types are more common in adult samples and were found in 13% of cases in our data from adult inpatients. Obviously, in those rare situations when both conditions are present, i.e., when *F* raw score values of 26 or greater are accompanied by a "floating" profile, the probability of a "fake bad" response style is further increased.

To empirically investigate the characteristics of fake bad profiles among adolescents, a research study is currently being completed by Archer, Gordon, and Kirchner (1986). Fake bad profile characteristics were examined by the administration of the MMPI to a group of 40 public high school students, ranging in age from 15 to 17 years, who were roughly equally divided in terms of sex and race (black-white). Students were excluded from this study if they had a history of psychiatric problems as reflected in prior or concurrent psychiatric treatment. Subjects were given the MMPI with the following instructions:

> "We would like you to respond to the MMPI as you believe you would if you were experiencing serious emotional or psychological problems. By serious problems, we mean problems that were severe enough that hospitalization for treatment would be necessary. As you read the items in the MMPI, please respond to them as if you were seriously disturbed and in need of hospital treatment for psychiatric care".

The mean profile produced by this group of students under fake bad instructions is presented in Fig. 3.4. The characteristics of this MMPI profile, consistent with findings from the adult literature as reported by Lachar (1974) and Graham (1977), show a grossly exaggerated picture of symptomatology that includes a mean F scale T-score value of 130, and clinical range elevations on all MMPI clinical scales except Mf and Si. Overall, the profile demonstrates the dramatic saw-toothed contours noted in studies of adults attempting to fake bad on the MMPI. This adolescent mean profile is quite similar to one reported by Lachar (1974), which had been produced by a 23-year-old male who was attempting to avoid court-martial in the U.S. Navy by presenting a picture of severe symptomatology. Less than 10% of the adolescent respondents in this study demonstrated any selectivity in their endorsement of pathological items, with the vast majority of adolescents apparently endorsing psychopathological items in the critical direction whenever such items were obvious or identifiable. The results of this study serve to suggest that adolescents, at least normal adolescents in public high school settings, may have substantial difficulty in simulating psychiatric illness. The F scale and clinical scale indices summarized below should adequately serve to screen for those adolescents who attempt to fake bad on the MMPI:

1. F scale raw score value of 26 or greater.
2. Presence of a floating profile characterized by nine or more scales elevated within clinical ranges.

The converse of the fake bad profile consists of deliberate or unconscious efforts to fake good or underreport symptomatology on the MMPI. Conceptually, the following guidelines may also be of general utility in detecting this attempt to distort MMPI features:

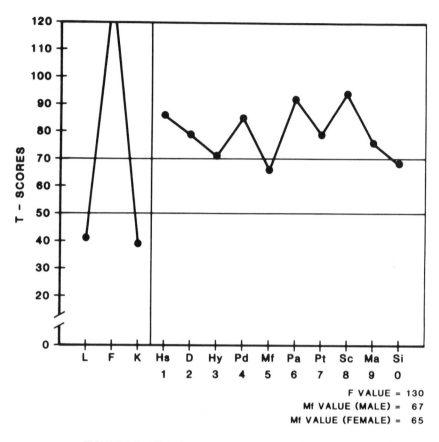

FIGURE 3.4   "Fake bad" profile on adolescent norms.

1. A "V" validity scale configuration.
2. All clinical scales equal to or less than T-score values of 65 in respondents with known psychopathology.

When elevations on both L and K exceed T-score values of 65 and the validity scales produce a "V" configuration, the possibility of a relatively crude "fake good" response style should be carefully considered. Roughly 2% of adolescent inpatients and 1% of adolescent outpatients produce this type of "fake good" validity configuration (Archer, in press). Additionally, when adolescents with known and marked degrees of psychopathology, such as adolescent psychiatric inpatients, produce no MMPI clinical scales in excess of T-score values of 65, the possibility of a more subtle "fake good" response pattern should be carefully evaluated. This "suppressed" profile is found for 11% of adolescent inpatients and 26% of adolescents in outpatient settings (Archer, in press). Similar to the cautions concerning the "fake bad" profile, when a rare response pattern is found in which both L and K are elevated above 65 and in which all clinical scales are below T-score values of 65 for groups such as inpatients, the possibility that such a profile represents a "fake good" response pattern is particularly marked.

In the data collected by Archer, Gordon, and Kirchner (1986), an examination was also conducted to ascertain the characteristics of adolescents who attempted to fake good on the MMPI. Studies with adult respondents have found that the ability to simulate a normal profile in adult psychiatric populations is significantly related to a favorable treatment outcome among schizophrenics (Newmark, Gentry, Whitt, McKee, & Wicker, 1983) and in general inpatient psychiatric samples (Grayson & Olinger, 1957). Additionally, Bonfilio and Lyman (1981) have investigated the degree to which college students could simulate a profile of a "well-adjusted college student" in relation to their actual MMPI profile features. Results from this study indicated that simulations produced by college students classified as neurotic, normal, and psychopathic based on their actual MMPIs administered under normal instructions were essentially within normal limits. Simulated profiles produced by college students labeled psychotic or hypomanic, however, contained clearly pathological or clinical range features. To investigate this issue in an adolescent sample, the MMPI was administered to a group of 22 adolescents, with a mean age of 14.76 years, in adolescent inpatient psychiatric settings. Ten of these adolescents were female and 12 were male and the mean length of time between their admission to the psychiatric unit and the administration of the MMPI under "fake good" instructions was approximately 40 days. This group of 22 adolescents were individually administered the MMPI with the following instructional set:

> We would like you to respond to the MMPI as you believe a well-adjusted teenager would who is not experiencing serious emotional or psychological problems. By well adjusted, we mean an adolescent who is doing well and is comfortable in school, at home, and with his or her peers. As you read the items, please respond to them as you believe a well-adjusted adolescent would who is not in need of psychiatric counseling and who is relatively happy and comfortable.

Based on the results of this administration, two distinct profiles emerged in relation to fake good instructional sets. One profile, produced by 8 subjects and termed an "ineffective" profile, consisted of very poor simulations of normalcy as defined by one or more clinical scales elevated in excess of a *T*-score value of 70. In contrast, a group of 14 subjects were able to simulate normalcy to the extent that none of their clinical scale values were elevated within clinical ranges, and this group were referred to as "effective" in their simulation attempts. Figure 3.5 presents the mean MMPI profiles for the effective and ineffective fake good groups.

Although many of the characteristics of this data sample are currently being analyzed, including the relationship between actual admission profiles and simulated fake good profiles for the subjects in the study, two findings are currently apparent regarding differences between the effective and ineffective group.

First, the ineffective group tended to have a younger mean age than respondents in the effective group, such that ineffective respondents

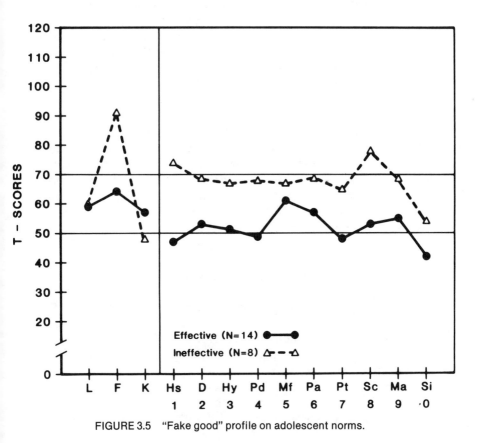

FIGURE 3.5   "Fake good" profile on adolescent norms.

tended to fall within the 12- to 14-year-old age grouping, or the lower segment of the adolescent ages sampled in this study. Second, the psychiatric diagnoses of adolescents in the ineffective group tended to be overrepresented by more "serious" diagnoses, with the two schizophrenics in this sample, and the majority of borderline personality disorders, found in the ineffective grouping. Thus, findings would suggest that younger adolescents and adolescents demonstrating evidence of more serious psychopathology are less able to simulate normalcy on MMPI items under fake good instructions. The mean profile for the ineffective group is marked by a very substantial elevation on the F scale in addition to clinical range elevations on scales Hs and Sc.

In contrast, older adolescents and adolescents with less severe diagnoses such as dysthymic disorder, conduct disorder, and other personality disorders (i.e., the other major psychiatric groupings employed in this study) were capable of producing a within normal limits MMPI profile that could potentially result in a substantial underestimate of their actual psychopathology. For the astute and careful MMPI interpreter, the elevations on scales L and K for the effective group may serve as a signal that a defensive response style had been employed, and that an attempt to appear virtuous and relatively free of psychiatric symptomatology had been undertaken by the respondents. On the other hand, the mean fake good profile for the effective group shows L and K scale elevations substantially below the clinical range L and K scale elevations reported by Graham (1977) for adults who were deliberately faking good on the MMPI.

Thus, conclusions from these data include the observations that the ability to simulate normalcy among adolescent psychiatric inpatients, similar to that of adult psychiatric patients, is related to the presence of less serious actual psychopathology and that many adolescents appear to be capable of faking good on the MMPI to a degree that is equivalent to or in excess of their adult counterparts.

STRATEGIES FOR CLINICAL INTERPRETATION

Given two possible sources of norms for interpreting adolescent MMPI responses (i.e., adolescent and adult) and the availability of codetype descriptors based on adult and adolescent respondents, there are obviously a variety of logical alternatives or approaches in attempting to interpret adolescent response patterns.

One might score adolescent responses on adult norms and then interpret MMPI profiles based on information derived from clinical correlate data established with adult respondents. Although such an approach is often seen in clinical practice with the MMPI, there is no research literature supporting this combination. An alternative approach would be to employ adult norms in scoring MMPI profiles, with subsequent profile interpretation based on adolescent data derived from Marks et al. (1974). This interpretive strategy is also widely employed in clinical practices with the MMPI, and examples of this can be seen in numerous published research studies. A third variant of the approaches described above consists of scoring adolescent response patterns on both adult and adolescent norms and, after examining clinical descriptors derived from both norms, selecting those statements that most closely correspond to the clinically observed symptomatology of the respondent. This approach served as the "conventional wisdom" for interpreting adolescent response patterns for the decade from the early 1970s to the early 1980s. The essential problem posed by all of the above approaches entails the degree to which MMPI profiles produced for adolescents using adult norms produce clinical impressions that are unwarranted. The above approaches, therefore, are inappropriate when applied to adolescent respondents and unsupported by the available research concerning adolescents and the MMPI.

Several interpretive approaches are available for use with adolescent respondents that involve the use of adolescent norms conversions. For example, one could score adolescent responses on adolescent norms and then interpret the resulting profile based on descriptive statements derived from adolescent respondents (Marks et al., 1974) or from data derived from adult respondents (e.g., Graham, 1977; Lachar, 1974) or from a combination of data generated by both adolescent and adult sources. The available literature supports the use of adolescent norm conversions for adolescent responses but does not allow for strong conclusions regarding correlate data sources. Research findings by Klinge and Strauss (1976) clearly indicate that adolescent norms produce the most accurate clinical descriptors for adolescent responses. This study used clinical correlate data derived exclusively from adult sources for both adolescent and adult norm conversions, however, and therefore was not relevant to the issue of clinical descriptor sources. Recent research by Wimbish (1984) examined adolescent responses scored on both adolescent and adult norms in combinations with clinical descriptor data from adolescent and adult sources. Her findings indicated adolescent norms combined with clinical descriptors derived from adolescent sources provided the most accurate statements for adolescents. Ehrenworth and Archer (1985) also examined clinicians' ratings of narrative accuracy for a group of adolescent inpatients whose profiles were scored on both adolescent and adult norms and interpreted using clinical descriptors from adolescent and adult codetype sources. In contrast to findings by Wimbish, results by Ehrenworth and Archer (1985) indicated that the use of clinical descriptors from adolescent sources (Marks et al, 1974) resulted in less accurate descriptors than those derived from adult sources (e.g., Graham, 1977; Lachar, 1974).

At the present time, a "commonsense" compromise appears to be most appropriate in terms of recommendations for the interpretation of adolescent profiles. This recommendation centers on using adolescent norms in converting adolescent raw scores and subsequently interpreting resulting profiles based on combining available information from both adolescent samples (i.e., Marks et al. 1974) and codetype descriptors available from the widely used adult "cookbooks" such as Graham (1977), Greene (1980), and Lachar (1974). Future research may aid in establishing the clear superiority of accuracy ratings for clinical descriptors derived from adolescent versus adult sources, but until such an empirical basis is clearly established the most reasonable course of action appears to involve utilizing available information from both sources.

ADOLESCENT PROFILES ON ADOLESCENT NORMS

Following the preceding recommendations for the interpretive strategy optimally employed with adolescent respondents, a number of additional observations and statements are appropriate concerning the general characteristics of adolescent respondents when raw score values are converted to adolescent norms. The conclusion that adolescent norm conversion is the most appropriate means of handling adolescent responses does not imply that such a procedure renders the interpretation or evaluation of adolescent response patterns to be either simple or straightforward. The most important "problem" that remains in attempting to interpret adolescent patterns scored on adolescent norms is that resulting profiles typically produce subclinical elevations, even for adolescents in inpatient psychiatric settings (e.g., Ehrenworth & Archer, 1985). The inherent contradiction in interpreting a normal range profile for an adolescent with known evidence of serious psychopathology has probably contributed to the continuation of the use of adult norms for adolescents. Thus, just as the application of adult norms to adolescent response patterns tends to produce profiles that overemphasize or exaggerate psychiatric symptomatology, so the application of the Marks et al. (1974) adolescent norms to adolescent responses produces patterns that may often underestimate the degree of psychopathology.

Normal range mean profiles for inpatient adolescent populations have been reported by Archer (1984), Archer et al. (1985), Archer, Stolberg, Gordon, and Goldman (1986), Ehrenworth and Archer (1985) and Klinge and Strauss (1976). For example, Archer, Stolberg, Gordon, and Goldman have presented the mean MMPI profiles for male and female adolescent inpatients and outpatients scored on adolescent norms as shown in Fig. 3.6. These mean profiles are similar to findings by Westendorp and Kirk (1982) for adolescents in outpatient and short-term private psychiatric hospital settings. Additionally, Archer et al. (1985) have presented mean MMPI profiles for a group of 146 male and female adolescent inpatients evaluated at hospital admission and grouped by principal psychiatric diagnoses as shown in Fig. 3.7. With the exception of adolescents labeled as borderline personality disorders and a residual group of 30 adolescents categorized as "other," the three remaining groups produced modal profiles within normal limits. The findings of Archer et al. (1985) illustrate that although mean profiles derived from heterogeneous groupings of inpatient adolescents produce values within normal limits, diagnostic breakdowns of these groups do isolate patterns of clinical range profiles for selected diagnostic categories. Nevertheless, the question remains why adolescents who have demonstrated sufficient psychopathology to warrant psychiatric hospitalization consistently obtain mean profiles that are within normal limits on adolescent norms.

Several sources of observation may be relevant to modal profiles by adolescents in inpatient settings. First, we have noted the difficulties inherent in the diagnosis of adolescents given the unique developmental characteristics of this age group. The literature relative to adolescent psychopathology underscores that many individuals experience heightened

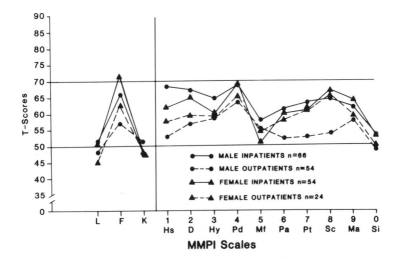

FIGURE 3.6   Mean MMPI for adolescent male and female inpatients and outpatients.

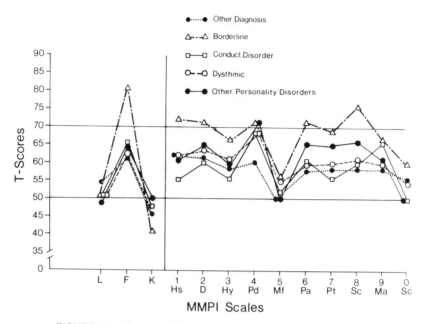

FIGURE 3.7   Mean MMPI T-scores for five diagnostic groups.

emotionality, feelings of alienation and isolation, as well as diminished impulse control during adolescence. Although this "turbulence" may not serve as a universal characteristic of adolescent development (Offer & Offer, 1975), data from the MMPI on the salient differences between adult and adolescent response patterns suggest substantially higher levels of self-reported symptomatology occur during adolescence. The implication of these findings is that the "dividing line" between normalcy and pathology during adolescence may be much less clear than during adult development. Adolescents who are not deviant in the statistical sense (i.e., who do not produce clinical elevations in excess of a T-score of 70 on the MMPI) may display behaviors or report experiences disturbing enough to be labeled "deviant" and even to result in hospitalization. Stated differently, the "typical" adolescent experiences sufficient psychological turbulence and distress such that relatively minor deviations in the course of normal development may warrant psychiatric intervention and response.

The result of this phenomenon for MMPI profile interpretation is that the application of the T-score criterion of 70, found useful in defining clinical symptomatology for adult respondents, may be of less utility with adolescents. A significantly greater proportion of adolescents than adults (26.6% versus 5%) produce normal range MMPI profiles upon admission to inpatient treatment facilities and 43% of adolescents in our outpatient sample were found to produce "within normal limits" profiles (Archer, in press). Research is clearly needed comparing groups of normal adolescents with adolescent psychiatric samples (both inpatient and outpatient) to aid in establishing the optimal elevation levels for defining "clinical" patterns. Until such time as this research has been undertaken the use of a rigid criterion based on T-score values of 70 does not appear to be supported. Adolescent profiles may yield greater information if the examiner is prepared to employ flexibility in his or her definition of clinical symptomatology with adolescent groups. Ehrenworth and Archer (1985) have recommended consideration of a T-score value of 65 in defining clinical range elevations in adolescents in inpatient settings. Employing this criterion in the inpatient and outpatient adolescent samples previously described (Archer, in press) reduced the frequency of normal range profiles to 11% and 26%, respectively.

A second observation relevant to the relatively low mean profiles typically found for adolescents relates to the absence of a K-correction procedure for adolescents. Bertelson, Marks, and May (1982), in noting the contrast between application of adult and adolescent norms to adolescent respondents, stated, "Since these adolescent norms do not include the K-correction, adolescent profiles are naturally lower than adult profiles plotted with K-corrections" (p. 317). Archer (1984), however, suggested that although this explanation may be relevant to the general differences in profile elevations produced by adult and adolescent norms, it does not account for specific discrepancies between adult and adolescent norms that are quite marked for scale Sc but are much less dramatic for scale Pt, whereas both scales receive an equal K-correction value using adult scoring procedures.

The absence of a K-correction procedure with adolescent norms does not directly explain the specific patterns of differences found between adult scoring procedures and adolescent scoring procedures for adolescent respondents. Rather, these differences reflect fundamental differences in frequency of endorsements occurring within the MMPI item pool. This does not imply, however, that the development of a K-correction procedure for adolescent respondents would not be valuable. A K-corrected procedure might serve to substantially increase the ability of the MMPI to detect psychopathological traits or characteristics for adolescent respondents in a manner similar to its usefulness with adults. Development of such adolescent K-correction procedures would very likely result in much different weighting patterns than those used with adult respondents, however, possibly involving a different set of clinical scales.

Evidence provided by Heilbrun (1963) indicates that the optimal K weights for various scales may vary widely from population to population. Specifically, Heilbrun investigated the degree to which an optimal K weighting system could be developed for the 10 MMPI clinical scales to identify adjustment problems within a college population. The resulting K-correction pattern devised for this population differs dramatically from the standard K-correction procedure, with major features involving a negative weighting of Hy and the deletion of weights from scales Hs, Pd, and Ma. Similarly, Greene (1980) has reviewed a series of studies that demonstrate the need to empirically validate the optimal K weights to be utilized with specific samples and populations. The development and use of specific K-correction factors for adolescent respondents, uniquely derived for adolescent populations and sensitive to variables such as type of setting and age of respondent, may serve to increase the overall accuracy of statements generated from adolescent MMPI profiles scored on adolescent norms. Gottesman and his colleagues and Colligan and Offord provide both K-corrected and non-K-corrected adolescent normative values in the appendices of this book. Although these authors recognize the potential limitations in applying adult-derived K weights to adolescent scores, K-corrected data are offered as a "starting place" for empirical research efforts in this area.

A final observation related to the frequent occurrence of within normal limits profiles for psychiatrically disturbed adolescents relates to the adequacy of the currently employed adolescent norms as developed by Marks et al. (1974). In this regard, it is helpful to briefly review the norm collection procedure utilized by Marks et al. Peter Briggs is reported in the Marks et al. text as having begun the process of norm development by selecting cases from the original Minnesota statewide sample that was collected by Hathaway and Monachesi (1963). Briggs selected, from the original Hathaway and Monachesi data, samples of 100 boys and 100 girls at the age groupings of 14, 15, and 16 as well as an additional 80 boys and 40 girls for the age grouping of 17. In order to obtain a more nationally representative sample, Marks et al. reported that an additional 1,046 profiles were collected in 1964/65 from urban and rural settings in both public and private schools in Alabama, California, Kansas, Missouri, North Carolina, and Ohio. By combining this data with the original data selected from the Hathaway and Monachesi sample, the adolescent norms were constructed based on mean raw score values and standard deviation data for samples ranging in size from 139 females and 166 males at the age group of 17 to 280 females and 271 males at the age group of 14. Marks, Seeman, and Haller employed all profiles selected in their samples regardless of elevations on scales L, F, and K, thus no profiles were eliminated from analysis because of validity criterion.

The adolescent norms developed by Marks, Seeman, and Haller were designed for use without a K-correction factor. Marks et al. indicated that such a procedure was employed because the original K scale weights were developed on relatively small samples of adults and their applicability to adolescents was questionable. Further, Marks et al. cited data indicating negative correlations between validity coefficients based on psychotherapists' descriptions and K scale magnitude for an adolescent sample.

Recently, Gottesman, Hanson, Kroeker, and Briggs have analyzed the original Minnesota statewide sample data collected by Hathaway and Monachesi to examine the normative values that would be derived from this entire sample, a procedure that allows for contrast with the normative values reported by Marks et al. The raw score and T-score normative values developed by Gottesman et al. are based on the responses of 6,871 male and 7,148 female 15-year-olds from the Hathaway and Monachesi sample and 1,810 male and 1,864 female 18-year-olds from the Minnesota statewide data (I. I. Gottesman and P. Briggs, personal communication, October, 1985). Unlike the Marks et al. procedure, the data developed by Gottesman et al. excluded certain profiles from analyses based upon a variety of criteria including F scale values that were equal to or greater than a raw score of 23, L scale values equal to or greater than 10, or more than 100 items left unanswered by the respondent. In addition, Gottesman et al. included age criteria such that respondents were not included from the 9th-grade sample of the statewide Minnesota project if they were older than 16.5 years old at the time of the assessment, and respondents were excluded from the 12th-grade retest segment of the Minnesota sample if they were older than 19.5 years at the time of that administration. Using these criteria, Gottesman et al. excluded 1,066 adolescents from the 15-year-old sample and 182 adolescents from the 18-year-old sample. The raw score means and T-score values for all of the standard MMPI scales, and selected special scales, are included in Appendix C of this book. In addition, these tables allow for a comparison between the normative raw score data reported by Gottesman et al. with raw score values reported by Marks et al. in their adolescent sample and with comparable data from the adult normative sample.

Close inspection of the contrast between normative raw score values for these samples indicate that the values reported for the entire statewide Minnesota sample typically fall between values reported by Marks et al. and adult expected values. For example, for 15-year-old males, the Gottesman et al. raw score mean values fall between Marks et al. and adult values for scales L, F, Hs, D, Hy, Pd, Mf, Pa, Pt, Sc, Ma, and Si. Similarly for males at the age grouping of 1, the Gottesman et al. norms occur between raw score values reported by Marks et al. and adult values on scales F, D, Hy, Pd, Pa, Pt, Sc, Ma and Si. For some of the scales mentioned above, the variation between the Marks et al. and Gottesman et al. norms are relatively minor, whereas on other scales several raw score point values separate these two estimates of adolescent norms. In nearly all cases, the raw score values reported in the Gottesman et al. data are in the direction of being lower than their counterparts in the Marks et al. norms.

These findings would appear to suggest that the norms reported by Marks, Seeman, and Haller, at least to the extent that they represent samples of the data collected by Hathaway and Monachesi, may have overestimated the occurrence of pathological item endorsements for adolescent respondents. This conclusion, however, must be tempered by at least two major qualifications. First, Marks et al. did not employ validity criteria in their selection of cases, and therefore would have been expected to produce a sample that contained respondents endorsing more items in the pathological direction than the procedure employed by Gottesman et al., which used a variety of validity cutoffs. Second, Marks, Seeman, and Haller are quite clear in indicating that their data collection procedures included a large number of respondents that were not contained within the original Hathaway and Monachesi data collection procedures, i.e., adolescent data collected in the mid-1960s from a variety of states. Thus the relatively higher raw score values reported by Marks, Seeman, and Haller may have been a reflection of the impact of this non-Minnesota, and more recent, data on their total norm sample. The issue of the accuracy of the Marks, Seeman, and Haller adolescent norms in terms of their representativeness of contemporary adolescent item endorsement patterns will ultimately be resolved as a product of the several adolescent norm projects being completed for the MMPI.

At the time of this writing in 1986, several independent efforts are currently underway to develop a "new" set of adolescent norms for the MMPI. This issue is discussed in much greater detail in the final chapter of this book. These efforts consist of the reanalysis of Hathaway and Monachesi's data currently being completed by Gottesman et al. based on the responses of approximately 15,000 adolescents in the late 1940s and early 1950s. Additionally, Colligan and his colleagues at the Mayo Clinic are establishing the normative response patterns for contemporary adolescents using the original form of the MMPI with approximately 1,300 teenagers from the American Midwest. Finally, a current restandardization project is being conducted at the University of Minnesota under the guidance of Grant Dahlstrom, John Graham, and James Butcher to produce new adolescent MMPI norms as well as a modified item pool specifically created for adolescent respondents. Data from all of these projects are likely to be of substantial interest to users of the MMPI with adolescents, and each project will probably contribute to our understanding of adolescent response patterns on the MMPI. Of particular relevance to our current discussion, the eventual publication of the norms developed by each of these projects will ultimately lead to an empirical method by which to evaluate the adequacy of the original adolescent norms as developed by Marks et al.

Preliminary data from the University of Minnesota Project (Williams, Butcher & Graham, 1986) and from the Mayo group (Colligan & Offord, 1986) derived on contemporary samples of adolescents currently suggest that the norms produced by Marks et al. (1974) may continue to serve as a reasonable reference point for evaluating the MMPI response patterns of adolescents in the 1980s.

4

CODETYPE CLINICAL CORRELATES FOR ADOLESCENTS

As we have noted in the previous chapters, sufficient data currently exist to strongly recommend the use of adolescent norms, but little data are available to guide the practitioner in the optimal selection of clinical descriptors for adolescents' MMPI profiles. Given the current "state of the art," it was noted that a commonsense compromise appears to be most appropriate in interpreting adolescent profiles involving the selection and utilization of compatible correlate information from both adolescent and adult cookbook sources. Although Marks et al. (1974) provide the only source of codetype descriptors based on investigations of adolescent psychiatric samples, several books are currently available that present MMPI correlates for adult codetypes. In particular, the codetype information provided by Graham (1977), Greene (1980), and Lachar (1974) are probably the most widely used MMPI sources for adult respondents. These texts represent concise summations of research findings from a variety of primary sources such as Carson (1969); Dahlstrom et al. (1972); Drake and Oetting (1959); Duckworth and Duckworth (1975); Fowler (1966); Gilberstadt and Duker (1965); Gynther, Altman, and Sletten (1975); and Marks and Seeman (1963). Thus, the information offered by Graham, Greene, and Lachar integrated data from various research and clinical sources and provided a compiled source of codetype descriptions.

In recommending the interpretation strategy of combining compatible statements from adolescent and adult clinical correlate sources, an assumption is made that descriptors found to be applicable to clinical codetypes in both adolescent and adult samples may be more "robust" and accurate for adolescent respondents than correlates that have not been "cross-validated" in this manner. It should be explicitly stated, however, that this assumption is speculative and represents this author's "best guess" given the research literature and clinical experience surrounding the interpretation of adolescent profiles. A major effort to cross-validate the Marks et al. descriptors has never been undertaken. Until such time as this type of research has been accomplished, however, clinicians will continue to be faced with the problem of selecting descriptors in the interpretation of adolescent MMPI data.

In recommending the use of adolescent descriptors generated by combining codetype information provided by Marks, Seeman, and Haller with adult sources, the implicit assumption was also made that these literature sources are readily available to the MMPI interpreter and that the necessary time is also available for the clinician to undertake this comparison task. Recognizing that sufficient resources and time may not always be present for the clinician, the purpose of this chapter is to provide this compiled information based on the author's completion of this task for a variety of commonly occurring codetypes.

THE CODETYPE INTERPRETATION APPROACH

As noted by Graham (1977) configural approaches to the interpretation of MMPI data have been viewed as the potentially richest source of diagnostic and descriptive information from MMPI data since the origination of this test instrument. Thus, early writings (Meehl, 1951, 1956b; Meehl & Dahlstrom, 1960) emphasized the interpretation of codetype MMPI information, and several of the earliest MMPI validity studies were focused on identifying reliable clinical correlates of MMPI two-point codetypes (e.g., Meehl, 1951).

Although several codetypes "cookbook" systems have been developed, such as those provided by Gilberstadt and Duker (1965) and Marks and Seeman (1963), which have employed very complex rules for classifying multiscale elevations, the more recent efforts and writings regarding codetype descriptors have tended to employ much simpler two-scale approaches in classifying MMPI profiles. These systems, such as those exemplified in Graham (1977) and Greene (1980), have typically assigned MMPI profiles to codetypes based on the two scales with the highest clinical range elevations. Several investigations, such as research by Lewandowski and Graham (1972), have demonstrated that reliable clinical correlates can be established for profiles that are classified based on these simpler two-point code systems. Recent data by Pancoast, Archer, and Gordon (in press) also indicate that assignments to simple codetype systems can be made with acceptable levels of reliability by independent raters. The obvious advantage of using the two-point code system is that a much larger proportion of profiles can be classified in a typical clinical setting when numerous stringent criteria are not required for such codetype assignments (Graham, 1977).

A high-point codetype is typically referred to by the numerical designation of the two scales most elevated in the profile, with convention dictating that the most elevated scale be designated first. Thus, if an adolescent produced his or her highest clinical elevations on scales *Pd* and *Ma* (in that order), the profile would result in classification as a 4–9 codetype. Throughout this textbook, individual MMPI scales have typically been referred to by their "names" or alphabetical abbreviations rather than numerical designations. This procedure has been followed to minimize confusion in scale delineations for the novice MMPI user. In discussing codetype classifications, however, MMPI scales are referred to in this chapter by their numerical designation in a manner consistent with the codetype literature. In addition to issues related to MMPI traditions, numerical designation of scales is probably the generally preferred practice among experienced MMPI users for a very important reason, i.e., the names that have been given to the clinical scales may often be misleading and may serve as inadequate descriptors of what that scale is currently believed to measure. For example, the Psychasthenia scale was originally developed to measure symptomatology related to what was later referred to as obsessive-compulsive neurosis. Psychasthenia is not a psychiatric label in common use today, and Graham (1977) has noted that scale *Pt* of the MMPI is currently thought of as a reliable index of psychological distress and discomfort, particularly related to symptoms of anxiety, tension, and apprehension.

Of primary importance in employing codetype descriptors with any population is clear recognition and awareness that the attribution of correlate statements to a particular client implicitly entails probability estimates. These estimates of accuracy may vary greatly based on the source of the descriptor statement (adequacy of research methodology, characteristics of population sampled, statistical strength of findings) and the individual characteristics of the client being assessed. Even under optimal conditions in which cross-validated research data exist that have led to the derivation of clinical correlates from samples highly similar to the individual being evaluated, a specific clinical correlate may be found not to apply to a specific client. Thus, as Greene (1980) noted, MMPI cookbooks even within adult populations "have not been the panacea that was originally thought" (p. 121). Nevertheless, they continue to serve as a valuable source of hypothesis concerning client characteristics when such cautions are borne in mind by the interpreter.

DERIVING A CODETYPE CLASSIFICATION
FOR ADOLESCENTS

In the adult codetype information as provided by such sources as Graham (1977) and Greene (1980), profiles are typically placed into two-point codetypes based on the two clinical scales that show the greatest degree of clinical range elevation. In these and most other systems, few high point codes are provided that involve scales 5 and 0, because these scales have often been excluded from the designation of clinical scales and were frequently excluded in codetype research in early MMPI investigations (Graham, 1977).

In general, two-point codes are used interchangeably; for example 2-7 codetypes are seen as equivalent to 7-2 codetypes, unless differences are specifically noted. Further, the absolute elevation of the two high scales is typically not considered beyond the assumption that they are occurring within clinical ranges, and the relative elevation of the two highest scales in relationship to the remaining profile is typically not considered or discussed in codetype narratives. In these and other sources, if a profile does not fit any of the two-point codetypes presented, the clinician is advised to employ an interpretation strategy based on clinical correlates found for individual MMPI scales that are elevated.

In Lachar's (1974) codetype system, more complex and specific codetype classification rules are frequently offered in relationship to actuarial statements, and some three- and occasionally four-point codes are contained within this system. When Lachar reports codetype information on the 2-7-8 profile, for example, which was derived from research from Marks and Seeman (1963), he also provides the profile codetype rules developed by Marks and Seeman to allow the clinician to independently evaluate the "goodness of fit" between a specific MMPI profile and the general codetype. Under the 2-7-8 profile, for example, the following rules are provided (1974, p. 59):

1. Scales 2, 7, and 8 over 70T.
2. Scale 2 minus 1 more than 15T.
3. Scale 2 cannot exceed 8 by more than 14T.
4. Scale 7 minus 4 more than 10T.
5. Scale 7 minus 6 more than 10T.
6. Scale 8 cannot exceed 7 by more than 4T.
7. Scale 7 and 8 greater than 1 and 3.
8. Scale 9 less than 70T.
9. Scale 0 over 70T.
10. Scale L and K less than 70T, F less than 80T.

In contrast to this codetype assignment system developed for adults, a somewhat different procedure was recommended by Marks et al. (1974) for classification of adolescent MMPI profiles into codetypes. Once an individual's MMPI profile has been plotted, the resulting configuration may be compared to the codetype profiles provided by Marks et al. in their mean profile index based on the two highest elevations occurring in the particular profile. If the codetype for the individual respondent corresponds to one of the two-digit codetypes presented by Marks et al., the clinician is referred to the codetype descriptor appropriate for that configuration. If the respondent's codetype is not classifiable, however, under this system, the authors recommend dropping the second high point and substituting the third highest scale to produce a new two-point code. If this procedure then results in a classifiable codetype, the clinician is encouraged to interpret that profile based on the clinical correlate information provided for that code. If the profile remains unclassifiable following this procedure, Marks et al. suggest that their actuarial interpretation system not be applied for that individual respondent. As in the adult literature, these authors encourage clinicians with unclassifiable profiles to employ a single-scale correlate interpretation strategy.

Because of the importance of the Marks, Seeman, and Haller actuarial system for adolescents, the following section presents a more detailed discussion of the procedures used by these authors in development of their actuarial system.

In terms of recommendations for the clinician in deriving codetype assignments, it would appear most appropriate at this time to employ a codetyping strategy that places an individual profile in a codetype based on the highest two-point characteristics occurring within clinical ranges for that profile. When such classification does not result in a codetype for which clinical correlate information is available from standard sources, it is suggested that the clinician interpret the profile based on single-scale correlates. The "substitution and reclassification" procedure suggested by Marks et al. (i.e., the substitution of the third most elevated profile scale for the second highest scale to achieve a two-point classification) is not recommended.

These recommendations are based on the view that very complex codetype rules may often be too conservative and result in actuarial systems that are unable to handle the majority of profiles found in the typical clinical setting. Similarly, the current recommendations are offered based on the belief that the Marks, Seeman, and Haller reclassification procedure for profiles that are initially unclassifiable may be too liberal and result in the classification of many profiles that may differ in salient and significant ways from the codetype to which they are eventually assigned.

THE MARKS, SEEMAN, AND HALLER ACTUARIAL
SYSTEM FOR ADOLESCENTS

As has been frequently noted throughout this text, the Marks et al. (1974) actuarial system for adolescents is currently the only source of clinical correlate data for adolescent profiles. For this reason, and because of the large sample size and objective methodology employed by these researchers, a more detailed review of the development of their system is warranted.

The main sample from which Marks et al. developed adolescent codetypes consisted of 834 teenagers who were involved in psychotherapy between the years 1965 and 1970. In acquiring this data set, the authors contacted 74 agencies in 30 states, ultimately involving 172 therapists, who agreed to participate in their study. This treatment sample consisted of white adolescents between the ages of 12 and 18 inclusive who had been involved in psychotherapy for a minimum of 10 therapy hours and who were not mentally retarded. Of the 172 psychotherapists who provided patient ratings, 116 were mental health professionals (psychiatrists, psychologists, or social workers) with at least 2 years of postgraduate therapy experience. Marks et al. report that this group of experienced therapists rated 746 (or 90%) of their adolescent patients. Therapists were requested to complete an adjective checklist, a case data schedule, and a Q-sort inventory for each of their patients. In addition, each adolescent patient completed a variety of self-administered objective questionnaires covering such topic areas as attitude toward self, attitudes toward others, motivational needs, and areas of conflict. Taken together, a preliminary correlate pool was available to Marks et al. that consisted of 2,302 descriptors potentially relevant to the adolescents in their study. The authors then selected from these potential correlates 1,265 descriptors that (a) occurred with substantial frequency; (b) were relevant to both male and female respondents; and (c) offered clinically relevant descriptors for codetype analyses.

The Marks et al. procedure for analyzing and evaluating these data consisted of converting adolescent MMPI raw scores to non-K-corrected age-appropriate norms based on their adolescent normative data. Profiles were then coded and grouped using two-point codetypes based on the 10 clinical MMPI scales. In cases in which adolescents produced more than two clinical scales that were equally elevated as profile high points, those profiles were classified into codetypes based on the use of elevated scales with the lowest numeric values, e.g., a 2-4-8 profile was classified as a 2-4 codetype. Profiles were subsequently combined based on two-point reversals (e.g., 2-4 = 4-2) and a minimum number of 10 was set for the creation of a code group for statistical analyses. This procedure resulted in classification of 749 of the 834 adolescents in their sample.

Rather than eliminating the remaining 10% of their sample (i.e., 85 cases), Marks et al. then made an important decision to increase sample sizes within codetypes. Specifically, the authors decided to reclassify the remaining profiles by discarding the second highest scale and substituting the third highest elevation within the profile for classification purposes. Under this reclassification procedure, then, a 1-7-8 profile would be codetyped as a 1-8/8-1. This resulted in a creation of codetypes that varied substantially in their degree of "purity," from such codetypes as 4-8/8-4, which were totally unaffected by this reclassification procedure, to codetypes such as 6-8/8-6 and 8-9/9-8 in which these reclassified codetypes constituted 24% and 46% of the total cases for those codes, respectively. In all, 29 adolescent codetypes with 10 or more cases per type were established by the use of these procedures. Statistical analyses were performed within codetypes when adequate sample sizes existed, e.g., high versus low codetype profiles or 3-1 versus 1-3 comparisons. In addition, analyses were performed between codetypes in which descriptors applicable to a particular codetype were evaluated in comparison with descriptors for the remaining codetypes.

Finally, Marks et al. collected an additional sample of adolescent data consisting of 419 inpatients and outpatients in treatment at the Ohio State University Health Center during the period of 1970 through 1973. Of particular significance was the fact that 61 cases in this sample consisted of black adolescents. The inclusion of this additional sample resulted in the addition of 10 or more cases to 22 of the previously existing 29 codetype classifications. The data collected in this sample involved certain variables not investigated in the original 1965-1970 sample, including information regarding drug use and abuse. The data from this additional sample were abstracted and added to supplement the narrative descriptive data for these 22 codetypes.

These procedures employed by Marks et al. resulted in an actuarial system that contains substantial strengths as well as areas of substantial problems. In contrast to prior research in the area, the investigation by Marks et al. had enormous advantages. For example, Hathaway and Monachesi published *An Atlas of Juvenile MMPI Profiles* in 1961 in which narrative information was provided for 1,088 adolescents on a case by case basis. Although the atlas was meant to serve as a reference book by which clinicians could profile an adolescent respondent and then search through the text for descriptions of adolescents with similar profile features the unwieldiness of this system and the lack of statistical evaluation render it of little practical value in this task. The Marks, Seeman, and

Haller work, in contrast, does offer the clinician a meaningful method of deriving clinical correlates for adolescent profiles based on a well-documented methodological and statistical procedure for identifying correlate information. Two primary problems, however, exist in the Marks et al. data that are related to the "over-analysis" of their findings.

First, their procedure of substituting the third highest elevation in a profile and using this value to replace the second most highly elevated scale in deriving two-point codes would appear to introduce a substantial degree of heterogeneity into the codetypes they constructed. The degree to which this procedure was worth the obtained benefit, i.e., the inclusion of additional cases in their codetypes, appears debatable. Second, their "within"-codetype analyses have led to the appearance of ambiguous descriptors within their actuarial system. For example, in the Marks et al. description of the 1-3/3-1 adolescent, they indicate that such adolescents are *not* irritable. This statement appears to be a result of their between-codetype analyses. However, probably as a result of their within-codetype analyses, the authors also indicated that "while 3-1s tend to be more nervous and anxious than 1-3s, 1-3s are more apt to be irritable, self-indulgent and flippant" (p. 179). These types of descriptions are apt to leave the clinical interpreter wondering to what extent the adjective "irritable" is applicable to this codetype. Similar problems may be noted in relationship to high versus low point codetype comparisons within other codetype groupings.

A final problem occurred in the relationship to the translation of statistical findings into the narrative format employed in the Marks et al. codebook. For example, the statement that "sex is definitely not an important personal value for these adolescents" in reference to the 2-3/3-2 codetype leaves the clinician with substantial confusion concerning the specific meaning implied by this statement. Certainly, as a result of its many strengths, and despite its areas of weakness, the Marks et al. actuarial system for adolescents has served as the predominant source of clinical correlate information for adolescent codetypes for over a decade. It should certainly continue to occupy this position until researchers are able to produce new samples of cross-validated clinical correlates.

TWO-POINT CODETYPES

In deriving the following codetype descriptors for adolescents, the 29 codetypes reported by Marks et al. were selected for development. In general, the clinical correlate information that is used from the Marks et al. data is based upon high point codetypes occurring within clinical ranges. This information was then compared with adult correlate information for these 29 high point pairs from Graham (1977), Greene (1980), and Lachar (1974). The typical narrative that was created by this method initially starts with statements found to be common across both the adolescent and adult descriptors for a particular MMPI configuration. Further, when sources of adult correlate data were not available for a particular codetype, a relatively rare occurrence, this has been noted in the first sentences of the narrative.

The last portion of each narrative description for the following codetype contains information unique to the Marks et al. descriptors, particularly concerning such variables as drug use, family characteristics, and therapists' evaluations. Occasionally, relevant information unique to adult clinical correlate data has also been introduced in this section.

In the majority of cases, the information presented by Marks, Seeman, and Haller and the information contained within the codetype narrative descriptions from adult samples are complementary and consistent. In these circumstances emphasis has been placed on stressing the common descriptors that appear to be applicable to both adults and adolescents within a particular codetype group. When marked or important differences occurred between descriptors derived from adolescent and adult clinical populations, the interpretive implications of these discrepancies are presented.

In addition to the 29 codetype narratives, the following section also contains information concerning characteristics of each of the 10 clinical MMPI scales. High and low single-scale correlates are suggested based on findings from adult samples combined with single-scale features found for adolescents by Hathaway and Monachesi (1963). Raw score mean differences between adolescents from the Marks et al. normative sample and from the adult normative sample are also included in the discussion of individual scales. The contrasts between adult and adolescent norm values may be reviewed in more detail by the reader in the Appendices provided by Colligan and Offord and by Gottesman, Hansen, Kroeker, and Briggs.

Scale 1 Codetypes

Scale 1 (Hypochondriasis) consists of 33 items developed to identify respondents who manifested a history of symptomatology associated with hypochondriasis, characterized by vague physical complaints and ailments and a preoccupation with body functioning, illness, and disease. Graham (1977) has reported that scale 1 appears to be the most unidimensional and homogeneous MMPI clinical scale in terms of item composition and content. All of the items on scale 1 relate to somatic concerns and complaints. Literature in adult samples has established that individuals who score high on scale 1 typically report many somatic symptoms and exaggerated complaints regarding physical functioning. Additionally, Greene (1980) has noted that adults who produce spike 1 MMPI elevations typically are not psychologically minded and often employ their physical complaints as a means of controlling and manipulating significant others in their environment.

Reports concerning physical functioning on scale 1 would also be expected to be influenced by an individual's actual physical condition, and respondents with physical illnesses typically produce moderate subclinical elevations on this measure. A comparison of the raw score mean values for adolescents versus adult normative subjects shows an inconsistent pattern of relatively small differences, with values seldom differing by more than 1.5 raw score points.

Profiles that produced a clinical spike on scale 1 were very unusual in the adolescent data gathered by Hathaway and Monachesi (1963), although a larger number of profiles were classified as producing their lowest value on this scale.

High Scores on Scale 1

The following is a summary of descriptors for high scale 1 scores:

- Excessive somatic and bodily concerns that are likely to be vague in nature.
- Increased likelihood of problems related to neurotic diagnoses.
- Likely to be seen by others as self-centered, pessimistic, dissatisfied, and cynical.
- Demanding, critical, selfish, and whining in interpersonal relationships.
- Likely to display little insight in psychotherapy.

Low Scores on Scale 1

Low scale 1 scores have been associated with the following characteristics:

- Few physical symptoms and freedom from somatic preoccupation.
- Higher levels of intelligence.
- More likely to come from urban rather than rural settings.
- Greater psychological sophistication and insight.

1-2/2-1

Adolescent and adult clients with this codetype frequently complain of physical symptoms including weakness, fatigability, and tiredness. These individuals often show a consistent pattern of somatic preoccupations and overreactions to minor physical dysfunction. Marked affective distress appears to be associated with the 1-2/2-1 codetype and these individuals are often described as ruminative, tense, anxious, and insecure. There are also frequent reports of depression, social withdrawal, and isolation.

In both the adult and adolescent literatures, the 1-2/2-1 codetype has been associated with a very low probability of the use of acting out as a primary defense mechanism. There are often marked interpersonal concerns and unmet needs for attention and approval by others. Thus, individuals who produce this codetype have been described as fearful and hypersensitive in their interactions with others, and often as dependent and indecisive.

Marks, Seeman, and Haller have reported that obsession and compulsion are the primary mechanisms of defense employed by the 1-2/2-1. Adolescents with this codetype in the Marks et al. sample often complained of being teased by others during their childhood and indicated that they were afraid of making mistakes during their adolescence. They appeared to be quiet, depressed teenagers who established very few friendships and often manifested obsessional defenses. Although Graham has reported that adults with the 1-2/2-1 profile often display excessive use of alcohol, the adolescents in the Marks et al. study with this codetype did not manifest significant drug involvements. Finally, Marks et al. noted these adolescents often had histories that included parental separations and divorce, academic problems including several cases of school phobias, and delayed academic progress.

1-3/3-1

Both adult and adolescent sources of clinical correlate data indicate that individuals with the 1-3/3-1 codetype typically present themselves as physically or organically ill. Indeed, when scales 1 and 3 are greater than a T-score value of 70, and both of these scales exceed the T-score value for scale 2 by at least 10 points, the profile may be described as a classic conversion "V." The types of physical complaints that have been noted in the general literture for the 1-3/3-1 include headaches, dizziness, chest pain, abdominal pain, insomnia, blurred vision, nausea, and anorexia. It would be expected that these physical symptoms would increase in times of psychological stress, and the clinician might be advised to attempt to identify secondary gain characteristics associated with this symptomatology.

In the adult and adolescent literatures the 1-3/3-1 codetype is associated more with neurotic and psychophysiological symptomatology rather than psychotic diagnoses. These respondents are frequently perceived as insecure and attention seeking. Behaving in socially acceptable ways appears to be important to the 1-3/3-1 person. Additionally, for both the adult and adolescent 1-3/3-1, there are problems in heterosexual adjustment and in establishing relationships with members of the opposite sex. Often, these problems are related to the lack of development of appropriate skills in these interpersonal areas. Additionally, primary defense mechanisms consist of somatization, denial, and externalization.

Data unique to the adolescent clinical sources for this profile indicate that 1-3/3-1 teenagers are more frequently referred for treatment because of problems or concerns in their academic setting. The majority of adolescents in the Marks et al. sample indicated that they were afraid of receiving poor grades, a fear that appears to be realistic in that 44% of the sample were a year behind their age-appropriate academic placement. In general, Marks et al. noted that adolescents with this codetype often display "diagnostic insight" into the descriptive features of their psychological problems, and at least are able to talk superficially about conflicts and are not evasive in psychotherapy. These features are in contrast to the descriptors in the adult literature indicating that 1-3/3-1 individuals typically display little willingness to acknowledge psychological factors in their life problems, and little insight into their problems. Of the 20 patients in the Marks et al. 1970–73 sample with the 1-3/3-1 codetype, over two thirds had no history of drug abuse or drug involvement.

1-4/4-1

The 1-4/4-1 codetype is relatively rare among adults, and it was not one of the larger codetypes in the Marks et al. (1974) text. In the adult and adolescent sources of clinical correlate information, the 1-4/4-1 individual appears to be defensive, negativistic, resentful, pessimistic, and cynical. Further, there are indications that these individuals may be described as self-centered and immature. The use of somatic complaints is a primary defense mechanism for both adolescents and adults, although this feature is more prevalent among adolescents producing more elevated scores on scale 1.

In addition to these features from the combined literature, a number of features appear to be uniquely related to the 1-4/4-1 codetype as found for adolescent respondents. In adolescents, more scale 4 features are reported as descriptive of these individuals, including defiance, disobedience, and provocative behaviors, particulrly manifested in the relationship between the adolescent and his or her parents. In the psychotherapy relationship, adolescents with this codetype have been described as superficial, cognitively disorganized, and providing evidence of moderately impaired judgment. Therapists rate adolescents with the 1-4/4-1 profiles as manifesting an overall degree of psychiatric disturbances, which is mild to moderate for 67% of the Marks et al. sample. In addition to the somatization, adolescents with this codetype often manifest acting out as a primary defense mechanism. Therapists describe adolescent patients with this codetype as aggressive, outspoken, resentful, headstrong, and egocentric. Despite the use of acting out as a primary defense mechanism, adolescents with this codetype in the Marks et al. sample were typically not found to be substance abusers.

1-5/5-1

The 1-5/5-1 is a relatively infrequent codetype among adults, and constituted one of the smaller codetype groupings in the Marks et al. study. In both sources of data, somatic complaints of a hypochondriacal nature appear to be frequently present, and patients with this codetype present themselves as physically ill. Additionally, these individuals are often seen as passive, and the adolescent data would indicate that teenagers with this codetype do not often enter into open conflict or disagreement with their parents.

Teenagers with this codetype were often referred for treatment by parents and by school officials. As patients, these teenagers were seen by their primary therapists as displaying mildly inappropriate affect, and compulsion appeared to be a primary defense mechanism distinctive to this codetype. Interestingly, many of the teenagers in this sample actually had experienced serious physical illnesses as children. Therapists described 1-5/5-1 adolescent patients as having difficulty in expressing or discussing their life problems and conflict areas, and these teenagers were seen as unreliable in terms of the information they provided to the therapist. They were not generally liked by others and had difficulty in forming close relationships. Teenage males with this profile type were described as effeminate.

1-6/6-1

Of the adult sources reviewed, only Greene provides a descriptive summary for the 1-6/6-1 profile. Greene's brief description for this codetype emphasizes the occurrence of hypochondriacal symptomatology combined with hostile and suspicious traits related to scale 6. Additionally, he notes that the personality structure of the adult 1-6/6-1 appeared resistant to change as a result of psychotherapy. In contrast, the results of investigation of adolescent 1-6/6-1 codetypes by Marks et al. produced a quite different descriptive picture. Confidence in any codetype descriptors for this configuration must be tempered, however, by awareness that little research has been done in adult settings and that the 1-6/6-1 codetype reported by Marks et al. was based on a very small sample size ($N = 11$).

Hypochondriacal tendencies and somatic complaints were *not* more likely to be shown by adolescents with the 1-6/6-1 codetype in contrast to other adolescent codetype groupings. Rather, these adolescents were primarily referred for psychotherapy because of excessive emotional overcontrol. Therapists viewed these teenagers as evasive and defensive and fearful of emotional involvement with others. More than half of these adolescents lived with their mothers in father-absent homes. When fathers were present in the families of these teenagers, their attitude toward the adolescent was reported to be rejecting. The 1-6/6-1 adolescents were viewed as egocentric and prone to rationalization as a defense mechanism. Data from the Marks et al. 1970–73 sample indicated some drug abuse involvement for this codetype, but it was not widespread or particularly characteristic of this code. Intense anger directed at parents was frequent for this group, including occasional violent outbursts. Suicidal attempts, perhaps representing an internalization of rage and anger, was also a characteristic of the 1970–73 adolescent sample.

1-8/8-1

Common features across the adolescent and adult literatures for the 1-8/8-1 codetype emphasize features of both scales 1 and 8. Patients with this profile type frequently present somatic concerns, such as headaches and insomnia, and often present themselves as physically ill. There are additional data from adolescent sources to suggest that adolescents with this codetype were, in fact, often ill with episodes of serious illness during their childhood. There are also frequent histories of poor social adjustment and social inadequacy, and individuals with the 1-8/8-1 profile appear to have difficulty in forming and maintaining interpersonal relationships. There is evidence across literatures that the 1-8/8-1 profile is often associated with delusional or disordered thinking, including symptoms related to difficulty in concentration and thought processes. Adolescents with the 1-8/8-1 codetype described themselves as distractible and forgetful.

Several clinical descriptors are uniquely available from the 1-8/8-1 profile from the Marks et al. study. These adolescents frequently reported problems during childhood involving being teased and harassed by peers, and often had difficulty in academic performance and reading.

Overall, their adjustment appeared to be problematic both in and outside of school settings and they tended to have substantial difficulty in making friends. Nearly one half of the 1-8/8-1 teenagers in the Marks et al. sample were a grade behind their expected academic placement.

Unique among the codetypes involving scale 1 in the Marks et al. data, the 1-8/8-1 adolescents were likely to be involved in drug abuse, and over 50% of the sample reported a drug use history. Additionally, attempted suicide was a high-frequency occurrence for these adolescents, with 65% of adolescents with this codetype attempting to take their own lives. Finally, intense family conflict was present for a very high percentage of the 1-8/8-1 teenagers, which often involved fighting and overt conflict with their parents. Two thirds of these adolescents were from families in which parents had divorced.

Scale 2 Codetypes

Scale 2 (depression) consists of 60 items that were created to assess or measure symptomatic depression. The essential characteristics of this MMPI dimension include poor morale, lack of hope in the future, and general dissatisfaction with one's life status and situation (Hathaway & McKinley, 1942). The major content areas involved in this scale include a lack of interest in activities or general apathy, physical symptoms such as sleep disturbances and gastrointestinal complaints and excessive social sensitivity and social withdrawal. Graham (1977) has described scale 2 as a sensitive measure of the respondent's life discomfort and dissatisfaction. He notes that although very elevated values on this scale are suggestive of clinical depression, more moderate scores have generally been seen as reflective of a general attitude or lifestyle characterized by apathy and poor morale.

The subscales derived by Harris and Lingoes (1955) for scale 2 include Subjective Depression, Psychomotor Retardation, Physical Malfunctioning, Mental Dullness, and Brooding. Comparison of adolescent normative data derived from Marks et al. with adult MMPI normative data indicated that adolescents typically endorse two to three more items in the critical direction than adults on scale 2.

Similar to scale 1 findings, scale 2 high points among the adolescents in the Hathaway and Monachesi (1963) Minnesota sample were very infrequent. Profiles containing their lowest values on scale 2 were relatively more common among these adolescents. Greene (1980) has reported that adult psychiatric patients who produce spike 2 profiles generally have the characteristics of clinically depressed individuals, i.e., feelings of inadequacy, lack of self-confidence, guilt and pessimism, and self-depreciation. Greene also noted that individuals who produce spike 2 profiles tend to be good psychotherapy candidates, and have shown significant improvement as a result of relatively brief psychiatric interventions. Perhaps these latter findings reflect the capacity of scale 2 elevations to measure a level of subjective distress that serves to motivate the client in psychotherapy efforts.

High Scores on Scale 2

The following provides a summary of high scale 2 features:

- Feelings of dissatisfaction, hopelessness, and unhappiness.
- General apathy and lack of interest in activities.
- Presence of guilt feelings and self-criticism.
- Lack of self-confidence and a sense of inadequacy and pessimism.
- A degree of emotional distress that may often serve as a positive motivator for psychotherapy efforts.

Low Scores on Scale 2

The following are characteristics that have been associated with low scale 2 scores:

- Higher levels of intelligence and academic performance.
- Freedom from depression, anxiety, and guilt.
- Self-confidence and emotional stability.
- The ability to function effectively across a variety of situations.
- Alert, competitive, and active.

2-3/3-2

There are substantial areas of overlap in the description in the 2-3/3-2 codetype for adolescent and adult psychiatric patients. They are characteristically described as emotionally overcontrolled, and unlikely to employ acting out as a primary defense mechanism. There are typically histories that reflect a lack of involvement or interest in relationships with others, and when relationships are established they tend to have dependent characteristics. Adjectives such as passive, docile, and dependent are frequently applied to individuals with a 2-3/3-2 profile, as well as characteristics such as unassertive, inhibited, insecure, and self-doubting. Both adolescents and adults with the 2-3/3-2 code are very achievement oriented, and set high goals for their own performance. These often unrealistic aspirations appear to be a contributor to their sense of inferiority and depression. Antisocial personality or psychopathic diagnoses are extremely rare for adolescents and adults who produce the 2-3/3-2 code. Additionally, there is little evidence of thought disorder or the presence of schizophrenic or psychotic diagnoses among these individuals. Defense mechanisms involving somatization and hypochondriasis are seen to be central to the 2-3/3-2 code. In particular, somatic weakness, fatigue, and dizziness appear to be common.

Data unique to adolescent findings for the 2-3/3-2 code indicate that the majority of these teenagers were referred for treatment because of poor peer relationships. These adolescents were seen as socially isolated and lonely individuals who had few friends inside the school environment and who were "loners" outside of academic settings. The 2-3/3-2 adolescent reported a relatively passive, compliant, and obedient childhood that often included an under-involved father in a professional occupation and mothers who may have been over-involved with these children. Sexual acting out and drug abuse do not appear to be high-frequency problem areas for these adolescents, and 76% of the teenagers in the Marks et al. 1970–73 sample reported no history of drug abuse. In the adult literature the 2-3/3-2 codetype is more prevalent among female patients, and the majority of patients with this codetype are seen as psychoneurotic or reactive depressive.

2-4/4-2

Among teenagers and adults, high-point codes involving scales 2 and 4 are typically produced by individuals who have had difficulties with impulsivity. They tend to undercontrol their impulses and to act without sufficient deliberation. There is often a marked disregard for accepted social standards, and problems with authority figures are manifested by inappropriate or antisocial behaviors and actions. Hypochondriacal and somatic defense mechanisms are not typically displayed by these individuals. Acting out, displacement, and externalization appear to be the primary defense features. There is often a history of legal violations including incidents of arrest, legal convictions, and court actions. Indeed, one half of the adolescents in the Marks et al. sample had been placed on probation or held in detention.

In the adult and adolescent literatures there are also frequent references to problems with substance abuse and alcohol. In the adult literature, the 2-4 profile is typically found as characteristic of mean profiles produced by groups of alcoholics (Sutker & Archer, 1979). Marks et al. also noted that adolescents with the 2-4/4-2 codetype reported a wide variety of drug use, which included all pharmacological categories except narcotics. Indeed, Marks et al. found patterns indicating drug addiction as well as drug abuse among their 2-4/4-2 sample.

In hospital settings, adolescents with the 2-4/4-2 profile were frequently found to be elopement risks. There were also frequent histories of promiscuous sexual behavior, truancy, and running away from home. In general, 2-4/4-2 adolescents indicated that much of their antisocial behaviors were attempts to escape or run away from what they perceived as intolerable and highly conflicted home situations. In the adult literature, the 2-4/4-2 code has been associated with a relatively poor prognosis for change. The major difficulty with adult psychiatric patients with this codetype has been their tendency to terminate psychotherapy prematurely when situational stress has been reduced but before actual personality change has occurred. Adolescents with this codetype are typically referred for treatment because of difficulties in concentration, and these adolescents often perceive their parents as unaffectionate and inconsistent. The majority of adolescents in the Marks et al. sample stated that they "had no one in the family" with whom to discuss their personal concerns, feelings, and thoughts.

2-5/5-2

The 2-5/5-2 codetype is quite rare among adults, and among commonly used sources only Greene (1980) reports information concerning this codetype. This author reported, based on findings from King and Kelley (1977), that male college students in outpatient psychotherapy who produced a 2-5/5-2 codetype were anxious, disoriented, and withdrawn and often had a history of somatic complaints. It was also noted that 2-5/5-2 college students displayed relatively poor heterosexual adjustment and dated infrequently.

Among adolescents, individuals with this codetype were typically referred for treatment because of poor sibling relationships, indecisiveness, shyness, extreme negativism, hypersensitivity, and suspiciousness. As a group, these adolescents were seen to be quite vulnerable to stress and were anxious, guilt-ridden, self-condemning, and self-accusatory. Similar to adults in the literature, they appeared to be quite anxious and indecisive and to have substantial difficulty in committing themselves to a definite course of action. The 2-5/5-2 adolescents typically displayed defense mechanisms involving obsession manifested in perfectionistic and meticulous concerns, and intellectualization. They were described as depressed, socially awkward and showing signs of poor heterosexual adjustment. Individuals with the 2-5/5-2 profile were not described as athletic and typically did poorly in sports, and males were described as not masculine.

In general, teenagers with this codetype were interpersonally shy, passive, and unassertive. Unsurprisingly, drug use and abuse was not found to be associated with adolescents who produced this codetype. Although many of these adolescents were seen to be intellectually and academically achieving at high levels, one third of them were "teased" by their peers in school settings.

2-7/7-2

The 2-7/7-2 codetype occurs with a relatively high frequency in adult psychiatric patients, and appears to be less prevalent among adolescents in psychiatric settings. The adjectives and descriptions for the 2-7/7-2 codetype, however, are quite consistent across both populations. Individuals with these profile types are anxious, tense, depressed, and highly intropunitive. They are often self-preoccupied and rigidly focused on their personal deficiencies and inadequacies. The adolescents in the Marks et al. 2-7/7-2 group consistently employed negative adjectives in self-descriptions.

Individuals with the 2-7/7-2 codetype tend to employ defenses that are obsessive-compulsive. They typically do not create problems for others, and when conflicts or difficulties arise they are handled by the 2-7/7-2 in a self-punitive and self-accusatory manner. These individuals are rigid in their thinking, and meticulous and perfectionistic in their everyday lives. They are seen by psychotherapists as self-defeating and behaviorally passive. Strong feelings of both depression and anxiety frequently co-occur for these individuals, and there is often a history of overreaction or overresponse to minor life stress events. These individuals are often described as overcontrolled and unable to deal with or express their feelings in an open manner. In interpersonal relationships, there is frequently a pattern of dependency, passivity, and lack of assertiveness. Adolescents and adults with the 2-7/7-2 codetype appear to have the capacity to form deep emotional ties with others, and the adolescents with this codetype typically reported close relationships with family members.

The primary reasons for referral among adolescents included tearfulness, restlessness, anxiety, excessive worry, and nervousness. Roughly 40% of the adolescents in the Marks et al. sample with this codetype indicated or expressed suicidal thoughts. Acting out behaviors such as drug use or school truancy were a markedly low-frequency event for these teenagers. Roughly one out of four of these teenagers with this codetype was categorized as exhibiting severe depression.

2-8/8-2

Both teenagers and adults with the 2-8/8-2 codetype are characterized by fearfulness, timidity, anxiety, and social awkwardness. They appear to prefer a large degree of emotional distance from others, and are fearful and anxious concerning interpersonal relationships. Among adolescents, isolation and repression have been reported as primary defense mechanisms. Impaired self-concept and poor self-esteem are also associated with the 2-8/8-2 codetype. In the adult literature, individuals with this codetype are often described as fearful of losing control, whereas the adolescent literature describes these individuals as highly emotional and characterized by deficits in the ability to moderate or modulate emotional expression. Further, adolescents with this codetype describe themselves as awkward and fearful of making mistakes. A high percentage of adolescents with this codetype in the Marks et al. study (44%) had a history involving an active suicide attempt. In the adult literature, the 2-8/8-2 codetype is also associated with suicidal preoccupation, and Graham (1977) noted that adults with this codetype frequently have suicidal thoughts that are accompanied by specific plans for suicidal actions.

For adolescents and adults, the 2-8/8-2 codetype is also frequently associated with more serious psychiatric symptomatology, particularly when elevations are marked on these scales. Schizophrenic, schizoaffective, and manic-depressive diagnoses are often attributed to adults with this codetype, and adolescents with these profile features have been found to display a higher than average frequency of such symptoms as hallucinations, preoccupation with bizarre or unusual concerns, and unusual sexual beliefs and practices. In the Marks et al. sample, over 25% of 2-8/8-2 codetype adolescents were found to have vague and nonlocalized organic deficits such as minimal brain damage or a history of seizure disorders and epilepsy.

2-0/0-2

Among both teenagers and adults, the 2-0/0-2 high-point code has been associated with symptomatology including depression, feelings of inferiority, anxiety, social introversion, and withdrawal. These individuals are typically described as conforming, passive persons who are highly unlikely to engage in antisocial or delinquent behaviors. Many 2-0/0-2 individuals show areas of social ineptitude and a general lack of social skills, and Greene (1980) has noted that social skills and assertiveness training may be beneficial in helping people with this codetype.

Adolescents with this codetype were typically referred for psychiatric treatment with presenting problems including tension and anxiety, apathy, shyness, lethargy, and inappropriate interpersonal sensitivity. As both children and adolescents, teenagers with the 2-0/0-2 codetype appear to be meek, socially isolated "loners" who conform to parental demands and who did not engage in alcohol or drug abuse. They expressed concerns to their therapists regarding feelings of inferiority, social rejection, and a self-perception as unattractive. They described themselves as awkward, dull, gloomy, cowardly, shy, silent, and meek. Primary defense mechanisms include social withdrawal, denial, and obsessive-compulsive mechanisms. The psychotherapists in the Marks et al. study tended to view adolescents with 2-0/0-2 codetype as schizoid, and individuals in this codetype grouping produced a very low frequency of substance or alcohol abuse. Based on findings from the Marks et al. 1970–73 sample, teenage girls with this profile wished to appear younger and less mature than their actual chronological age, and both boys and girls were seen as socially awkward, unpopular, and maintaining few significant friendships.

Scale 3 (Hysteria)

Scale 3 (Hysteria) consists of 60 items originally designed to identify individuals who utilize hysterical reactions to stress situations. The hysterical syndrome, as reflected in the item pool for scale 3, includes specific somatic concerns as well as items related to the presentation of self as well socialized and well adjusted. Greene (1980) noted that although these two areas of item content are often unrelated, or even negatively correlated, in well-adjusted individuals, they tend to be positively correlated and closely associated for individuals with hysterical features. Graham (1977) has noted that it is not possible to obtain a T-score value in excess of 70 on scale 3 without endorsing a substantial number of items in both content areas.

The subscales derived by Harris and Lingoes (1955) for scale 3 include Denial of Social Anxiety, Need for Affection, Lassitude-Malaise, Somatic Complaints, and Inhibition of Aggression. In the adult literature, marked elevations on scale 3 are typically associated with the pathological condition of hysteria. More moderate elevations have been found to be associated with a number of characteristics that include social extroversion, superficial relationships, exhibitionistic behaviors, and self-centeredness, but do not necessarily involve the classical hysterical syndrome. In normal samples, there is some tendency for adolescents to endorse more scale 3 items than adults, with this difference ranging from approximately 1.5 raw score points at age 15 versus Minnesota adults to roughly 2.5 raw score points at age 17 versus Minnesota adults.

Hathaway and Monachesi (1963) found that scale 3 MMPI profile high points tended to occur with a greater frequency than scale 1 or 2 high points among Minnesota normal adolescents. They speculated that children who employ somatic complaints or "play sick" as a way of avoiding

school and manipulating their parents would be expected to show elevations on this scale. Further, these authors noted that moderate elevations
on scale 3 might be expected among well-behaved and intelligent children who expressed what the authors referred to as "middle-class social
conformity." In fact, Hathaway and Monachesi found that high scale 3
profiles were related to higher levels of intelligence and achievement and
that these children often had parents who had professional occupations.
In contrast, profiles that contain scale 3 as a low point were associated
with lower academic achievement and a lower socioeconomic background than high scale 3 adolescents.

High Scores on Scale 3

The following is a summary of characteristics concerning high scale 3
profiles:

- Achievement oriented, socially involved, friendly.
- Patterns of overreaction to stress often involving development of
  physical symptoms.
- Self-centered, egocentric, and immature.
- Higher levels of educational achievement.
- Strong needs for attention and affection.
- Often from families of higher socioeconomic status.
- Psychologically naive with little insight into problem areas.

Low Scores on Scale 3

The following are characteristics of individuals who produce low scores
on Scale 3:

- Narrow range of interests.
- Limited social involvement and avoidance of leadership roles.
- Unfriendly, tough minded, realistic.
- Unadventurous, unindustrious, low achievement needs.

3-4/4-3

There appear to be at least three areas of common features among adolescents and adults who exhibit the 3-4/4-3 codetype. First, these individuals
are often found to display hypochondriacal or somatic complaints,
including symptoms of weakness, easy fatigability, loss of appetite, and
headaches. Second, both teenagers and adults with the 3-4/4-3 code tend
not to perceive themselves as emotionally distressed, although they are
often perceived as such by therapists. Finally, both age groups tend to

manifest problems in impulse control and often report histories that include both antisocial behaviors and suicidal attempts.

These problems in impulse control are manifested in several ways. Sexual promiscuity appears to be relatively common among females with this codetype during both adolescence and adulthood, and problems with substance abuse and dependence also appear prevalent. Adolescents with this codetype frequently have a history of theft, school truancy, and running away from home. As psychiatric inpatients, 3-4/4-3 adolescents often pose an AWOL risk for the hospital unit. Drug use is also associated with this codetype, particularly among the adolescent sample. In the Marks et al. study, 63% of adolescents with this codetype reported a drug abuse history in their 1970–73 sample. Further, roughly one third of these adolescents had made suicide attempts, a finding also found characteristic for adult 3-4/4-3 codes.

In the adult literature, the 3-4/4-3 individual is typically described as chronically angry and harboring hostile and aggressive impulses. Particularly when scale 4 is higher than scale 3, "overcontrolled hostility" is expected as manifested by episodic outbursts that could take the form of aggressive or violent behavior. Graham (1977) has noted that prisoners with the 4-3 codetype frequently have histories of assaultive and violent crimes.

Among adolescents, 3-4/4-3 teenagers are typically referred for treatment for sleep difficulties and for suicidal thoughts. They were often known as "roughnecks" in school and their main problems and concerns relate to conflicts with their parents. Therapists of these teenagers frequently describe them as depressed, although also indicating that they perceived adequate ego strength among these teenagers. As Marks et al. noted, however, several of the scale 4 adult descriptors are not applicable for adolescents. The overcontrolled hostility syndrome attributed to the 3-4/4-3 among adults, for example, does not necessarily appear to be applicable to teenagers with these MMPI features.

3-5/5-3

This profile is extremely rare in the adult literature, and Greene (1980) has stated, "there is no information on the 3-5/5-3 high point pair. A college educated male with hysteroid features would be expected to achieve this high point pair" (p. 129). No discussion of this codetype is available in either Graham (1977) or Lachar (1974). Among adolescents, this codetype also appears to be rare. Marks et al. were able to identify only 13 teenagers who produced this codetype in their study, all of whom were male.

Among adolescents the 3-5/5-3 codetype has many features that would be associated with the individual scale high points for scales 3 and 5.

None of the adolescents in the Marks et al. codetype were referred to treatment by court agencies or authorities, an unusual finding in adolescent psychiatric populations. Many of the teenagers with this codetype came from homes in which moral and religious values were firmly and perhaps rigidly enforced, and the teenagers in this sample viewed the moral and ethical judgments of their parents as highly predictable.

3-5/5-3 adolescents were seen by their therapists as moderately depressed. Yet perhaps consistent with scale 3 utilization of denial, several of these adolescents described themselves as elated. A major symptom pattern connected with this codetype was one of withdrawal and inhibition. Although these adolescents were perceived as basically insecure and having strong needs for attention, they were also perceived as shy, anxious, inhibited, and socially uncomfortable. Often these teenagers were also found to be affectively shallow and their rate of speech was described as rapid. They did not employ acting out as a primary defense mechanism, and in fact tended to overcontrol their impulses. When adolescents with this code type were involved with drug abuse, the substances employed were alcohol, marijuana, amphetamines, and sopors. Interestingly, 43% of the teenagers in the Marks sample were found to have weight problems including both obesity and anorexia.

3-6/6-3

There are a variety of characteristics that appear to be commonly displayed by adolescents and adults who produce the 3-6/6-3 profile type. They tend to be generally suspicious and distrustful individuals who manifest poor interpersonal relationships and have substantial difficulty in acknowledging the presence of psychological problems and conflicts. In general, both teenagers and adults with this codetype utilize the defenses of rationalization and projection, and often have difficulty in understanding why others are concerned regarding their behavior. Among adolescents, descriptors such as suspicious and paranoid were often used to characterize these 3-6/6-3 teenagers. In general, individuals with this codetype appear to be difficult to get along with, self-centered, and distrustful and resentful of others. They maintain an egocentric and guarded stance concerning the world around them.

Among adolescents, the most distinctive characteristic of this group is a relatively high incidence of suicide attempts, and one third of the adolescents in the Marks et al. study were seen for psychotherapy following such behaviors. In the Marks et al. 1970–73 sample, this profile was associated with substance abuse, but not as extensively as other adolescent codetypes. In this sample, roughly 50% of these adolescents acknowledged drug involvement. Interestingly, 40% of this group were academically superior students.

Scale 4 (Psychopathic Deviate)

Scale 4 (Psychopathic Deviate) consists of 50 items originally designed to identify or diagnose the psychopathic personality, now referred to under DSM III as antisocial personality disorder. The 50 items in this scale cover a diverse array of content areas including family conflict, problems with authority figures, social isolation, delinquency, sexual problems, and absence of satisfaction in everyday life. Scale 4 has a substantial degree of item overlap with many of the validity and clinical scales, and it contains an almost equal number of true and false responses that are keyed in the critical direction.

In the adult literature, individuals who score high on scale 4 are typically described in pejorative or unfavorable terms that include strong features of anger, impulsivity, interpersonal and emotional shallowness, interpersonal manipulativeness, and unpredictability. Thus, a marked elevation on scale 4 is typically taken to indicate the presence of antisocial behaviors and attitudes, although Greene (1980) noted that such elevations do not necessarily imply that these traits will be expressed overtly. The degree to which antisocial behaviors are manifested is typically seen as related to the individual's standing on additional MMPI clinical scales, particularly scales 9 and 0. Higher scale 9 values, and lower scale 0 values, in combination with an elevated 4, increase the likelihood for the overt behavioral expression of antisocial attitudes and cognitions. Harris and Lingoes (1955) have identified six content subscales within scale 4, which they labeled Familial Discord, Authority Conflict, Social Imperturbability, Social Alienation, Self Alienation, and Alienation.

Scores on scale 4 have been identified as varying in relationship to respondent's age and race. Graham (1977), for example, has noted that black subjects tend to score higher on scale 4 than white subjects, potentially reflecting a tendency among blacks to view social regulations and conventions as unfair or as racially or culturally biased. There is quite clear evidence that scale 4 values also differ as a function of adolescence versus adulthood in both normal and clinical populations.

In normal samples, adolescents tend to endorse in the critical direction roughly 4 more items than do adult respondents (see the Gottesman et al. tables in Appendix C). Hathaway and Monachesi (1963) found scale 4 was the most frequent high point for normal adolescents in the Minnesota statewide sample, with the highest frequencies of scale 4 elevations among girls and adolescents from urban settings. The Minnesota sample data also indicated that scale 4 elevations increased as a function of severity of delinquent behavior. Further, high scale 4 profiles for both boys and girls were associated with higher rates of "broken" homes.

Within clinical samples, although codetypes involving scale 4 are relatively frequent in adult populations, they could be described as ubiquitous in adolescent settings. Nine of the 29 codetypes reported for adolescents by Marks et al. involve a scale 4 high point, and nearly one half of their clinical cases produced a high point code that included scale 4. Thus, we know that scale 4 items tend to be endorsed by more adolescents than adults, and that high scale 4 codetypes are more frequently found in adolescent psychiatric samples in contrast to their adult clinical counterparts.

High Scores on Scale 4

High scale 4 scores have been related to the following characteristics:

- Poor school adjustment and school conduct.
- Increased probability of delinquent behavior.
- Increased probability of family history involving parental separation or divorce.
- Higher frequencies of urban backgrounds.
- Difficulty in incorporating the values and standards of society.
- Rebelliousness and hostility toward authority figures.
- Inability to delay gratification.
- Poor planning ability and impulsivity.
- Little tolerance for frustration and boredom.
- Primary reliance on acting out defense mechanisms.
- Increased probability of parent-adolescent conflicts and discord.
- Risk taking and high sensation-seeking behaviors.
- Selfishness, self-centeredness, and egocentricity.
- Ability to create a good first impression, extroverted outgoing style.
- Relative freedom from guilt and remorse, and relatively little affective distress.

Low Scores on Scale 4

The following features have been associated with individuals who score low on scale 4:

- Conventional, conforming, and compliant with authority.
- Lowered probability of delinquency.
- Concerns involving status and security rather than competition and dominance.
- Accepting, passive, and trusting in interpersonal styles.

4-5/5-4

The adult and adolescent literatures for the 4-5/5-4 profile codetype are substantially discrepant. Adults with these profile characteristics are typically discussed in terms of immaturity, emotional passivity, and conflicts centered around dependency. Greene (1980) has noted that this adult codetype is almost exclusively produced by male respondents, as a result of the infrequency with which scale 5 is clinically elevated among females. Adults with this codetype are frequently rebellious in relation to social conventions and norms, and this nonconformity is often passively expressed through selection of dress and speech and social behavior. Although these individuals appear to have strong need for dependency, there are also conflicts created by their fear of domination by others. This latter pattern appears most marked in relationship to males, with 4-5/5-4 men often entering into heavily conflicted relationships with females.

Although adults with these codetypes typically display adequate control, there are also indications that these individuals are subject to brief periods of aggressive or antisocial acting out. Sutker, Allain, and Geyer (1980) have reported that the 4-5/5-4 codetype is found among 23% of women convicted of murder. Among male college students, King and Kelley (1977) have related this codetype to students who are typically passive, who manifest heterosexual adjustment problem, and who often experience general and transient interpersonal difficulties. This sample did not display significant evidence of personality disorders, nor was homosexuality apparently characteristic of this group. Greene (1980) has recommended that detection of homosexual drive or behaviors in adults with this codetype is most effectively achieved when the clinician directly raises this issue with the respondent in clinical interview.

Among adolescents, Marks et al. indicated that teenagers with this codetype appear to get along well with their peer group, and are gregarious and extroverted in their social interactions. In contrast to teenagers with other codetypes, the 4-5/5-4 adolescent was described by therapists as better adjusted, easier to establish rapport with, and demonstrating greater ego strength. Further, therapists felt that teenagers with this codetype typically displayed relatively effective defenses in terms of protection from conscious awareness of depression or anxiety. The typical defense mechanisms utilized by these adolescents included acting out and rationalization. In contrast to 5-4s, 4-5 adolescents appear to have greater difficulty in controlling their tempers, and they described themselves as argumentative, opinionated, and defensive. Over half of the adolescents in the 4-5 codetype were rated by their therapists as having a good prognosis. In contrast to the adult literature, over 80% of the 4-5/5-4 adolescents in the Marks et al. study were engaged in heterosexual dating, a figure substantially higher than the base rate for other adolescent codetype groups.

Respondents with this profile configuration in the Marks et al. 1970–73 sample reported a relatively high frequency (i.e., 72%) of drug abuse history. The drug use found for these teenagers appears to involve a broad variety of drug categories. In addition, adolescents in this sample had a high rate of antisocial behaviors, including shoplifting, auto theft, breaking and entering, and drug dealing. As a group, they were described as emotionally reactive and prone to temper tantrums and violent outbursts. Finally, teenagers in this sample also evidenced significant problems in school adjustment, including histories of truancy, school suspension, and failing academic grades.

4-6/6-4

A relatively consistent picture emerges from the adolescent and adult literature for individuals with the 4-6/6-4 codetype. They are uniformly described as angry, resentful, and argumentative. Adolescents referred for treatment with this codetype typically present symptomatology involving defiance, disobedience, and negativism, and treatment referrals are often made from court agencies.

4-6/6-4 individuals appear to typically make excessive demands on others for attention and sympathy, but are resentful of even mild demands that may be placed on them in interpersonal relationships. They are generally suspicious of the motives of others, and characteristically avoid deep emotional attachments. The adolescents with this codetype appear to be aware of deficits in their interpersonal relationships and often reported that they were disliked by others. For adults and teenagers, however, there is very little insight displayed into the origins or nature of their psychological problems. Individuals with this codetype tend to deny serious psychological problems, and they rationalize and transfer the blame for their life problems onto others. In short, they characteristically accept no responsibility for their behavior and are not receptive to psychotherapy efforts. Although adolescents with this codetype were rated by others as aggressive, bitter, deceitful, hostile, and quarrelsome, they often appear to view themselves as attractive, confident, and jolly.

Among adolescents, the 4-6/6-4 codetype is almost inevitably associated with conflicts with parents, which often take the form of chronic intense struggles. These adolescents typically undercontrol their impulses and act without thought or deliberation. Problems with authority figures are prevalent among these teenagers. Narcissistic and self-indulgent features appear prevalent in this codetype for both adolescents and adults. Therapists describe the 4-6/6-4 adolescent as provocative, and indicated that major defense mechanisms included acting out and projection. About half of the adolescents with this codetype in the Marks et al. sample reported a history of drug abuse, most frequently involving the use of alcohol.

4-7/7-4

The 4-7/7-4 codetype appears to be characteristic of adolescents and adults who employ acting out as a primary defense mechanism, but experience substantial feelings of guilt, shame, and remorse concerning the consequences of their behavior. Thus, they tend to alternate between exhibiting behaviors that show a disregard for social norms and standards, and maintaining excessive and neurotic concerns regarding the effects of their behavior. Underlying these impulse control problems and tendencies to behave in a provocative and antisocial manner, these individuals appear to be insecure and dependent. They have excessive needs for reassurance and attention.

In the adolescent codetype data, the 4-7/7-4 teenager was described by therapists as impulsive, provocative, flippant, and resentful. At the same time, they demonstrated evidence of substantial conflicts concerning emotional dependency and sexuality. The majority of these teenagers expressed substantial feelings of guilt and shame and were viewed by their therapists as guilt-ridden and self-condemning.

4-8/8-4

The 4-8/8-4 codetype is associated with marginal social adjustment for adolescents and adults. Marks et al. have described the 4-8/8-4 adolescent as "one of the most miserable and unhappy groups of adolescents we studied" (1974, p. 218). They are frequently perceived as angry, odd, peculiar, and immature individuals who display impulse control problems and frequently have chronic interpersonal conflicts with those around them. Among adolescents, only 16% of teenagers with this codetype were rated as showing a definite improvement as a result of psychotherapy, and only 9% were rated as showing a good prognosis for future adjustment. Adolescents with this codetype were often evasive in psychotherapy, and frequently attempted to handle their problems by denying their presence.

Teenagers with these profile characteristics displayed patterns of very poor academic achievement, and were often seen in psychotherapy as frequently as three times a week. Their family lives were described as chaotic, and unusual symptomatology such as anorexia, encopresis, enuresis, and hyperkinesis were often noted. Although excessive drinking and drug abuse are common among adults with this codetype, the 4-8/8-4 teenager did not appear to be among the heavier drug abuser groups. Although 8-4 adolescents were described as more regressed than 4-8s, the 4-8 adolescent was also noted to display thought patterns that were unusual and sometimes delusional. Thus, individuals with this codetype display antisocial features related to elevations on scale 4 in combination with schizoid or schizophrenic symptomatology characteristic of elevations on scale 8.

4-9/9-4

A striking degree of congruency exists in the descriptions of both teenagers and adults who produce a 4-9/9-4 codetype. These individuals almost always display a marked disregard for social standards and values and are likely to display difficulties in the areas of acting out and impulsivity. They are characteristically described as egocentric, narcissistic, selfish, and self-indulgent and are often unwilling to accept responsibility for their own behavior. They are seen as high sensation seekers who have a markedly low frustration tolerance and are easily bored. In social situations, the 4-9/9-4s are often extroverted and make an excellent "first impression." They also, however, appear to manifest chronic difficulties in establishing close and enduring interpersonal relationships, and are highly manipulative and shallow in dealings with others. Classic features of the antisocial personality type clearly have a high degree of relevance for individuals with this codetype in adolescent and adult settings.

Huesmann, Lefkowitz, and Eron (1978) have reported findings that indicate that the summation of T-score values on scales F, 4, and 9 serves as a viable predictor of aggression in older adolescents. In the Marks et al. research, the 4-9/9-4 adolescent was invariably referred for treatment because of defiance, disobedience, impulsivity, provocative behaviors, and truancy from school. In most cases, there were constant conflicts between the adolescents and their parents concerning their history of misbehaviors. Intriguingly, fewer adolescents in the 4-9/9-4 codetype are raised in their natural homes than youngsters from any other codetype. Specifically, 17% of adolescents in this codetype grew up in foster or adoptive homes, and 20% did not reside with their parents at the time of their evaluation in this study. As a group, these adolescents appeared to be socially extroverted and reported an earlier age of dating than other teenagers. Nearly 50% of the teenagers with this codetype had a history of legal involvements that included placements in detention or on probation. Ninety-three percent of these teenagers employed acting out as their primary defense mechanism, and problems with affective distress such as anxiety or feelings of inadequacy were not found for these teenagers.

Therapists described adolescents with this codetype as resentful of authority figures, socially extroverted, narcissistic, egocentric, selfish, self-centered, and demanding. Further, this group was noted to be impatient, impulsive, pleasure seeking, reckless, and emotionally and behaviorally undercontrolled. Sixty-one percent of the adolescents with this codetype in the Marks et al. 1970–73 sample reported a history of drug abuse. These teenagers, however, appeared to be selective in the substances they experimented with and did not use more dangerous drugs such as hallucinogens or opiates. Eighty-three percent of 4-9/9-4s in this sample were either chronically truant from school, had run away from home, or had run away from the treatment setting, and many of these adolescents had engaged in all of these activities. Marks et al. described these adolescents as provocative and seductive problem children with long histories of lying, stealing, and other antisocial behaviors. These authors used the phrase "disobedient beauties" in reference to the 4-9/9-4 codetype. In the adult literature, these MMPI features have been repeatedly related to a poor prognosis for personality or behavioral change as a result of psychotherapy.

4-0/0-4

As noted by Greene (1980), the 4-0/0-4 codetype is extremely rare in adults and little empirical data exist to describe these individuals. Conceptually, there is an inherent conflict presented by high point elevations on both scales 4 and 0. Individuals who typically score high on scale 4 characteristically are relatively comfortable around others and often show extroverted traits. Thus, co-elevations on these scales would be an unusual or infrequent occurrence. Marks et al. (1974) were able to identify 22 adolescents who produced the 4-0/0-4 codetype, evenly divided between high and low point codes.

Surprisingly, 4/0-0/4 adolescents appear to display more feature related to elevations on scale 6 than they did characteristics related to elevations on either scale 4 or 0. Thus, they were described as suspicious and distrustful by their therapists. Additionally, they frequently expressed grandiose ideas and their main defense mechanism consisted of projection. They are resentful, argumentative adolescents who perceive themselves as shy and socially uncomfortable. Therapists describe the 4-0/0-4 adolescents as not talkative, passively resistant, and relatively uninvolved in activities around them. They have few close friends, and experienced problems in establishing friendships as one of their problem areas. They were judged to display moderate ego strength, and to demonstrate a pattern of overreaction to minor stresses.

Scale 5 (Masculinity-Femininity)

Scale 5 (Masculinity-Femininity) consists of 60 items that are heterogeneous in terms of content areas. The scale was originally developed by Hathaway and McKinley to identify homosexual males, but the authors encountered problems in identifying or defining a relatively pure diagnostic grouping to create a single criterion group. The primary criterion group finally selected consisted of 13 homosexual males who were selected based on their relative freedom from neurotic, psychotic, or psychopathic tendencies.

Fifty-five of the items in scale 5 are keyed in the same direction for both sexes, with the five remaining items that deal with overt sexual material keyed in opposite directions for males and females. T-score conversions are reversed for men and women so that a high raw score value for males results in a high T-score placement, whereas a high raw score value for females is converted to a low T-score value.

Much controversy and confusion has surrounded the meaning and interpretation of scale 5, particularly over recent years. Graham (1977) has noted that scores on scale 5 have been related to intelligence, education, and socioeconomic level. As suggested by Greene (1980), the usefulness of scale 5 in diagnosing homosexuality appears to be substantially limited since elevations on this scale may reflect the influence of a variety of factors in addition to homosexuality. He noted that when scale 5 produces the only clinical range elevation in an MMPI profile, those individuals are unlikely to be seen as manifesting a psychiatric disorder.

Markedly low scores on the Mf scale for women appear to indicate a substantial identification with traditional feminine roles, which may include passivity, submissiveness, and the adoption of a caricature of traditional femininity. Low-scoring males have been described by Greene (1980) as displaying an "almost compulsive" masculine identification in an inflexible manner. High scores in excess of a T value of 60 on the Mf scale appear to be associated with women who are not interested or invested in a traditional feminine role, and moderate elevations for men have been related to aesthetic interests. This range of elevation is typically found for most college-educated males. Clinical range elevations on scale 5 have been related to passivity for males.

There appears to be relatively little difference in mean raw score Mf values between normal male adolescents and adults, but there is a tendency for female adolescents to produce raw score values that are 2 to 3 points lower than adult females. Data from Hathaway and Monachesi (1963) found that boys in their Minnesota normal sample who produced their highest values on scale 5 tended to be of higher socioeconomic status, with parents from professional and semiprofessional occupations, and tended to have higher intelligence scores and academic grades. They also exhibited a lower frequency of delinquency and antisocial behaviors. In contrast, boys who scored lowest on scale 5 tended to display patterns of school underachievement and delinquency, and were of lower intelligence than high scale 5 boys. Similarly, Minnesota normal female adolescents who scored low on scale 5 were higher in terms of intelligence scores and displayed evidence of higher levels of academic achievement. High-scoring female adolescents on scale 5 were less clearly defined, but appeared to do less well in school and more frequently to come from rural environments.

High Scores on Scale 5

The following is a summary of descriptors for high scale 5 males:

- Intelligent, aesthetic interests, higher levels of academic achievement.
- Possible areas of insecurity or conflict regarding sexual identify.
- Comfortable in expressing feelings and emotions with others.
- Passive and submissive in interpersonal relationships.
- Lower likelihood of antisocial or delinquent behaviors.

The following is a summary of high scale 5 characteristics for females:

- Vigorous and assertive.
- Competitive, aggressive, tough minded.
- Greater problems in terms of school conduct.
- Possibility of "masculine" interests in school and sports.

Low Scores on Scale 5

The following is a summary of low scale 5 characteristics for males:

- Presentation of self with extremely masculine emphasis.
- Higher frequency of delinquency and school conduct problems.
- Overemphasis on strength often accompanied by crude and coarse behaviors.
- Lower intellectual ability and achievement.
- Relatively narrow range of interests defined by the traditional masculine role.

The following are low scale 5 characteristics for females:

- Presentation of self in stereotyped female role.
- Passive, yielding, and submissive in interpersonal relationships.
- Lower socioeconomic background.
- Higher levels of academic performance.

5-6/6-5

No information is available concerning the 5-6/6-5 codetype among adults in the widely used adult source books. Marks et al. presented the 5-6/6-5 codetype based on findings from 11 adolescents. Thus, we might begin by noting that very little is currently known concerning the characteristics of individuals who produce this MMPI configuration.

Most of the descriptors identified for the 5-6/6-5 profile among adolescents appear to be related to the scale 6 elevation. Although teenagers with this codetype were able to acknowledge psychological problems with their therapists, they were also hesitant to establish deep or frequent contacts with their therapists. In general, they were seen as fearful of emotional involvement with others. Thirty-six percent of this group were given a poor prognosis by their therapists, a percentage that is roughly three times higher than that found by Marks et al. for therapists' ratings for other codetypes. Additionally, the 5-6/6-5 adolescents were described as resentful and insecure, and acting out was a primary defense mechanism.

A majority of the teenagers in this small codetype grouping had a history of drug abuse, which entailed a variety of psychoactive drug classes. Additionally, a history of violent actions appeared to be associated with the 5-6/6-5. Legal actions and arrests were prevalent for such offenses as assault and battery and assault with a deadly weapon. Marks et al. described this group as preoccupied with themes of death, murder, and brutality.

5-9/9-5

Like the previous codetype, the 5-9/9-5 profile has produced little attention in the adult literature. Marks et al. identified 10 teenagers with the 5-9 code and 10 teenagers with the 9-5 code in their creation of this codetype grouping.

In general, teenagers who produced the 5-9/9-5 code appeared to display substantially less psychopathology than other codetypes. Their overall degree of disturbance was typically judged to be mild to moderate. Primary defense mechanisms for this code appear to be rationalization for the 5-9 group, and denial for the 9-5 codetype. Psychotherapists found that conflicts regarding emotional dependency and assertion were primary among these adolescents. One third of the adolescents in the Marks et al. sample reported that they were raised during their childhood by their mothers in single-parent households.

A slight majority of these adolescents, i.e., 56%, were found to have a history of drug abuse in the 1970–73 Marks et al. sample. Most uncharacteristically, in contrast to adolescents with other codetypes, members of this code group typically did well in school. None of these teenagers had been suspended or expelled from school, and in general they appeared to be a group that valued academic achievement and emphasized aesthetic interests. Parents of the teenagers with this codetype reported that they were unmanageable and rebellious. Family conflicts, rather than peer conflicts, appear to be characteristic of this group.

5-0/0-5

Consistent with the other high point codes involving scale 5, little information is available on adults with the 5-0/0-5 codetype. The Marks et al. 5-0/0-5 codetype was created based on a sample of 11 adolescents.

Consistent with the elevations on scales 5 and 0, adolescents with the 5-0/0-5 codetype were seen as cautious, anxious, and inhibited teenagers who are fearful of emotional involvement with others. They did not employ acting out as a defense mechanism, and in general exhibited few problems in impulse control and did not report histories of antisocial behaviors. In fact, the teenagers with this codetype typically exhibit overcontrol and are ruminative and overideational. Slightly over one third of the teenagers in the 5-0/0-5 codetype were involved in special classroom settings, such as classes for emotionally disturbed children.

The majority of these adolescents perceived their major problems involving their social awkwardness and difficulties in forming friendships with others. In general, they described themselves as awkward, shy, timid, inhibited, cautious, and submissive. Therapists tended to view these adolescents as manifesting severe anxiety. Major conflicts for these teenagers typically involve sexuality and difficulties in assertive behavior. The general picture that emerges for this codetype group is one of individuals who retreat into personal isolation rather than reaching out to others in interpersonal relationships.

Scale 6 (Paranoia)

Scale 6 (Paranoia) consists of 40 items that were created to assess an individual's standing in relation to such symptomatology as ideas of reference, suspiciousness, feelings of persecution, moral self-righteousness, and rigidity. Although many of the items on scale 6 deal with overtly psychotic symptoms such as ideas of reference and delusions of persecution, there are also large groups of items dealing with interpersonal sensitivity, cynicism, and rigidity that are not necessarily psychotic markers or symptoms. Further, Graham (1977) has noted that it is possible to achieve a T-score value in excess of 70 on scale 6 without endorsing overtly or blatantly psychotic symptomatology. Harris and Lingoes (1955) have identified three subscale areas for scale 6 that include Persecutory Ideas, Poignancy, and Naivete.

Although individuals who produce marked clinical elevations on scale 6 usually have paranoid symptomatology, some paranoid patients are able to achieve within normal limits values on this scale. Greene (1980), for example, has noted that T-score values ranging from 45 to 59 on scale 6 typically are produced by individuals in two categories: (1) respondents without paranoid symptomatology, and (2) individuals who have well-established paranoid symptomatology but maintain sufficient reality contact to avoid endorsing obvious items in the critical direction on this dimension.

Extreme elevations on scale 6 (T-score values in excess of 75) typically identify persons with a psychotic degree of paranoid symptomatology such as paranoid schizophrenics and individuals manifesting paranoid states. Moderate elevations in the range of T-score values of 65 to 75 are often produced by people who are relatively free of psychotic symptomatology, but are characterized by excessive sensitivity to the opinions and actions of others, a suspicious and guarded interpersonal stance, and the use of rationalization and projection as primary defense mechanisms. They frequently present as hostile, resentful, and argumentative individuals who are rigid and inflexible.

Mild elevations on scale 6, within the range of T-score values of 55 to 65, have often been seen as positive signs when the respondent is not in a psychiatric setting. Individuals within this range are frequently described as sensitive to the needs of others, and trusting and frank in interpersonal relationships. Graham (1977) has also noted that individuals within this range on scale 6 may be submissive and dependent in interpersonal relationships and describe themselves as prone to worry and anxiety. Greene (1980) notes that mental health workers frequently score within the range of T-score values of 60 to 69 on scale 6, perhaps reflective of interpersonal sensitivity.

Scale 6 appears to be one of the MMPI scales that are significantly affected by the application of adult versus adolescent norms in converting raw scores to T-scores values. Typically, the adolescents in the Marks et al. norm sample critically endorsed two to three more items than was found for adults in the Minnesota normative sample. Data from Hathaway and Monachesi (1963), based on Minnesota normal adolescents, indicated that boys who score high on scale 6 are more likely to drop out of school, perhaps as a function of their interpersonal sensitivity in the school environment. In contrast, girls in this sample who scored high on scale 6 tended to have higher IQ scores and better academic grade averages, and were considered well adjusted by others. Hathaway and Monachesi observed that moderate elevations on scale 6 appear to be an academic and social asset for girls, whereas boys with elevations on scale 6 tended to get into greater academic and social difficulties, possibly reflecting increased aggressiveness for the males.

High Scores on Scale 6

The following is a summary of characteristics for individuals who produce marked elevations on scale 6 ($T \geq 76$):

- Anger, resentment, hostility.
- Disturbances in reality testing.
- Delusions of persecution or grandeur.
- Ideas of reference.
- Use of projection as a primary defense mechanism.
- Diagnoses often associated with schizophrenia and thought disorder.

The following are features frequently associated with moderate elevations on scale 6 ($T = 65\text{--}75$):

- Marked interpersonal sensitivity.
- Suspicion and distrust in interpersonal relationships.
- Tendencies towards hostility, resentfulness, and argumentativeness
- Problems in school adjustment for boys.
- Difficulties in establishing therapeutic relationships due to interpersonal guardedness.

The following are associated with low scale 6 features ($T = 35\text{--}45$):

- Lower levels of intelligence and academic achievement.
- Presentation of self as cheerful and balanced.
- Cautious and conventional.
- Interpersonally insensitive, unaware of the feelings and motives of others.
- If psychiatric patient, possibility of overcompensation for paranoid symptoms.

6-8/8-6

The 6-8/8-6 codetype is indicative of serious psychopathology for teenagers and adults. This codetype has clearly been associated with paranoid symptomatology, including delusions of grandeur, feelings of persecution, hallucinations, and outbursts of hostility. Individuals with this codetype appear to be socially isolated and withdrawn, and their behavior is frequently unpredictable and inappropriate. Difficulties in thought processes are often apparent, ranging from deficits in concentration to bizarre and schizophrenic ideation. It would appear that the 6-8/8-6 individual frequently has difficulty in differentiating between fantasy and reality, and often withdraws into autistic fantasy in response to life stress.

Adolescents with 6-8/8-6 codetype are typically referred for treatment in response to the occurrence of bizarre behaviors or excessive fantasy. As children, this group appeared to be subjected to physical punishment as a primary form of discipline, and nearly half of the adolescents with this codetype in the Marks et al. sample had received beatings as punishments for misbehaviors. Additionally, the majority of these adolescents had fathers who had committed either minor or major legal offenses, and 30% of these teenagers had attended five or more school settings within their elementary education years.

The 6-8/8-6 adolescent often had a violent temper and when angry these teenagers appeared to express this feeling directly by either hitting others or throwing objects. They were not liked by their peers and they often perceived their peer group as picking on them or teasing them. In general, these adolescents were preoccupied with their physical appearance, and ratings by their psychotherapist indicated that they were, indeed, below average in appearance. The predominant affective distress for these teenagers included moderate depression and feelings of guilt and shame. Adolescents with this codetype were frequently delusional and displayed grandiose ideas. In the Marks et al. 1970–73 sample, slightly over half of these teenagers had used drugs, although much of this drug use had been connected with suicide attempts. As might be expected for a group of adolescents who produce this codetype, these teenagers typically displayed no insight into their psychological problems.

Scale 7 (Psychasthenia)

Scale 7 (Psychasthenia) consists of 48 items designed to measure psychasthenia, a neurotic syndrome that has more recently been conceptualized as obsessive-compulsive neurosis. Such individuals are characterized by excessive doubts, compulsions, obsessions, and high levels of tension and anxiety. Because this symptom pattern is more typically found among outpatients, the original criterion group employed by McKinley and Hathaway in the development of this scale was restricted to a relatively small number (20) of inpatients with this condition. McKinley and

Hathaway were reluctant to use outpatients in their criterion group because of their inability to confirm diagnoses for patients in this setting (Greene, 1980). The content areas of scale 7 cover a wide array of symptomatology including unhappiness, physical complaints, deficits in concentration, obsessive thoughts, anxiety, and feelings of inadequacy. Harris and Lingoes (1955) did not identify subscales for scale 7, perhaps reflective of the relatively high degree of internal consistency found for this MMPI measure.

In general, individuals who score high on scale 7 (T-score values of 70 and above) are described as anxious, tense, and indecisive individuals who are very self-critical and perfectionistic. At extreme elevations, there are often patterns of intense ruminations and obsessions constituting disabling symptomatology. Low scores on this scale are frequently indicative of self-confident, secure, and emotionally stable individuals who are achievement and success oriented. Greene (1980) notes that females typically endorse more scale 7 items than men.

There are differences between adolescent and adult normal respondents on scale 7, with adolescent males typically critically endorsing roughly five more items than their adult counterparts, and female adolescents typically endorsing two to three additional items than adult women. Data from normal adolescents by Hathaway and Monachesi (1963) showed that scale 7 high point elevations were more common in adult than adolescent profiles, although scale 7 was the most frequently elevated neurotic scale in adolescent MMPI profiles. In general, a meaningful correlate pattern for scale 7 elevations in adolescence did not emerge in the Hathaway and Monachesi findings.

High Scores on Scale 7

The following is a summary of characteristics associated with high scale 7 scores:

- Anxious, tense, and apprehensive.
- Self-critical, perfectionistic approach to life.
- Feelings of insecurity, inadequacy, and inferiority.
- Emotionally overcontrolled and uncomfortable with feelings.
- Introspective and ruminative.
- Lacking in self-confidence and ambivalent in decision-making situations.
- Rigid, moralistic, conscientious.
- At marked elevations, obsessive thought patterns and compulsive behaviors.

Low Scores on Scale 7

The following are features associated with low scale 7 scores:

- Lack of emotional distress and freedom from anxiety and tension.
- Capable and self-confident in approach to problems.
- Perceived as warm, cheerful, and relaxed.
- Flexible, efficient and adaptable in response to environment.

7-8/8-7

The 7-8/8-7 profile for both adults and adolescents appears to be related to the occurrence of inadequate defenses and poor stress tolerance. These individuals are frequently described as socially isolated, withdrawn, anxious, and depressed. There is also evidence that individuals with the 7-8/8-7 codetype feel insecure and inadequate. They have substantial difficulty in modulating and expressing their emotions in appropriate ways.

The 7-8/8-7 codetype among adolescents appears to be related to the presence of substantial tension and impairments in ego defense systems. These adolescents were described as anxious and depressed. They were typically inhibited and conflicted in terms of their interpersonal relationships, particularly relationships involving emotional dependency. Many of these teenagers expressed fears of failure in school, and Marks et al. report that roughly one half of this sample had failed at least one academic grade.

In the adult literature, the relationship in elevation between scales 7 and 8 is frequently cited as highly significant in interpretation of this profile. Scale 7 is seen as a suppressor of scale 8 symptomatology such that profiles displaying relatively higher elevations on scale 7 are seen as more neurotic, whereas profiles containing the highest elevation on scale 8 are frequently seen as related to more schizophrenic symptomatology. Marks et al. have noted that there is no evidence of this phenomenon in the adolescents in their 7-8/8-7 codetype. Specifically, based on their data from the 1970–73 sample, they observed that 7-8s and 8-7s were both quite deviant in thought and behavior and that nearly one half of these adolescents had experienced either auditory or visual hallucinations.

7-9/9-7

Across both adult and adolescent respondents, the 7-9/9-7 codetype appears to be associated with tension, anxiety and rumination. Over three quarters of adolescents with this codetype were characterized by their therapists as worriers who were vulnerable to both real and unrealistic threats and fears. For adults with this codetype, Greene (1980) has recommended that the possibility of manic features be investigated and that psychopharmacological medications be considered in terms of the reduction of very high levels of anxiety and tension. Among adolescents, Marks et al. have described the 7-9/9-7 codetype as related to insecurity and strong needs for attention, probable conflicts involving emotional dependency issues, and fear of loss of control. They are tense and have difficulty "letting go," but do not show evidence of scale 9 manic characteristics such as elation.

In general, these teenagers appeared to be defensive in discussing their psychological problems, and very sensitive to demands placed upon them by others. Within the adolescent sample, scale 7 properties were more predominant for this codetype than scale 9 characteristics.

7-0/0-7

The 7-0/0-7 codetype appears to be rare among adults, and Marks et al. were able to identify only 11 adolescents with this codetype in their research sampling. For adolescents and adults, this codetype is seen to be related to the presence of neurotic symptomatology including excessive anxiety, tension, social introversion, and shyness.

The predominant reasons for treatment referrals for the 7-0/0-7 adolescent consisted of shyness and extreme sensitivity. Although defiant and disobedient behaviors were relatively common for this group, these characteristics tended to occur with a lower base rate frequency for the 7-0/0-7 codetype than for other adolescent groups. Interestingly, almost one half of these adolescents had family members with a history of psychiatric disorder.

Psychotherapists felt positively about adolescents with this codetype and indicated that they displayed moderate motivation for treatment, good treatment prognosis, and good cognitive-verbal insight. These teenagers performed well in academic settings and maintained high needs for achievement. Reaction formation and isolation appear to be the predominant defense mechanisms for the 7/0-0/7 adolescent. These individuals become intropunitive in response to stress or frustration, and have a decided tendency toward emotional overcontrol. Marks et al. noted that these adolescents are basically insecure and tend to have conflicts regarding emotional dependency and assertion.

Scale 8 (Schizophrenia)

Scale 8 (Schizophrenia) consists of 78 items and constitutes the largest scale in the MMPI. Scale 8 was developed to identify patients with schizophrenia, and deals with content areas involving bizarre thought processes, peculiar perceptions, social isolation, difficulties in concentration and impulse control, and disturbances in mood and behavior. Harris and Lingoes (1955) have identified six subscales within the schizophrenia scale that they have labeled: Social Alienation; Emotional Alienation; Lack of Ego Mastery, Cognitive; Lack of Ego Mastery, Conative; Lack of Ego Mastery, Defective Inhibition; and Bizarre Sensory Experiences.

Individuals who score high on scale 8 are typically described as alienated, confused, delusional, often displaying psychotic features, socially isolated, withdrawn, shy, and apathetic. Extreme elevations on scale 8, particulary *T*-score values in excess of 100, are typically produced by clients who are not schizophrenic but are experiencing intense, acute situational stress. Greene (1980) has noted that adolescents undergoing severe identity crisis may frequently score in this extreme range. In general, the exclusive reliance on scale 8 to diagnose schizophrenia in either adolescents or adults appears to produce a relatively high rate of false positives. Individuals who score markedly low on scale 8 have typically been described as conventional, cautious, compliant persons who may be overly accepting of authority and who place a premium on practical and concrete thinking.

Graham (1977) has noted that scores on scale 8 have been related to both race and age. Black subjects, most consistently male black respondents, have tended to score higher on scale 8 than their white counterparts. These elevations have been attributed by Gynther and others to the result of the black experience of social alienation and estrangement.

Scale 8 shows the largest degree of differences in mean raw score endorsement patterns between adolescent and adult normals among the MMPI dimensions, with adolescents typically critically endorsing between five and eight more scale 8 items than their adult counterparts. Hathaway and Monachesi (1963) found that boys were more likely than girls to have profiles that featured scale 8 as the highest point. Both adolescent males and females who produced high scale 8 scores were likely to be lower in intelligence and in academic achievement than other adolescents, and high scale 8 girls were more likely to drop out of school.

High Scores on Scale 8

The following are characteristics associated with high scale 8 scores:

- Withdrawn, seclusive, and socially alienated.
- Confused and disorganized.
- Schizoid features.
- Feelings of inferiority, incompetence, and dissatisfaction.

- Reluctant to engage in interpersonal relationships, including psychotherapeutic relationships.
- Nonconforming, unconventional, and socially deviant.
- At marked elevations associated with delusions, hallucinations, and other schizophrenic symptoms.

Low Scores on Scale 8

The following are characteristics associated with low scale 8 scores:

- Conforming, conventional, and conservative.
- Unimaginative and cautious in approaches to problem solving.
- Practical and achievement oriented.
- Responsible and dependable.

8-9/9-8

The occurrence of an 8-9/9-8 codetype in either adolescence or adulthood appears to be related to the presence of serious psychopathology. Individuals who produce this MMPI configuration have been referred to as immature, self-centered, argumentative, and demanding. Although these individuals seek a great deal of attention, they are resentful and hostile in interpersonal relationships and display little capacity to form close friendships with others. Acting out, often of an unpredictable nature, is a salient defense mechanism for this codetype.

Many of the respondents with the 8-9/9-8 codetype also display evidence of thought disorder, including grandiose ideas, as well as evidence of hyperactivity and a very rapid personal tempo. Marks et al. noted that adolescents with the 9-8 codetype appear to "think, talk, and move, and at an unusually fast pace" (1974, p. 239). For adults and adolescents, this codetype has been associated with the presence of both schizophrenic and paranoid symptomatology. Within the Marks et al. 1970–73 sample, this codetype was not particularly associated with substance abuse or addiction.

Scale 9 (Hypomania)

Scale 9 (Hypomania) consists of 46 items originally developed to identify patients manifesting hypomanic symptomatology. The content areas covered in this scale are relatively broad and include grandiosity, egocentricity, irritability, elevated mood, and cognitive and behavioral overactivity. Harris and Lingoes (1955) have identified four subscales contained within the hypomania scale: Amorality, Psychomotor Acceleration, Imperturbability, and Ego Inflation.

Greene (1980) has noted that scale 9 elevations are often difficult to interpret in isolation. In this sense, elevations on scale 9 are often seen as facilitating or moderating the expression of qualities or characteristics identified by elevations in other clinical scales such as *D* and *Pd*. High scores on scale 9 have been related to impulsivity, excessive activity, narcissism, social extroversion, and a preference for action in contrast to thought and reflection. In addition, individuals who score high on this scale may also display manic features such as flight of ideas, delusions of grandeur, and hyperactivity. Markedly low scores on scale 9 (*T*-scores below 40) have been related to lethargy, apathy, listlessness, and decreased motivational states. Additionally, low scores on scale 9 have often been related to the presence of serious depressive symptomatology including vegetative signs.

Graham (1977) has noted that scores on scale 9 appear to be related to race and age. Black subjects and younger respondents typically score higher on this MMPI measure. Adolescent normals from the Marks et al. sample typically endorsed three to four more items in the clinical direction on scale 9 than did adult respondents from the MMPI normative sample. Hathaway and Monachesi (1963) found low scores on scale 9 in their sample of normal adolescents to be associated with lower rates of delinquency. In general, the teenagers who scored low on this scale in the Minnesota sample were well behaved and conforming, and demonstrated high levels of achievement in the academic setting. Extrapolating current findings from Colligan and Offord (1986) and Williams et al. (1986), it appears probable that contemporary adolescent mean raw score values for scale 9 will be substantially higher than those found by Marks et al. (1974) in their adolescent samples.

High Scores on Scale 9

The following are features associated with high point elevations on scale 9:

- Accelerated personal tempo and excessive activity.
- Preference for action rather than thought and reflection.
- Impulsivity and restlessness.
- Lack of realism, and grandiosity in goals setting and aspirations.
- Outgoing, socially extroverted, gregarious.
- Talkative and energetic.
- Egocentricity and self-centeredness.
- Greater likelihood of school conduct problems and delinquent behaviors.
- Flight of ideas, euphoric mood, grandiose self-perceptions.

Low Scores on Scale 9

The following are characteristics or features associated with low scale 9 scores:

- Low energy level.
- Quiet, seclusive, withdrawn.
- Overcontrolled, inhibited, overly responsible.
- Decreased probability of acting out or antisocial behaviors.
- Depressed, anxious, emotionally uncomfortable.
- Apathetic, lethargic, difficult to motivate.

Scale 0 (Social Introversion)

Scale 0 (Social Introversion) consists of 70 items that were designed to assess the individual standing on the dimension of social introversion-extroversion. High or elevated scores on this scale reflect greater degrees of social introversion. Although Harris and Lingoes did not attempt to create specific subscales for the social introversion scale, Graham (1977) has indicated that two broad clusters of items occur in the *Si* scale. These groups consist of items related to social participation and items related to general neurotic maladjustment and self-depreciation. Graham notes that high scores on scale 0 can occur by the endorsement of either, or both, of these clusters.

Individuals who produce elevated scores on scale 0 are socially introverted, insecure, and markedly uncomfortable in social situations. They tend to be shy, timid, submissive, and lacking in self-confidence. When high scores occur for scale 0, the potential for impulsive behaviors and acting out is decreased, and the likelihood of neurotic rumination is increased. Individuals who produce low scores on the *Si* scale are described as socially extroverted, gregarious, friendly, and outgoing. These individuals appear to have strong affiliation needs and are interested in social status and social recognition. In addition, low scorers may be subject to impulse control problems, and their relationships with others may be more superficial than sincere and long enduring.

A comparison of adolescent norms with adult norms for scale 0 indicates that adolescents typically endorse three or more additional items in the extroverted direction than do normal adults. Greene (1980) has also noted that adolescents and college students typically scored toward the extroverted pole of the *Si* scale. Hathaway and Monachesi (1963) found an interesting pattern of correlates for scale 0 scores in their sample of Minnesota normal adolescents. Social introversion was a relatively frequent finding among boys and girls from rural farm settings, whereas so-cial extroversion was characteristic of adolescents from families with par-ents in professional occupations. Intriguingly, low scale 0 profiles were found for children with higher intelligence levels but with spotty records of academic achievement. Hathaway and Monachesi interpreted this finding as indicating that there was a potential conflict between an ado-lescent's social success and his or her academic achievement.

High Scores on Scale 0

The following are features that have been associated for individuals who score high on scale 0:

- Social introversion and social discomfort.
- Reserved, timid, and socially retiring.
- Decreased probability of delinquent or anti-social behaviors.
- Submissive, compliant, and accepting of authority.
- Lacking in self-confidence.
- Overcontrolled, difficult to get to know, interpersonally sensitive.
- Reliable, dependable, cautious.

Low Scores on Scale 0

The following are features associated with individuals who score low on scale 0:

- Sociable, extroverted, gregarious.
- Intelligent, with possible history of academic underachievement.
- Active, energetic, talkative.
- Interested in social influence, power, and recognition.
- Socially confident and competent.

5

ADDITIONAL FACTORS
AFFECTING INTERPRETATION

In the previous chapters we have discussed criteria for evaluating the utility of administering MMPIs to adolescents, general interpretive approaches for adolescent profiles, and clinical correlate descriptors for adolescent codetypes. In this chapter we discuss a variety of additional factors that may significantly impact the interpretation of adolescent MMPI profiles. We begin with important extra-test information that may affect interpretation, including race, gender, and age of respondent. These discussions incorporate the available literature concerning the direction and extent of effects produced by these demographic variables on the interpretation process. We then cover a variety of standard MMPI clinical scale indices related to the prediction of acting out or aggressive behaviors. Finally, we review a variety of MMPI special scales that may be found to be useful in generating interpretive data for adolescence.

RACE

A substantial amount of research literature has established that demographic variables such as race, gender, and age may significantly influence the MMPI profiles of adult respondents (Dahlstrom et al., 1975). Gynther (1972), for example, reviewed the literature relative to the influence of race on adult MMPI scores and concluded that distinctive racial differences reliably occurred that reflected variations in the respective cultural and environmental backgrounds of black and white respondents. In particular, Gynther interpreted findings from analyses of item differences as indicating that higher scores for blacks on scales *F*, *Sc*, and *Ma* reflected differences in perceptions, expectations, and values rather than differential levels of adjustment. He called for the development of MMPI norms for black respondents in order to allow for more accurate assessment of psychopathology in black populations.

Several studies that have examined the variable of subject race within adolescent populations serve to support Gynther's conclusions regarding the presence of racial differences in MMPI scale values. Ball (1960) examined MMPI scale elevations for a group of 31 black and 161 white ninth graders and found that black males tended to score higher on scale *Hs* than white male students, and that black female students produced significantly higher elevations on scales *F, Sc,* and *Si* than white females. Similarly, McDonald and Gynther (1962) examined the MMPI response patterns of black and white students within segregated high schools settings. Findings indicated that black students produced higher scores than their white counterparts on scales *L, F, K, Hs, D,* and *Ma.* Further, black female students had significantly higher scores on all MMPI scales, with the exception of scales *K* and *Sc,* than did white female students.

More recently, research results have suggested that where blacks and whites have experienced common cultural influences and socioeconomic backgrounds, racial differences are less likely to be found in MMPI profile elevations. Klinge and Strauss (1976) and Lachar and his associates (1976) reported no significant MMPI differences between samples of black and white adolescents. These results were attributed to the observation that the black and white respondents in these investigations had been raised and educated in equivalent environments. Bertelson et al. (1982) matched 462 psychiatric patients (of whom 144 were adolescents) on variables such as gender, age, residence, education, employment, and socioeconomic status. No significant MMPI differences were found for the matched racial samples in this study. Archer, Gordon, and Kirchner (1986) recently administered the MMPI to 58 white and 36 black male and female adolescents in a predominantly middle-class public high school setting. Subjects were matched for age and educational setting. MMPIs were profiled using the Marks et al. adolescent norms. The profiles resulting from this assessment, shown in Fig. 5.1, illustrate minimal racial differences (*T*-score mean differences < 3 points) across MMPI scales.

Finally, Marks et al. (1974) included 61 black subjects in their clinical population used to derive clinical correlate descriptors of adolescent codetype profiles. These subjects were part of their Ohio State University Health Center sample used for creating codetype data. The authors found few black-white differences among the descriptors generated for their adolescent codetypes and hence statements regarding race of subject are seldom made in the Marks et al. text.

Greene (1980; in press) has recently surveyed the literature on the issue of racial differences in MMPI response patterns. His review of studies examining black-white differences within normal samples revealed no MMPI scale that consistently demonstrated racial differences across 10 independent investigations. Greene noted that scales *F* and *Ma* were most likely to be significantly affected by race, but that significant differences were not found for scale *Sc*, which had been reported by Gynther (1972) as one of the scales typically elevated among black populations. Further, Greene noted that the actual mean differences in studies reporting significant differences between black and white respondents typically were equal to or less than 5 *T*-score points. Additionally, reviewing a series of 11 studies on the effects of race on MMPI scale elevations in prison and psychiatric populations, Greene found a consistent pattern of black-white differences on scales *Sc* and *Ma* such that black populations typically produced higher elevations (usually less than 5 *T*-score points) on

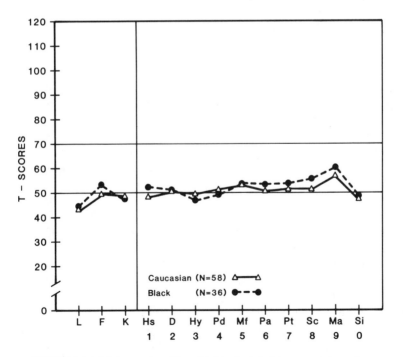

FIGURE 5.1   Adolescent profiles   for black and white respondents in a high-school sample.

these measures. Thus, although differences have been found in clinical populations, the clinical significance of these findings appears to be limited. Greene concluded, "it appears that the critical question of the validity of the MMPI with blacks remains unanswered" (1980, p. 220).

In summary, the literature on racial differences on the MMPI has produced mixed findings and does not allow for a firm conclusion. If social differences that are independent of socioeconomic factors do occur in MMPI profiles, however, it appears likely that the interpretation significance of such differences are relatively limited in both clinical and nonclinical settings.

GENDER

Hathaway and Monachesi (1963), in their Minnesota statewide sample, identified gender differences in item endorsement patterns and in frequency of high point codetypes. The authors identified the presence of 63 items in which the difference in percentage of "true" endorsements by boys and girls was 25 points or more. Table 5.1 presents 20 items selected from this list illustrating male-female differences in item endorsement. In categorizing these items, Hathaway and Monachesi (1963) stated, "It is informative to employ generalized adjectives like 'sensitive' or 'fearful' or 'candid.' Such adjectives organize the pattern of correlated items expressing the feminine role, whereas 'inquisitive' or 'desirous of active outdoor activities' or 'aggressive' might better characterize the male role" (p. 41).

Additionally, significant gender differences were found in the number of items omitted by adolescent respondents. Although religion and sex were the content areas of items most frequently omitted by both boys and girls, items related to sex were more often left unanswered by female than male respondents.

In terms of codetype profile, girls more frequently displayed peak elevation on scale *Si* whereas boys were more likely to have high scale *Sc* codetypes. Hathaway and Monachesi noted that gender differences were likely to be more marked when adolescents were viewed against a backdrop of adolescent norms than when adolescent respondents were profiled against adult norms. Interactional effects between gender of respondent and type of norms utilized to score the profile (adolescent vs. adult) have also been reported by Ehrenworth (1984), Klinge and Strauss (1976), and by Lachar et al. (1976). The direction and meaning of these interactional findings, however, have been markedly complex and inconsistent. In the study by Ehrenworth (1984), for example, *T*-score values for male adolescent inpatients on scales *F*, *Pt*, and *Sc* were significantly

TABLE 5.1

MMPI Items on Which the Difference in Percentages of "True" Response by Boys
and Girls of the Statewide Sample Was 25 Points or More

	Boys (N = 100)	Girls (N = 100)	Diff.
I like mechanics magazines...	83%	11%	72%
I enjoy reading love stories...	17	87	70
I have often wished I were a girl. (Or if you are a girl) I have never been sorry that I am a girl...	7	70	63
I like adventure stories better than romantic stories...........	88	27	61
I would like to be a nurse...	1	55	54
I very much like hunting...	89	38	51
I like movie love scenes...	28	77	49
I am embarrassed by dirty stories...	21	69	48
I think I would like the kind of work a forest ranger does.......	76	29	47
I used to keep a diary...	3	47	44
I must admit that I have at times been worried beyond reason over something that really did not matter..................	46	83	37
I like dramatics...	36	73	37
My feelings are not easily hurt...	74	38	36
I dread the thought o an earthquake...	42	78	36
If I were an artist I would like to draw children......................	24	59	35
What others think of me does not bother me......................	53	21	32
I cry easily...	10	39	29
I daydream very little...	66	37	29
I like poetry...	17	44	27
I believe women ought to have as much sexual freedom as men...	74	47	27

higher than female values when adult norms were employed, but nonsignificant when adolescent norms were used. In contrast, females produced higher *Si* *T*-scores than males using adolescent norms, with less marked sex differences using adult norms.

Moore and Handal (1980) examined the MMPI profile elevations of 16- and 17-year-old male and female volunteers from school settings in the St. Louis area. These data were analyzed by sex of respondent for adult *K*-corrected *T*-scores. They reported substantial evidence that males tended to score significantly higher than females on scales *F, Pd, Mf, Pt, Sc,* and *Ma*. Gender MMPI differences were more prevalent in this sample than racial differences, with males producing MMPI profiles suggestive of greater impulsivity, problems with the authority, identity confusion, and rebelliousness than their female counterparts. Similarly, Ehrenworth and Archer (1985) examined the MMPI profiles of adolescents in psychiatric treatment and found that males produced higher *T*-score elevations than females on several scales when adult norms were employed. Differences in profile elevations by gender were minimal, however, when adolescent norms were used in this sample. Equivalent profiles for males and females were also reported by Archer (1984) for inpatient samples employing adolescent norms.

On the profile clinical correlate level, Marks et al. (1974) stated they found no significant differences between males and females relative to clinical correlates of codetype descriptors. The Marks et al. text, therefore, presents codetype narratives that are not differentiated by sex of respondent.

In summary, it is clear that significant gender differences in item endorsement patterns occur for adolescent respondents, and these differences are reflected in the development of separate T-score conversions for male and female respondents in adolescent and adult norms. The degree to which gender differences occur following T-score conversions, however, is currently unclear. Thus far, it may be inferred that the degree to which gender differences are found for MMPI profile patterns of adolescents is related to whether adolescent or adult norms are utilized. Recent findings suggest that when adult norms are employed the gender differences that occur are likely to reflect higher profile elevations for male respondents. Until such time as further research is completed in this area, firm conclusions cannot be drawn concerning the degree to which reliable gender differences occur in the response patterns of adolescents in various settings.

AGE

Differences between adult and adolescent response patterns have been briefly discussed in the first chapter of this book. On the item endorsement level, Hathaway and Monachesi (1963) presented a variety of items showing dramatic differences in endorsement frequency as a function of adolescent versus adult status of respondents. Tables 5.2 and 5.3 present selected aspects of these data.

A remaining question concerns the degree to which age differences within adolescent age ranges significantly affect profile evaluation and interpretation. Similar to the issue concerning gender differences, the creation and utilization by Marks et al. (1974) of separate adolescent T-score conversions with groupings by ages 17, 16, 15, and 14 and below indicate that item endorsement differences as a function of age are known to occur for adolescents. Further, Hathaway and Monachesi (1963) identified a series of 24 items in a random sample of their statewide data that showed more than 39% instability in the direction of item endorsement from the time of assessment in the ninth grade to reevaluation during the senior year of high school. Table 5.4 shows the breakdown for these items analyzed separately for male and female respondents.

TABLE 5.2
MMPI Items with Adolescent-Adult Male Differences of 32 Points or More
in Percentages of True Responses

Item	Adult Males (N = 226)	Adolescent Males (N = 100)	Differences
I am neither gaining nor losing weight	84%	26%	58%
*My relatives are nearly all in sympathy with me	65	18	47
*Sometimes at elections I vote for men about whom I know very little	62	18	44
I would like to hunt lions in Africa	20	63	43
*I like poetry	59	17	42
*I worry over money and business	53	15	38
I like to attend lectures on serious subjects	62	28	34
*I never worry about my looks	52	19	33
I would like to be an auto racer	17	50	33
*Someone has been trying to influence my mind	40	8	32

Additionally, 29 items for boys and 30 items for girls were identified that showed more than a 17% change in item endorsement direction between 9th and 12th grade. The authors noted that item endorsement instability may be the result of item unreliability as well as "true" shifts in personality that occurred during this 3-year period of adolescent development. These changes in item endorsement were found to be specifically related to the gender of respondent, i.e., no common items appeared on the lists for both males and females. Finally, items that were most likely to shift in endorsement direction tended to involve personal attitudes or perceptions rather than biographical information.

Additionally, Hathaway and Monachesi investigated the stability of high point codetype profiles for adolescents in their test-retest assessments during the 9th and 12th grades. The authors examined the frequency with which high point profiles were maintained on 12th-grade reevaluation, and the conditions under which profiles were likely to change. They found substantially more profile stability when the initial responses from the 9th grade produced T-scores that were equal to or greater than T-score values of 70. In particular, high Pd scale stability was found for both boys and girls when extreme item endorsement patterns

TABLE 5.3
MMPI Items with Adolescent-Adult Female Differences of 40 Points or More
in Percentages of True Responses

Item	Adult Females (N = 315)	Adolescent Females (N = 100)	Differences
*My relatives are nearly all in sympathy with me	73%	22%	51%
I would like to be a private secretary	21	72	51
Usually I would prefer to work with women	6	54	48
*I like poetry	87	44	43
*I worry over money and business...............................	58	16	42
I feel that it is certainly best to keep my mouth shut when I'm in trouble	82	40	42
I have very few fears compared to my friends	74	32	42
It does not bother me that I am not better looking..................	83	42	41
When I get bored I like to stir up some excitement.............	43	83	40
Dirt frightens or digusts me	61	21	40

($T > 70$) were produced on 9th-grade assessment. More than half of the high Pd scale children continued to have Pd as one of the highest two scales in their second profile. In contrast, other scales such as Mf, Hs and D were found to be highly unstable, with values on these scales frequently moving from high point to low point codetype characteristics. Based upon these analyses they concluded, "It is clear that predictions from the individual MMPI scale should be made with caution if the prediction period is to cover several years" (1963, p. 71). These data clearly reflected both cross-sectional differences in item endorsement patterns as a function of age, and the occurrence of longitudinal changes in item endorsement patterns for individuals assessed repeatedly across a period of several years.

TABLE 5.4

Items to Which Responses by a Statewide Random Sample of 100 Boys and 100 Girls Showed More Than 39 Percent Instability Between the Ninth and Twelfth Grades

Item	Percentage of Changing Responses	
	"True" to "False"	"False" to "True"
BOYS		
Once in a while I think of things too bad to talk about	22	20
My speech is the same as always (not faster or slower, or slurring; no hoarseness)	21	19
I like dramatics	20	21
My conduct is largely controlled by the customs of those about me	19	23
It makes me uncomfortable to put on a stunt at a party even when others are doing the same sort of things	24	20
I should like to belong to several clubs or lodges	19	24
I dream frequently about things that are best kept to myself	22	20
People often disappoint me	24	19
I feel unable to tell anyone about myself	24	21
When I was a child I didn't care to be a member of a crowd or gang	19	21
When I am cornered I tell that portion of the truth which is not likely to hurt me	26	21
It is unusual for me to express strong approval or disapproval of the actions of others	22	22
GIRLS		
These days I find it hard not to give up hope of amounting to something	28	24
Most people willl use somewhat unfair means to gain profit or an advantage rather than lose it	21	19
I know who is responsible for most of my troubles	24	22
It makes me impatient to have people ask my advice or otherwise interrupt me when I am working on something important	22	18
I am always disgusted with the law when a criminal is freed through the arguments of a smart lawyer	20	20
I like to keep people guessing what I'm going to do next	19	21
I am apt to hide my feelings in some things, to the point that people may hurt me without their knowing about it	23	18
If given the chance I would make a good leader of people	23	18
I have never been made especially nervous over trouble that any members of my family have gotten into	22	20
I prefer work which requires close attention, to work which allows me to be careless	21	23
I do not try to cover up my poor opinion or pity of a person so that he won't know how I feel	23	20
I think Lincoln was greater than Washington	22	20

Do MMPI profiles of adolescents at different age groups yield differences in interpretive accuracy and validity? Three studies have direct relevancy for this issue. Findings by Lachar et al. (1976), Ehrenworth and Archer (1985), and Wimbish (1984) have reported no evidence of significant age effects for clinician accuracy ratings of adolescent narratives when adolescent norms were employed in converting MMPI raw scores to T-score values. Lachar et al. (1976) did find, however, significant age differences when comparing the accuracy ratings produced from MMPI profiles using adolescent and adult K-corrected norms. Specifically, the authors found that interpretations of profiles from adolescent norms produce statistically higher accuracy ratings than statements from adult norms for adolescents in the 12- to 13-year-old age group. These norm differences were nonsignificant for accuracy data in the mid- and later adolescent groupings. Examination of mean values show that although accuracy ratings remained relatively constant for adolescent norms across three age groups (12 to 13, 14 to 15, and 16 to 17), ratings for profiles based on adult norms were substantially more inaccurate for the 12- to 13-year-old period than for the other two age groupings.

In summary, it can be concluded that there are known and substantial differences in item endorsement patterns as the function of the age of adolescent respondents on the MMPI. Thus far, findings suggest that accuracy of narrative statements based upon age-appropriate norms tend to be relatively unaffected by age of adolescent.

ASSESSING POTENTIAL FOR ACTING OUT AND IMPULSIVITY

As previously noted, initial research applications of the MMPI to adolescents were based on attempts to predict the development of delinquent behaviors. Hathaway and Monachesi (1963) reported that certain personality configurations appeared to be associated with differentially higher rates of delinquency. Following their analyses of high point code distributions from the Minnesota ninth-grade sample, they identified specific MMPI scale features relevant to the prediction of delinquency that they referred to as excitatory and suppressor scales. Excitatory scales were defined by elevations on *Pd, Sc,* and *Ma* and associated with elevated rates of delinquent behavior during follow-up periods. Suppressor codetypes were associated with reduced rates of delinquent behavior. Monachesi and Hathaway summarized these data as follows:

> Scales 4, 8, and 9, the excitatory scales, were found to be associated with
> high delinquency rates. When profiles were deviant on these scales, singly

or in combination, delinquency rates were considerably larger than the overall rate. Thus, it was found that boys with the excitatory MMPI scale codes (where scales 4, 8, and 9 in combination were the most deviant scales in the profile) had a delinquency rate of 41.9% in contrast to the overall rate of 34.6%. Again, scales 0, 2, and 5 are the suppressor scales and were the dominant scales in the profiles of boys with low delinquency rates (27.1% as against 34.6%). The variable scales 1, 3, 6, and 7 were again found to have little relationship with delinquency. Of great interest is the fact that some of these relationships are even more marked for girls. In this case, the MMPI data are so closely related to delinquency that it found that girls with the excitatory code profile had a delinquency rate twice as large as the overall rate. Again, the more deviant scores on scales 4, 8, and 9, the higher the delinquency rate. Girls with inhibitor or suppressor scale scores have lower delinquency rates than the overall rate (1969, p. 217).

Systematic follow-up and extensions of this work typically based upon further analyses of the Minnesota statewide sample, have provided consistent support for the concept that elevations on scales *Pd, Sc* and *Ma* serve an "excitatory" function and are predictive of higher rates of "acting out" or delinquent behavior in adolescent samples (e.g., Briggs et al., 1961; Rempel, 1958; Wirt & Briggs, 1959). Findings by Briggs et al. (1961) indicated that the accuracy of prediction to delinquent behaviors increased when MMPI data were combined with data regarding a family history of severe disease or death. Specifically, Briggs et al. found that when elevations on excitatory scales were combined with positive histories for family trauma, the frequency of delinquent behavior was twice that of the general population. Similarly, Rempel (1958) reported that he could accurately identify 69.5% of the delinquents based on analysis of MMPI scales. When MMPI data were combined with school record data in a linear regression procedure the accurate identification rate for delinquent boys rose to 74.2%. More recently, Huesmann et al. (1978) found that a simple linear summation of the sums of scales *Pd, Ma* and *F* served as the best predictor of delinquent and aggressive behavior in a sample of 426 nineteen-year-old adolescents. This procedure was effective in predicting concurrent incidents of aggression and delinquency as well as retroactively accounting for significant proportions of variance in the ratings of aggressiveness for subjects at age 9.

The majority of studies on the effects of excitatory and suppressor scales have typically employed the use of adult *K*-corrected norms with adolescent respondents. The fact that such studies have consistently reported significant results suggests that the effects of excitatory and suppressor scales are probably quite marked. Given the greater reliance on acting out defenses during adolescence in both normal and clinical settings, such research findings are highly relevant to the description and prediction of adolescent behavior. Purer estimates of predictive accuracy involving less "noise" due to norm distortions might be found if future research in this area employs appropriate adolescent norms.

ASSESSING SUBSTANCE ABUSE: THE MAC SCALE

MacAndrew (1979) has suggested that the MacAndrew Alcoholism Scale (MAC) may be useful for assessing substance abuse problems in adolescent respondents and he has reported impressive accuracy rates for identification of substance abuse problems in samples of older adolescents and young adults. The available literature, although very limited, supports the utility of the MAC scale with adolescent samples.

The MAC scale was developed by contrasting the MMPI item endorsements of 300 male outpatient alcoholics with those of 300 male psychiatric outpatients (MacAndrew, 1965). Final items were selected for the MAC scale based on ability to separate these two groups and excluding the two items related directly to alcohol consumption. The final 49 items selected by these procedures correctly classified 81.5% of subjects in cross-validation samples of male alcoholic and nonalcoholic psychiatric outpatients (MacAndrew, 1965). Based on a review of the MMPI literature in the substance abuse area, Sutker and Archer (1979) concluded that the research findings on the MAC scale supported the view that it is the "most promising of current MMPI-derived alcoholism scales" (p. 127).

In general, the MAC literature from adult populations indicates this scale is useful in identifying a variety of substance abuse and dependency problems in addition to alcohol (e.g., Kranitz, 1972; Lachar, Berman, Grissell, & Schoof, 1976; Lachar, Godowski, & Keegan, 1979). Further, MAC scores tend to be highly stable over time and may be effective in identifying individuals who do not manifest drug abuse problems at the time of testing but will manifest drug involvement problems at a later point (Hoffman, Loper, & Kammeier, 1974; Huber & Danahy, 1975). In contrast to the extensive literature on the characteristics of the MAC scale in adult populations, few studies have examined the properties of this scale in adolescent groups.

Rathus, Fox, and Ortins (1980) administered a short form of the MAC scale to 1,672 high school students. They found MAC scores significantly related to marijuana use patterns as well as to such antisocial behaviors as crimes against persons and property. The authors concluded that adolescent MAC scores may be generally sensitive to antisocial behaviors rather than specifically related to substance abuse. Wolfson and Erbaugh (1984) investigated the ability of the MAC scale to identify drug abusers by comparing the scores of four groups of adolescents that included normal high school students, inpatient psychiatric patients without significant history of substance abuse, outpatient psychiatric patients without history of substance abuse, and adolescents in residential treatment for drug abuse. The results of mean comparison for MAC scores indicated that this special MMPI scale was of significant utility in discriminating between groups of adolescents with and without significant substance abuse histories. The authors recommended a raw score "cutoff" value of 24 for female adolescents and of 26 for male adolescents. Klinge et al. (1978) found the MAC scale to be of utility in separating adolescents with and without a drug abuse history in a sample of adolescent psychiatric inpatients. Their optimal cutoff score of 23 for respondents of either gender, however, was able to correctly identify only 65% of their drug user sample and 55% of their nonuser psychiatric inpatient group. Finally, significant relationships between drug involvement and MAC scores have been reported for adolescent samples of substance abusers in hospital or residential settings by Klinge (1983) and by Sutker, Moan, Goist, and Allain (1984). Further, Wisniewski, Glenwick, and Graham (1985) found MAC scores related to abuse of a variety of drugs in a sample of 403 Caucasian adolescents in the Ohio school system.

The exact cutoff scores of greatest utility in identifying substance abuse among adolescent respondents is thus far unclear. Current recommendations for adolescent MAC cutoff scores range from Wolfson and Erbaugh's (1984) suggestion of 24 for females and 26 for males to Graham's (1985) suggestion of 28 for both genders. Additionally, Graham (1985) has noted that recent studies with adult populations have indicated that the MAC may be of limited utility with black respondents. Specifically, Graham (1985) and Graham and Mayo (1985) have reported that although black substance abusers tend to score high on the MAC scale, high scores have also been found for many blacks who do not abuse drugs or alcohol, resulting in an elevated rate of "false positives." Although these data were based on investigations of adult samples, findings are of sufficient importance to imply substantial caution in attempting to interpret MAC scores of black adolescents.

OTHER SPECIAL SCALES: THE *A*, *R*, AND *Es* SCALES

With the exception of these limited findings regarding the MAC scale, no empirical investigations have been conducted concerning the properties of other special MMPI scales with adolescent respondents. Three additional scales are mentioned, however, in light of their widespread usage in adult samples and their *potential* utility with adolescent respondents. These are Welsh's Anxiety (*A*) and Repression (*R*) scales and Barron's Ego

Strength (*Es*) Scale. Based on follow-up analyses of the Minnesota statewide sample, Gottesman has very recently developed adolescent normative information for these special MMPI scales, which appear in Appendix C of this book. These norms are available for 15- and 18-year-old male and female adolescents. Additionally, Watson, Harris, Johnson, and LaBeck (1983) have provided adolescent norms for numerous special scales, including the *Es* scale, based on a sample of 1,022 adolescents with mixed psychiatric diagnoses from the Missouri Mental Health Department. Typically, however, adult norms are employed for conversion of adolescent responses to these special scales in the absence of published, comprehensive adolescent norm values from normal populations.

The use of adult special scale norms for adolescents is a quite problematic practice that represents an "interim" strategy that should be replaced by use of adolescent norms for these scales as these data become available. Given the differences found between adolescent and adult normative values on standard MMPI scales, it seems reasonable to assume that significant differences will also occur between adult and adolescent norm values for special MMPI scales. A review of Gottesman et al. adolescent normative data for special scales suggests that the *R* and *MAC* scales are particularly affected by differences between adult- and adolescent-based *T*-score conversion values, with much fewer effects found for norms on the *A* and *Es* scales. In general, a given raw score value will convert to substantially higher *T*-score values in the Gottesman et al. norms for the *R* scale, and substantially lower *T*-score values on the *MAC*, in contrast to adult *T*-score conversions. At this time, however, the Gottesman et al. adolescent norms provide data only for ages 15 and 18, and the ability to generalize these norms to other age grouping is unknown. The current necessity of employing adult norm conversions for adolescent special scale values is one of the major limitations of these measures when employed in the assessment of adolescents.

As noted by Graham (1977), the large volume of factor analytic literature on the MMPI has typically found two basic MMPI dimensions accounting for a majority of score variance. Welsh (1956) developed the Anxiety (*A*) and Repression (*R*) scales to assess the respondent's standing along these first and second dimensions, respectively. The Anxiety scale is a 39-item instrument keyed in such a manner that higher scores on the *A* scale are associated with greater degrees of psychopathology. High scores are said to be reflective of individuals who are maladjusted, anxious, distressed, pessimistic, inhibited, and uncomfortable (Graham, 1977). Although these adjectives are largely negative in tone, it has also been noted that high scores on the *A* scale may be associated with sufficient emotional distress to serve as a motivator for positive change in the psychotherapeutic process. In contrast, low scores on the *A* scale are related to a preference for activity, freedom from anxiety and discomfort, sociability, manipulativeness, and impulsivity (Graham, 1977).

Welsh's Repression Scale consists of 40 items with high scores for adult respondents related to unexcitability, submissiveness, conventionality, and internalization of affect. Low R scores are related to excitability, enthusiasm, impulsivity, aggressiveness, argumentativeness, and a tendency to be self-seeking and self-indulgent. It should be explicitly noted that A and R scale correlates have not been cross-validated within adolescent populations and, therefore, the attribution of these descriptors to adolescents is not supported by empirical data. Given the potential relevance of these dimensions to adolescent behavior, however, it is recommended that adolescent profiles be scored for the A and R scales and that impressions based on these special scales be cross-validated against other standard MMPI features as well as the adolescent's clinical history.

The A scale may serve as a useful overall estimate of the adolescent's level of psychopathology and distress, and R scale values may be found useful in separating adolescents who employ neurotic and repressive defense structures (i.e., high R scores) from those adolescents who tend to employ defense structures emphasizing acting out (i.e., low R scores). The main limitation of these scales with adolescent inpatients has been the restricted range of values typically found in this setting. Specifically, A scale values for inpatient adolescents usually vary between T-score values of 60 and 75 on adult norm conversions, and R scale values have typically ranged between T-score values of 40 to 50. These findings may reflect the fact that adolescents hospitalized for psychiatric treatment consistently display relatively high levels of overall distress and employ acting out, rather than neurotic styles, as primary defense mechanisms.

The Ego Strength (Es) scale is a 68-item measure developed by Barron (1953) to predict the responses of adult neurotic patients to individual psychotherapy. Items were empirically selected by comparing item response frequencies of 17 patients who were judged improved following 6 months of insight-oriented psychotherapy with the response frequencies of 16 patients who were rated unimproved. In general, higher scores indicate a greater capacity for positive response to insight-oriented psychotherapy, whereas scores below a T-score value of 50 raise questions concerning the availability of the patient's internal resources to respond to insight-oriented treatments. In addition, Graham (1977) noted that high Es scores may be produced by highly defensive patients and that under such circumstances these scores should not be interpreted as reflecting a high potential for psychotherapeutic gain. Conversely, low Es scores have also been found among individuals in acute crisis and should not be interpreted under such conditions as indicating poor prognosis for psychotherapeutic gains.

Although not validated in adolescent samples, *Es* scores may be of potential utility in aiding the psychotherapist in determining the adolescent's availability for insight-oriented psychotherapy. Scores above $T = 50$ may reflect the adolescent's ability to prosper from insight-oriented interventions, whereas scores substantially below *T*-score values of 50 indicate that other interventions of a more supportive or behavioral style may be more effective during initial therapy stages. Graham (1977) has reported that scores frequently increase as a function of duration of psychotherapeutic intervention. Reviews of the *Es* scale in adult populations have been provided by Dahlstrom et al. (1975); Graham (1977), Greene (1980), Meltzoff and Kornreich (1970), and others. Evaluations of the *Es* scale have been quite mixed, with largely negative reviews by both Dahlstrom, Welsh, and Dahlstrom and by Greene. The use of the *Es* scale is clearly controversial for both adults and adolescent populations, and MMPI interpreters who employ this measure should be aware that predictions from the *Es* scale are often likely to be misleading in terms of treatment prognosis. This point is illustrated in several of the case examples provided in the next chapter.

6

CLINICAL
CASE EXAMPLES

The purpose of this section is to provide clinical case examles of interpretation approaches for seven adolescents in psychiatric or forensic evaluation settings. These clinical cases were selected from assessment records to illustrate a variety of the diagnostic and treatment issues found in adolescent psychiatric populations. In particular, these cases illustrate major principles related to determining profile validity, deciding treatment planning, dealing with multiple high point codetypes, and interpreting special scale data for adolescents. The interpretations provided for these cases are not exhaustive, and it is likely that the reader may observe additional characteristics and features highly relevant to the diagnosis or treatment of these adolescents. Clinical correlate descriptions are based on combinations of sources involving both adolescent and adult correlate studies. Selected Rorschach data are included in the discussions of each clinical example to provide additional personality data and to offer a limited illustration of the utility of this instrument in enriching adolescent MMPI interpretations. These Rorschach data are presented in a very abbreviated form, and a much more extensive evaluation of Roschach data and indices is recommended in comprehensive psychological evaluations of adolescents.

As shall be seen, the clinical case presentations include discussions of the standard 10 clinical scales as well as the 4 special scales (i.e., *A, R., Es,* and *MAC*), which have previously been reviewed. Additionally, the clinical examples illustrate uses of the MMPI for diagnostic and treatment planning purposes, as well as MMPI assessment to provide information regarding treatment evaluation and outcome.

CLINICAL CASE EXAMPLE I: FEMALE INPATIENT

Mary R. is a white female from an upper middle-class background who was 13 years, 7 months old at the time of her first admission to an adolescent psychiatric inpatient unit. At admission, she produced on the Wechsler Intelligence Scale for Children-Revised (WISC-R) a Full Scale IQ score of 103, a Verbal IQ Score of 95, and a Performance IQ Score of 114. The results of her Rorschach administration, scored using the Comprehensive System, resulted in an $X + \%$ = .72, W to M ratio of 19:2, Zd = -3.0, white space = 9, texture =0, D = -1 and $ADJ\ D$ = 0. These Rorschach findings would suggest that Mary has adequate reality testing capacity $(X + \%)$, but was unrealistic and grandiose in terms of her aspiration level and goal setting $(W$ to $M)$ and tended to be underincorporative in terms of integrating her perceptions of her environment (Zd). Mary's Rorschach findings also suggest that she experienced less need for interpersonal closeness and was more negative and oppositional (white space) than most adolescents. Finally, the D and adjusted D results indicate that Mary's antisocial behaviors probably reflected controlled and directed responses on her part rather than chaotic undercontrolled actions.

Upon inpatient admission Mary's presenting problems included a history of running away from home. She often stayed away from home for intervals as long as 2 to 3 weeks. During these runaway episodes, Mary would engage in shoplifting as a way of meeting her basic needs. Mary also had a history of alcohol abuse and school truancy, and family interview findings indicated a chronic history of family conflict and dysfunction. Mary presented for psychological evaluation dressed in "Punk" attire, with her hair cut at various lengths and dyed a variety of colors. She tended to wear provocative clothing that displayed embroidered slogans bearing political or Punk ideology. Figure 6.1 presents Mary's admission and discharge MMPI profiles on adolescent norms.

An inspection of Mary's validity scale data at treatment admission shows a mean value on the F scale in the range typically found for adolescents in inpatient settings. Mary's T-score values on L and K are also relatively close to mean expected values for adolescents. Mary, therefore, is reporting a substantial degree of unusual symptomatology and appears reasonably open to discussing her problems in therapy.

A review of Mary's standard clinical scale data indicates the presence of a 4-9 clinical codetype. Marks et al. (1974) have noted that 4-9 codetypes are common among adolescents who are referred for treatment because of disobedience, defiance, impulsivity, and school truancy. These authors also observed that such adolescents are likely to be runaways who are described by their parents as difficult to control. Their chief defense mechanism is acting out, and therapists describe adolescents who pro-

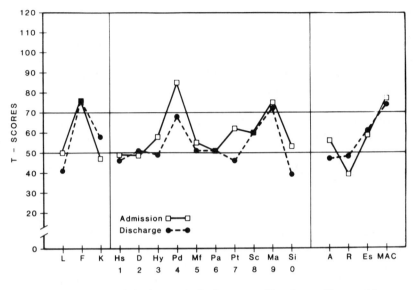

FIGURE 6.1   Admission and discharge profiles for a 13-year-old female.

duce 4-9 profiles as insecure, resentful of authority figures, socially extroverted, and likely to initially arouse liking in others. Marks et al. noted that 4-9s are often described as provocative, seductive, and handsome, and they referred to adolescents with this codetype as "disobedient beauties." Congruent with this picture, the correlate data from adult populations indicate individuals with the 4-9 codetype are often in trouble with their environment because of antisocial behaviors. Terms including selfish, self-indulgent, and impulsive are frequently applied to adult 4-9 codetypes, and the diagnosis of antisocial personality is also typically associated with this code. Consistent with antisocial features, it was quite notable that Mary's depression scores were markedly low for an adolescent in inpatient treatment. Her *Pt* scale score, although somewhat elevated, was also clearly within normal limits suggesting relatively little affective distress given her life circumstances.

A survey of Mary's special scale scores also produced a number of interesting observations. Mary's *A* and *R* scale scores suggested that she was in relatively little general distress at the time of this assessment and that she did not tend to utilize repression as a primary defense mechanism. Such findings are consistent with the features of a 4-9 codetype in which acting out is employed as a primary defense mechanism. Mary's Ego Strength Score would superficially appear to indicate that she was a good candidate for insight-oriented psychotherapy. In this regard, it is accurate that Mary would not be described as fragile and could be expected to respond to confrontive or insight-oriented psychotherapies without fear of sudden deterioration. Mary was not, however, an adolescent who had a high potential for positive therapeutic gain as a result of treatment. Indeed, the 4-9 codetype has been repeatedly identified as characteristic of individuals who are unlikely to show basic personality structure changes as a function of treatment (Sutker, Archer, & Kilpatrick, 1981). Of particular interest among the special scale features is Mary's MacAndrew score, i.e., a raw score value of 29. This value would classify Mary as a probable substance abuser, a hypothesis that is supported by the clinical history data for this patient.

Following 5 months of intensive inpatient care, Mary again received the MMPI at the time of discharge to evaluate treatment effects and to aid in discharge planning. Although not presented in the figure for this patient, the application of adolescent and adult K-corrected norms for this discharge profile produced very significant differences in clinical impressions for this patient. Although adolescent norms continued to produce a 4-9 profile, adult K-corrected norms would produce a 4-9-8 profile, the latter's features of schizophrenia apparently unrelated to this patient's symptomatology. Thus very different views of treatment outcome were produced by adolescent and adult norms, with adult norm characteristics yielding a false-positive picture of thought disorder features.

Beginning with the discharge assessment validity scales, it can be seen that substantial changes have occurred for this patient, particularly in relationship to scale K elevation. The validity scale configuration for this patient at discharge appears valid and indicates that Mary was substantially guarded in reporting symptomatology. The K value found for this patient is indicative of an adolescent who is concerned with self-protection and who is not currently receptive to psychiatric or psychological treatment. This K scale value reflects a general unwillingness to discuss personal issues and a desire to present a picture of positive adjustment.

Although a general lowering of clinical scale elevations have occurred for Mary, it is also apparent that her basic 4-9 MMPI configuration has remained constant from admission to discharge. The relatively small degree of affectve distress Mary was experiencing at the time of admission had dissipated by discharge. Mary could be described as emotionally comfortable and relatively free of subjective distress at inpatient treatment termination. Additionally, her *Si* scores had moved in the direction of greater social extroversion consistent with a picture of increased interpersonal comfort.

The MMPI special scales of *Es* and *MAC* were remarkably consistent from admission to discharge. The only notable changes in terms of special scale values consisted of a slight decrease in *A* scale values consistent with the general lowering of the overall clinical profile, and a slight increase in R scale values suggesting that Mary may have somewhat reduced her overall reliance on acting out as an exclusive defense mechanism.

Overall, the results of pre-versus-post MMPI administrations for this patient indicated that 5 months of inpatient treatment had made little relative impact in changing this individual's overall characterologically oriented personality structure. The discharge profile certainly served to suggest that further inpatient treatment would probably not result in any significant gains, particularly in the sense that Mary's subjective distress had reduced to a level at which she would be unlikely to be motivated for further therapy efforts. It is interesting to note, in relationship to the Marks et al. (1974) description of 4-9 codetypes as "disobedient beauties," that Mary was perceived by peers and staff on the inpatient unit as sexually seductive and interpersonally manipulative. She tended to form rapid and superficial relationships with others and was highly successful in avoiding dealing with the underlying reasons for her hospitalization. Clinical notes by both the individual and family therapist involved in this case reflected the perception that Mary had made relatively minimal progress during her inpatient stay. Treatment staff felt that she presented a moderate to high degree of risk for engaging in impulsive and antisocial actions following discharge in a manner similar to her prehospitalization record. Mary's discharge diagnosis was Mixed Personality Disorder with Antisocial and Narcissistic features.

The poor prognosis offered for Mary is relatively consistent with the available literature concerning treatment outcome for adult patients who present in psychiatric facilities with 4-9 profiles. Lachar (1974) reports that the 4-9 codetype is a "very stable" personality pattern that carries a poor prognosis for behavioral improvement as result of treatment. Further, Lachar reports that roughly 80% of patients treated with an admission codetype of 4-9 are rated as demonstrating no change at the time of discharge. Marks and Seeman (1963) found that patients in a psychiatric teaching hospital who produced a 4-9 profile at admission also produced a 4-9 mean profile at discharge.

Mary was readmitted to a separate inpatient treatment unit, approximately one year following her original discharge, for impulsive, antisocial behaviors and running away from home. This patient's readmission profile, as well as her original admission and discharge profile are presented in Fig. 6.2.

Examination of Mary's readmission profile in comparison with prior testing reveals an impressive degree of personality consistency despite inpatient and outpatient therapeutic intervention. At the time of Mary's readmission she continued to display a quite clearly delineated *Pd-Ma* profile suggestive of substantial personality disorder at ranges very simi-

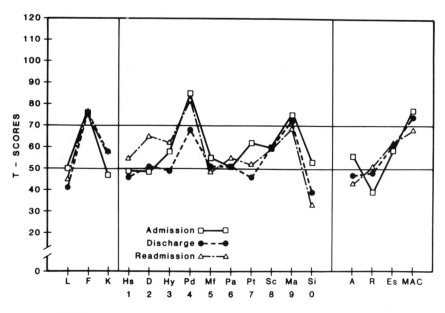

FIGURE 6.2   Admission and discharge profiles for a 13-year-old female with readmission profile at age 15.

lar to her original admission profile. Although some minor differences may be noted between her initial and readmission MMPI profile elevations, such as higher readmission T-score values on scale K and the neurotic triad, the general clinical picture for this girl had remained essentially unchanged. The repeated MMPI assessments of this girl served both to indicate the difficulties that were likely to occur in her treatment and to document the relatively limited effects of therapeutic intervention.

CLINICAL CASE II: WHITE MALE ADOLESCENT

The next profile that we examine was produced by a 17-year-old white male adolescent at the time of his first admission to an adolescent inpatient psychiatric unit. Harold had a Full Scale WISC-R IQ score of 98, a Verbal IQ of 97, and a Performance IQ of 99. Rorschach data for this patient assessed at admission resulted in an $X+\%$ of .71 and an $F+\%$ of .67 indicating adequate perceptual accuracy and conventionality. The record also included five white spaces, no texture responses, and one vista suggesting marked oppositional features, a guarded interpersonal stance, and the presence of an uncomfortable, ruminative, self-inspection process. There were two pure color responses and two color-form (CF) responses in his record, with three out of four of these color responses associated with minus form quality levels, indicating poor emotional controls and modulation and maladaptive or inappropriate responding in emotionally charged situations. Finally, the patient's D and adjusted D values were − 2, suggestive of a relatively long-standing poor tolerance for stress and marked potential for impulsive behaviors.

At the time of his admission, Harold's presenting problems included suicidal and self-destructive ideations and behaviors and a history of impulsive actions that often placed him at risk for physical injury in his environment. For example, the patient would frequently ride his motorcycle at very high speeds (e.g., in excess of 100 mph) under conditions that contained high probabilities for serious or fatal injury. The patient also had a history of polydrug abuse, dating to age 7, which included use of cocaine, marijuana, and alcohol. Harold was awaiting court sentencing for convictions on charges of breaking and entering and vandalism. Harold had a history of parental neglect and physical abuse that dated to his early childhood. The patient's biological father was an alcoholic who had frequently beaten him.

At the time of admission, Harold performed well on the mental status exam and demonstrated no signs of psychotic symptomatology such as disorientation or thought confusion. Harold did indicate that he had fears of "becoming homosexual" and related this concern to his impression that his father might be homosexual and "that kind of thing tends to run in families." The patient's admission MMPI profile, scored on both adolescent and K-corrected norms, are presented in Fig. 6.3. The adult profile is offered for this patient to illustrate the contrast in interpretation that frequently occurs by use of these two sets of norms.

It is immediately apparent from these profiles that although adult and adolescent norms produce essentially the same profile configuration high points, very marked and dramatic differences are present, particularly in relationship to scale Sc. Scale Sc dominates the adult profile produced by this patient in a manner that clearly indicates a strong possibility of paranoid schizophrenic ideation and symptomatology. The application of adolescent norms essentially produces a 4-6 profile with scale 8 as a secondary elevation at a much lower range. The adolescent norm profile produced a much more accurate description of the clinical symptomatology and psychosocial history of this patient than did the MMPI profile produced by adult norms.

Beginning with the validity scale configuration on adolescent norms, it might be noted that Harold's raw score F value was 26. This raises an immediate question concerning the degree to which we might expect

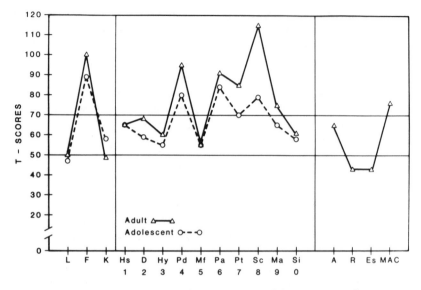

FIGURE 6.3   Profiles derived from adult and adolescent norms for a 17-year-old male.

Harold's profile to be interpretable or clinically useful. Given Harold's reading level (ninth grade), and the individual administration procedures employed for this patient, we were able to rule out the possibilities that Harold was unable to accurately read the MMPI item pool or that he responded to the test in a random or disorganized fashion. Therefore, we cautiously proceeded to interpret Harold's MMPI profile based on an awareness derived from the F scale that he was reporting a substantial degree of highly infrequent or unusual symptomatology.

In terms of clinical scale elevations produced by adolescent norms, Harold produced a 4-6 MMPI profile that also contained clinical elevations on scales 8 and 7. Clinical correlate data for Marks et al. (1974) indicate that 4-6 adolescents are frequently described as rebellious, defiant, disobedient, tense, restless, and negativistic. Acting out and projection are the main defense mechanisms for these patients. Clinical correlate data from adult patients with 4-6 codetypes suggest descriptors of anger, suspiciousness, hostility, and irritability and when such profiles are combined with elevations on scale 8, patients tend to be fairly evenly divided into psychotic and personality-disordered diagnoses. In addition to anger and hostility, prominent affective experiences for this patient appear to include substantial tension and anxiety as reflected in the clinical range elevation on the *Pt* scale. Additionally, salient features also include a degree of agitation as manifested by elevation of scale *Ma,* and a marked degree of social introversion reflected in this patient's *Si* score.

Turning to this patient's special scale scores, Harold's overall level of psychological distress as measured by the A scale would be described as marked and substantial. It is notable, however, that the A scale is probably serving as an underestimation of his overall level of maladjustment when contrasted with the clinical profile produced on the standard scales. Both the R and Es scale values for this patient are low, serving to provide warnings to the therapist in terms of the type and intensity of psychotherapeutic efforts. Given the extreme symptomatology reported by Harold, a therapist may well wish for a higher R scale score indicating a greater capacity on Harold's part to be able to repress or "seal over" issues that threaten his overall stability. Further, the relatively low T-score value on the Es scale might suggest that therapy efforts would best be initiated in terms of supportive or behavioral psychotherapy, rather than interpretive or insight-oriented psychotherapy. The latter therapy approaches may exceed Harold's ability to tolerate or incorporate observations that could directly threaten his ability to deal with his external and intrapsychic environment. Finally, Harold's MacAndrew scale raw score value of 29 would result in a positive indication for substance abuse. This judgment is supported by the patient's clinical history as well as cross-validated in Marks et al.'s (1974) description of the features 4-6 codetypes among adolescents.

Perhaps the most puzzling feature of the adolescent norm profile for this patient is the clinical elevation on the Sc scale, which is too high to ignore, but does not clearly indicate the presence of an ongoing schizophrenic process. The function of the scale 8 elevation in Harold's profile may be best understood in conjunction with the history of his treatment while in inpatient hospitalization.

In general, Harold initially presented to the Unit as a guarded, hostile, and easily irritated adolescent who typically maintained rigid control over his impulses and generally tended to behave in an overcontrolled and conventional manner. During the early stages of inpatient treatment it was noted that Harold appeared to have substantial sensitivity to the psychopathological patterns and symptoms of others and he tended to freely comment on these issues in a manner that often appeared to be critical and "cutting." Harold tended to display much more resistance and lack of insight, however, concerning his own problems. Specifically, Harold appeared to have great difficulty in talking about his thoughts and feelings surrounding the abusive episodes involved in his early childhood.

Several weeks after his inpatient admission, Harold was denied a unit privilege that he was seeking and responded with intense rage and anger toward the treatment staff. Harold rapidly escalated out of control and eventually required physical restraint and seclusion procedures as his behavior and verbalizations became increasingly irrational and physically threatening. During this rage experience, which lasted roughly 4 hours, Harold displayed overtly psychotic behaviors and appeared to "break with reality" in a manner that required strong external controls to ensure his safety and the safety of those around him. This type of episode was repeated three times during his 5 months of hospitalization, with two of the three episodes being "touched off" by Harold being confronted to experience his feelings concerning his sense of abandonment and rejection by his parents. Thus, Harold's elevation on scale 8 in his admission MMPI profile appeared to represent his transient experiences of "psychosis," which were infrequent and were contained within relatively brief episodes. If Harold had been pushed too quickly into dealing with his affect, it is probable that the frequency of psychotic episodes would have dramatically increased and little psychotherapeutic gain would have resulted. The MMPI *Es* scale, in combination with his elevation on the *Sc* scale, served as a valid warning to psychotherapists regarding Harold's fragility. Harold's discharge diagnosis was Borderline Personality Disorder. An MMPI discharge profile was not available for this patient.

CLINICAL CASE III: 17-YEAR-OLD BLACK MALE

Frederick M. was a 17-year-old black male at the time of his evaluation. This testing was conducted as part of court evaluation processes in relationship to a first-degree murder charge. The results of a Wechsler Adult Intelligence Scale-Revised (WAIS-R) administration for this individual resulted in a Full Scale IQ of 80, a Performance IQ score of 87, and a Verbal IQ score of 78. These test results were relatively consistent with findings from a 1977 evaluation performed by the public school system. Additionally, the results of the current administration of the Rorschach resulted in a 15-response protocol that included an $X+$% of .73, and $F+$% of .75, and a score of 2 on the schizophrenic index, findings suggestive of adequate reality testing. The patient had three positive signs on the suicide constellation and no positive signs on the depression index, indicating negative findings for serious depression or suicidal potential. The patient's $W:M$ ratio was 9:3, his Zd score $= -5.5$, and he had no texture responses in the record. These last findings revealed an excessively high aspirational level, a tendency to underincorporate in processing information, and a guarded interpersonal stance. The patient's D value was 0 and his FC to $CF+C$ ratio was 0:3, including two pure-color responses. This pattern would suggest that although Frederick had adequate stress tolerance, he was likely to respond to emotional stimuli in a poorly controlled manner. The patient's MMPI profile is presented in Fig. 6.4.

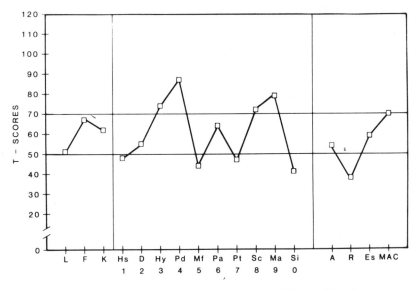

FIGURE 6.4   Forensic evaluation profile for a 17-year-old male.

Frederick was referred for psychological testing by his defense attorney following charges of first-degree murder and unlawful use of a firearm in committing a felony. He appeared for testing neatly groomed and was a tall, athletically built, handsome man. Given his limited verbal IQ, special efforts were made to ensure that he fully understood the meaning of MMPI items, and he appeared to have no significant problems in this regard. Frederick had been charged with a premeditated murder of his lover's ex-boyfriend during which he lay in ambush for the victim and shot him repeatedly with a large caliber handgun. The prosecution in this case perceived the slaying as stemming from a premeditated arrangement initiated by the defendant's girlfriend, for which Frederick allegedly received a sum of money for the killing, rather than related to an "act of passion." Following the slaying, the defendant and his girlfriend were also accused of attempting to dispose of the body by attaching weights to the body and placing it in a nearby river. The girlfriend of the defendant was also being tried on accessory charges.

The psychological issues related to these charges involved the presence or absence of significant emotional disturbance in the defendant, as well as his capacity to stand trial as an adult. During the preliminary interview, the defendant indicated that he perceived himself as a highly talented individual whose substantial educational and career potential had been frustrated by "bad luck." This perception stood in contrast to the results of intelligence testing that indicated marked limitations in the educational potential that was possible for him. At one point, Frederick discussed his desire to attend college and indicated that he wished to become a business executive because he desired "prestige and power." At no point in the psychological evaluation was the client directly questioned concerning details of the alleged crimes. Independent evaluations of this patient were also conducted by two psychiatrists and one social worker.

The pattern of this individual's validity scale configuration suggests the presence of a moderate degree of unusual symptomatology coupled with a test-taking attitude that could be described as moderately defensive. Overall, the validity scale configuration for this individual suggests a valid protocol produced by an individual who is endorsing some deviant or unusual symptomatology, but who is unlikely to display much psychological awareness of problem areas. Further, his K scale elevation indicates that he typically would be expected to display relatively little insight concerning psychological problems and relatively little "openness" to psychological help.

The clinical scale elevations displayed by this client reveal peak elevations on scales Pd, Ma, Hy and Sc. A 4-9-3-8 codetype is unavailable in either adult or adolescent codetype sources, but a viable approach to understanding this client may be achieved by viewing this clinical profile as a combination of several two-point codetypes. Starting with the 4-9 features of this profile, the major codetype for this profile, it might be expected that this individual will show salient features of what Marks et al. (1974) described as their "disobedient beauties." Thus, we might expect a history of impulsive, provocative, and defiant behaviors with a marked possibility that this client grew up in a family that showed substantial evidence of dysfunction. Extensive use of acting out as a primary defense mechanism and problems with impulse control and delay of gratification are likely. The data collected by Marks, Seeman, and Haller in their 1970–1973 sample also indicate that there is a very marked possibility of substance use and abuse, an issue that is also examined in relationship to this patient's MacAndrew score. From the adult literature on the 4-9 codetype, such as Graham (1977), we might also expect this client to be narcissistic, selfish, and self-indulgent and to have a history of delinquent behaviors and marked disregard for social standards and value. Although this client is likely to make a good "first impression" with others, his relationships would tend to be superficial and shallow. Referring to the original data on adolescent respondents provided by Hathaway and Monachesi (1963), we find that the elevations displayed by this client on scales Pd, Sc, and Ma all serve to suggest difficulties in impulse control and marked potential for delinquent behaviors and antisocial acts.

If we also consider the 4-8 aspects of this profile, clinical correlate data for adolescents provided by Marks et al. (1974) indicate an immature personality marked by extreme narcissism. The Marks et al. data show such adolescents typically displayed minimal motivation in psychotherapy efforts and only 16% of their 4-8 sample showed definite improvement as a result of therapy. Consistent with the 4-9 profile, acting out is the primary defense mechanism for the 4-8 codetype, although projection is also employed as a secondary defense mechanism among 4-8 respondents. Problems in impulse control are noted, and the 4-8 adolescent is described as provocative, argumentative, resentful, and evasive. Therapists described 4-8s in the Marks et al. sample as negativistic and superficial. Forty-three percent of the 4-8s in this sample either had been held in detention or had been placed on probation. In his description of the 4-8 codetype, Graham notes that when crimes are committed by these individuals such criminal activities tend to be vicious and assaultive, and are often poorly planned, poorly executed, and senseless. He further notes that when these individuals become involved interpersonally, they often display little empathy for others and typically relate to others exclusively through attempts to manipulate them in efforts to satisfy their own needs or desires.

Finally, one could evaluate this profile in terms of integration of the 4-3 codetype characteristics. Taking this approach, Marks, Seeman, and Haller note that 3-4/4-3 codetype adolescents frequently come from homes that have experienced separation or divorce. Symptom patterns frequently involve hostility and aggression, and there is often a history of stealing, truancy, and running away from home. Advising caution in attempting to interpret this codetype, Marks, Seeman, and Haller noted that only 1 of their 38 adolescents in the 3-4/4-3 codetype was from a black racial background. In the adult literature, Graham noted that the most salient characteristics of the 3-4/4-3 codetype is chronic, intense anger displayed by individuals who harbor substantial hostility and aggressive impulses. When *Pd* exceeds the elevation of *Hy*, Graham also notes that the individual is likely to be overcontrolled much of the time, but is subject to brief episodes of aggressive and violent acting out. Graham notes that prisoners with the 4-3 codetype often present histories involving assaultive and violent crimes. Additionally, these individuals frequently appear to be superficially conforming, but underlying this are substantial feelings of rebelliousness. Their interpersonal stance is often marked by demands for attention and approval from others.

Taken together, the information derived from these codetypes produces a number of descriptors that are common across these interpretation strategies. Specifically, there appears to be ample support for the view that this client is immature, narcissistic, impulsive, and prone to hostile or aggressive actions. Further, there is substantial cross-validation for the perception that he is likely to display superficial and shallow interpersonal relationships that are often manipulative. The general personality configuration displayed by this patient corresponds to a personality disorder involving antisocial and narcissistic features. Lachar, in his 1974 text, has classified the 4-9, 4-8, and 4-3 profile codetypes as "characterological."

A review of the special scale configuration for this patient appears consistent with the information derived from analysis of the clinical profile. Specifically, the patient displays relatively little general psychological distress on scale A, a finding that is consistent with his low levels of affective distress on scales D and Pt. This response pattern may serve as a particularly negative sign in that the patient had substantial environmental reasons for distress; i.e., at the time of the evaluation he was awaiting trial on first-degree murder charges. Additionally, his relatively low score on scale R would suggest that he is an outgoing, impulsive, dominant, aggressive, and self-indulgent individual who would not be described as repressive in terms of his defense style. Indeed, there is ample evidence that this patient is much more likely to employ acting out as a major defense mechanism. The relatively high ego strength scale value for this patient would probably be quite misleading if interpreted as indicating a good potential for insight-oriented psychotherapy. A much more likely interpretation of this elevation would be that this patient's general defensiveness, as displayed by his scale K elevation, is also being reflected in the elevation on the Es scale. Finally, this patient's raw score value of 29 on the MacAndrew scale would result in a positive judgment for substance abuse or substance dependence, a finding consistent with the clinical correlate data derived from his clinical scale profile.

Following this assessment, a psychological evaluation report was submitted to the defendant's attorney summarizing the results of psychological testing. The primary use involved in this assessment, from the defense standpoint, was the degree to which test findings supported a judgment that this client displayed a "diminished capacity." Results of the psychological evaluation were consistent with the reports of two of the psychiatrists, based on extensive psychiatric interviews, and the social worker, based on the patient's family interview and social history, in indicating a characterological or personality disorder for this client. The psychological evaluation was not employed by the defense during the trial of this individual, who entered a plea of "not guilty." The defendant was convicted as charged.

CLINICAL CASE IV: WHITE MALE ADOLESCENT

Steven H. was a 13-year-old white male at the time of first admission to an adolescent inpatient psychiatric setting. At admission, Steven's responses to the WISC-R produced Full Scale, Verbal, and Performance IQ values of 90. In addition, Steven's Rorschach responses resulted in the following values: schizophrenic index $= 0$, depression index value $= 0$, $X+\% = .86$, and $F+\% = .82$. Thus, Steven's Rorschach protocol was negative for indicators of schizophrenia and depression, and his reality testing and ability to perceive his environment in a conventional manner appeared unimpaired. Steven had a Zd value of -4, and he produced 5 white space responses in his record, indicating a tendency to underincorporate the environment in terms of information processing and to respond oppositionally to task demands. Steven's suicide constellation resulted in 6 positive signs scored on adult norms and 4 positive signs on adolescent norms, which, although less than the conventional cutoff total number of indicators, might be sufficient to raise clinical questions regarding suicidal potential.

Steven was admitted for psychiatric evaluation and treatment following a suicide attempt by drug overdose. This attempt, although potentially serious in nature, involved the self-administration of a non-lethal dosage of medications that had been prescribed for his mother. In addition, Steven's presenting complaints included a long history of family conflict, particularly involving the relationship between Steven and his mother, which often resulted in loud and angry exchanges between them. On rare occasions these mother-son conflicts included physical aggression on Steven's part that constituted a threat to the safety of his mother. Steven also had a very turbulent relationship history with his two younger siblings, which was manifested by Steven's "tormenting" of them. In particular, Steven appeared to have mastered a variety of ways to place his younger brother and sister in positions where they received punishment for his misdeeds. His academic performance in the classroom had been steadily declining, with several changes of classroom setting resulting from Steven's sullen and hostile behavior in his educational placements. Steven also had an infrequent history of physically attacking his classmates, on one occasion with sufficient intensity to require medical treatment for his "victim." More typically, however, Steven tended to be generally noncooperative in the classroom setting in a passive-aggressive manner. He was described by teachers and classmates as a "loner" who tended to have few peer interactions. At inpatient admission, his mental status exam did not reveal evidence of symptomatology related to psychotic process, and his affect appeared to be a mixture of anger and depression. Steven's admission and discharge MMPI profiles are shown in Fig. 6.5. A review of the validity scale data at admission indicated a raw score of 16 on the F scale, a value frequently found for adolescents in an inpatient setting (Archer, in press). His scores on L and K suggest an openness to seeking help and willingness to work in a meaningful way in psychotherapeutic efforts. A quick scan of Steven's clinical scales

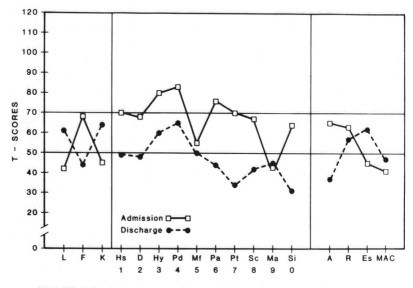

FIGURE 6.5   Admission and discharge profiles for a 13-year-old male.

suggest the presence of five clinical scales below a *T*-score of 70 on adolescent norms, indicating a selectivity in the item endorsement pattern produced by this patient. Steven's clinical profile is interesting from the standpoint that a 4-3 codetype emerges from this patient accompanied by "other" codetype features. It could be argued, for example, that Steven manifests 4-6 codetype features as well as characteristics of the primary 4-3 codetype.

The adolescent codetype information from Marks et al. (1974) indicates that over half of adolescents who produce a 4-3 profile have suicidal thoughts and that the focal concern of these teenagers often involves conflict with parents. Additionally, Marks et al. described the 4-6 codetype as related to defiance, disobedience, restlessness, and a negativistic stance. Adolescents with 4-6 codetypes tended to show a deterioration in their attitude toward school and frequently were in trouble in their relationships within the school environment. The literature from adult correlate data (e.g. Graham, 1977; Greene, 1980; Lachar, 1974) indicates that 4-3 codetypes are related to substantial hostile and aggressive impulses that might be manifested in brief episodes of aggressive or violent behaviors. It is also typically noted that the 4-3 individuals tend to project blame on others and have many features of the passive-aggressive personality style. Similarly, adults with 4-6 codetypes are described as passive-dependent and resentful of demands placed on them by others. They are also typically described as hostile, irritable, and sullen. In the adult literature for both 4-3 and 4-6 codetypes, vague somatic complaints have frequently been found, including headaches and gastrointestinal problems.

When we examine Steven's clinical profile in terms of potential for the use of acting out as a primary defense mechanism, his relative elevation on scale Pd appears to be counterbalanced by his low scores on the Ma scale and his introverted charcteristics on the Si scale. Therefore, overt use of acting out as a primary defense mechanism does not appear likely for this patient. It should be noted, however, that his relative elevations on scales Hy and Pd would suggest that Steven would be subject to manifesting episodes of violent or aggressive behavior when placed under sustained stress (i.e., the overcontrolled hostility syndrome). Based on his scores from scales D and Pt, his degree of affective distress might be described as moderate and within clinical ranges. Further, his elevations on Pd and Pa indicate a substantial degree of frustration, anger, suspiciousness, and hostility is likely to be harbored by this teenager, and his relative elevations on Sc and Si suggest a pattern of substantial isolation and alienation from others. The general slope of Steven's overall profile suggests a disturbance in personality features, which if manifested by an adult would be referred to as characterological in nature. Overall, the picture is one of an angry, sullen, hostile, and distrustful adolescent who is markedly alienated from others and who is likely to display passive-aggressive behaviors with occasional explosive outbursts.

Review of Steven's special scales lend additional interpretive information for his profile. Steven's relatively high scores on A and R suggest that he might be described as anxious, uncomfortable, and pessimistic and that he is typically conventional, inhibited, and internalizing. Similarly, Steven's T-score value of approximately 45 on the Es scale suggests that he might be experiencing feelings of helplessness, chronic fatigue, inhibition, and rigidity, and that he may manifest difficulties in responding positively to insight therapies. Finally, Steven's MAC raw score of 19 would suggest that he does not appear to be at risk for the development or experience of substance abuse or substance dependency problems.

Steven received approximately 4 months of inpatient treatment during which time he manifested many of the characteristics and features noted above. Specifically, Steven frequently presented himself as isolated, sullen, and angry. Although he occasionally flirted with an "openness to treatment" stance, he more typically assumed a pessimistic, critical, and angry position. His most typical way of dealing with stress and anxiety was to withdraw socially from others and to assume a sarcastic and critical posture. When under sustained pressure, however, Steven would occasionally display angry outbursts that resembled temper tantrums characteristic of much younger children. As the isssue of Steven's suicide attempt was explored, it became apparent that Steven's intention was not self-destruction, but rather the punishment of his mother for what Steven perceived as her unavailability to him. Steven had carefully studied the medications he took and knew that the dosage level he had self-administered was within a non-lethal range. Steven maintained a marked distance from both peers and staff on the unit throughout his inpatient treatment and was described by his individual and family psychotherapist as showing only minimal gains as a result of therapy efforts.

At the conclusion of his inpatient treatment, Steven was readministered the MMPI to evaluate treatment effects. The results of the discharge MMPI evaluation reveal several striking features in contrast to his admission profile. It is immediately apparent that substantial validity scale changes have occurred reflected in increased elevations on scales L and K and a dramatic reduction in scale F elevation. The scale F decrease would suggest a reduction in unusual or infrequent symptomatology for this patient. This observation should not be comforting to the interpreter, however, when it is reviewed in conjunction with the relative increases in L and K, which reflect a much more guarded, rigid, and defensive posture on the part of this patient. Thus, Steven appeared to have "closed up shop" by the time of his discharge in terms of his accessibility to psychological issues or interventions. The patient's validity scale configuration indicates that Steven may well have "psychologically left the hospital" substantially before his discharge date.

Examination of the clinical scales shows that Steven continued to maintain a 4-3 codetype as the most salient features of his MMPI profile. Thus, he maintained substantial feelings of hostility and anger, and his susceptibility to brief episodes of aggressive outbursts or behaviors remains relatively unaffected by therapeutic interventions. Dramatic changes in profile features, however, are evident for Steven, including reductions in the report of affective distress. Specifically, Steven demonstrates marked reductions on scales D, Pt, and A indicative of his self-report of substantially greater emotional comfort. Additionally, the patient shows marked reductions on scales Pa and Sc as well as significant movement on the Si scale in the direction of social extroversion reflecting substantially greater interpersonal comfort.

Inspection of MMPI special scales indicate that Steven reported a much lower level of overall maladjustment on the A scale, and the MacAndrew discharge score is identical to his admission value. Steven's Ego Strength scale showed a dramatic shift from admission to discharge, with a relatively higher elevation on the Es scale apparent at the time of the second evaluation. Particular caution, however, should be taken in attempting to interpret this elevation as a positive prognostic sign. Indeed, relatively high elevations on the Es scale may be produced as a function of a defensive response style typically reflected in L and K scale elevations

(Graham, 1985). Thus, it is likely that the *Es* change manifested by this patient simply reflected his increased defensiveness and rigidity (negative prognostic signs), rather than an actual increase in his ability to respond to insight-oriented therapy.

In summary, the discharge MMPI profile produced by this patient appears to characterize an adolescent who has made minimal therapy gains. Changes on the discharge MMPI profile primarily reflected his attempts to "say the right thing" to facilitate his hospital discharge. The marked elevations on *L* and *K* along with the continued elevations on scales *Pd and Hy* serve as indicators of a poor prognosis following discharge. The initial accessibility that was displayed by Steven at the time of his admission rapidly shifted to a defensive stance as he became accustomed to a secure environment that removed him from the immediate sources of distress and pressure. By the time of his discharge, Steven might be described as emotionally "sealed over" and unavailable. Steven was discharged to outpatient psychotherapy, which he refused to attend following the initial four sessions. Although Steven's mother was alarmed by this noncooperation in attendance, she felt unable to compel Steven to attend and treatment was discontinued. Three weeks after his refusal to attend individual therapy, Steven also ceased attendance at family therapy sessions.

Approximately 6 months following discharge from the inpatient setting, Steven was readmitted to inpatient care following continued chronic family conflict coupled with an episode in which Steven had threatened a fellow classmate with a razor. The patient is currently undergoing the second hospitalization at a different facility, and reports of his current progress are unavailable. Figure 6.6 shows Steven's original admission and discharge MMPI profile in relationship to his readmission profile obtained at the time of his second hospitalization.

The results of this patient's readmission MMPI profile reflect on overall level of symptomatology that was relatively consistent with that found for his initial hospital admission profile. Specifically, it can be noted that the *K* scale elevation has once again returned to a level consistent with an openness to psychiatric assistance, and his readmission *F* scale score shows a relatively equivalent level of overall severe symptomatology to the original admission level. In terms of the clinical scale profiles, scales *Pt* through scales *Si* are relatively unchanged from the first to the second administration. Differences in the left-hand side of the clinical profile would suggest a moderate increase in neurotic types of symptomatology with a corresponding decrease in personality disorder and charcterological-like features. These findings are reflected in relatively higher scores on scales 1 and 2 and relatively lower scores on scales 3 and 4 at the time of the second hospital admission. The clinical profile produced by Steven at the

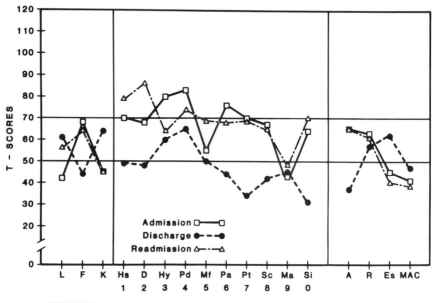

FIGURE 6.6   Admission and discharge profiles for a 13-year-old male with readmission profile at age 14.

time of his second hospital admission is a 2-1-4 profile, however, which is still consistent with the view that Steven manifests combinations of neurotic and personality disorder symptomatology. Steven's readmission MMPI profile is not inconsistent with his discharge diagnosis of mixed personality disorder with passive-aggressive features at the time of his first hospitalization. Finally, it may be noted that Steven's special scale values from the admission profiles from his first and second hospitalization were essentially unchanged. The ability to contrast these three MMPI profiles for this patient tends to reinforce the conclusion that Steven's discharge MMPI profile was not a reflection of substantial gains made as a result of psychotherapy, but rather served as a fake good attempt by this patient to facilitate his discharge from the hospital setting.

CLINICAL CASE V: WHITE FEMALE ADOLESCENT

Debra was a 14-year-old white female at the time of her admission for inpatient psychiatric care. Evaluation on the WISC-R resulted in a Full Scale IQ score of 97, a Performance IQ of 104, and a Verbal IQ score of 97. Rorschach data at the time of admission indicated a schizophrenic index value of 4, an $X+\% = .46$, and a D value of -2. These findings raise serious questions concerning this adolescent's reality testing and thought processes as well as her impulse control and stress tolerance. The suicide constellation value was 8 on adult criterion and the depression index score was 3. The values are also sufficient to cause clinical concerns, and to justify clinical precautions, in terms of self-injurious and suicidal behaviors related to marked depression. Additionally, there were three pure-color responses indicative of emotional lability and problems in modulation of responses to emotional stimuli.

The patient was admitted following a suicidal gesture in which she held a knife to her stomach in the presence of her mother and talked about her intention to kill herself "if not now, then eventually."

The patient had experienced escalating conflicts with her parents that resulted in her running away from home for overnight periods on several occasions during the prior year. Debra's parents stated that she typically showed poor judgment, yet they often placed her in a parental role with her two siblings who were 2 and 7 years old. On one occasion Debra had let her younger brother pour lighter fluid over his arm, which he then lit to "see what would happen." In general, Debra was seen as a "bad girl" within her family, and her refusal to comply with family instructions or responsibilities was viewed as indicators of her poor motivation and character. Debra also reported a variety of unusual and delusional beliefs, including the contention that her biological father had not died 4 years prior to her hospitalization but rather had "disappeared" and might return to her family. Additionally, Debra had a history of marginal academic performance and was perceived by her teachers as "odd and unusual." Debra had not, however, been evaluated for the presence of emotional disturbance, nor had she been placed in special education classrooms. Debra's admission MMPI profile scored on adolescent norms is shown in Fig. 6.7.

Debra's validity scale configuration produces an inverted V which is often associated with a fake bad response set among adults. Her raw score value on the F scale of 21 obviously represents a substantial elevation even for adolescents in inpatient settings. Her F scale elevation does not, however, necessarily invalidate the results of her clinical profile. In general, the validity scales for this girl suggest that she is responding to the MMPI by the endorsement of a substantial number of items related to serious psychopathology and that she approached the testing in a psychologically exhibitionistic or self-punitive manner. Thus, the validity scale configuration for this adolescent indicated that Debra is either a substantially disturbed teenager or a teenager who wishes to appear substantially distressed. A cautious evaluation of her clinical profile should have

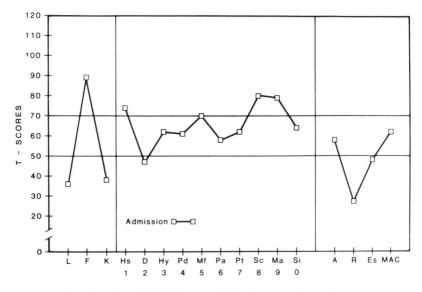

FIGURE 6.7   Admission profile for a 14-year-old female.

relevance in determining which of these descriptions apply for this patient.

Debra's clinical profile shows a substantial degree of selectivity in her item endorsement patterns. Her overall profile corresponds to an 8-9 codetype with secondary clinical range elevations on scales *Hs* and *Mf*. If Debra wished to appear psychiatrically disturbed, she demonstrated an unusually selective approach to simulating psychiatric disturbance (Archer, Gordon, and Kirchner, 1986). Therapists in the Marks et al. (1974) investigation described 8-9 codetype adolescents as impulsive and having little capacity to form close interpersonal relationships. These adolescents were also found to be more likely than other emotionally disturbed groups to show signs of thought disturbance, including hallucination and sensory disturbances, and to be characterized as paranoid and schizoid. Graham (1977) described the 8-9 codetype among adults as characterized by hyperactivity, emotional lability, and serious psychological disturbance, particularly if scales *Sc* and *Ma* are substantially elevated. He noted that difficulties in concentration and thinking were often present and that this codetype had been associated with various forms of schizophrenia. Additionally, the elevation of scale *Hs* in conjunction with this 8-9 profile type would suggest that Debra tends to employ somatization as a primary defense mechanism. She is likely to have a history of vague physical complaints that are seen as odd or peculiar by others.

Finally, her elevation on *Mf* suggests that Debra may have a decided preference for activity in a manner traditionally viewed as masculine, and she may be described as active and vigorous. This preference for activity, when combined with her elevations on scales *Sc* and *Ma*, suggests that Debra has marked potential for impulsive actions that are poorly planned and undercontrolled. Stated differently, Debra is likely to proceed impulsively with actions based on highly idiosyncratic or unusual perceptions of her environment. Before leaving the clinical portion of her profile, it is interesting to note that on the affective dimensions of the MMPI measured by scales *D* and *Pt*, Debra reported relatively little emotional distress at the time of her admission. This relative absence of emotional pain may reflect the successful or effective operation of her defense mechanisms (somatization and flights into fantasy and activity) as a means of protecting her from painful feelings.

Several interesting features may be noted in reference to Debra's special scale scores. Her relatively moderate elevation on the *A* scale probably represents a reasonably accurate estimate of her overall level of psychological distress. Debra's markedly low score on the Repression scale (i.e., a raw score value of 8) would indicate that she could be described as impulsive, aggressive, and argumentative. Indeed, her relatively low score on the *R* scale is not a positive prognostic indicator for this adolescent, but rather indicates the degree to which her defense mechanisms are geared toward impulsive activity. The patient's ego strength or *Es* scale score of 50 would suggest that Debra has a moderate potential for therapeutic gain from insight interventions. Although this prediction was in conflict with the author's clinical impressions in this regard, the accuracy from the *Es* scale tended to be borne out by Debra's ability to respond positively to insight-oriented individual and group interventions during her course of inpatient treatment. Whether this ability was measured by the *Es* scale, or existed independently of the factors related to *Es*, is unclear. Finally, Debra produced a raw score value of 24 on the MacAndrew Scale, which tends to fall in a gray area concerning applications of cutoff rules. If one employs the recommended cutoff score of 28 offered by Graham (1985), then Debra would not be identified as a marked risk for substance abuse behaviors. In contrast, employing the cutoff score of 24 for females recommended by Williams (1985), Debra would be identified as positive for substance abuse problems. In fact, Debra did have a positive history of substance abuse involving amphetamines, barbituates, alcohol, and marijuana such that the cutoff score recommended by Williams would have resulted in a true-positive classification for these behaviors. Utilizing the stricter *MAC* criteria recommended by Graham, however, it should still be noted that further questioning in this area would have been appropriate. Debra's diagnosis at the time of discharge was schizotypal personality disorder. A discharge MMPI profile was unavailable for this patient.

Results of both MMPI and Rorschach admission assessments suggested that Debra was subject to significant impairments in thought processes consistent with the features of social isolation, odd speech, inadequate rapport in face-to-face interactions due to constricted affect, and magical thinking noted under the diagnostic criterion for schizotypal personality disorder. Indeed, Debra's speech often showed unusual qualities manifested by the selection of inappropriate or highly unusual words or phrases to express her thoughts. Further, her affect was typically very blunted and she was unable or incapable of establishing any close relationships with either treatment staff or peers during the early stages of her treatment. Following 2 weeks of inpatient care, a decision was made to try a course of antipsychotic medication targeted on a reduction of thought disorder symptomatology. Debra responded well to this pharmacological intervention, and following approximately 5 weeks of treatment began to deal with materials involving incidents of her sexual abuse by her father. Appropriate state protective service workers were notified of this newly revealed history, and their investigation revealed independent evidence of the validity of the patient's claims. Debra made excellent progress in terms of being able to "work through" the emotional components of these incidents and was discharged on psychoactive medications to outpatient therapy following 3½ months of inpatient care.

CLINICAL CASE EXAMPLE VI:
WHITE MALE ADOLESCENT

Same K. was a 16-year, 2-month-old white male adolescent who was admitted for 6 weeks of inpatient treatment in an adolescent facility. Sam's responses on the WISC-R resulted in a Full Scale IQ score of 100, a Verbal IQ score of 99, and a Performance IQ score of 101. His Rorschach responses resulted in a high Dd frequency and substantial elevations in shading responses suggestive of a perfectionistic stimulus monitoring style and substantial emotional discomfort and anxiety. An above average number of both white spaces response and popular responses were also present indicating potential for oppositional tendencies expressed in an indirect and passive aggressive manner. Sam's record contained a high W to M ratio weighted on the W side and no texture responses, indicating an unrealistically high level of aspirations and a guarded interpersonal stance. Additionally, there was a significant difference between the patient's $F+\%$ level, which tended to be above expectations for a 16-year-old adolescent, and his $X+\%$ percentage, which tended to be roughly one standard deviation below age expectations. These findings reflect a tendency for Sam's responses to become less conventional and reality oriented in situations in which his responses include a variety of non-form determinants.

Sam was admitted for psychiatric hospitalization following a suicide attempt involving a serious drug overdose. This overdose involved medications that were accessible to him in the family medicine chest. The patient was transferred directly from a general hospital emergency room to the psychiatric treatment setting. Sam's presenting problems also included an escalating sense of depression, anxiety, and tension that initially appeared following his diagnosis of Tourette's Syndrome, a neurological dysfunction. At admission, Sam performed well on mental status examination and displayed little affect. He was described by unit staff as reserved, cooperative, and well mannered and he quickly adapted to hospital routine. Sam typically expressed little feeling on the Unit, with the exception of substantial anxiety and tension in psychotherapy groups. He was perceived by his Unit peer group as reserved, shy, and odd. Sam's admission and discharge MMPI profiles are presented in Fig. 6.8.

The validity scale scores for this patient at admission indicated that a complex judgment regarding profile validity would be required that would include a cautious evaluation of a variety of factors. Sam's raw score value of 28 on scale F is markedly high, suggesting that this patient's MMPI profile may have been the result of reading problems, psychotic confusion, or a conscious or unconscious "fake bad" response set. Again, the first two possibilities were capable of being ruled out given the educational reading test results for this patient (WRAT reading level of 10th grade) and the information derived from clinical evaluation and mental status examination. The issue remained, however, concerning the degree to which this patient was attempting to report "excessive" symptomatology in a manner designed to exaggerate his clinical picture. Using the criteria recommended earlier in this book, we might turn to the clinical scale elevations to examine whether nine or more clinical scales are elevated in excess of a T-score value of 69, i.e., whether a "floating" clinical profile was produced. Such an examination clearly revealed that Sam did not produce a floating profile, and that five of the clinical scales produced T-score values less than 70. In general, it appeared that Sam endorsed symptomatology in a selective and meaningful manner that might be subject to valid interpretation. Thus, the decision was made to cautiously continue the clinical interpretation of this profile, bearing in mind that the patient was endorsing a very high rate of unusual or infrequent items and may have consciously selected to distort his response pattern or to use the MMPI as a means of "crying out for help."

Continuing with the interpretation of the validity scales, Sam pro-

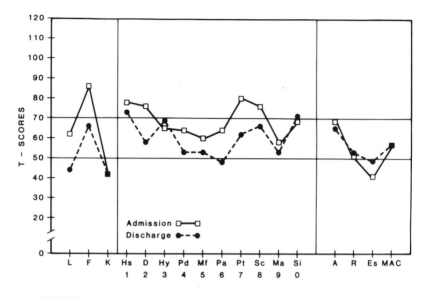

FIGURE 6.8   Admission and discharge profiles for a 16-year-old male.

duced an unusual pattern of L and K scale elevation such that L resulted in a T-score value of approximately 60, whereas K score values for this patient tended to occur below the mean T-score value of 50. Thus, Sam appeared to respond to the MMPI in a rigid manner, denying common faults or human failings while acknowledging clinical symptomatology in an open and help-seeking manner. This L-K pattern is often found in combination with elevations on psychotic scales and suggests a very rigid individual who might be highly moralistic concerning common human failings while also very self-critical concerning personal psychological adjustment.

Clinical range elevations at treatment admission may be seen for this patient on scales Hs, D, Pt, and Sc. A 7-1-2-8 profile is unavailable in Marks et al. (1974), but a reasonable approach to this very complex profile might consist of combining the Marks et al. description of 1-2/2-1 profiles and their descriptors of 7-8/8-7 profile types. The descriptors available for the 1-2 codetype involve adjectives including shy and oversensitive. Individuals with this codetype are described as socially isolated, fearful of making mistakes, and unlikely to utilize acting out as a defense mechanism. These individuals typically react to frustration by punishing themselves, and a significant proportion have histories of suicide attempts. The Marks et al. 7-8 profile describes adolescents who have difficulty in making friends, are afraid of school failure, and often experience tension, anxiety, and guilt. In the general adult literature, 7-8 profile types are described as worriers who are vulnerable to both real and imagined sources of threat. The closest codetype to Sam's profile in the adult literature is produced by Lachar's 2-7-8 profile type. It should be noted, however, that Sam's admission profile is not a "typical" 2-7-8 codetype and would satisfy only 6 of the 10 criteria required by Marks and Seeman (1963) for profile classification in this codetype. Adult patients presenting with this codetype typically present symptomatology involving tension, anxiety, fearfulness, and difficulty in concentration. Depression, worry, and an obsessional-ruminative, perfectionistic orientation often associated with suicidal ideations was present in 65% of these 2-7-8 cases. Thus, Sam's clinical profile characteristics are highly congruent with a picture of neurotic symptomatology involving anxiety, depression, insecurity, and obsessional defenses. It is important to note that Sam's profile scored on adult norms produced a 6-8 profile type, which is related to paranoid schizophrenic ideational disturbances and features. These charcteristics are totally unsupported by the clinical history and admission workup of this patient.

In terms of probable defense mechanisms for this patient, it seems likely that Sam would be subject to manifesting obsessional defenses as well as somatization. One should exercise substantial care, however, in interpreting Sam's *Hs* elevation given this patient's history of physical disorder (i.e., Tourette's syndrome). Osborne (1979) has demonstrated that adult patients with documented physical disorders score in elevated ranges on the *Hs* scale in a manner that is often difficult to distinguish from that of psychiatric patients with psychosomatic or hysteria symptoms. Recent research by Ball, Archer, Struve, Hunter, and Gordon (in press) has also indicated that higher *Hs* scale elevations are found among adolescent psychiatric inpatients who produce mild EEG abnormalities.

Additionally, Sam might be described as socially withdrawn and isolated and his 2-7 MMPI profile features tend to interrelate to his *L* and *K* scale characteristics in presenting a picture of a rigid and inflexible adolescent who is perfectionistic and maladaptive in his responses to environmental distress. In terms of Sam's potential for acting out and antisocial behavior, the elevations on scales *D* and *Si* combined with relatively low scores on *Pd* and *Ma* suggest that Sam is unlikely to engage in these behaviors as a means of coping with stress in his environment.

A very important point might be made in reference to Sam's potential for suicidal behavior. Data from Clopton (1978, 1979) and others strongly indicate that there is no typical or characteristic profile for individuals who attempt suicide, and therefore it is not possible to employ Sam's MMPI profile in predicting whether he will attempt suicide again in the future. Although this limitation is widely ignored by MMPI interpreters in their attempts to employ characteristics and combinations of scales 2, 4, and 9 to derive an actuarial statement regarding suicidal potential, the available literature indicates that such a strategy is likely to be of little value and potentially dangerous in terms of generating a false "sense of confidence" regarding the prediction of such a highly important class of behaviors. These statements are not to suggest that MMPI indices are unrelated to general impulsivity or various types of depression, but rather that *specific* predictions regarding suicidal behaviors are not supported by the literature.

Finally, a review of Sam's special scale scores at admission indicated a T-score value of 69 on the A scale. This would suggest a near-clinical level of general distress that is borne out by Sam's clinical scale profile and history. Sam's R scale T-score of 51 would suggest that Sam does not tend to use repression extensively as a primary defense mechanism. Indeed, his clinical scale profile much more strongly suggests the coping style of a "sensitizer" rather than a repressor in terms of dealing with environmental and intrapsychic stress. Further, Sam's Es score suggests that this patient did not show marked promise as a candidate for insight-oriented psychotherapy efforts at admission. In this regard, Sam's admission level of affective distress, involving substantial feelings of anxiety and depression, was likely to interfere with his ability to prosper from interpretive psychotherapeutic efforts. This situation, however, could be subject to change as Sam's emotional distress decreased in a supportive and secure environment. Finally, Sam's raw score of 24 on the MacAndrew scale would result in a general classification as negative for substance abuse using the recommended cutoff points offered by either Graham (1985) or Williams (1985). In this regard, Sam's clinical case history would suggest that, with the exception of his suicide attempt by drug overdose, a history of involvement in drugs or alcohol was not present.

To return to our original question, did Sam's MMPI profile allow for valid interpretation or were his responses the reflection of a "fake bad" response set that should not be interpreted as an accurate picture of his current psychological functions? In response to this issue, we would suggest a qualified affirmative response to the interpretability of this profile. It appears likely that Sam tended to exaggerate certain clinical features as a general reflection of his overall tendency to sensitize to stress. In this sense, Sam's tendency to readily endorse MMPI items, and to occasionally "over-respond" to items, probably served as an accurate picture of his psychological functioning at that time. Therefore, we cautiously assume that this admission MMPI profile, despite the high F value reported, represents a reasonably valid and accurate picture of Sam's psychological functioning at treatment admission.

Following 6 weeks of inpatient psychotherapy, Sam was readministered the MMPI at the time of hospital discharge. Several very positive changes may be noted in Sam's personality features when admission levels of symptomatology are compared to discharge MMPI profile characteristics. Beginning with the validity scales, it is quite notable that both scales L and F have substantially decreased, suggesting a reduction in more extreme symptomatology as well as less rigid use of crude defense mechanisms. Sam's K scale raw score value of 10 remains the same from pre- to post-administration, suggesting that Sam continues to maintain a help-seeking stance that may also contain an aspect of psychological "exhibitionism." In terms of clinical profile characteristics, Sam also has substantially reduced his level of affective distress to subclinical ranges indicative of a greater degree of subjective comfort. The raw scores on the Hs scale dropped only 2 points from admission to discharge, perhaps reflecting the ongoing physical concerns that Sam was experiencing. Similarly, Sam's Si score did not change as function of treatment, suggesting that Sam has remained a relatively isolated and socially introverted adolescent despite treatment efforts. Very encouraging reductions occurred in relationship to the Pa and Sc scales, reflecting a substantially less alienated, distrustful, and suspicious stance at the time of discharge. Overall, Sam's profile changed from admission codetype of 7-1-2-8 to a discharge codetype of 1-0 with secondary elevations on 3 and 8. Interestingly, both Sam's admission and discharge codetype are essentially reflective of neurotic processess, but this patient's discharge characteristics appear substantially more flexible and adaptive than those reported at admission.

A review of special scales indicates that a change of 4 raw score points occurred on the A scale, suggestive of less overall distress. Additionally, Sam's Es scale raw scores climbed from 39 to 44, indicating that Sam appeared to be a more promising candidate for insight-oriented outpatient efforts following his discharge from residential treatment. Sam's MAC scale score of 24 was identical to his admission levels, reflective of the overall stability of the MacAndrew scale in a manner consistent with the longitudal studies reported in the adult literature (e.g., Hoffman et al., 1974).

Overall, Sam responded well to inpatient therapies and was discharged to outpatient psychotherapy. A central issue in Sam's treatment consisted of the degree to which psychoactive medications might have been useful in reducing his overall psychological distress to a level more consistent with his ability to benefit from therapeutic efforts. In this regard, Sam's progress in the secure hospital environment was sufficient to indicate that such medication was not necessary for reduction of affective distress. In making decisions about the use of psychoactive medication, it is often highly useful to review the adolescent's *MAC* scale score to evaluate the potential for abuse of psychoactive medications. In Sam's case, although his MacAndrew scale scores did not contraindicate the use of psychoactive medications, his history involving an attempted suicide by drug overdose suggested substantial caution in this regard.

CLINICAL CASE EXAMPLE VII: ELIZABETH M.: A 13-YEAR-OLD WHITE FEMALE ADOLESCENT

Elizabeth was a 13-year-old white female adolescent at the time of her outpatient evaluation. Elizabeth had been adopted at age 2 and her adoptive parents provided her with an upper middle-class lifestyle. Elizabeth's mother was a mental health professional, and Elizabeth's father was an upper level manager in a large telecommunications corporation. At the time of her evaluation, Elizabeth's parents had brought her to the outpatient psychotherapy clinic for evaluation and treatment based on their perception that Elizabeth was displaying problems in the area of impulse control and anger, dishonesty, and academic performance. Further, they perceived her behaviors at home as contributing to substantial family dysfunction. Elizabeth's parents indicated that they were unsure that outpatient psychotherapy would be sufficient to meet Elizabeth's psychiatric needs, and strongly recommended that inpatient care be immediately undertaken for their daughter. The outpatient therapist contacted the author to evaluate the degree of psychopathology displayed by Elizabeth in order to engage more comprehensively in treatment placement and planning.

The results of Elizabeth's WISC-R administration produced a Verbal IQ score of 105, a Performance IQ score of 106 and a Full Scale IQ score of 105. The Rorschach record for this patient indicated the presence of 1 white space response, 1 texture response, 6 popular responses, an $F+\% = .88$, and an $X+\% = .86$. All of these values are within normal ranges for a 13-year-old female based on Exner's norms for nonpatient adolescents. Additionally, the patient produced an egocentricity ratio of .57, and a D value of -1, both of which were also within expected ranges. The only relative deviations for this patient from expected normative values occurred on the affective ratio, where the patient's obtained value of 1.0 was substantially higher than mean expectations, and the production of 1 vista response in her record, which was also higher than typical records for this age group. These findings would suggest Elizabeth, at the time of her assessment, was involved in an introspective process and attempting to gain perspective on herself in a manner that was resulting in some negative or painful affect (the vista response) and that she was somewhat more responsive to affective stimulation (the affective ratio value) than is typically found for 13-year-old girls.

The MMPI profile produced by this girl at the time of evaluation appears in Fig. 6.9. A review of the validity scale scores for this patient indicates a valid profile produced by an individual who is likely to be experiencing some acute disturbances. She appeared to be engaging in a relatively open admission of pathology, including symptoms of poor self-concept or poor self-esteem. There appeared to be an openness to seeking psychological help as manifested by the relatively low K produced by this patient.

An inspection of Elizabeth's clinical scale profile indicates within normal range functioning on all dimensions if we employ a T-score value of 70 as the definition of clinical psychopathology. Using a more liberal criterion of a T-score value of 65, it might be noted that Elizabeth manifests a relative elevation on the Psychopathic Deviancy scale or scale Pd of the MMPI. Based upon information from the adult correlate literature, we might anticipate that Elizabeth may have problems in the area of impulsivity and frustration tolerance and there may be a tendency toward antisocial or inappropriate behaviors. Inspection of the Harris-Lingoes subscale values for scale Pd indicated that much of the elevation on this

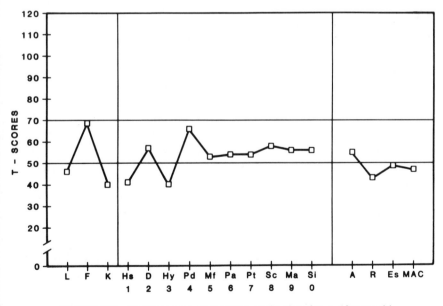

FIGURE 6.9   Profile of an outpatient evaluation for a 13-year-old female.

measure was the result of family conflict and discord. Additionally, examining the information provided by Lachar (1974), we might further modify our comments regarding the *Pd* scale in light of the moderate score for Elizabeth on scale *Ma*. This *Pd* scale elevation, then, in conjunction with her *Ma* scale value might further indicate that Elizabeth is currently experiencing substantial dissatisfaction with people around her, and is more likely to engage in a passive rebellious stance than in overtly antisocial behaviors. Thus, Elizabeth's anger and frustration may be specifically directed toward individuals within her family environment, and may not necessarily be reflective of a general development of the antisocial personality. Remaining values on clinical scales for this patient occur within *T*-score values ranging from 40 to 58, ranges in which interpretations stressing clinical psychopathology would be inappropriate. The MMPI clinical scale findings, in combination with findings from the Rorschach, would suggest that this patient is essentially operating within normal ranges of personality functioning. Features unique to this girl included a degree of rebelliousness or anger, evidence of a painful introspective process, and a tendency toward becoming readily engaged in affective stimulation.

Findings from the MMPI special scales also appear within normal ranges. Her level of affective distress on the *A* scale is relatively consistent with values on the *D* scale and *Pt* scale in suggesting a minor deviation from age expectations, which might be summarized as a subclinical and relatively moderate degree of affective distress. Findings from scale *R* also indicate that this patient is unlikely to engage in a repressive defense style, and findings from the *Pd* would suggest that she is more likely to engage in behavioral attempts to discharge aversive emotional states (i.e., passive-aggressive behaviors and acting out) than in repression or denial. Elizabeth's MacAndrew scale value would not result in a positive judgment for substance abuse, and this negative finding also corresponds to her parents' reports that did not indicate a history of substance abuse. Finally, Elizabeth's ego strength or *Es* scale score indicates that she may present substantial potential for insight-oriented psychotherapeutic efforts.

An immediate question that would occur from most interpreters at this point concerns the degree to which Elizabeth presents significant psychopathology that would warrant a DSM-III diagnosis or recommendations for psychotherapy. Stated differently, the most salient question from this assessment is the degree to which Elizabeth's test responses deviate from normal functioning sufficiently to warrant psychiatric concern. If one compared Elizabeth's profile to the profile provided by Marks et al. (1974) for their average or mean adolescent patient, based on the 822 patients utilized in their codetype descriptors, several factors appear important. Bearing in mind that the Marks et al. sample was largely from outpatient adolescents, it still appears notable that Elizabeth is reporting levels of psychopathology that are substantially below those reported for the Marks et al. adolescents. With the exception of her *Pd* scale value, all other clinical scales for Elizabeth fall substantially below the mean profile produced by Marks et al. Thus, if we were to compare this patient to the typical outpatient sample produced by these authors, one would conclude that she is displaying substantially less marked psychopathology than the typical adolescent outpatient. Similarly, with the exception of her elevations on scales *D* and *Pd*, Elizabeth appears to be reporting less symptomatology than was found by Archer, Stolberg, Gordon, and Goldman (1986) in their sample of female adolescent outpatients. Although not discounting the significance of Elizabeth's elevations on the *Pd*, and her moderate subclinical elevations on affective scales such as *D* and *Pt*, one might reasonably wonder why a teenage girl whose parents reported such a marked history of symptomatology produced essentially subclinical findings on both the MMPI and the Rorschach.

This case example was selected to illustrate a specific point concerning the assessment of adolescents in psychiatric settings for diagnostic and treatment-planning purposes. Specifically, this point involves the importance of the individual assessment of parental features, as well as an understanding of family dynamics, before diagnostic formulations are offered and treatment recommendations are suggested concerning adolescent patients. Although it is recognized that such procedures are not always possible, it has been our experience that psychological assessment of both adolescent and parents is typically quite feasible in the vast majority of families who present adolescents for either inpatient or outpatient services.

The rationale we have offered families for parental and family assessment procedures has been quite simple, but apparently also effective. We have explained to families that we believe that the treatment of the adolescent requires the full involvement of those individuals who are most important to them in their lives. In this sense then, we solicit the assistance and help of parents by truthfully underscoring for them the importance of their involvement in treatment efforts. As part of their involvement, we also explain to parents that we routinely request their participation in psychological assessment. In doing so, we emphasize that their assessment results are confidential, and are to be seen only by members of the treatment team who are directly involved in the treatment of their child. Further, we offer to provide individual feedback to the parents concerning the results of their MMPI assessment. With the use of this rationale, we have experienced over a 95% participation rate for parents in terms of their involvement in psychological testing at the time of the evaluation of their child.

Figures 6.10 and 6.11 represent the MMPI profiles produced by Elizabeth's mother and father at the time of her evaluation. As shown in inspection of these figures, both Elizabeth's mother and father produced clinical range MMPI profiles suggestive of substantial psychiatric symptomatology, particularly of a characterological nature. Viewed against a backdrop of these parental MMPI charcteristics, some of the presenting problems reported for Elizabeth by her parents began to "make more sense" to both the examiner and the outpatient therapist. Specifically, Elizabeth's mother, who produced a 4-6 profile codetype that was also marked by a low *Mf* value and a clinically elevated *Si* score, had repeatedly indicated that Elizabeth was an uncaring and insensitive child who made endless demands upon her for attention and affection but was incapable of reciprocating these emotions. She was characteristically suspicious of Elizabeth's motivations and her capacity to form meaningful emotional involvements with others. Mrs. M. was markedly unrealistic in terms of the academic and social goals she had set for her daughter. In discussing Elizabeth, it was apparent that her mother was intensely frustrated and furious at her daughter's perceived inability to respond to her

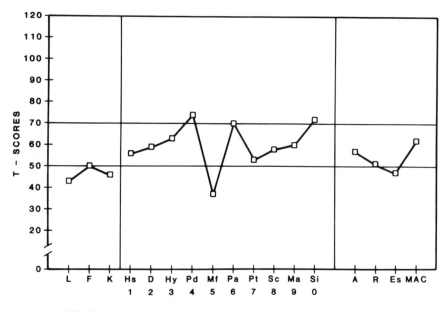

FIGURE 6.10   Profile for a 42-year-old female (maternal MMPI).

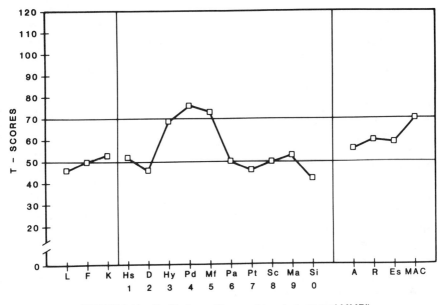

FIGURE 6.11   Profile for a 46-year-old male (paternal MMPI).

needs, and she viewed Elizabeth as ungrateful and selfish. Much of the maternal reports concerning this child's behavior problems appeared to have a markedly exaggerated tone, i.e., her reports of school failure did not match the school records obtained for this child and her complaints of behavior problems in the classroom were not verified by Elizabeth's current teachers.

Elizabeth's father, who produced a 4-5 codetype with a marked secondary elevation on scale *Hy*, was much less critical of his daughter's behavior, but indicated that he concurred with his wife's recommendations for inpatient psychotherapy because "she threatened to leave me if I refused to go along with her." In general, Elizabeth's father was a "recovering alcoholic" who had a long history of alcohol abuse and dependence. Family therapy efforts with Elizabeth and her parents soon indicated that Elizabeth's father often indirectly and subtly reinforced Elizabeth's conflicts and expressions of anger with her mother. In this sense, Elizabeth's frequent conflicts with her mother appear to serve as a vicarious release for Mr. M., who typically overcontrolled his feelings of hostility and frustration with his wife.

Based on the results of the psychological evaluations, it was recommended to the therapist in this case that Elizabeth and her parents be involved in outpatient family therapy sessions with particular emphasis on understanding the role of Elizabeth's behavior within the dynamics of this family unit. Family therapy was conducted for 4 months, at which time primary focus had shifted from Elizabeth to the now overt degree of conflict and hostility present between Elizabeth's parents. As a result of family therapy, it became rapidly apparent that Elizabeth's mother often perceived her husband as "hiding behind" Elizabeth's behaviors in attempts to "get back at her." It also became apparent that the quality of their marital life had deteriorated substantially, including Mr. M.'s involvement in an ongoing extramarital affair and his increasing emotional distancing from his wife.

At the conclusion of 4 months of outpatient family therapy, both parents reported a substantial improvement in Elizabeth's behaviors and a marked decrease in their concerns regarding her "psychopathology." The family therapist reported that this shift represented more of a change in their perception of Elizabeth's typical behaviors, rather than any dramatic change in her characteristic exchanges with others.

It was decided to continue family therapy sessions within a couples therapy format, which excluded Elizabeth from direct participation. This decision was made as a tangible way of de-emphasizing Elizabeth's role in the expression and operation of marital discord between her parents. Elizabeth spent eight sessions in individual psychotherapy primarily focused on facilitating her developing sense of self, particularly within the context of a family that was likely to continue to experience some degree of dysfunction for a substantial length of time.

In this clinical case example, it is apparent that a full and comprehensive understanding of the life problems evidenced by this adolescent required a tangible knowledge of the personality features of the adolescent, her parents, and the underlying dynamics within her family. The next chapter presents a review and discussion of the psychological interrelationships that have been found between adolescents and their parents in a variety of psychiatric and nonpsychiatric settings.

7

FAMILIAL INTERRELATIONSHIPS IN MMPI RESPONSE PATTERNS

Numerous theories of psychological development postulate a meaningful relationship between personality characteristics of family members, manifested both cross-generationally (e.g., parent and child similarities) and within generational boundaries (e.g., intersibling relationships). This research focus has received substantial attention from MMPI researchers over the past three decades with literature reviews in the parental-offspring area provided by Hafner, Butcher, Hall and Quast (1969) and Lachar and Sharp (1979). The latter authors observed that investigations of intrafamily personality similarities have substantial importance and relevance to theoretical models of psychological development, as well as implications for applied treatment issues such as the selection of intervention setting (inpatient or outpatient) and type or combinations of therapies (e.g., individual or family). Further, the examination of personality characteristics within family members with varying degrees of shared genetic background provides a methodology to investigate genetic influences on personality development and the inheritability of certain psychological features. The purpose of this chapter is to provide a current, broad review of this complex literature on familial interrelationships in MMPI response patterns.

STUDIES INVESTIGATING GENETIC INFLUENCES ON THE ORGANIZATION AND DEVELOPMENT OF PERSONALITY AMONG SIBLINGS

To what extent does shared genetic inheritance result in similarities in personality characteristics within biologically related individuals on measures such as the MMPI? In addressing this area, two primary research approaches have been pursued.

One approach has consisted of investigating intrafamily personality characteristics in samples of adoptive families. In these types of studies comparisons are typically made involving biologically unrelated children reared within the same family environments and biologically related children reared in similar and different family environments. If genetic factors play a substantial role in the development of personality characteristics, one would expect that biologically related pairs of individuals would show a higher degree of similarity in personality features than unrelated or adoptive siblings when environmental factors are held constant.

A primary source of experimental data on this issue has been derived from the Texas Adoption Project, which has investigated the characteristics of adopted and biological children in several hundred families containing adopted children (Horn, Loehlin, & Willerman, 1979; Loehlin, Horn, & Willerman, 1981; Loehlin, Willerman, & Horn, 1982; Loehlin, Willerman, & Horn, 1985). The data for these studies have been based, in part, on agency files of a private home for unwed mothers that contained test data from the unwed biological mothers of these children, obtained at the time of their residence in the home prior to the birth of the child. These data were combined with assessments of the adoptive parents and biological and adoptive children, typically following adoption procedures and placement. Thus, comparisons were possible between biological parents and their offspring, as well as adoptive parents and their natural and adoptive children.

In 1982, Loehlin et al. investigated MMPI responses of unwed mothers and adoptive parents in a sample of 300 Texas adoptive families. In addition, adoptive family members over the age of 8 were given an age-appropriate form of the Cattell personality measures such as the Sixteen Personality Factor Questionnaire or the Jr.-Sr. High School Personality Questionnaire (Cattell, Eber, & Tatsuoka, 1970; Cattell & Cattell, 1969). Further, one of the adoptive parents, usually the mother, rated all younger children in the family, age 3 or older, on 24 bipolar 9-point scales intended to assess their standing on Cattell's personality factors. Major findings from this study indicated a low but statistically significant correlation on the extroversion dimension between unwed mothers and their biological children raised in adoptive environments. Surprisingly, however, the adoptive children of biological mothers who produced more elevated MMPI profiles tended to be rated by their adoptive parents as *more* emotionally stable than children of biological mothers who reported lower levels of maladjustment on the MMPI. This latter finding was interpreted as consistent with the view that individuals with genotypes that rendered them vulnerable to insensitive or non-nurturing environments may tend to show high levels of adjustment in warm, supportive environments provided by the adoptive families. This perspective does not account, however, for the differentially higher level of adjustment for this genetically "at risk" group of children.

In 1985, Loehlin et al. published further data from this project involving 220 families with adoptive children who were at least 14 years of age. The primary dependent measures in this study involved the California Personality Inventory (CPI; Gough, 1964) and the Thurstone Temperament Scale (TTS: Thurstone, 1953). The CPI consists of 480 true-false self-descriptive items designed to assess personality traits within the range of normal functioning, and the TTS consists of 140 true-false self-descriptive items designed to measure relatively permanent traits that are typically manifested by well-adjusted individuals. Comparisons were made in correlational patterns between adoptive children and their nonbiological adoptive parents, and between biological children and their biological parents within the same adoptive families. Additionally, biological siblings and nonbiological siblings within adoptive families were investigated in terms of their personality congruence on these dependent measures.

The results from this study indicated little similarity between parents and their nonbiological children or between adoptive nonrelated siblings reared within the same families. The average correlation on the CPI and TTS for these groupings typically yielded values around $r = .05$ (range $= -.07$ to $.20$). The authors noted that the presence of a biological relationship tended to raise correlations to an average mean coefficient value of $.15$ (range $= -.27$ to $.42$). The authors interpreted these data, combined with prior findings from Scarr, Webber, Weinberg, and Wittig (1981), as suggesting that there is typically little similarity in personality characteristics produced by the effects of a shared social environment under conditions in which family members do not share a common genetic inheritance. They also noted, however, that the results of their data indicated that genetic effects made a fairly modest total contribution to personality development and that shared genetic structure did not appear to have a pervasive or overwhelming influence on personality development. Thus, the authors concluded, "this suggests that something else—configural genetic effects, idiosyncratic experiences, measurement problems—carries the main share of the action" (1985, pp. 389–390).

Another approach to understanding the genetic influences in personality development involves the use of biological twins to investigate the heritable component in variations observed in personality traits and types. In these studies, comparisons are made on standard personality measures involving pairs of monozygotic and dizygotic biological twins. These research studies, which have typically examined twins during their adolescence, have employed various statistical techniques for comparing the magnitudes of correlation coefficients for monozygotic and dizygotic pairs to serve as an estimate of the genetic or heritability variance accounted for in these data. A small number of studies have been done in this area that have relevance to the MMPI.

Gottesman (1963) examined overall indices of MMPI profile similarity in a sample of 34 pairs of monozygotic and 34 pairs of dizygotic adolescent twins from public high schools in Minnesota. He reported greater evidence of MMPI profile similarity among monozygotic pairs, with particularly marked correlations on scales *D, Pd, Pt, Sc,* and *Si,* in a manner consistent with the existence of significant genetic influences on the development and organization of personality.

Dworkin, Burke, Maher, and Gottesman (1977) reported findings from a longitudinal study of shared personality characteristics among monozygotic and dizygotic twins in the Boston area, assessed during adolescence (mean age 15.9 years) and retested at follow-up during adulthood (mean age 27.9 years). In terms of profile contour, or the configurations of MMPI profiles, the authors reported no evidence of significant genetic variation in MMPI profiles assessed during either adolescence or adulthood. There was, however, evidence of heritability for MMPI profile elevation indices during adolescence but not during adulthood. Profile elevation in this study referred to the overall mean level of elevation across scales. In examining these data on an individual scale level, Dworkin, Burke, Maher, and Gottesman (1976) reported significantly higher MMPI clinical scale correlations for 25 pairs of adolescent monozygotic twins, in comparison with 17 pairs of dizygotic twins, on MMPI scales *D, Pd, Pa,* and *Sc.* Assessed during adulthood, monozygotic twins produced higher correlational values only on scales *K* and *Ma.* Additionally, two special MMPI scales (i.e., *Dy* or Dependency and *A* or Anxiety) demonstrated evidence of significant heritability during both the adolescent and adult assessments. Table 7.1 presents the data from Dworkin et al. (1976) on individual MMPI scale correlations as assessed during adolescence and adulthood from monozygotic and dizygotic twins.

Although displaying some differences in individual scale correlational values, the results from the Boston sample of adolescents are generally consistent with the report by Gottesman (1963) on the twin study of adolescents in the Minnesota area. Taken together, the results of these studies suggest significant heritability in personality features as assessed by the MMPI. Perhaps more important, results from Dworkin et al. (1976) also indicate significant differences in patterns of heritability related to the developmental period at which assessment occurs. As noted by these authors, Fuller and Thompson (1960) have speculated that the decreases in heritability may be a result of increases in environmental variance as individuals are exposed to increasingly divergent environmental settings, and environments that may serve to suppress phenotypic expression.

TABLE 7.1

Adolescent and Adult Minnesota Multiphasic Personality Inventory Intraglass Correlation Coefficients and F Ratios

	Adolescent						Adult				
Scale	RMZᵃ	RDZ	MZ Within-Pair MS	DZ Within-Pair MS	F (17.25)	Fᵇ (68.79)	RMZᵃ	RDZ	MZ Within-Pair MS	DZ Within-Pair MS	F (17.25)
Hypochondriasis (Hs)	.07	.47	36.48	39.09	1.07	1.00	.42	.30	30.20	55.65	1.84
Depression (D)	.43	.15	34.10	92.27	2.71*	1.80**	.49	.56	42.50	37.29	.88
Hysteria (Hy)	.23	.20	35.08	69.62	1.98	1.51*	.16	.40	53.36	46.68	.87
Psychopathic Deviate (Pd)	.49	.30	32.62	75.44	2.31*	1.64*	.44	.34	58.66	68.21	1.16
Masculinity-Femininity (Mf)	.64*	.17	37.82	106.97	2.83**	1.36	.79	.81	34.34	42.97	1.25
Paranoia (Pa)	.19	-.19	52.56	161.21	3.07**	1.69*	.21	-.27	91.20	68.09	.75
Psychasthenia (Pt)	.41	.14	51.30	77.15	1.50	1.46	.28	.19	71.54	75.32	1.05
Schizophrenia (Sc)	.47	.24	47.08	100.44	2.13*	1.48*	-.15	.55	76.04	50.32	.66
Hypomania (Ma)	.46	.31	57.76	91.32	1.58	1.17	.72**	.08	37.44	76.79	2.05*
Social Introversion (Si)	.45	.26	33.04	50.56	1.53	1.69*	.50	.25	44.14	67.35	1.53
K	.45	.29	53.62	47.32	.88	1.13	.47**	-.27	47.42	73.82	1.56
Anxiety (A)	.58*	-.04	49.20	54.06	1.10	1.12	.71**	.00	25.42	69.88	2.75*
Repression (R)	.37	-.04	81.22	92.03	1.13	1.24	.40	.12	50.58	74.88	1.48
Ego Strength (Es)	.35	.14	43.24	72.50	1.68	1.35	.53	-.06	30.12	63.82	2.12*
Dependency (Dy)	.53**	-.21	53.92	72.85	1.35	.85	.76**	-.05	26.26	86.18	3.28**

Note. MZ = Monozygotic; DZ = dizygotic.
ᵃSignificance levels given in RMZ column are for RMZ > RDZ.
ᵇRevised values for entire adolescent sample (cf. Gottesman, 1965, for preliminary analysis).
* p < .05. ** p < .01

Thus, as adolescent twins become adults, there may be less environmental similarity present, resulting in decreased expression of phenotypic variance. Another possible influence related to this pattern of data suggested by Dworkin et al. (1976), however, is that MMPI scales or dimensions may measure different traits at different ages. Thus, in this view the personality characteristics or constructs measured, for example, by scale *Sc* may be qualitatively different during adolescence than adulthood. This interpretation is particularly intriguing in that other sources of data on differences in MMPI response patterns (e.g. Hathaway & Monachesi, 1963) serve to support the view that adolescents and adults respond in significantly different ways to numerous MMPI items. Indeed, this observation serves as the basic foundation of support for the use of age-appropriate MMPI norms for adolescent respondents (Archer, 1984). These item endorsement differences may be reflective of differences in semantic and psychological "meanings" of particular items, and hence scales, as a function of the developmental stage of the respondent.

In conclusion, the MMPI literature comparing biological and nonbiological siblings, and monozygotic and dizygotic twins, serves to suggest that both environment and genetic inheritance impact on psychological development as assessed by the MMPI. The effects of both the family environment and genetic inheritance variables in these studies appear to be limited, however, and considerably less than what one might have anticipated given the primary importance placed on "nature and nurture" influences in prevalent theories of personality development. Substantial and impressive correlations in personality features between siblings are found only under conditions in which both identical genetic inheritance and similar family environments are present. Additionally, the work of Dworkin and his colleagues serves to indicate that the degree and type of genetic influences found in personality development among biological twins are significantly affected by the point in development at which personality assessment is undertaken. Thus, the expression of genetic influences on personality appears subject to change across developmental stages in response to complex genetic/environmental interactions.

STUDIES OF MMPI FEATURES OF PARENTS OF EMOTIONALLY DISTURBED CHILDREN

Another important focus in understanding familial influences on the development of personality has been investigations of MMPI features demonstrated by parents of emotionally disturbed children, typically in contrast with MMPI profiles produced by groups of normal adults (e.g., Adrian, Vacchiano, & Gilbart, 1966; Goodstein & Rowley, 1961; L'Abate,

1960; Lauterbach, London, & Bryan, 1961; Liverant, 1959; Marks, 1961; Wolking, Quast, & Lawton, 1966). Six of these studies employed either the MMPI adult normative data or Goodstein and Dahlstrom's (1956) sample of normal parents for control group comparisons. Adrian et al. (1966), in perhaps the most carefully matched control effort, used parents of normal children from PTA organizations. The results of these investigations have consistently shown evidence of greater psychopathology among the MMPI profiles of parents of psychiatrically disturbed children in contrast to adults in normal populations.

Pursuing this issue further, several studies have compared the MMPI profiles of parents of disturbed children with those of adults in psychiatric treatment. Lauterbach et al. (1961) found that parents of emotionally disturbed children had significantly fewer pathological MMPI profiles than adult Veterans Administration inpatients with neurotic diagnoses. McAdoo and Connolly (1975) and McAdoo and DeMeyer (1978) compared the MMPI profiles of parents of disturbed children with MMPI profiles produced by adult psychiatric patients who were also parents of disturbed children. These authors reported significantly higher MMPI scale elevations for parents of disturbed children who were themselves in psychiatric treatment.

These collective studies establish that parents of children with psychiatric disorders demonstrate a greater degree of personality disturbance than adults from normal populations, but less serious evidence of psychopathology than comparable groups of adults receiving treatment for psychiatric disturbance. Several qualifications of these findings, however, appear appropriate.

First, although the parents of children labeled psychiatrically disturbed demonstrate greater pathology than normal groups of adults, the clinical significance of these findings (in contrast to the statistical significance) are not clear-cut. For example, Lachar and Sharp (1979) noted that mean MMPI scale differences between parents of psychiatrically disturbed children and normal adults were typically less than 5 T-score points. Similarly, Wolking, Dunteman, and Bailey (1967) concluded that although significant MMPI scale differences appeared to exist between various parent groups, the magnitude of these differences was typically too small to be of clinical relevance in individual cases.

Second, although differences between parents of psychiatrically disturbed children and other groups of adults have been demonstrated, efforts to delineate a specific or consistent pattern of personality features for parents of disturbed children have been less successful. Hafner et al. (1969), in their review of this literature, observed that although the Hy and Pd scales tended to be elevated in parents of disturbed children, no stable codetype configurations have been consistently found for these parental groups. They postulated that the variability in parental profile features may be a function of the quite heterogeneous samples of psychiatric disturbances found across children in these studies, complicated by lack of diagnostic specificity within individual studies.

Perhaps the most significant issue raised in relationship to these studies centers on the interpretation of findings that higher levels of psychopathology are typically produced by parents of psychiatrically disturbed children. A simplistic review of this research might lead to the postulation of a causal relationship in which parental psychopathological features directly lead to the subsequent development of child pathology. Erickson (1968) proposed, however, a "stress-reaction" hypothesis in which elevated parental profiles are viewed as a reflection of parents' stress reactivity in response to the burdens involved in serving as the primary caretaker for children displaying deviant psychological development.

In order to explore this hypothesis, several studies have employed research designs in which the parents of emotionally disturbed children are compared and contrasted with parents of children displaying deviant development involving the presence of nonpsychiatric medical syndromes or conditions. Erickson (1968), for example, found no significant differences between the MMPI profiles of parents of retarded children without evidence of emotional disturbance and parents of retarded children in which psychiatric disorders were evident. Similarly, Miller and Keirn (1978) failed to find significant differences in the MMPI profiles of parents of retarded children and the parents of children with primary psychiatric disturbances. In contrast, however, there are a number of studies that have failed to produce support for the stress-reaction postulation. For example, Wolking et al. (1966) reported significantly higher elevations in the MMPI profiles of parents of emotionally disturbed children than in the parents of retarded children, and Routh (1970) found equivalent MMPI profiles between normal adults and parents of retarded children. Similarly, researchers have not found parental MMPI elevations to be related to severity of problems in child stutterers (Goodstein & Dahlstrom, 1956), children with cleft palate (Goodstein, 1960a, 1960b), infants with gastrointenstinal problems (Pinneau & Hopper, 1958) or children with enuresis (Stehbens, 1970). These latter findings stand in contrast to expectations derived from Erickson's hypothesis that would predict greater parental disturbance as a result of greater deficits or degrees of disturbance in child functioning.

Taken together, the literature discussed in the previous section would be consistent with Hafner et al.'s (1969) conclusion that "parents of children who are psychiatrically disturbed are themselves more disturbed than parents in general. However, there is some indication that they are not as disturbed as adult psychiatric patients" (p. 185). Additionally, it may be seen that the issue of causality in this relationship is complex and that simple unidimensional causal models are probably inappropritae when applied to these data.

STUDIES DIRECTLY COMPARING MMPI RESPONSE PATTERNS OF ADOLESCENTS AND THEIR PARENTS

While the literature thus far reviewed has served to suggest an association or relationship between parent and child features, the specific characteristics of this relationship have remained obscure.

A limited number of investigations have attempted to identify meaningful relationship patterns by comparing parent and adolescent MMPI responses in both normal samples (Butcher & Messick, 1966; Gjerde, 1949; Hill & Hill, 1973; Sopchack, 1958) and in samples of families with adolescents in psychiatric treatment (Archer, Sutker, White & Orvin, 1978; Lauterbach, Vogel, & Hart, 1962; Mlott, 1972; Smith, Burleigh, Sewell, & Krisak, 1984). Findings have ranged from investigations that have emphasized the degree of dissimilarity between parent and child features, particularly in samples of more disturbed adolescents (e.g., Archer et al., 1978; Lauterbach et al., 1962) to investigations that have found significant patterns of interrelationships for MMPI scales, especially correlations between same-sex parent/offspring dyads (Smith et al., 1984; Sopchak, 1958).

Illustrating this literature, Sopchak (1958) correlated raw score MMPI scale values, using the Spearman Rank Order technique, for the responses of 25 male and 25 female normal college students and their parents. Highly significant correlations were reported between same-sex parent-offspring combinations. Specifically, five clinical scales were correlated significantly between fathers and sons, and nine scales significantly interrelated for mothers and daughters. Sopchak concluded that the substantial intercorrelations between MMPI scores for same-sex parents and offspring resulted from a process of role identification or sex role modeling.

In contrast, Lauterbach et al. (1962) intercorrelated *T*-score values from 24 male adolescents referred for outpatient psychiatric treatment with their parents' MMPI scores. Lauterbach and his associates reported only one clinical scale (i.e., the *Pa* scale) significantly interrelated between fathers and sons, and only the *Hy* clinical scale significantly related between mothers and sons. The authors concluded that disturbed male children may show fewer effects related to identification with their parents than would be found in samples of normal or well-adjusted male adolescents. Similarly, Archer et al. (1978) correlated MMPI *T*-scores for 28 male and 23 female adolescent inpatients with their parents' MMPI responses. In addition, an overall measure of profile dissimilarity was calculated between adolescents and their parents, and analyzed based upon adolescent groupings related to primary psychiatric diagnostic category. Findings revealed relatively few significant MMPI intercorrelations between parents and adolescents, and a marked pattern of greater dissimilarity between parent and adolescent features as the severity of adolescent psychopathology increased. As in Lauterbach et al.'s (1962) conclusion, Archer et al. suggested that parent-child personality congruence may be more characteristic of functioning within normal families than within families involved in psychiatric treatment.

Most recently, Smith et al. (1984) correlated MMPI T-score values of 34 male and 25 female adolescent inpatients with T-score values of their mothers in a repeated measures design, with repeated MMPI administrations reoccurring across various stages of treatment. The authors found significant correlations between profiles of mothers and daughters, but not between mothers and sons. Further, the degree of intercorrelation between mother and daughter MMPI features tended to decrease as a funcion of the length of time the adolescent had been in treatment. The authors concluded that there was evidence of a significant relationship between maternal adjustment and deviant behavior in female adolescent offspring, and that the decrease in associations found across time might be accounted for by the impact of treatment in reducing the "pathological" influence of maternal characteristics.

In general, the interpretability of this literature has been obscured by pervasive methodological problems. All of the studies thus far discussed have utilized relatively small samples of families, and most, with the exception of Archer et al. (1978) and Butcher and Messick (1966), have employed simple univariate correlational analyses of individual MMPI scales as the exclusive statistical approach. Among correlational studies, only Sopchak (1958) employed a correction procedure for the use of multiple correlations to control for experiment-wise rates, i.e., the increased probability of obtaining significant findings when multiple correlations are performed. Additionally, at least four of these studies (Archer et al., 1978; Butcher & Messick, 1966; Lauterbach et al., 1962; Mlott, 1972) scored and statistically evaluated adolescent MMPI responses that had been converted to adult K-corrected T-scores. This scoring procedure undoubtedly resulted in substantial and marked distortions in correlational values when viewed in comparison to the use of age-appropriate adolescent norms or correlations based on raw score values.

To attempt to address some of these methodological issues, a recent study performed by Archer, Stolberg, Gordon, and Goldman (1986) examined the MMPI responses of 199 families with adolescents entering inpatient and outpatient psychiatric settings (total N = 542). Figure 7.1 presents the mean MMPI T-scores for adolescent male and female patients in inpatient and outpatient settings, and Fig. 7.2 presents the mean MMPT T-scores for fathers and mothers of these adolescents.

Statistical analyses indicated that parents of inpatient adolescents, as well as inpatient adolescents, reported significantly higher mean T-score values across a variety of MMPI scales than did their outpatient counterparts. A linear combination of adolescent and maternal MMPI scale data, in a stepwise discriminant function analysis, resulted in an accurate classification of 75% of all children assigned to inpatient treatment and 74% of outpatients. Further, the results of chi-square analysis indicated that the occurrence of clinical range maternal profiles ($T \geq 70$ on any clinical scale) was significantly related to an increased frequency of marked clinical profiles for both male and female outpatients. It was quite notable that paternal MMPI features bore little systematic relationship to MMPI characteristics of their offspring in either inpatient or outpatient treatment settings. Table 7.2 presents the intercorrelation matrix for MMPI raw score values between adolescent patients and their parents, with significance values corrected for multiple tests using the Bonferroni multistage procedure (Larzelere & Mulaik, 1977). It can be noted from this table that the overall pattern of adolescent-parent correlations indicated modest but significant relationships (r = .22 to r = .37) between type and intensity of

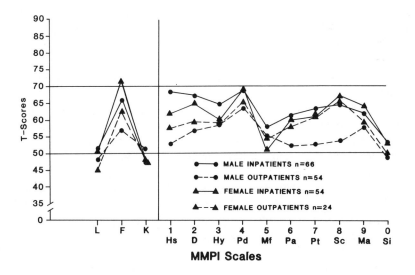

FIGURE 7.1   Mean MMPI T-scores for adolescent males and female inpatients and outpatients.

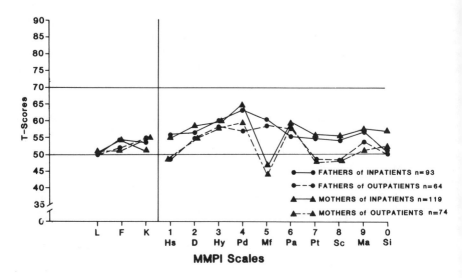

FIGURE 7.2   Mean MMPI T-scores for fathers and mothers of inpatient and outpatient adolescents.

psychological symptomatology reported by adolescents at treatment entrance and parental psychopathology, particularly maternal self-reports.

These findings provide the first clear indications in the MMPI literature that the degree of parental psychopathology is related to adolescent degree of disturbance. Similar to prior findings, results from this study demonstrated that parents of psychiatrically disturbed adolescents produce elevated MMPI profiles. Beyond this point, however, the Archer, Stolberg, Gordon, and Goldman (1986) data indicated that higher levels of adolescent psychopathology, as reflected in both greater MMPI scale elevations and placement in inpatient services, were related to higher parental MMPI elevations on eight clinical scales. Highly congruent with the Lachar and Sharp (1979) data, the *Pd* scale was most frequently involved in parental elevations, with 3-4, 2-4, and 4-6 codetypes most frequently found for maternal profiles (in that order) and 2-4, 3-4, and 4-5 profiles most common among fathers, respectively. Further, similar to Lachar and Sharp's (1979) data, in excess of 41% of paternal profiles and 46% of maternal profiles produced at least one clinical scale *T*-score elevation within clinical range ($T \geq 70$). Finally, the Archer et al. data have provided evidence of a differential parent-adolescent relationship as a function of sex of parent. Maternal-adolescent correlations showed stronger relationship than did interrelationships between psychiatrically disturbed adolescents and their fathers. This finding is also consistent with Lachar and Sharp's (1979) analyses of data from the Lafayette Clinic.

TABLE 7.2
Correlations for MMPI Raw Scores of Adolescent Patients and their Parents

MMPI Scales	Total Sample			Male Patients		Female Patients	
	(n = 161) Patient-father	(n = 192) Patient-mother	(n = 156) Mother-father	(n = 98) Son-father	(n = 115) Son-mother	(n = 63) Daughter-father	(n = 77) Daughter-mother
L	.01	.08	.28*	−.11	.05	.17	.10
F	.03	.18	.14	−.07	.17	.24	.21
K	.00	.23*	.14	.05	.27*	−.08	.17
Hs(1)	.17	.32*	.24*	.24	.31*	.03	.34*
D(2)	.11	.10	.22*	.08	.08	.15	.14
Hy(3)	.15	.27*	.04	.24	.20	.01	.34*
Pd(4)	.27*	.29*	.30*	.20	.29*	.36*	.29*
Mf(5)	.23*	.05	.12	.37*	.01	.07	.21
Pa(6)	−.02	.17	.00	−.02	.21	.00	.12
Pt(7)	.09	.25*	.21*	.07	.20	.13	.32*
Sc(8)	−.02	.28*	.14	.06	.24*	−.15	.34*
Ma(9)	.15	.05	.09	.17	.09	.10	.01
Si(0)	.10	.15	.28*	.11	.21	.09	.09

*$p < .05$ when corrected using a two-tailed multistage Bonferroni procedure with an adjusted stage one value of $p < .0038$.

SUMMARY AND CONCLUSIONS

The concept that important and meaningful relationships occur between parent and adolescent personality functioning is congruent with basic assumptions of numerous theoretical frameworks ranging from Gottesman's (1962) behavioral genetics perspective of personality development to the postulations of numerous family therapy theorists (e.g., Bowen, 1961; Guerin, 1976; Minuchin & Fishman, 1981). Within the clinical domain, such underlying assumptions have served as the basic foundation for efforts to involve family members in psychiatric treatment efforts of children and adolescents. The literature reviewed in this chapter serves to indicate a significant relationship between MMPIs derived within families, whether specifically involving parent-child comparisons or sibling-sibling comparisons.

Findings from twin studies and studies of adoptive families serve to support the view that both environmental and genetic components contribute to the personality development. It is also quite notable, however, that a majority of variance in personality features appears to be currently unaccounted for by either the genetic or environmental factors that have been investigated.

Findings from the MMPI literature on parental-adolescent MMPI features indicate a significant, but relatively modest, interrelationship between parental and adolescent features. Further, positive findings in several of these studies appear to indicate stronger relationships between parents and children of the same sex, although this conclusion is still quite tentative. The data by Archer, Stolberg, Gordon, and Goldman (1986) and Lachar and Sharp (1979), in contrast, indicate that maternal features seem to be much more centrally related to both male and female adolescent characteristics than may be noted in the relationships of fathers to their offspring.

Although the literature demonstrates important relationships between parental and adolescent psychological functioning, substantial caution should be exercised in attempting to attribute causal models to these results. Psychoanalytic writers have frequently viewed child psychopathological development as a result of maternal pathogenic characteristics behavior (e.g., Sperling 1970; Spitz, 1970). In contrast, however, Erickson (1968) has noted that elevated MMPI profiles typically found for parents of psychiatrically disturbed children may, at least in part, be reflective of parental reaction or response to the daily intense stress involved in caring for a psychiatrically disturbed child.

In attempting to account for this body of literature, the attribution of unidirectional models of causality may ultimately prove to be unproductive, simplistic, and reductionistic. More promising conceptualizations have been offered by Bell (1979) and others that view the parent-offspring interaction as reciprocal and bidirectional in nature, such that "the responses of each participant serve not only as the stimuli for the other but also change as a result of the same stimulus exchanges, leading to the possibility of altered responses on the part of the other" (p. 822). Viewing the development of personality exclusively from the framework of genetics or environment, in isolation, is also likely to produce an inaccurate and incomplete picture. Thus far, it seems quite clear that even our most complex multidisciplinary and interactional models have proven insufficient in reliably accounting for the majority of variance in domains of personality functioning as measured by the MMPI.

Several directions for further investigations appear indicated. The literature on parent-child relationships, including MMPI studies in this area, have typically been conducted employing families with at least one psychiatrically disturbed member. Thus, as noted by Hafner et al. (1969), there have been few reference data based on studies of normal families through which to evaluate patterns such as those found in studies of families in treatment settings. Although studies of normal families would be expected to use less pathology-oriented instruments than the MMPI, meaningful comparisons with MMPI literature should be possible. Indeed, the research findings of Dworkin et al. (1977) indicate that the California Personality Inventory may produce different patterns of relationships between family members than MMPI assessment, based on greater sensitivity of the CPI to normal range functioning. The use of both the MMPI and CPI may produce a more comprehensive view of intrafamily congruence in future research.

Recent research by Smith et al. (1984) has indicated that the nature and strength of MMPI relationships between mothers and inpatient adolescents may vary substantially as a function of time of assessment during the adolescent's treatment process. Additionally, the findings of Dworkin et al. (1976) have demonstrated that the degree of relationship between personality features of twins tends to vary as a function of the developmental period at assessment. Longitudinal research, therefore, appears to be required to provide a view of how these relationships unfold across time as well as aiding in determining the degree to which such relationships reflect long-standing personality trait characteristics or more transient and acute state processes and responses (Spielberger, 1966).

Finally, as noted by both Hafner et al. (1969) and Lachar and Sharp (1979), although most of the MMPI studies of relationships between parents and offspring have typically assumed that evidence of shared characteristics between parent and child is mediated, at least in part, through specific patterns of interactional behaviors, little effort has been made to identify these mediating patterns. In what ways are specific parental MMPI patterns related to typical parenting behaviors, and what probable effects would certain classes of offspring behavior have on the psychological features of parents?

In one of the few attempts to investigate the relationship of parental MMPI profiles to independent ratings of parenting behaviors, Lachar and Sharp (1979) found that maternal elevations, particularly on scales *F, D, Pd, Pa* and *Sc,* were positively related to therapists' ratings of greater maternal difficulty in setting consistent or appropriate limits on children's behaviors. Further, the higher the maternal score on the *Es* scale, the less excessive physical punishment was manifested in the family and the greater the tendency toward overt concern and protectiveness of children. Finally, the lower the father's *Es* score, the greater the paternal tendency, rated by family clinicians, to minimize the child's problems.

More systematic research efforts are needed to explore empirical correlates of MMPI features as displayed in the family context. A most useful future development in this area of MMPI research would consist of the construction of a meaningful classification system to identify salient categories of parenting and adolescent behaviors. This type of objective rating instrument would allow for a systematic investigation approach capable of identifying relationships between certain parental or adolescent MMPI profile features and the occurrence of salient classes of interpersonal behaviors within family environments.

A final clinical observation also appears indicated. The current literature supports the involvement of parents of psychiatrically disturbed children in psychiatric treatment efforts. Perhaps the clearest finding from this literature is that parents of psychiatrically disturbed children typically display substantial features of psychological distress and maladjustment. This conclusion is particularly marked for the parents of children in inpatient treatment settings. Therefore, the involvement of parents in treatment programs that are responsive to the psychological features of the parents, as well as the symptomatology of the adolescent patient, appears to have firm empirical grounding. Clearly, such treatment involvement does not require a causal assumption of a parental role in the etiology of the child's disorder. These treatment efforts may be more parsimoniously based upon the recognition of the marked degree of psychological pain and disturbance commonly reported among parents of children experiencing deviant psychological development.

8

SUMMARY AND FUTURE DIRECTIONS

SUMMARY AND CONCLUSIONS

The purpose of this volume has been to review the available MMPI literature related to adolescence and to offer a series of recommendations concerning the use of this instrument with adolescent respondents. In summarizing these suggestions, four general statements may be offered.
First, the available literature strongly supports the conversion of adolescent raw score values to adolescent norms rather than adult norms. At
this time, the most appropriate adolescent norms to employ consist of
those established by Marks et al. (1974) which appear in Appendix A. Second, the subsequent interpretation of adolescent MMPI profiles appears
to be best undertaken through examination of codetype information from
adolescent sources as provided by Marks et al. (1974) integrated with additional information provided in adult sources of clinical correlate data
such as those provided by Graham (1977), Greene (1980), and Lachar
(1974). Third, substantial flexibility should be employed in interpreting
validity scale characteristics of adolescent respondents, particularly in relationship to elevations on scale F, which appear to carry substantially different implications for adolescents than for adult respondents. The use of
rigid and conservative F scale validity criteria for adolescents, particularly
in clinical settings, is counterproductive Finally, the available data support the utilization of the MAC scale with adolescent respondents, but
substantial caution should be exercised in interpreting MAC scores from
non-white respondents. In addition, special scales such as Welsh's A and
R and the Harris-Lingoes subscales may provide useful information regarding adolescent features, although current knowledge concerning
these measures among adolescent samples is quite limited. Overall,

179

with the above considerations in mind, it can be concluded that the MMPI is a meaningful and useful instrument to employ with adolescent respondents.

The MMPI will undoubtedly experience dramatic growth and development in the next few years in terms of its applications to adolescent populations. One factor will remain valid for the MMPI, however, for the near future. We know substantially less about the characteristics of this assessment instrument in adolescent samples than we do in adult samples. This observation is not made to discourage the use of the MMPI with adolescents, but it is offered to reinforce the view that interpretation of the MMPI with adolescents is substantially more tentative and qualified than with adult respondents. Our knowledge base for adolescents is dramatically limited when compared to the thousands of studies that have been performed with the MMPI in adult samples. As noted in chapter 2, the limited research attention given to this area probably reflects the difficulty and confusion surrounding the use of the MMPI with adolescents as well as the general scarcity of psychological research on adolescent development. The total of 96 MMPI publications on adult substance abusers for the 5-year period of 1972 to 1977 (Butcher & Owen, 1978), for example, roughly equals the cumulative productivity for MMPI studies with adolescents for the 40-year period of 1945–1985. Both the researcher and the clinician, therefore, are well advised to respect the limits of our current knowledge in attempting to understand adolescent development and psychopathology through the MMPI.

A respect for these limitations suggests that the MMPI is currently best used in adolescent samples as a means of deriving an overall estimate and description of psychopathology rather than in attempts to identify specific DSM III differential diagnoses. Further, the researcher and clinician should remember that charcteristics reported by adolescents on the MMPI may be relatively transient and unstable during this developmental period. Therefore, particular caution should be exercised in interpreting adolescent MMPI profile characteristics as indicative of longstanding, trait personality features. Finally, the current available data suggest that narrative statements derived from MMPI responses of adolescents may result in lower clinician-judged accuracy ratings than has been found for adults. Therefore, MMPI-based statements regarding adolescents should be carefully and cautiously cross-validated against data from other test instruments as well as information from clinical observations. It should be noted, however, that this procedure also serves as good clinical practice with adult respondents even though a great wealth of information concerning MMPI clinical correlates is available for this group.

Paul Meehl (1945) stated, "The final test of the adequacy of any technique is its utility in clinical work" (p. 303). Our current understanding of the MMPI and adolescents indicates that although this instrument appears to be of substantial utility in understanding psychopathology within this developmental age group, we currently lack clear and precise guidelines for the interpretation of MMPI profiles with adolescent populations. If adequate research attention is focused on gaining a better understanding of the MMPI with adolescents, however, there are ample grounds to expect substantial clarifications in this area over the next few years. We now review three current research projects being conducted on adolescent norm development.

AN OVERVIEW OF THREE NORM DEVELOPMENT PROJECTS

The Mayo Clinic Project

Colligan and his colleagues at the Mayo Clinic have been conducting MMPI studies in both adult and adolescent normal populations to develop contemporary norms for these age groups. The results of their normative investigations within adult populations have been reported by Colligan, Osborne, Swenson, and Offord (1983, 1984). Colligan and Offord (1986) have recently completed collection of the adolescent component of these data and have presented preliminary findings.

Colligan and Oxford (1986) noted that there have been many cultural changes in American society during the decades since the collection of the Marks et al. (1974) adolescent data that could potentially affect adolescent MMPI endorsement patterns. In investigating contemporary adolescent patterns on the current MMPI form, the authors randomly sampled from roughly 12,000 households in Minnesota, Iowa, and Wisconsin that were within a 50-mile radius of Rochester, Minnesota. Telephone interviews established that slightly more than 10% of these households contained adolescents between the ages of 13 and 17, inclusive. After excluding adolescents with potentially handicapping disabilities and limiting participation to one adolescent of each sex per household, 1,412 households were targeted for adolescent MMPI testing. MMPI test materials were mailed to these households, resulting in return rates of 83% for female adolescents and 72% for male adolescents or a total of 691 and 624 completed tests for females and males, respectively. Appendix B of this text contains detailed information from this investigation concerning sample size, return rates, and raw score MMPI data with and without K-correction. Additionally, this appendix provides numerous MMPI mean profile comparisons involving adolescent data derived by Colligan and Offord (1986), Marks et al. (1974), and Hathaway and Monachesi (1963), and the adult normative data from the original Minnesota sample (Dahlstrom et al., 1972) and contemporary adult norms from the Mayo Clinic (Colligan et al., 1983). The adolescent raw score data developed by Colligan and Offord are grouped by sex for ages 13, 14, 15, 16, and 17 . Some current trends in these data are discussed later in this chapter. It is anticipated that adolescent T-score conversions based on these findings will be published by 1987.

In their development of adult norms, Colligan and his colleagues have employed a procedure that converts MMPI raw scores to T-score values utilizing a normalized T-score procedure that is different from the linear transformation traditionally used with the MMPI. Thus, the T-score values produced by the contemporary norms developed by Colligan are seen by some MMPI researchers as producing MMPI profiles that would be substantially and significantly different from the traditional T-score conversion procedures. Hsu (1984) has suggested that the effects of the procedure used by Colligan has been to "normalize" MMPI profiles or reduce the amount of clinical elevation typically found. In sum, the Colligan et al. T-score transformation procedures have been viewed as discontinuous with the development of the MMPI, and profiles produced by the Colligan norms seen as possibly inconsistent with the research literature that has been gathered using the standard MMPI norm conversion procedure.

In response to these views, Colligan, Osborne, and Offord (1984) have submitted that their normalized T-score procedures do not result in "distortion" of MMPI profiles but rather serve to provide more accurate information concerning the respondents' relative standing in relationship to samples of "normals." They argue that the traditional conversion procedures used with the MMPI have ignored the fact that scores on particular MMPI scales are seldom normally distributed, and that several of the scales demonstrate a significant skewness on the right-hand side of the distribution. Thus, T-score values of 70 on scale 2 for adult females, for example, do not represent a score occurring within the upper 2.3% of the adult normative distribution but actually represent a score occurring in the top 7.3% of the normative group as a result of the skewness of the distribution of scores on this measure. Adding to the complexity of this issue is the Colligan et al. observation that skewness and kurtosis are not constant across all scales, but rather vary significantly in relation to the particular MMPI scale in question. Thus, Colligan et al. have suggested that the use of the traditionally derived norms does not allow for reliable comparison of elevations across various scales and that numerically equivalent

T-score values on different scales represent varying departures from the mean. Further, these authors argued that the use of the original normative data may often mislead the interpreter into overestimating the degree of psychopathology represented by a particular *T*-score elevation. The controversy surrounding traditional versus normalized *T*-score transformation procedures is likely to continue until sufficient research data have been acquired to empirically resolve this issue.

The Gottesman, Hanson, Kroeker, and Briggs Norm Project

Concurrent with the Mayo Clinic efforts, Gottesman, Hanson, Kroeker, and Briggs have developed adolescent norms based on the responses of approximately 14,000 fifteen-year-olds and 3,500 eighteen-year-olds derived in the original Hathaway and Monachesi statewide sample from Minnesota. Their sample sizes and validity criteria, raw score mean data, and *T*-score conversions based on a normalized *T*-score procedure similar to that employed by Colligan et al. appear in Appendix C of this text for male and female adolescents at age 15 and 18.

The Gottesman et al. normative data are based on current analyses of the Hathaway and Monachesi (1963) Minnesota samples of 9th-grade adolescents tested between 1948 and 1954 and retested in 12th grade during 1956-1957. Gottesman et al. employed a variety of criteria in selecting the original MMPI test protocols for analysis. Analyses were based on subjects who met the following criteria:

1. *L* scale raw score value less than 10.
2. *F* scale raw score value less than 23.
3. *?* scale value less than 40.
4. Ninth-grade respondent less than 16½ years of age.
5. Twelfth-grade respondent less than 19½ years of age.

These procedures excluded 1,066 fifteen-year-olds and 182 eighteen-year-olds from the eventual Gottesman et al. normative samples. These exclusion procedures are the most conservative among MMPI adolescent norm development projects. Perhaps this factor contributed to the lower mean raw score clinical scale values found by Gottesman et al. in comparison with values by Marks et al. (1974) and Colligan and Offord (1986). The look-up tables provided in Appendix C allow for direct *T*-score conversions of raw score values for standard MMPI scales, Welsh's *A* and *R*, Barron's *Es* scale, and *MAC* scale, and many other special scales. Figures 8.1 and 8.2 provide an estimated profile generated by placement of the Gottesman et al. mean raw score values for 15-year-old male and female adolescents on the adolescent norms developed by Marks et al. (1974).

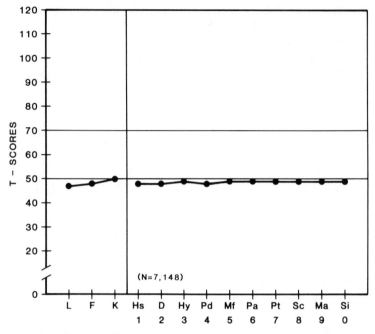

* T - SCORE VALUES ESTIMATED FROM MEAN RAW SCORE DATA FROM
GOTTESMAN, HANSON, KROEKER, AND BRIGGS (1986)

FIGURE 8.1   Mean MMPI profile for Gottesman et al. 15-year-old adolescent females using Marks et al. adolescent norms.

Although the Gottesman et al. data are based on MMPI responses of adolescents in the 1940s and 1950s, their current analyses are the first to comprehensively evaluate this very large adolescent sample. Thus, the product of the Gottesman et al. project are "new" in the sense of fully analyzing all of the Minnesota adolescent sample and in deriving both standard scale and numerous special scale norms from these data.

The MMPI Restandardization Project

The MMPI Restandardization Project is a complex and comprehensive effort by the University of Minnesota Press which may derive not only contemporary adolescent and adult norms but also new MMPI test booklets containing unique adult and adolescent item pools.

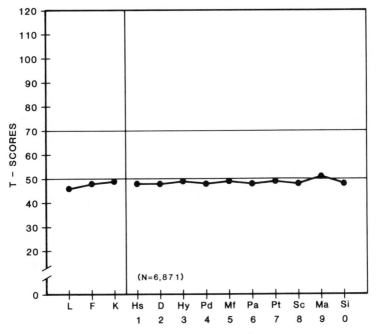

* T – SCORE VALUES ESTIMATED FROM MEAN RAW SCORE DATA FROM
GOTTESMAN, HANSON, KROEKER, AND BRIGGS (1986)

FIGURE 8.2   Mean MMPI profile for Gottesman et al. 15-year-old adolescent males using Marks et al. adolescent norms.

For many years, a variety of problems have been recognized in relationship to the current MMPI item pool that suggested the need for both
restandardization and revision. In 1972, James Butcher edited a book
dealing with these issues from the perspectives of a variety of MMPI ex-
perts. The factors supporting the University of Minnesota Press Project
have been multiple.

First, a number of items on the MMPI have become quite dated in
terms of their content. There are also at least 12 items in the MMPI item
pool that are sexist in terms of language usage, and an additional number
of items that are worded awkwardly, often producing unnecessary com-
plication in content understanding. Second, 40 years of experience with
the MMPI have identified a variety of items, approximately 50 in number,
that do not significantly contribute to MMPI interpretation and have been
referred to as "lazy" items. Third, there have been numerous reasons to

believe that significant shifts may have occurred in normative endorsement patterns on the MMPI item pool for both adolescent and adult respondents. Related to this point, there has been ample evidence that comprehensive and accurate norms for adolescents had never been established in the sense of ethnic or geographic balance.

Based on these concerns, the current MMPI restandardization and revision efforts were initiated in the early 1980s by the University of Minnesota Press in conjunction with National Computer Systems (NCS). When the University of Minnesota Press awarded the MMPI distribution contract to NCS, a steering committee including Grant Dahlstrom, James Butcher, and John Graham was formed to advise the University of Minnesota Press on those actions and activities necessary for the restandardization project. The financing for the data collection portion of the restandardization project is being provided by the University of Minnesota Press. By early 1986, data collection of adult norms had been completed in Seattle, Washington; San Diego, California; Minneapolis, Minnesota; Kent, Ohio; Philadelphia, Pennsylvania; and Norfolk, Virginia. The new adult norm sample will consist of approximately 3,000 adult respondents, drawn at random from the above-mentioned communities; several hundred of them have received test-retest administrations of the MMPI. In addition several special populations, i.e., roughly 1,500 college students and between 1,200 and 1,400 military personnel, have been studied. The target date for publication of the new adult norms for the MMPI is December, 1986, with the projection that adolescent norms may be available in 1987. As of this writing, roughly 20% of the collection of adolescent norms has been obtained and a final selection of all the sites to be included in the sampling of adolescent data has not been completed.

In both the adult and adolescent experimental forms, the initial 550 items of the MMPI item pool have been retained with relatively minor revisions affecting about 14% of these items to improve content clarity or quality. The 16 repeated items have been eliminated from these item pools, thereby "making room" for new items but eliminating the possibility of calculating a TR index for dissimulation. Following the first 550 items, the adult and adolescent experimental forms each contain an additional and differing set of 154 new items such that different 704-item test booklets were created for adults and adolescents.

Butcher reports that over 30 individuals were involved across an 18-month period in the revision and redesign of the original adult item pool, as well as the addition of new items to the adult form with specific emphasis on the creation of content sensitive to therapy potential and therapy change. In addition, some items were added because of their potential relevancy to new DSM-III diagnostic categories and symptomatology. In the normative sampling for the adult form, respondents' information has been routinely gathered on life events and demographic and psychosocial history, and many subjects have also been rated by significant others in their environment in terms of prominent personality and relationship characteristics.

Items unique to the new adolescent form include a variety of statements specifically created because of their potential relevance to adolescent development and adolescent psychopathology. Butcher and Graham (personal communications, January 24, 1986) have indicated that these new items for the adolescent form were based on the clinical and research judgments of Graham, Butcher, and Williams. Specifically, John Graham reviewed factor analytic studies of existing measures currently employed with adolescents, and generated items related to these broad factor dimensions. James Butcher and Carolyn Williams undertook a more theoretical and clinical/intuitive approach in which they identified items frequently cited by clinicians, or discussed in clinical/theoretical articles, as symptoms or characteristics frequently found for adolescents exhibiting pathological development. Thus, for the first time items specifically designed to assess adolescent symptomatology will be present in the MMPI. These new item content areas will include (1) negative peer group influence; (2) alcohol and drug abuse; (3) problems in relationships with parents; (4) school and achievement problems; (5) eating disorders; and (6) identity problems.

To summarize, major features of the restandardization project have been quite similar for both the adult and adolescent forms. For both versions, clinical research studies will occur concurrently with the gathering of new normative values, but will not be published until the new normative data have been publicly distributed. The experimental forms of the adult and adolescent MMPI contain 704 items. For both forms, the first section of the booklets consists of 550 items necessary to score basic scales and the established special scales, followed by a second section with the remaining new experimental item pool for which scale membership and clinical correlates have not yet been established.

NEW NORMS FOR ADOLESCENTS: CURRENT TRENDS

The question of greatest relevance to this volume concerns the degree to which the current norm development projects and revision effects will affect future MMPI usage, particularly with adolescents. The current data collection efforts geared toward gathering new normative values on adolescents across several geographic areas within the United States should produce, for the first time, a contemporary, national normative basis for using the MMPI with adolescents. As we have discussed throughout this volume, the adult normative values tend to produce gross exaggerations in terms of clinical symptomatology for adolescents, and the norms developed by Marks, Seeman, and Haller have provided an estimate of adolescent response patterns that *may* be substantially dated in relation to adolescents in the mid-1980s.

Current data from the University of Minnesota (Williams et al., 1986), researchers at the Mayo Clinic (Colligan & Offord, 1986), and Archer, Gordon, and Kirchner (1986) provide information suggesting that the adolescent response patterns of contemporary subjects will be relatively consistent with the values reported by Marks et al. in 1974. When differences occur in response patterns for contemporary adolescents in contrast to the Marks et al. norms, these differences appear to be most likely manifested in a more frequent endorsement of pathological items on the clinical MMPI scales for contemporary adolescents.

Preliminary analyses have been completed at the University of Minnesota on a relatively small number of adolescents who have responded to the new experimental adolescent form of the MMPI in sampling procedures in Minnesota and Ohio (Williams et al., 1986). This sample consisted of 172 male adolescents and 202 female adolescents who met the following criteria: (1) Cannot Say or uncompleted items not to exceed 29; (2) F scale T-score values not to exceed 99; and (3) ages between 12 and 18, inclusive. The data from these adolescents were then compared with the responses of 172 adult males and 202 adult females randomly selected from the pool of adult respondents in the restandardization projects in Ohio and Minnesota. Adolescent data were also compared and contrasted with normative findings from Marks et al. (1974).

Significant elevation differences were found between adult and adolescent respondents in these preliminary samples that strongly indicate that separate adolescent norms for the MMPI will be developed as a result of the restandardization projects. For example, male adolescents produced significantly higher mean raw score values than male adults on MMPI scales F, Pd, Sc, and Ma. Further, differences between adolescent and adult females on the new form of the MMPI involve a variety of validity and clinical scales in addition to F, Pd, Sc, and Ma. Also, in contrast to the mean raw score values reported for adolescent respondents by Marks et al. (1974), mean raw score values for both male and female adolescents in the University of Minnesota sample tended to be higher on scales Mf, Pt, Sc, and Ma and lower on validity scales L and K. The magnitude of clinical scale differences between the Marks et al. mean raw score values and the University of Minnesota data tended to range between 3 and 5 raw score points across these latter MMPI scales. On most other scales, a substantial degree of congruency was noted between the University of

Minnesota raw score values and the raw score values reported by Marks et al.

The University of Minnesota sample is a relatively small and limited subsection of the eventual 2,000 to 3,000 adolescents that will probably be employed in the creation of new norm values for this instrument. Current findings are highly tentative and are subject to important modifications as much larger samples of adolescents are included with these data. These preliminary data, however, strongly suggest that highly significant and substantial differences will continue to be found between adult and adolescent response patterns on the new forms of the MMPI, and that adolescent response patterns on the new form will not be radically different from the adolescent norms currently in use.

Recent data by Archer, Gordon, and Kirchner (1986) on the current MMPI form appear very consistent with the preliminary data from Williams et al. (1986). The Archer et al. findings, shown in the Fig. 8.3, were based on responses of 96 male and female normal adolescents between the ages of 14 and 18, inclusive, and profiled on the adolescent

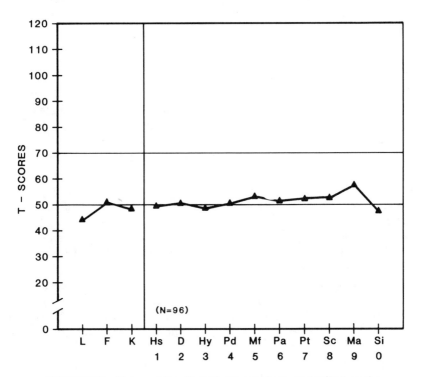

FIGURE 8.3   Male and female high-school students profiled on the Marks et al. adolescent norms.

norms developed by Marks et al. (1974). Although the Archer, Gordon, and Kirchner (1986) sample size was very small and, therefore, any conclusions drawn must be quite limited, the similarity of these results based on adolescents from the mid-Atlantic region to those derived from Williams et al. in the Midwest strengthen the view that new adolescent norms will present variations on, rather than radical departures from, the Marks et al. (1974) adolescent norms.

Additional data on contemporary adolescent response patterns are also available for roughly 1,300 adolescents evaluated by Colligan and Offord (1986). The MMPI scale mean raw score values reported by Colligan and Offord are also generally similar to the mean raw score values found by the University of Minnesota, with values seldom varying substantially even though Colligan and Offord (like Archer, Gordon, & Kirchner, 1986) were employing the current form of the MMPI whereas Williams, Butcher, and Graham were employing the revised form of the MMPI with midwestern adolescents. When MMPI scale differences are present between the Mayo Clinic and University of Minnesota Press samples of adolescents, the tendency is toward slightly lower clinical scale mean raw score values in the Colligan and Offord norms, suggesting that the University of Minnesota sample values will exhibit some regression toward the mean as more adolescents are included in the eventual development of these norms. Further, very similar to the current University of Minnesota findings, the most consistent pattern of differences between adolescent mean raw score values found by Colligan and Offord and raw score means reported by Marks, Seeman, and Haller, is in the direction of higher mean values on clinical scales Mf, Pt, Sc, and Ma, and somewhat lower mean raw score values on validity scales L and K, for adolescents in the Colligan and Offord sample. These differences across clinical scales also tend to be in the range of 2 to 5 raw score points for both males and females. Figures 8.3 and 8.4, taken from Colligan and Offord (1986), present the raw score values for 15-year-old male and female adolescents from the Mayo Clinic sample plotted on the adolescent norms provided in Marks et al. (1974) for 15-year-old respondents.

The current research findings by Williams et al. (1986), Colligan and Offord (1986), and Archer, Gordon, and Kirchner (1986), therefore, provide us with a foundation upon which to speculate concerning the eventual characteristics of the new MMPI norms currently being developed at the University of Minnesota on the new adolescent form of the MMPI. Although the final normative values produced in the restandardization project for adolescents are currently unknown, the high degree of congruency between the University of Minnesota and the Mayo Clinic projects strongly supports the view that the eventual University of Minnesota norms for adolescents will not be a radical departure from the current

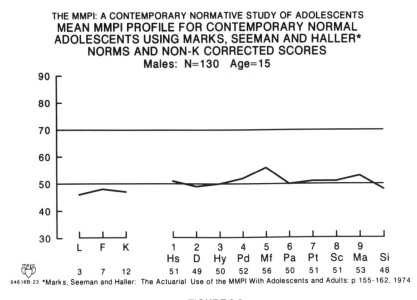

THE MMPI: A CONTEMPORARY NORMATIVE STUDY OF ADOLESCENTS
MEAN MMPI PROFILE FOR CONTEMPORARY NORMAL
ADOLESCENTS USING MARKS, SEEMAN AND HALLER*
NORMS AND NON-K CORRECTED SCORES
Males: N=130 Age=15

946 16B-23 *Marks, Seeman and Haller: The Actuarial Use of the MMPI With Adolescents and Adults: p 155-162, 1974

FIGURE 8.3

THE MMPI: A CONTEMPORARY NORMATIVE STUDY OF ADOLESCENTS
MEAN MMPI PROFILE FOR CONTEMPORARY NORMAL
ADOLESCENTS USING MARKS, SEEMAN AND HALLER*
NORMS AND NON-K CORRECTED SCORES
Females: N=127 Age=15

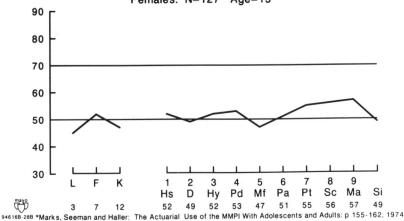

946 16B-28B *Marks, Seeman and Haller: The Actuarial Use of the MMPI With Adolescents and Adults: p 155-162, 1974

FIGURE 8.4

FIGURES 8.3 and 8.4   Normative data collected by Colligan and
Offord and plotted on the Marks et al. adolescent norms.

TABLE 8.1
Selected Features of Current Adolescent MMPI Projects

Project Features	Projects			
	Univ. of Minn. Press	Colligan & Offord	Gottesman et al.	Marks et al.
Sample sizes (males & females combined)	2,000 to 3,000 (projected)	1,315 (5 age groups)	15 yr. olds. = 12,953	1,806 (4 age groups)
Sample locations and dates	Multiple sites (locations to be determined)	3 Mid-West States (1985-1986)	Minnesota (1947–1957)	Minnesota (1947–1954); Alabama, California, Kansas, Missouri, North Carolina, Ohio (1964–1965)
Age groupings for T-scores	Currently Unknown	Possible Groupings for 13, 14, 15, 16, and 17; (fewer groupings probable)	15, 18	14 and below, 15, 16, 17
T-score development procedure	Linear Transformation (probable)	Normalized T-score (probable)	Normalized T-score	Linear Transformation
Year of Norm Publication	1987–1988 (probable)	1987 (probable)	1987 (see Appendix C)	1972 (Dahlstrom Welsh and Dahlstrom); 1974 (Marks, Seeman Haller)

Sampling Procedure	Stratified random procedure; supervised group testing	Telephone contacts and mail-out procedures	Hathaway and Monachesi 9th and 12th grade Minnesota samples	Hathaway and Monachesi Minnesota samples combined with additional data
Exclusive Criteria	To be determined	Presence of physical or psychiatric disorders	$F \geq 23$ $L \geq 10$ $? \geq 100$ Age cutoffs	Psychiatric treatment at time of testing (1964–1965)
MMPI form employed	Standard item pool (revised) plus experimental items	Standard	Standard	Standard
Selected unique features	National sampling including minority subjects; inclusion of experimental items; eventual products to include new norms and forms	Normalized T-score procedures; use of standard form with contemporary adolescents	Large sample size; data for 15 and 18 yr. olds; norms available for numerous special scales	Extensive research and clinical literature; availability of clinical correlate data in Marks et al. (1974)

norms as developed by Marks et al. (1974). In addition to marked differences traditionally found between adolescents and adults on scales *F, Pd,* and *Sc,* it appears likely that substantial differences will eventually be found between adults and adolescents for MMPI scale *Ma* in contemporary samples.

Beyond issues related to norm development, it is important to note that the new MMPI item pool being evaluated for adolescent populations by the University of Minnesota Press will require many years of continuing research efforts to generate a clinical correlate base to interpret adolescent profiles. This means, in a practical sense, that the 40 years of research findings that have been accumulated on the use of MMPI with adolescents will continue to be of central importance in attempting to interpret adolescent profiles for the foreseeable future. Although we do not know the degree to which profiles generated on the new norms will be similar to profiles currently generated on Marks et al. adolescent norms, preliminary findings seem to suggest that most profiles will be essentially similar in terms of general elevation and configurations, particularly in clinical settings. Additionally, contrasting the adolescent response patterns produced by Williams et al. (1986) with data by Colligan and Offord (1986) and Archer, Gordon, and Kirchner (1986) suggests raw score values for the standard MMPI scales will be equivalent for the old and new forms. Thus, the "meaning" of adolescent profiles utilizing the new form and norms, in terms of clinical interpretation, description and prediction, will continue to rest upon the literature that has been developed over the past four decades.

The interpretive recommendations in this book will remain relevant long after the publications of new normative values for adolescents. It is hoped, however, that interpreting adolescent profiles will become substantially more straightforward as normative confusion regarding the MMPI is reduced and fewer "compensations" must be made for potential norm distortions and errors. Each of the current adolescent norm development projects is serving to provide us with new and useful information concerning the MMPI response patterns of adolescents. Each effort has unique sets of strengths as well as limitations. Table 8.1 presents comparative information on selected features of the three current norm development projects as well as the traditional MMPI adolescent norms provided by Marks et al. (1974).

Information on these investigations is provided to encourage both clinical and research examinations of their relative utility in understanding adolescent functioning and psychopathology. Clinicians, for example, may wish to plot adolescent responses against one or more of these sets of "new" norms, to examine for themselves the impact of these normative values on specific clinical cases. Controlled research investigations are also clearly needed to evaluate the effects of these various normative values in relation to the ability to accurately identify clearly defined sets of clinical syndromes and disorders. The eventual product of these projects will be a clearer and more precise understanding of the definitions of normal and abnormal behavior among adolescents as reflected in MMPI item endorsements. This understanding, in turn, has the potential to significantly reduce the amount of confusion that has existed around the MMPI since it was first applied to adolescent respondents in the mid-1940s.

ADOLESCENT NORMS
FOR MALES AND FEMALES AT
AGES 17, 16, 15, AND 14 AND BELOW

Philip A. Marks
  Incline Village, Nevada

Peter F. Briggs
  San Diego, California

Provided in:
Marks, P. A., Seeman, W., and Haller, D. L. (1974). The actuarial use of the MMPI with adolescents and adults (pp. 155™162). Baltimore, MD: William and Wilkins.

Originally published in:
Dahlstrom, W. G., Welsh, G. S., and Dahlstrom, L. E. (1972). An MMPI handbook: Vol. 1. Clinical Interpretation (pp. 388™399). Minneapolis: University of Minnesota Press.

SECTION 1

T-score Conversions for Basic Scales without K-corrections for Minnesota Adolescents Age 14 and Below

Males

Raw Score	?	L	F	K	1(Hs)	2(D)	3(Hy)	4(Pd)	5(Mf)	6(Pa)	7(Pt)	8(Sc)	9(Ma)	0(Si)
0	41	32	36	23	34					23	30	32		
1		37	38	25	37					25	32	33		
2		42	40	27	40					27	33	35		
3		46	42	29	43					30	34	36		
4		51	44	31	46		20			33	36	37	21	
5		56	46	33	49	21	22	21		35	37	38	23	
6		61	48	35	52	23	25	23		38	38	39	25	
7		66	50	37	55	26	27	25		41	40	40	27	20
8		71	52	39	58	28	29	28	20	44	41	41	29	22
9		76	54	41	61	30	31	30	22	46	43	42	31	23
10	44	80	56	43	64	32	33	32	24	49	44	43	33	24
11		85	58	45	67	35	36	35	27	52	45	44	35	26
12		90	60	48	70	37	38	37	29	55	47	45	37	27
13		95	62	50	73	39	40	39	31	57	48	46	39	28
14		100	64	52	76	41	42	42	34	60	49	47	41	30
15		105	66	54	79	43	44	44	36	63	51	48	43	31
16			68	56	82	46	47	46	38	65	52	50	45	33
17			70	58	84	48	49	49	41	68	54	51	47	34
18			71	60	87	50	51	51	43	71	55	52	49	35
19			73	62	90	52	53	53	46	74	56	53	52	37
20	47		75	64	93	55	56	56	48	76	58	54	54	38
21			77	66	96	57	58	58	50	79	59	55	56	40
22			79	68	99	59	60	60	53	82	60	56	58	41

Females

Raw Score	?	L	F	K	1(Hs)	2(D)	3(Hy)	4(Pd)	5(Mf)	6(Pa)	7(Pt)	8(Sc)	9(Ma)	0(Si)
0	41	31	36	22	36					28	29	32		
1		36	39	24	39					30	30	34		
2		41	41	27	41					32	32	35	20	
3		46	44	29	44			21	120	34	33	36	22	
4		50	46	31	46	20		23	118	36	34	37	24	
5		55	49	33	49	22		25	115	38	36	38	26	20
6		59	51	35	51	24	20	27	113	40	37	40	28	21
7		64	54	38	54	26	22	29	111	43	39	41	30	23
8		69	56	40	56	28	24	31	109	45	40	42	32	24
9		73	59	42	59	30	27	34	107	47	43	43	35	25
10	44	78	61	44	61	32	29	36	104	49	44	45	37	26
11		83	64	47	64	34	31	38	102	51	44	46	39	28
12		87	66	49	66	36	33	40	100	54	46	47	41	29
13		92	69	51	69	38	35	42	99	56	47	48	43	30
14		97	71	53	71	41	38	44	97	58	49	49	45	32
15		101	74	56	74	43	40	46	95	60	50	51	47	33
16			76	58	76	45	42	49	92	62	52	52	49	34
17			79	60	79	47	44	51	90	65	53	53	51	35
18			81	62	81	49	46	53	88	67	54	54	54	37
19			84	65	84	51	49	55	86	69	56	56	56	38
20	47		86	67	86	53	51	57	84	71	57	57	58	39
21			89	69	89	55	53	59	81	73	59	58	60	40
22			91		91	57	55	61	79	75	60	59	62	42

Males

Raw Score	?	L	F	K	1 (Hs)	2 (D)	3 (Hy)	4 (Pd)	5 (Mf)	6 (Pa)	7 (Pt)	8 (Sc)	9 (Ma)	0 (Si)
23			81	70	102	68	61	62	55	84	62	57	60	42
24			83	72	105	70	63	65	57	87	63	58	62	43
25			85	74	108	72	66	67	60	90	65	59	64	45
26			87	76	111	74	68	69	62	93	66	60	66	46
27			89	79	114	76	70	72	65	95	67	61	68	47
28			91	81	117	79	73	74	67	98	69	62	70	49
29			93	83	120	81	75	76	69	101	70	63	72	50
30	50		95	85	123	83	78	79	72	104	71	65	74	51
31			97			85	80	81	74	106	73	66	76	53
32			99			87	82	83	76	109	74	67	78	54
33			101			89	84	86	79	112	75	68	80	56
34			103			92	87	88	81	114	77	69	82	57
35			105			94	89	90	83	117	78	70	84	58
36			107			96	91	93	86	120	80	71	86	60
37			109			98	93	95	88		81	72	88	61
38	53		111			100	95	97	91		82	73	90	62
39			113			102	97	100	93		84	74	92	64
40			115			104	100	102	95		85	75	94	65
41			117			106	101	104	98		86	76	96	66
42			119			108	103	106	100		88	77	98	68
43						110	106	109	102		89	78	100	69
44						112	108	111	105		91	80	101	70
45						114	110	113	107		92	81	103	72

Females

Raw Score	?	L	F	K	1 (Hs)	2 (D)	3 (Hy)	4 (Pd)	5 (Mf)	6 (Pa)	7 (Pt)	8 (Sc)	9 (Ma)	0 (Si)
23				71	94	59	58	64	77	62	78	60	64	43
24				73	96	62	60	66	75	63	80	62	66	44
25				76	99	64	62	68	73	64	82	63	68	45
26				78	101	66	64	70	70	66	84	64	70	47
27				80	104	68	66	72	68	67	86	65	72	48
28				82	106	70	69	74	66	69	89	67	75	49
29				85	109	72	71	76	64	70	91	68	77	51
30	50			87	111	74	73	79	62	72	93	69	79	52
31			114		113	76	75	81	59	73	95	70	81	53
32			116		116	78	78	83	57	74	97	71	83	54
33			119		118	80	80	85	55	76	99	73	85	56
34						83	82	87	53	77	102	74	87	57
35						85	84	89	51	79	104	75	89	58
36						87	86	92	48	80	106	76	91	59
37						89	89	94	46	82	108	77	94	61
38	53					91	91	96	44	83	110	79	96	62
39						93	93	98	42	84	113	80	98	63
40						95	95	100	40	86	115	81	100	64
41						97	98	102	37	87		82	102	66
42						99	100	104	35	89		84	104	67
43						102	102	107	33	90		85	106	68
44						104	104	109	31	92		86	108	69
45						106	106	111	29	93		87	110	71

(Continued)

SECTION 1 (Continued)

Males

Raw Score	?	L	F	K	1(Hs)	2(D)	3(Hy)	4(Pd)	5(Mf)	6(Pa)	7(Pt)	8(Sc)	9(Ma)	0(Si)
46						112	113	116	109		93	82	105	73
47						115	115	118	112		95	83		75
48						117	118	120	114		96	84		76
49						119	120		117			85		77
50	56								119			86		79
51												87		80
52												88		81
53												89		83
54												90		84
55												91		85
56												92		87
57												93		88
58												95		89
59												96		91
60	58											97		92
61												98		93
62												99		95
63												100		96
64												101		98
65												102		99

Females

Raw Score	?	L	F	K	1(Hs)	2(D)	3(Hy)	4(Pd)	5(Mf)	6(Pa)	7(Pt)	8(Sc)	9(Ma)	0(Si)
46						108	109	113	26		94	88	113	72
47						110	111	115	24		96	90		73
48						112	113	117	22		97	91		75
49						114	115	119	20			92		76
50	56					116	118					93		77
51						118	120					95		78
52						120						96		80
53												97		81
54												98		82
55												99		83
56												101		85
57												102		86
58												103		87
59												104		88
60	58											106		90
61												107		91
62												108		92
63												109		94
64												110		95
65												112		96

Females

Raw Score	?	L	F	K	1 (Hs)	2 (D)	3 (Hy)	4 (Pd)	5 (Mf)	6 (Pa)	7 (Pt)	8 (Sc)	9 (Ma)	0 (Si)	Raw Score
66												113		97	66
67												114		99	67
68												115		100	68
69												117		101	69
70	62											118		102	70
71												119			71
72												120			72
73															73
74															74
75															75
76															76
77															77
78															78

Males

Raw Score	?	L	F	K	1 (Hs)	2 (D)	3 (Hy)	4 (Pd)	5 (Mf)	6 (Pa)	7 (Pt)	8 (Sc)	9 (Ma)	0 (Si)	Raw Score
66												103		100	66
67												104		102	67
68												105		103	68
69												106		104	69
70	62											107		106	70
71												108			71
72												110			72
73												111			73
74												112			74
75												113			75
76												114			76
77												115			77
78												116			78

SECTION 2
T-score Conversions for Basic Scales without K-corrections for Minnesota Adolescents Age 15

Males

Raw Score	?	L	F	K	1 (Hs)	2 (D)	3 (Hy)	4 (Pd)	5 (Mf)	6 (Pa)	7 (Pt)	8 (Sc)	9 (Ma)	0 (Si)
0	41	32	37	22	36					27	29	33		
1		37	38	24	39					29	31	34		
2		42	40	26	41					31	32	35		
3		46	41	28	44		20			33	34	36	21	
4		50	43	30	46		22			35	35	37	22	
5		55	45	32	48	20	24	22		37	37	38	24	
6		59	46	34	51	22	26	24	20	40	38	39	26	
7		63	48	37	53	24	28	26	20	42	39	40	28	20
8		67	50	39	55	27	30	28	22	44	41	41	30	21
9		72	52	41	58	29	32	30	24	46	42	42	32	23
10	44	76	53	43	60	31	34	32	26	48	44	43	34	24
11		80	55	45	62	33	36	34	28	50	45	44	36	25
12		85	57	47	65	36	38	37	31	52	46	45	38	27
13		89	58	49	67	38	40	39	33	54	48	46	40	28
14		93	60	51	69	40	42	41	35	56	49	47	42	30
15		98	62	53	72	43	44	43	37	58	51	48	43	31
16			63	55	74	45	46	45	39	60	52	49	45	32
17			65	58	76	47	48	47	41	63	54	50	47	34
18			67	60	79	49	50	49	43	65	55	51	49	35
19			68	62	81	52	52	52	45	67	56	52	51	36
20	47		70	64	84	54	54	54	47	69	58	53	53	38
21			72	66	86	56	57	56	49	71	59	54	55	39
22			73	68	88	58	59	58	51	73	61	55	57	40

Females

Raw Score	?	L	F	K	1 (Hs)	2 (D)	3 (Hy)	4 (Pd)	5 (Mf)	6 (Pa)	7 (Pt)	8 (Sc)	9 (Ma)	0 (Si)
0	41	31	36	21	37				120	26	29	32		
1		36	38	23	39				118	29	31	34	20	
2		40	41	25	41				115	31	32	35	22	
3		45	43	27	43				113	33	33	36	24	
4		49	45	29	46			21	111	36	35	37	26	
5		53	47	32	48			23	109	38	36	39	28	
6		58	50	34	50	21	21	25	107	40	37	40	29	21
7		62	52	36	52	24	23	27	105	42	39	41	31	22
8		66	54	38	55	26	25	30	103	44	40	42	33	23
9		70	57	40	57	28	27	32	101	47	41	43	35	24
10	44	75	59	42	59	30	29	34	100	49	43	44	37	26
11		79	61	45	61	32	31	36	98	51	44	45	39	27
12		83	63	47	64	34	33	38	96	53	45	46	41	28
13		88	66	49	66	37	35	40	94	55	47	47	42	30
14		92	68	51	68	39	37	42	92	58	48	48	44	31
15		96	70	53	70	41	39	44	90	60	49	49	46	32
16			73	56	72	43	42	46	88	62	51	50	48	33
17			75	58	75	45	44	48	86	64	52	51	50	35
18			77	60	77	47	46	51	84	66	53	53	52	36
19	47		79	62	79	49	48	53	82	68	55	54	54	37
20			82	64	81	52	50	55	79	71	56	55	56	39
21			84	67	84	54	52	57	77	73	58	56	57	40
22			86	69	86	56	54	59	75	75	59	57	59	41

Females

Raw Score	0 (Si)	9 (Ma)	8 (Sc)	7 (Pt)	6 (Pa)	5 (Mf)	4 (Pd)	3 (Hy)	2 (D)	1 (Hs)	K	F	L	?
23	42	61	58	60	77	73	61	56	58	88	71	89		
24	44	63	59	62	79	71	63	58	60	90	73	91		
25	45	65	60	63	82	69	65	60	62	93	75	93		50
26	46	67	61	64	84	67	67	62	65	95	77	95		
27	48	69	62	66	86	65	69	64	67	97	80	98		
28	49	70	63	67	88	63	71	66	69	99	82	100		
29	50	72	61	68	90	61	74	68	71	102	84	102		
30	52	74	65	70	93	59	76	70	73	104	86	104		
31	53	76	66	71	95	57	78	72	75	106		107		
32	54	78	68	72	97	55	80	74	78	108		109		
33	55	80	69	74	99	53	82	76	80	110		111		
34	57	82	70	75	101	51	84	79	82			114		
35	58	83	71	76	103	49	86	81	84			116		
36	59	85	72	78	106	47	88	83	86			118		
37	61	87	73	79	108	45	90	85	88			120		
38	62	89	74	80	110	42	92	87	90					
39	63	91	75	82	112	40	95	89	93					
40	64	93	76	83	114	38	97	91	95					53
41	66	95	77	85		36	99	93	97					
42	67	96	78	86		34	101	95	99					
43	68	98	79	87		32	103	97	101					
44	70	100	80	89		30	105	99	103					
45	71	102	82	90		28	107	101	106					

Males

Raw Score	0 (Si)	9 (Ma)	8 (Sc)	7 (Pt)	6 (Pa)	5 (Mf)	4 (Pd)	3 (Hy)	2 (D)	1 (Hs)	K	F	L	?
23	42	59	56	62	75	53	60	61	61	91	70	75		
24	43	61	57	64	77	56	62	63	63	93	72	77		
25	44	63	58	65	79	58	64	65	65	95	74	78		50
26	46	65	59	66	81	60	66	67	67	98	76	80		
27	47	66	60	68	83	62	69	70	69	100	78	82		
28	48	68	61	69	86	64	71	71	71	102	81	83		
29	50	70	62	71	88	66	73	73	74	105	83	85		
30	51	72	63	72	90	68	75	75	77	107	85	87		
31	52	74	64	73	92	70	77	79	79	109		88		
32	54	76	65	75	94	72	79	81	81	112		90		
33	55	78	66	76	96	74	81	83	83	114		92		
34	56	80	67	78	98	76	84	86	86			93		
35	58	82	68	79	100	79	86	88	88			95		
36	59	84	69	81	102	81	88	90	90			97		
37	60	86	70	82	104	83	90	92	92			98		
38	62	87	71	85	106	85	92	95	95			100		
39	63	89	72	86	109	87	94	97	97			102		
40	64	91	73	88	111	89	96	99	99			103		53
41	66	93	74	88		91	99	101	101			105		
42	67	95	75	89		93	101	104	104			107		
43	69	97	76	90		95	103	106	106			108		
44	70	99	77	92		97	105	108	108			110		
45	71	101	78	93		99	107	111	111			112		

(Continued)

SECTION 2 (Continued)

Males

Raw Score	?	L	F	K	1 (Hs)	2 (D)	3 (Hy)	4 (Pd)	5 (Mf)	6 (Pa)	7 (Pt)	8 (Sc)	9 (Ma)	0 (Si)
46			114			113	108	109	101		95	79	103	73
47			115			115	110	111	104		96	80		74
48			117			117	112	114	106		98	81		75
49			119			120	114	116	108			82		77
50	56		120				116	118	110			83		78
51							118		112			84		79
52							120		114			85		81
53									116			86		82
54									118			87		83
55									120			88		85
56												89		86
57												90		87
58												91		89
59												92		90
60	58											93		91
61												94		93
62												95		94
63												96		95
64												97		97
65												98		98
66												99		99
67												100		101

Females

Raw Score	?	L	F	K	1 (Hs)	2 (D)	3 (Hy)	4 (Pd)	5 (Mf)	6 (Pa)	7 (Pt)	8 (Sc)	9 (Ma)	0 (Si)
46						108	103	109	26		91	83	104	72
47						110	105	111	24		93	84		73
48						112	107	113	22		94	85		75
49	56					114	109	115	20			86		76
50						116	111	118				87		77
51						119	113					88		79
52							115					89		80
53							118					90		81
54							120					91		82
55												92		84
56												93		85
57												94		86
58												95		88
59												97		89
60	58											98		90
61												99		92
62												100		93
63												101		94
64												102		95
65												103		97
66												104		98
67												105		99

Males

Raw Score	?	L	F	K	1 (Hs)	2 (D)	3 (Hy)	4 (Pd)	5 (Mf)	6 (Pa)	7 (Pt)	8 (Sc)	9 (Ma)	0 (Si)
68												101		102
69												102		103
70	62											103		105
71												104		
72												105		
73												106		
74												107		
75												108		
76												109		
77												110		
78												111		

Females

Raw Score	?	L	F	K	1 (Hs)	2 (D)	3 (Hy)	4 (Pd)	5 (Mf)	6 (Pa)	7 (Pt)	8 (Sc)	9 (Ma)	0 (Si)
68												106		101
69												107		102
70	62											108		103
71												109		
72												110		
73												112		
74												113		
75												114		
76												115		
77												116		
78												117		

SECTION 3

T-score Conversions for Basic Scales without K-corrections for Minnesota Adolescents Age 16

Males

Raw Score	?	L	F	K	1 (Hs)	2 (D)	3 (Hy)	4 (Pd)	5 (Mf)	6 (Pa)	7 (Pt)	8 (Sc)	9 (Ma)	0 (Si)
0	41	31	35	20	33					34	28	30		
1		35	37	22	36					35	30	32		
2		40	39	24	39					36	31	33		
3		44	40	27	42					37	33	35		
4		49	42	29	45					39	34	36		
5		53	44	31	47	20	21	21		40	36	37	21	
6		58	46	33	50	22	23	23		42	37	38	23	
7		62	47	36	53	24	26	25		43	39	39	25	
8		67	49	38	56	27	28	28	20	45	40	40	28	20
9		71	51	40	59	29	30	30	22	46	42	41	30	21
10	44	76	53	42	62	31	32	32	24	48	43	42	32	22
11		80	54	45	64	33	34	34	27	49	45	43	34	24
12		85	56	47	67	36	37	36	29	51	46	44	36	25
13		89	58	49	70	38	39	38	31	52	48	45	38	27
14		94	60	51	73	40	41	41	35	54	49	46	40	28
15		99	61	54	76	42	43	43	36	55	51	48	43	29
16			63	56	78	45	45	45	39	57	52	49	45	31
17			65	58	81	47	47	47	41	58	54	50	47	32
18			66	60	84	49	50	49	43	60	55	51	49	34
19			68	63	87	51	52	51	46	61	56	52	51	35
20	47		70	65	90	54	54	53	48	63	58	53	53	37
21			72	67	93	56	56	56	50	64	59	54	55	38
22			73	70	95	58	58	58	53	66	61	55	58	39

Females

?	L	F	K	1 (Hs)	2 (D)	3 (Hy)	4 (Pd)	5 (Mf)	6 (Pa)	7 (Pt)	8 (Sc)	9 (Ma)	0 (Si)	Raw Score
41	29	35	22	35					21	27	32			0
	34	37	24	37					24	29	33			1
	38	39	26	40					27	30	34			2
	42	41	28	42				120	29	32	35			3
	47	44	30	44			20	118	32	33	36	21		4
	51	46	33	47		20	23	116	35	34	38	23		5
	56	48	35	49	20	22	25	113	37	36	39	26		6
	60	50	37	51	22	24	27	111	40	37	40	28		7
	64	53	39	54	24	26	29	109	42	38	41	30	20	8
	69	55	41	56	26	28	31	106	45	40	42	33	21	9
44	73	57	44	58	28	30	33	104	48	41	43	35	23	10
	78	59	46	61	30	32	36	102	50	42	44	37	24	11
	82	62	48	63	32	34	38	100	53	44	45	39	26	12
	86	64	50	65	34	36	40	98	55	45	46	41	27	13
	91	66	52	67	36	38	42	96	58	46	47	43	28	14
	95	68	55	70	38	40	44	94	61	48	48	45	29	15
		71	57	72	40	42	47	91	63	49	49	48	31	16
		73	59	74	43	44	49	89	66	50	50	50	32	17
		75	61	77	45	46	51	87	68	52	51	53	33	18
		77	63	79	47	48	53	84	71	53	52	55	34	19
47		80	66	81	49	50	55	82	74	54	53	57	36	20
		82	68	84	51	52	57	80	76	56	54	59	37	21
		84	70	86	53	54	60	77	79	57	55	62	38	22

Females

Raw Score	?	L	F	K	1 (Hs)	2 (D)	3 (Hy)	4 (Pd)	5 (Mf)	6 (Pa)	7 (Pt)	8 (Sc)	9 (Ma)	0 (Si)
23			86	72	88	55	56	62	75	81	58	56	64	39
24			89	74	91	57	57	64	73	84	60	58	66	41
25			91	77	93	59	59	66	70	87	61	59	68	42
26			93	79	95	61	61	68	68	89	62	60	71	43
27			95	81	98	63	63	71	66	92	64	61	73	44
28			98	83	100	65	65	73	64	94	65	62	75	46
29			100	85	102	67	67	75	61	97	66	63	77	47
30			102	88	105	69	69	77	59	99	67	64	80	48
31			104		107	71	71	79	57	102	69	65	82	49
32			107		109	73	73	82	54	105	70	66	84	51
33			109		112	75	75	84	52	107	71	67	86	52
34			111			77	77	86	50	110	73	68	89	53
35			113			79	79	88	47	112	74	69	91	54
36			116			81	81	90	45	115	75	70	93	55
37			118			83	83	92	43	118	77	71	95	57
38			120			85	85	95	40	120	78	72	98	58
39						87	87	97	38		79	73	100	59
40						89	89	99	36		81	74	102	60
41						92	91	101	34		82	75	104	62
42						94	93	103	31		83	77	106	63
43						96	95	106	29		85	78	109	64
44						98	97	108	27		86	79	111	65
45						100	99	110	24		87	80	113	67

Males

Raw Score	?	L	F	K	1 (Hs)	2 (D)	3 (Hy)	4 (Pd)	5 (Mf)	6 (Pa)	7 (Pt)	8 (Sc)	9 (Ma)	0 (Si)
23			75	72	98	60	61	60	55	62	62	56	60	41
24			77	74	101	63	63	62	57	64	64	57	62	42
25			79	76	104	65	65	64	60	65	66	58	64	44
26			80	79	107	67	67	66	62	67	67	59	66	45
27			82	81	109	69	69	69	65	68	69	61	68	46
28			84	83	112	71	71	71	67	70	71	62	70	48
29			86	85	115	74	74	73	69	72	73	63	73	49
30	50		87	88	118	76	76	75	72	73	75	64	75	51
31			89			78	78	77	74	74	76	65	77	52
32			91			80	80	79	76	76	78	66	79	54
33			92			83	82	82	79	77	80	67	81	55
34			94			85	85	84	81	79	82	68	83	56
35			96			87	87	86	83	80	83	69	85	58
36			98			89	89	88	85	82	85	70	88	59
37			99			92	91	90	86	83	87	71	90	61
38			101			94	93	92	89	85	89	72	92	62
39			103			96	96	95	91	86	90	74	94	63
40	53		105			98	98	97	93	87	92	75	96	65
41			106			101	100	99	95	89	94	76	98	66
42			108			103	102	101	98	90	95	77	100	68
43			110			105	104	103	100	92	97	78	103	69
44			112			107	106	105	103	93	99	79	105	71
45			113			110	109	107	105	95	101	80	107	72

(Continued)

SECTION 3 (Continued)

Males

Raw Score	?	L	F	K	1 (Hs)	2 (D)	3 (Hy)	4 (Pd)	5 (Mf)	6 (Pa)	7 (Pt)	8 (Sc)	9 (Ma)	0 (Si)
46		115				112	111	110	110		96	81	109	73
47		117				114	113	112	112		98	82		75
48		118				116	115	114	114		99	83		76
49		120				119	117	116	117			84		78
50	56						120	118	119			85		79
51												86		81
52												88		82
53												89		83
54												90		85
55												91		86
56												92		88
57												93		89
58												94		90
59												95		92
60	58											96		93
61												97		95
62												98		96
63												99		98
64												101		99
65												102		100

Females

Raw Score	?	L	F	K	1 (Hs)	2 (D)	3 (Hy)	4 (Pd)	5 (Mf)	6 (Pa)	7 (Pt)	8 (Sc)	9 (Ma)	0 (Si)
46						102	101	112	22		89	81	115	68
47						104	103	114	20		90	82		69
48						106	105	116			91	83		70
49	56					108	107	119				84		72
50						110	109					85		73
51						112	111					86		74
52						114	113					87		75
53						116	115					88		77
54						118	117					89		78
55						120	119					90		79
56												91		80
57												92		82
58												93		83
59												94		84
60	58											95		85
61												97		86
62												98		88
63												99		89
64												100		90
65												101		91

Females

Raw Score	?	L	F	K	1 (Hs)	2 (D)	3 (Hy)	4 (Pd)	5 (Mf)	6 (Pa)	7 (Pt)	8 (Sc)	9 (Ma)	0 (Si)
66												102		93
67												103		94
68												104		95
69												105		96
70	62											106		98
71												107		
72												108		
73												109		
74												110		
75												111		
76												112		
77												113		
78												114		

Males

Raw Score	?	L	F	K	1 (Hs)	2 (D)	3 (Hy)	4 (Pd)	5 (Mf)	6 (Pa)	7 (Pt)	8 (Sc)	9 (Ma)	0 (Si)
66												103		102
67												104		103
68												105		105
69												106		106
70	62											107		107
71												108		
72												109		
73												110		
74												111		
75												112		
76												114		
77												115		
78												116		

SECTION 4

T-score Conversions for Basic Scales without K-corrections for Minnesota Adolescents Age 17

Males

Raw Score	?	L	F	K	1(Hs)	2(D)	3(Hy)	4(Pd)	5(Mf)	6(Pa)	7(Pt)	8(Sc)	9(Ma)	0(Si)
0	41	30	32	20	35						27	31		
1		34	34	23	38					22	28	32		
2		38	36	25	40					25	30	33		
3		43	39	27	43	21				28	32	34		
4		47	41	29	45	23	21			31	33	35	20	
5		51	43	31	48	24	23			34	35	36	22	
6		55	45	34	50	26	25	20		37	36	37	24	
7		59	47	36	53	28	27	23	20	40	38	38	26	
8		63	50	38	55	30	29	25	22	43	39	39	28	
9		68	52	40	58	32	30	27	24	46	41	40	31	20
10	44	72	54	42	60	34	32	29	26	49	42	41	33	21
11		76	56	45	63	35	34	32	29	52	44	43	35	23
12		80	58	47	65	37	36	34	31	55	45	44	37	24
13		84	60	49	68	39	38	36	33	58	47	45	39	26
14		88	63	51	70	41	40	39	35	61	48	46	41	27
15		93	65	53	73	43	42	41	37	64	50	47	43	29
16			67	56	75	44	44	43	40	67	52	48	45	30
17			69	58	78	46	46	46	42	70	53	49	48	32
18			71	60	80	48	48	48	44	72	55	50	50	33
19			73	62	83	50	49	50	46	75	56	51	52	35
20	47		76	64	85	52	51	52	48	78	58	52	54	36
21			78	67	88	54	53	55	50	81	59	53	56	38
22			80	69	90	55	55	57	53	84	61	55	58	39

Females

Raw Score	?	L	F	K	1(Hs)	2(D)	3(Hy)	4(Pd)	5(Mf)	6(Pa)	7(Pt)	8(Sc)	9(Ma)	0(Si)
0	41	28	32		31						25	29		
1		33	35	21	34					21	27	31		
2		37	37	23	36				120	24	28	32		
3		41	40	26	38				117	27	30	33	22	
4		45	42	28	41				115	30	31	35	24	
5		49	45	31	43	20	20		113	33	33	36	26	
6		54	47	33	45	22	21	21	111	38	34	37	28	
7		58	49	36	48	24	23	24	108	41	36	38	30	
8		62	52	38	50	26	25	26	106	44	37	39	32	
9		66	54	41	52	28	27	28	104	47	39	40	34	21
10	44	70	57	44	55	30	29	31	102	50	40	41	37	22
11		74	59	46	57	31	31	33	100	53	42	43	39	23
12		79	62	49	59	33	32	35	98	56	43	44	41	25
13		83	64	51	61	35	33	37	96	59	44	45	43	26
14		87	67	54	64	37	35	40	94	61	46	46	45	27
15		91	69	56	66	39	37	42	92	64	47	47	47	28
16			72	59	68	41	39	44	89	67	49	48	50	29
17			74	61	71	43	41	47	87	70	50	49	52	30
18			77	64	73	45	43	49	85	73	52	50	54	31
19			79	66	75	47	45	51	83	76	53	52	56	33
20	47		81	69	77	49	47	54	80	79	55	53	58	34
21			84	71	80	50	49	56	78	82	56	54	60	35
22			86	74	82	52	51	58	76	84	58	55	63	37

Females

Raw Score	0 (Si)	9 (Ma)	8 (Sc)	7 (Pt)	6 (Pa)	5 (Mf)	4 (Pd)	3 (Hy)	2 (D)	1 (Hs)	K	F	L	?
23	38	65	56	59	87	74	61	53	54	84	89	76		
24	39	67	57	60	90	71	63	55	56	87	91	79		
25	41	69	58	62	93	69	65	57	58	89	94	81		
26	42	71	60	63	96	67	67	59	60	91	96	84		
27	43	73	61	65	99	65	70	61	62	93	99	86		
28	45	76	62	66	102	62	72	63	65	96	101	89		
29	46	78	63	68	105	60	74	65	67	98	104	91		
30	47	80	64	69	108	58	77	67	69	100	106	94		50
31	49	82	65	71	110	56	79	69	71	103	109			
32	50	84	66	72	113	53	81	71	73	105	111			
33	51	86	68	74	116	51	84	73	75	107	113			
34	53	89	69	75	119	49	86	75	78		116			
35	54	91	70	77		47	88	77	80		118			
36	55	93	71	78		44	91	79	82					
37	57	95	72	79		42	93	81	84					
38	58	97	73	81		40	95	83	86					
39	59	99	74	82		38	98	85	88					
40	61	101	76	84		36	100	87	90					53
41	62	104	77	85		33	102	89	93					
42	63	106	78	87		31	104	91	95					
43	65	108	79	88		29	107	93	97					
44	66	110	80	90		27	109	95	99					
45	67	112	81	91		24	111	97	101					

Males

Raw Score	0 (Si)	9 (Ma)	8 (Sc)	7 (Pt)	6 (Pa)	5 (Mf)	4 (Pd)	3 (Hy)	2 (D)	1 (Hs)	K	F	L	?
23	41	60	56	62	87	55	59	57	57	93	71	82		
24	42	62	57	64	90	57	62	59	59	95	73	84		
25	44	65	58	65	93	59	64	61	61	98	75	87		
26	45	67	59	67	96	61	66	63	63	100	78	89		
27	47	69	60	69	99	63	69	65	64	103	80	91		
28	49	71	61	70	102	66	71	67	66	105	82	93		
29	50	73	62	72	105	68	73	68	68	108	84	95		
30	52	75	63	73	108	70	75	70	70	110	86	97		50
31	53	77	64	75	111	72	78	72	72	113	100			
32	55	79	66	76	114	74	80	74	73	115	102			
33	56	82	67	78	117	77	82	76	75	118	104			
34	58	84	68	79	120	79	85	78	77		106			
35	59	86	69	81		81	87	80	79		108			
36	61	88	70	82		83	89	82	81		110			
37	62	90	71	84		85	91	84	83		113			
38	64	92	72	86		87	94	86	84		115			
39	65	94	73	87		90	96	87	86		117			
40	67	96	74	89		92	98	89	88		119			53
41	68	99	75	90		94	101	91	90					
42	70	101	77	92		96	103	93	92					
43	71	103	78	93		98	105	95	93					
44	73	105	79	95		100	108	97	95					
45	74	107	80	96		103	110	99	97					

(Continued)

SECTION 4 (Continued)

Males

Raw Score	?	L	F	K	1 (Hs)	2 (D)	3 (Hy)	4 (Pd)	5 (Mf)	6 (Pa)	7 (Pt)	8 (Sc)	9 (Ma)	0 (Si)
46						99	101	112	105		98	81	109	76
47						101	103	114	107		99	82		77
48						102	105	117	109		101	83		79
49						104	107	119	111			84		80
50	56					106	108		114			85		82
51						108	110		116			86		83
52						110	112		118			88		85
53						112	114		120			89		86
54						113	116					90		88
55						115	118					91		89
56						117	120					92		91
57						118						93		92
58	58											94		94
59												95		95
60												96		97
61												97		98
62												99		100
63												100		101
64												101		103
65												102		104

Females

Raw Score	?	L	F	K	1 (Hs)	2 (D)	3 (Hy)	4 (Pd)	5 (Mf)	6 (Pa)	7 (Pt)	8 (Sc)	9 (Ma)	0 (Si)
46						103	99	114	22		93	82	114	69
47						105	101	116	20		94	84		70
48						108	103	118			95	85		71
49						110	105					86		73
50	56					112	107					87		74
51						114	109					88		75
52						116	111					89		77
53						118	113					90		78
54						120	115					92		79
55							117					93		81
56						119						94		82
57												95		83
58												96		85
59												97		86
60	58											98		87
61												100		89
62												101		90
63												102		91
64												103		93
65												104		94

Males

Raw Score	?	L	F	K	1 (Hs)	2 (D)	3 (Hy)	4 (Pd)	5 (Mf)	6 (Pa)	7 (Pt)	8 (Sc)	9 (Ma)	0 (Si)
66												103		106
67												104		107
68												105		109
69	62											106		110
70												107		112
71												108		
72												109		
73												111		
74												112		
75												113		
76												114		
77												115		
78												116		

Females

Raw Score	?	L	F	K	1 (Hs)	2 (D)	3 (Hy)	4 (Pd)	5 (Mf)	6 (Pa)	7 (Pt)	8 (Sc)	9 (Ma)	0 (Si)
66												105		95
67												106		97
68												108		98
69												109		99
70	62											110		101
71												111		
72												112		
73												113		
74												114		
75												116		
76	000											117		
77												118		
78												119		

Appendix **B**

TODAY'S ADOLESCENT AND THE MMPI: PATTERNS OF MMPI RESPONSES FROM NORMAL TEENAGERS OF THE 1980s

Robert C. Colligan, Ph.D.
Kenneth P. Offord, M.S.

From the Section of Psychology and the Section of Medical Research Statistics, Mayo Clinic and Mayo Foundation, Rochester, Minnesota

The MMPI is aging. More than 45 years have passed since the original adult norms were established (Hathaway & McKinley, 1940; Hathaway & Monachesi, 1963; McKinley & Hathaway, 1943). Later, specific norms for adolescents were developed (Marks & Briggs, 1967; Marks, Seeman, & Haller, 1974). However, about 40% of the adolescent MMPIs used in the Marks and Briggs (1967) norms were drawn from existing samples that had been obtained during 1947 and 1954 and were supplemented by a new sample obtained in 1964 and 1965. Changes in the patterns of MMPI responses among adults since the original norms were first developed have been well documented (Colligan, Osborne, Swenson, & Offord, 1983, 1984, 1985). It is obvious that there have been equally significant changes in the role of adolescents in our society during the past 20-35 years since the development of the adolescent norms. However, new adolescent norms have not been developed and the old adolescent norms have not been reevaluated to determine whether they are still appropriate for contemporary use.

To evaluate possible changes in adolescent MMPI response patterns during the past three decades, a random sample of 11,933 households in an area of approximately 8,000 square miles surrounding Rochester, Minnesota, was contacted. Telephone interviewers obtained demographic information about family members and determined whether there were physically or mentally handicapping conditions among potential adolescent respondents aged 13–17 years. Only about one household in 10 included adolescents in the desired age range. Approximately 2½% of the households refused participation. Approximately 2% of potential respondents were excluded because they had conditions believed to be potentially handicapping to a degree that might engender an atypical response bias. In addition, we were unable to contact the intended household in about 9% of the cases because of a mismatch between telephone numbers and household names, business lines, and nonworking telephone numbers. These procedures yielded 1,412 households with subjects in the desired age range. Only one adolescent of each sex was accepted from each household. Response rate was very satisfactory, ranging from 81%-85% for the female and 67%-79% for the male adolescents. The final sample consisted of 1,315 adolescents (691 females, 624 males; age, 13–17 years).

Tables of sample sizes and return rates are presented separately for age and sex groups. Incomplete MMPIs were excluded; all others were included. In addition, tables of raw scores without K-correction, showing comparisons with the Marks and Briggs (1967) norms, are provided. A similar set of tables listing K-corrected scores is also presented. Mean profiles are provided as well for a variety of norm comparisons.

In summary, the contemporary normal reference sample of adolescents described above is the only one of its kind since random-sampling procedures and specific criteria for defining normality were used. Just as patterns of MMPI responses among adults have changed, it is equally clear that MMPI response patterns among adolescents have changed as well. In general, contemporary adolescent MMPI patterns vary from contemporary adult patterns in a manner similar to that in which adolescents of the past differed from the original MMPI norms of more than 45 years ago. The data suggest that clinicians should take a somewhat more conservative approach in interpreting MMPI profiles from adolescents. Clinicians using the Marks and Briggs (1967) norms should also consider plotting the mean MMPI profile from this contemporary sample of normal adolescents for the same age and sex as the patient, as this procedure is likely to increase the accuracy of the interpretive statements that are made.

REFERENCES

Colligan, R. C., Osborne, D., Swenson, W. M., & Offord, K. P. (1983). *The MMPI: A contemporary normative study*. New York: Praeger.

Colligan, R. C., Osborne, D., Swenson, W. M., & Offord, K. P. (1984). The MMPI: Development of contemporary norms. *Journal of Clinical Psychology, 40*, 100–107.

Colligan, R. C., Osborne, D., Swenson, W. M., & Offord, K. P. (1985). Using the 1983 norms for the MMPI: Code type frequencies in four clinical samples. *Journal of Clinical Psychology, 41*, 629–633.

Hathaway, S. R., & McKinley, J. C. (1940). A multiphasic personality schedule (Minnesota). I. Construction of the schedule. *Journal of Psychology, 10*, 249–254.

Hathaway, S. R., & Monachesi, E. D. (1963). *Adolescent personality and behavior: MMPI patterns of normal, delinquent, dropout, and other outcomes*. Minneapolis: University of Minnesota Press.

Marks, P. A., & Briggs, P. F. (1967). Adolescent norms tables for the MMPI. (Tables 6 through 9.) In W. G. Dahlstrom, G. S. Welsh, & L. E. Dahlstrom (Eds.), An MMPI handbook: Vol. 1. Clinical interpretation (rev. ed., pp. 388–399). Minneapolis: University of Minnesota Press.

Marks, P. A., Seeman, W., & Haller, D. L. (1974). *The actuarial use of the MMPI with adolescents and adults*. Baltimore: Williams & Wilkins.

McKinley, J. C., & Hathaway, S. R. (1943). *The identification and measurement of the psychoneuroses in medical practice: The Minnesota Multiphasic Personality Inventory*. Journal of the American Medical Association, 122, 161–167.

RETURN RATES AND BASIC MMPI SCALE
RAW SCORE DATA

THE MMPI: A CONTEMPORARY NORMATIVE STUDY OF ADOLESCENTS

SAMPLE SIZES AND PERCENT RETURN RATES FOR MMPIs
SENT TO NORMAL ADOLESCENTS AGREEING TO PARTICIPATE
IN THE ADOLESCENT MMPI NORMATIVE STUDY

Males

Age	Sent	Returned	%
13	165	112	68
14	186	147	79
15	185	130	70
16	183	122	67
17	163	113	69
Totals	882	624	71

mayo
94616B-49

THE MMPI: A CONTEMPORARY NORMATIVE STUDY OF ADOLESCENTS

SAMPLE SIZES AND PERCENT RETURN RATES FOR MMPIs
SENT TO NORMAL ADOLESCENTS AGREEING TO PARTICIPATE
IN THE ADOLESCENT MMPI NORMATIVE STUDY

Females

Age	Sent	Returned	%
13	168	136	81
14	182	153	84
15	150	127	85
16	169	138	82
17	166	137	83
Totals	835	691	83

mayo
94616B-48

Means and Standard Deviations of Raw Scores for Basic MMPI Scales,
With K Correction for Contemporary Normal Adolescents at Five Ages

Females

Age, yr	n	L X̄	L SD	F X̄	F SD	K X̄	K SD	1(Hs)[a] +.5K X̄	1(Hs)[a] +.5K SD	2(D) X̄	2(D) SD	3(Hy) X̄	3(Hy) SD	4(Pd)[a] +.4K X̄	4(Pd)[a] +.4K SD
13[b]	136	2.9‡	1.5	7.5†	4.9	11.4‡	4.4	12.3	3.5	19.3	4.6	19.9	4.7	22.9	4.5
14	153	3.0‡	2.0	6.9†	4.8	12.3†	4.8	12.4	3.9	19.0	4.9	20.2	4.3	23.5	4.8
15	127	2.5‡	1.6	6.8	5.5	11.6‡	4.6	13.0	4.6	19.2	5.2	20.7	4.8	23.8	5.1
16	138	2.3‡	1.5	7.6	5.4	11.1‡	4.2	13.5	4.9	21.0	5.7	21.1	5.1	24.3	5.3
17	137	2.7‡	1.4	5.8†	4.6	12.3	4.6	12.7	3.9	18.9‡	4.7	20.9	4.7	23.5	4.5

Age, yr	n	5(Mf) X̄	5(Mf) SD	6(Pa) X̄	6(Pa) SD	7(Pt)[a] +1.0K X̄	7(Pt)[a] +1.0K SD	8(Sc)[a] +1K X̄	8(Sc)[a] +1K SD	9(Ma)[a] +0.2K X̄	9(Ma)[a] +0.2K SD	0(Si) X̄	0(Si) SD
13[b]	136	35.1	4.5	10.5	3.4	29.3	5.6	31.3	7.8	22.4	4.8	30.0	7.3
14	153	35.4	4.7	11.2	4.0	29.4	5.8	31.8	8.1	23.0	5.0	28.5	8.4
15	127	36.3†	4.6	11.4	3.9	30.7	6.3	32.3	7.9	23.5	4.6	28.5	8.9
16	138	36.7‡	4.4	11.8*	4.2	31.4	6.5	32.6	9.1	22.9	5.0	30.9	9.1
17	137	36.9‡	4.1	11.1*	3.4	29.4	5.1	29.0	7.0	21.9	4.7	26.8‡	8.3

[a] Marks and Briggs (1967) did not provide K-corrected scores but they are presented here for those who wish to plot the profile according to the suggestion of Hathaway and Monachesi (1963).

[b] Specific norms for age 13 yr are not available in Marks and Briggs (1967) but are presented as age 14 yr and younger.

Significance values are for comparisons with norms of Marks and Briggs.

*p <0.05.

†p <0.01.

‡p <0.001.

Means and Standard Deviations of Raw Scores for Basic MMPI Scales,
Without K Correction for Contemporary Normal Adolescents at Five Ages

Females

Age, yr	n	L X̄	L SD	F X̄	F SD	K X̄	K SD	1(Hs) X̄	1(Hs) SD	2(D) X̄	2(D) SD	3(Hy) X̄	3(Hy) SD	4(Pd) X̄	4(Pd) SD
13[a]	136	2.9‡	1.5	7.5‡	4.9	11.4‡	4.4	6.4*	3.8	19.3	4.6	19.9	4.7	18.3‡	5.0
14	153	3.0‡	2.0	6.9†	4.8	12.3†	4.8	6.0	4.2	19.0	4.9	20.2	4.3	18.6‡	5.2
15	127	2.5‡	1.6	6.8	5.5	11.6‡	4.6	6.9*	5.4	19.2	5.2	20.7	4.8	19.1†	5.7
16	138	2.3‡	1.5	7.6	5.4	11.1‡	4.2	7.7*	5.5	21.0	5.7	21.1	5.1	19.8‡	5.8
17	137	2.7‡	1.4	5.8†	4.6	12.3	4.6	6.3†	4.3	18.9‡	4.7	20.9	4.7	18.5	4.9

Age, yr	n	5(Mf) X̄	5(Mf) SD	6(Pa) X̄	6(Pa) SD	7(Pt) X̄	7(Pt) SD	8(Sc) X̄	8(Sc) SD	9(Ma) X̄	9(Ma) SD	0(Si) X̄	0(Si) SD
13[a]	136	35.1	4.5	10.5	3.4	17.9†	8.1	19.9†	10.1	20.1‡	5.2	30.0	7.3
14	153	35.4	4.7	11.2	4.0	17.2†	8.1	19.5†	10.3	20.5†	5.2	28.5	8.4
15	127	36.3‡	4.6	11.4	3.9	19.1†	9.1	20.6†	10.8	21.2†	4.9	28.5	8.9
16	138	36.7‡	4.4	11.8*	4.2	20.3†	8.8	21.5‡	11.4	20.7‡	5.2	30.9	9.1
17	137	36.9‡	4.1	11.1*	3.4	17.1	7.5	16.7	9.2	19.5‡	5.0	26.8‡	8.3

[a] Specific norms for age 13 yr are not available in Marks and Briggs (1967) but are presented as age 14 yr and younger.

Significance values are for comparisons with norms of Marks and Briggs.

*p <0.05.

†p <0.01.

‡p <0.001.

Means and Standard Deviations of Raw Scores for Basic MMPI Scales,
With K Correction for Contemporary Normal Adolescents at Five Ages

Males

Age, yr	n	L X̄	L SD	F X̄	F SD	K X̄	K SD	1(Hs)[a]+.5K X̄	1(Hs)[a]+.5K SD	2(D) X̄	2(D) SD	3(Hy) X̄	3(Hy) SD	4(Pd)[a]+.4K X̄	4(Pd)[a]+.4K SD
13[b]	112	3.2*	1.8	7.5	4.6	12.4	5.0	12.4	3.9	18.3	5.2	17.9	4.3	23.4	4.5
14	147	3.2*	2.1	8.8†	5.6	11.3‡	4.8	12.2	3.6	18.3	4.6	18.2	4.5	24.5	5.2
15	130	2.8‡	1.7	7.1	5.4	12.1*	5.0	12.0	3.5	17.8	4.5	18.2	4.5	23.8	5.2
16	122	3.1‡	2.0	8.3	5.7	12.1*	4.6	12.9	3.9	18.2	4.6	18.8	4.5	24.3	4.8
17	113	3.0‡	1.8	7.0*	4.9	12.4	4.9	11.8	3.9	17.0‡	4.8	19.0	5.0	23.2	5.0

Age, yr	n	5(Mf) X̄	5(Mf) SD	6(Pa) X̄	6(Pa) SD	7(Pt)[a]+1.0K X̄	7(Pt)[a]+1.0K SD	8(Sc)[a]+1K X̄	8(Sc)[a]+1K SD	9(Ma)[a]+0.2K X̄	9(Ma)[a]+0.2K SD	0(Si) X̄	0(Si) SD
13[b]	112	22.9‡	5.0	10.9	3.9	27.4	5.2	31.1	7.5	22.8	4.5	29.3	8.3
14	147	23.3‡	4.4	11.2*	4.7	28.2	5.7	31.9	8.6	23.4	5.5	30.0	8.8
15	130	23.7‡	4.8	11.2	3.5	27.3	5.2	30.3	7.3	22.6	4.0	27.6	9.0
16	122	23.9‡	5.2	11.5	3.6	29.2	5.5	32.6	8.3	24.0	4.0	28.7	8.2
17	113	23.8‡	4.9	11.1	4.1	27.3	5.8	29.3	8.1	23.2	4.1	25.7†	8.7

[a] Marks and Briggs (1967) did not provide K-corrected scores but they are presented here for those who wish to plot the profile according to the suggestion of Hathaway and Monachesi (1963).

[b] Specific norms for age 13 yr are not available in Marks and Briggs (1967) but are presented as age 14 yr and younger.

Significance values are for comparisons with norms of Marks and Briggs.

*$p < 0.05$.

†$p < 0.01$.

‡$p < 0.001$.

Means and Standard Deviations of Raw Scores for Basic MMPI Scales,
Without K Correction for Contemporary Normal Adolescents at Five Ages

Males

Age, yr	n	L X̄	L SD	F X̄	F SD	K X̄	K SD	1(Hs) X̄	1(Hs) SD	2(D) X̄	2(D) SD	3(Hy) X̄	3(Hy) SD	4(Pd) X̄	4(Pd) SD
13[a]	112	3.2*	1.8	7.5	4.6	12.4	5.0	5.9	4.4	18.3	5.2	17.9	4.3	18.4	4.9
14	147	3.2*	2.1	8.8†	5.6	11.3‡	4.8	6.3†	3.9	18.3	4.6	18.2	4.5	19.9†	5.5
15	130	2.8‡	1.7	7.1	5.4	12.1*	5.0	5.6	3.9	17.8	4.5	18.2	4.5	18.9	5.5
16	122	3.1‡	2.0	8.3	5.7	12.1*	4.6	6.6	3.9	18.2	4.6	18.8	4.5	19.5*	5.0
17	113	3.0‡	1.8	7.0*	4.9	12.4	4.9	5.4	4.0	17.0‡	4.8	19.0	5.0	18.3	5.0

Age, yr	n	5(Mf) X̄	5(Mf) SD	6(Pa) X̄	6(Pa) SD	7(Pt) X̄	7(Pt) SD	8(Sc) X̄	8(Sc) SD	9(Ma) X̄	9(Ma) SD	0(Si) X̄	0(Si) SD
13[a]	112	22.9‡	5.0	10.9	3.9	15.0	8.0	18.7*	10.5	20.3‡	4.8	29.3	8.3
14	147	23.3‡	4.4	11.2*	4.7	16.9†	8.4	20.6‡	11.1	21.2‡	5.9	30.0	8.8
15	130	23.7‡	4.8	11.2	3.5	15.2	7.8	18.2	9.5	20.2‡	4.4	27.6	9.0
16	122	23.9‡	5.2	11.5	3.6	17.1†	7.7	20.5†	10.4	21.5‡	4.3	28.7	8.2
17	113	23.8‡	4.9	11.1	4.1	14.9	8.2	16.9	10.0	20.7‡	4.5	25.7†	8.7

[a] Specific norms for age 13 yr are not available in Marks and Briggs (1967) but are presented as age 14 yr and younger.

Significance values are for comparisons with norms of Marks and Briggs.

*$p < 0.05$.

†$p < 0.01$.

‡$p < 0.001$.

MEAN MMPI PROFILES FOR THE MINNESOTA STATEWIDE SAMPLES USING *K*-CORRECTED ADULT ORIGINAL NORMS

THE MMPI: A CONTEMPORARY NORMATIVE STUDY OF ADOLESCENTS

MEAN MMPI PROFILE FOR THE 1954 MINNESOTA STATEWIDE SAMPLE OF NINTH GRADE STUDENTS USING ORIGINAL ADULT NORMS AND K CORRECTED SCORES

FEMALES: N=5,207   CA=14.4 YR

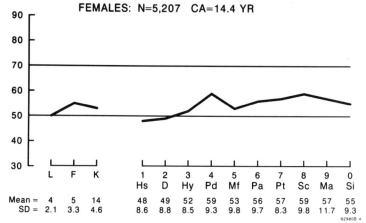

	L	F	K		1 Hs	2 D	3 Hy	4 Pd	5 Mf	6 Pa	7 Pt	8 Sc	9 Ma	0 Si
Mean =	4	5	14		48	49	52	59	53	56	57	59	57	55
SD =	2.1	3.3	4.6		8.6	8.8	8.5	9.3	9.8	9.7	8.3	9.8	11.7	9.3

929808 4

THE MMPI: A CONTEMPORARY NORMATIVE STUDY OF ADOLESCENTS

MEAN MMPI PROFILE FOR THE 1954 MINNESOTA STATEWIDE SAMPLE OF NINTH GRADE STUDENTS USING ORIGINAL ADULT NORMS AND K CORRECTED SCORES

MALES: N=4,944   CA=14.6 YR

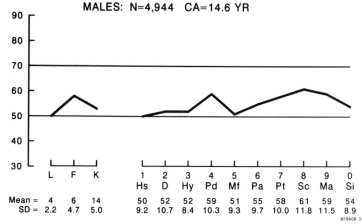

	L	F	K		1 Hs	2 D	3 Hy	4 Pd	5 Mf	6 Pa	7 Pt	8 Sc	9 Ma	0 Si
Mean =	4	6	14		50	52	52	59	51	55	58	61	59	54
SD =	2.2	4.7	5.0		9.2	10.7	8.4	10.3	9.3	9.7	10.0	11.8	11.5	8.9

929808 3

THE MMPI: A CONTEMPORARY NORMATIVE STUDY OF ADOLESCENTS

MEAN MMPI PROFILE FOR THE 1957 MINNESOTA STATEWIDE SAMPLE OF TWELFTH GRADE STUDENTS USING ORIGINAL ADULT NORMS AND K CORRECTED SCORES

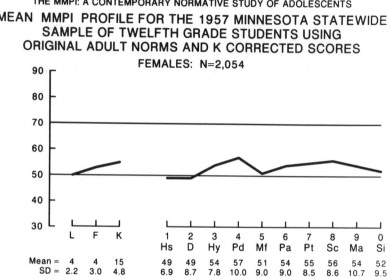

FEMALES: N=2,054

Mean =	4	4	15		49	49	54	57	51	54	55	56	54	52
SD =	2.2	3.0	4.8		6.9	8.7	7.8	10.0	9.0	9.0	8.5	8.6	10.7	9.5
	L	F	K		1 Hs	2 D	3 Hy	4 Pd	5 Mf	6 Pa	7 Pt	8 Sc	9 Ma	0 Si

THE MMPI: A CONTEMPORARY NORMATIVE STUDY OF ADOLESCENTS

MEAN MMPI PROFILE FOR THE 1957 MINNESOTA STATEWIDE SAMPLE OF TWELFTH GRADE STUDENTS USING ORIGINAL ADULT NORMS AND K CORRECTED SCORES

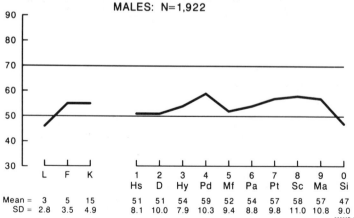

MALES: N=1,922

Mean =	3	5	15		51	51	54	59	52	54	57	58	57	47
SD =	2.8	3.5	4.9		8.1	10.0	7.9	10.3	9.4	8.8	9.8	11.0	10.8	9.0
	L	F	K		1 Hs	2 D	3 Hy	4 Pd	5 Mf	6 Pa	7 Pt	8 Sc	9 Ma	0 Si

MEAN MMPI PROFILES FOR MARKS, SEEMAN, AND HALLER SAMPLE OF NORMAL ADOLESCENTS USING ORIGINAL ADULT NORMS AND CONTEMPORARY ADULT NORMS

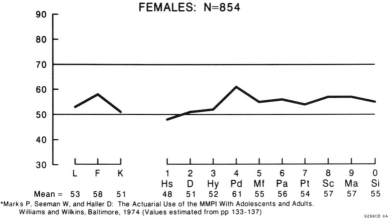

THE MMPI: A CONTEMPORARY NORMATIVE STUDY OF ADOLESCENTS

MEAN MMPI PROFILE FOR MARKS, SEEMAN AND HALLER* SAMPLE OF NORMAL ADOLESCENTS AGES 9-18 USING ORIGINAL ADULT NORMS AND NON-K CORRECTED SCORES

FEMALES: N=854

	L	F	K		1 Hs	2 D	3 Hy	4 Pd	5 Mf	6 Pa	7 Pt	8 Sc	9 Ma	0 Si
Mean =	53	58	51		48	51	52	61	55	56	54	57	57	55

*Marks P, Seeman W, and Haller D: The Actuarial Use of the MMPI With Adolescents and Adults.
Williams and Wilkins, Baltimore, 1974 (Values estimated from pp 133-137)

92980B 8A

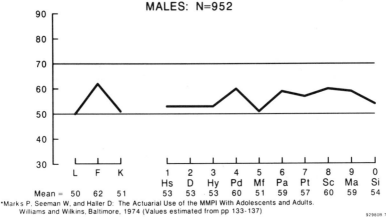

THE MMPI: A CONTEMPORARY NORMATIVE STUDY OF ADOLESCENTS

MEAN MMPI PROFILE FOR MARKS, SEEMAN AND HALLER* SAMPLE OF NORMAL ADOLESCENTS AGES 9-18 USING ORIGINAL ADULT NORMS AND NON-K CORRECTED SCORES

MALES: N=952

	L	F	K		1 Hs	2 D	3 Hy	4 Pd	5 Mf	6 Pa	7 Pt	8 Sc	9 Ma	0 Si
Mean =	50	62	51		53	53	53	60	51	59	57	60	59	54

*Marks P, Seeman W, and Haller D: The Actuarial Use of the MMPI With Adolescents and Adults.
Williams and Wilkins, Baltimore, 1974 (Values estimated from pp 133-137)

92980B 7

THE MMPI: A CONTEMPORARY NORMATIVE STUDY OF ADOLESCENTS

MEAN MMPI PROFILE FOR MARKS, SEEMAN AND HALLER* SAMPLE OF NORMAL ADOLESCENTS AGES 9-18 USING CONTEMPORARY ADULT NORMS AND NON-K CORRECTED SCORES

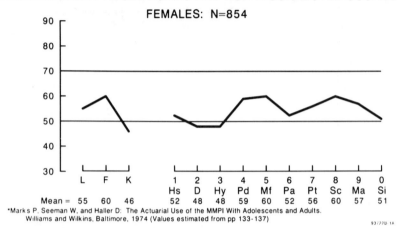

FEMALES: N=854

	L	F	K		1 Hs	2 D	3 Hy	4 Pd	5 Mf	6 Pa	7 Pt	8 Sc	9 Ma	0 Si
Mean =	55	60	46		52	48	48	59	60	52	56	60	57	51

*Marks P, Seeman W, and Haller D: The Actuarial Use of the MMPI With Adolescents and Adults.
Williams and Wilkins, Baltimore, 1974 (Values estimated from pp 133-137)

93772B·1A

THE MMPI: A CONTEMPORARY NORMATIVE STUDY OF ADOLESCENTS

MEAN MMPI PROFILE FOR MARKS, SEEMAN AND HALLER* SAMPLE OF NORMAL ADOLESCENTS AGES 9-18 USING CONTEMPORARY ADULT NORMS AND NON-K CORRECTED SCORES

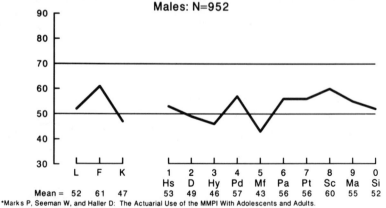

Males: N=952

	L	F	K		1 Hs	2 D	3 Hy	4 Pd	5 Mf	6 Pa	7 Pt	8 Sc	9 Ma	0 Si
Mean =	52	61	47		53	49	46	57	43	56	56	60	55	52

*Marks P, Seeman W, and Haller D: The Actuarial Use of the MMPI With Adolescents and Adults.
Williams and Wilkins, Baltimore, 1974 (Values estimated from pp 133-137)

937228 4

MEAN MMPI PROFILES FOR CONTEMPORARY NORMAL ADOLESCENTS SAMPLED BY COLLIGAN AND OFFORD USING ORIGINAL ADULT K-CORRECTED SCORES

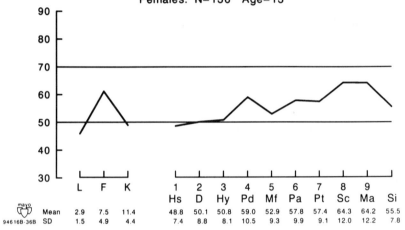

THE MMPI: A CONTEMPORARY NORMATIVE STUDY OF ADOLESCENTS
MEAN MMPI PROFILE FOR CONTEMPORARY NORMAL
ADOLESCENTS USING ORIGINAL ADULT NORMS
AND K CORRECTED SCORES
Females: N=136   Age=13

	L	F	K		1 Hs	2 D	3 Hy	4 Pd	5 Mf	6 Pa	7 Pt	8 Sc	9 Ma	Si
Mean	2.9	7.5	11.4		48.8	50.1	50.8	59.0	52.9	57.8	57.4	64.3	64.2	55.5
SD	1.5	4.9	4.4		7.4	8.8	8.1	10.5	9.3	9.9	9.1	12.0	12.2	7.8

94616B-36B

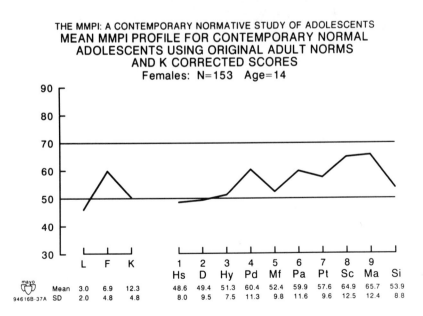

THE MMPI: A CONTEMPORARY NORMATIVE STUDY OF ADOLESCENTS
MEAN MMPI PROFILE FOR CONTEMPORARY NORMAL
ADOLESCENTS USING ORIGINAL ADULT NORMS
AND K CORRECTED SCORES
Females: N=153   Age=14

	L	F	K		1 Hs	2 D	3 Hy	4 Pd	5 Mf	6 Pa	7 Pt	8 Sc	9 Ma	Si
Mean	3.0	6.9	12.3		48.6	49.4	51.3	60.4	52.4	59.9	57.6	64.9	65.7	53.9
SD	2.0	4.8	4.8		8.0	9.5	7.5	11.3	9.8	11.6	9.6	12.5	12.4	8.8

94616B-37A

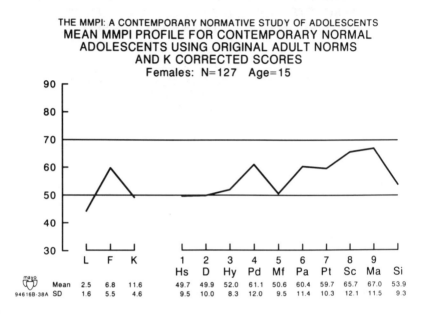

THE MMPI: A CONTEMPORARY NORMATIVE STUDY OF ADOLESCENTS
MEAN MMPI PROFILE FOR CONTEMPORARY NORMAL ADOLESCENTS USING ORIGINAL ADULT NORMS AND K CORRECTED SCORES
Females: N=127   Age=15

	L	F	K	1 Hs	2 D	3 Hy	4 Pd	5 Mf	6 Pa	7 Pt	8 Sc	9 Ma	Si
Mean	2.5	6.8	11.6	49.7	49.9	52.0	61.1	50.6	60.4	59.7	65.7	67.0	53.9
SD	1.6	5.5	4.6	9.5	10.0	8.3	12.0	9.5	11.4	10.3	12.1	11.5	9.3

94616B-38A

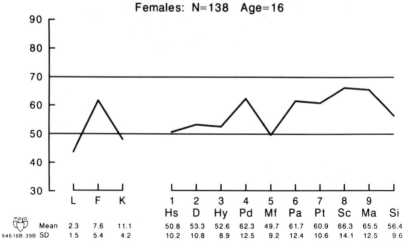

THE MMPI: A CONTEMPORARY NORMATIVE STUDY OF ADOLESCENTS
MEAN MMPI PROFILE FOR CONTEMPORARY NORMAL ADOLESCENTS USING ORIGINAL ADULT NORMS AND K CORRECTED SCORES
Females: N=138   Age=16

	L	F	K	1 Hs	2 D	3 Hy	4 Pd	5 Mf	6 Pa	7 Pt	8 Sc	9 Ma	Si
Mean	2.3	7.6	11.1	50.8	53.3	52.6	62.3	49.7	61.7	60.9	66.3	65.5	56.4
SD	1.5	5.4	4.2	10.2	10.8	8.9	12.5	9.2	12.4	10.6	14.1	12.5	9.6

94616B-39B

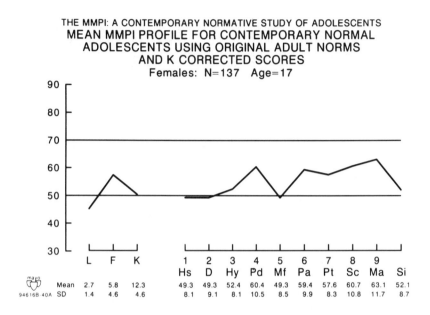

THE MMPI: A CONTEMPORARY NORMATIVE STUDY OF ADOLESCENTS
MEAN MMPI PROFILE FOR CONTEMPORARY NORMAL
ADOLESCENTS USING ORIGINAL ADULT NORMS
AND K CORRECTED SCORES
Females: N=137   Age=17

	L	F	K	1 Hs	2 D	3 Hy	4 Pd	5 Mf	6 Pa	7 Pt	8 Sc	9 Ma	Si
Mean	2.7	5.8	12.3	49.3	49.3	52.4	60.4	49.3	59.4	57.6	60.7	63.1	52.1
SD	1.4	4.6	4.6	8.1	9.1	8.1	10.5	8.5	9.9	8.3	10.8	11.7	8.7

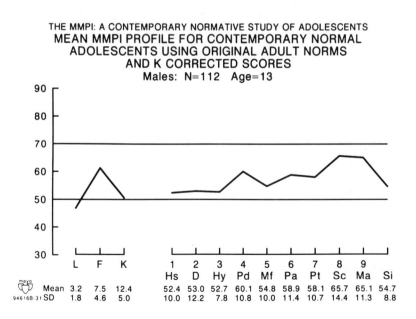

THE MMPI: A CONTEMPORARY NORMATIVE STUDY OF ADOLESCENTS
MEAN MMPI PROFILE FOR CONTEMPORARY NORMAL
ADOLESCENTS USING ORIGINAL ADULT NORMS
AND K CORRECTED SCORES
Males: N=112   Age=13

	L	F	K	1 Hs	2 D	3 Hy	4 Pd	5 Mf	6 Pa	7 Pt	8 Sc	9 Ma	Si
Mean	3.2	7.5	12.4	52.4	53.0	52.7	60.1	54.8	58.9	58.1	65.7	65.1	54.7
SD	1.8	4.6	5.0	10.0	12.2	7.8	10.8	10.0	11.4	10.7	14.4	11.3	8.8

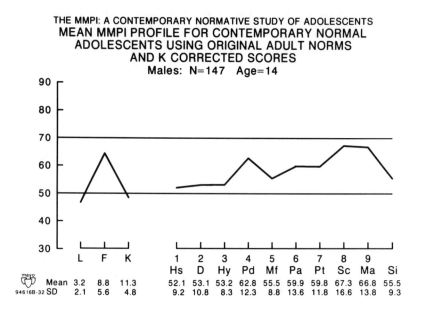

THE MMPI: A CONTEMPORARY NORMATIVE STUDY OF ADOLESCENTS
**MEAN MMPI PROFILE FOR CONTEMPORARY NORMAL
ADOLESCENTS USING ORIGINAL ADULT NORMS
AND K CORRECTED SCORES**
Males: N=147 Age=14

	L	F	K		1 Hs	2 D	3 Hy	4 Pd	5 Mf	6 Pa	7 Pt	8 Sc	9 Ma	Si
Mean	3.2	8.8	11.3		52.1	53.1	53.2	62.8	55.5	59.9	59.8	67.3	66.8	55.5
SD	2.1	5.6	4.8		9.2	10.8	8.3	12.3	8.8	13.6	11.8	16.6	13.8	9.3

946 16B-32

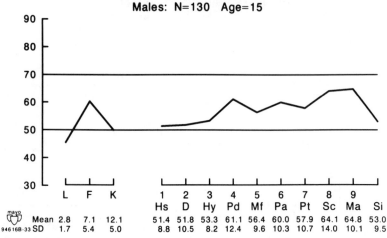

THE MMPI: A CONTEMPORARY NORMATIVE STUDY OF ADOLESCENTS
**MEAN MMPI PROFILE FOR CONTEMPORARY NORMAL
ADOLESCENTS USING ORIGINAL ADULT NORMS
AND K CORRECTED SCORES**
Males: N=130 Age=15

	L	F	K		1 Hs	2 D	3 Hy	4 Pd	5 Mf	6 Pa	7 Pt	8 Sc	9 Ma	Si
Mean	2.8	7.1	12.1		51.4	51.8	53.3	61.1	56.4	60.0	57.9	64.1	64.8	53.0
SD	1.7	5.4	5.0		8.8	10.5	8.2	12.4	9.6	10.3	10.7	14.0	10.1	9.5

946 16B-33

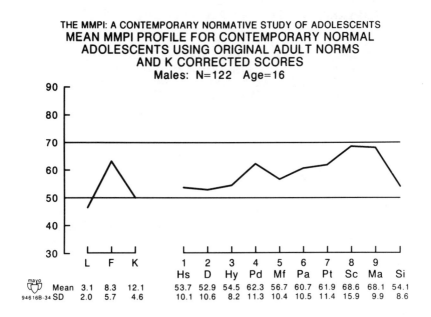

THE MMPI: A CONTEMPORARY NORMATIVE STUDY OF ADOLESCENTS
**MEAN MMPI PROFILE FOR CONTEMPORARY NORMAL
ADOLESCENTS USING ORIGINAL ADULT NORMS
AND K CORRECTED SCORES**
Males: N=122   Age=16

	L	F	K		1 Hs	2 D	3 Hy	4 Pd	5 Mf	6 Pa	7 Pt	8 Sc	9 Ma	Si
Mean	3.1	8.3	12.1		53.7	52.9	54.5	62.3	56.7	60.7	61.9	68.6	68.1	54.1
SD	2.0	5.7	4.6		10.1	10.6	8.2	11.3	10.4	10.5	11.4	15.9	9.9	8.6

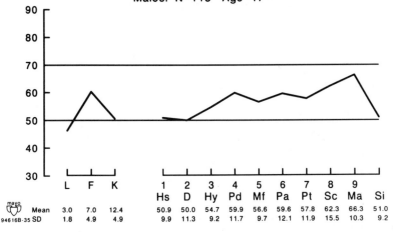

THE MMPI: A CONTEMPORARY NORMATIVE STUDY OF ADOLESCENTS
**MEAN MMPI PROFILE FOR CONTEMPORARY NORMAL
ADOLESCENTS USING ORIGINAL ADULT NORMS
AND K CORRECTED SCORES**
Males: N=113   Age=17

	L	F	K		1 Hs	2 D	3 Hy	4 Pd	5 Mf	6 Pa	7 Pt	8 Sc	9 Ma	Si
Mean	3.0	7.0	12.4		50.9	50.0	54.7	59.9	56.6	59.6	57.8	62.3	66.3	51.0
SD	1.8	4.9	4.9		9.9	11.3	9.2	11.7	9.7	12.1	11.9	15.5	10.3	9.2

MEAN MMPI PROFILES FOR CONTEMPORARY NORMAL ADOLESCENTS SAMPLED BY COLLIGAN AND OFFORD USING MARKS, SEEMAN, AND HALLER ADOLESCENT NORMS

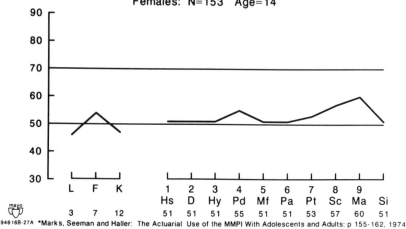

THE MMPI: A CONTEMPORARY NORMATIVE STUDY OF ADOLESCENTS
MEAN MMPI PROFILE FOR CONTEMPORARY NORMAL ADOLESCENTS USING MARKS, SEEMAN AND HALLER* NORMS AND NON-K CORRECTED SCORES
Females: N=136   Age=13

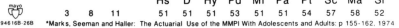

	L	F	K		1 Hs	2 D	3 Hy	4 Pd	5 Mf	6 Pa	7 Pt	8 Sc	9 Ma	Si
	3	8	11		51	51	51	53	51	51	54	57	58	52

94616B-26B   *Marks, Seeman and Haller: The Actuarial Use of the MMPI With Adolescents and Adults: p 155-162, 1974

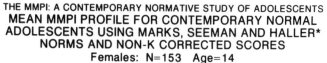

THE MMPI: A CONTEMPORARY NORMATIVE STUDY OF ADOLESCENTS
MEAN MMPI PROFILE FOR CONTEMPORARY NORMAL ADOLESCENTS USING MARKS, SEEMAN AND HALLER* NORMS AND NON-K CORRECTED SCORES
Females: N=153   Age=14

	L	F	K		1 Hs	2 D	3 Hy	4 Pd	5 Mf	6 Pa	7 Pt	8 Sc	9 Ma	Si
	3	7	12		51	51	51	55	51	51	53	57	60	51

94616B-27A *Marks, Seeman and Haller: The Actuarial Use of the MMPI With Adolescents and Adults: p 155-162, 1974

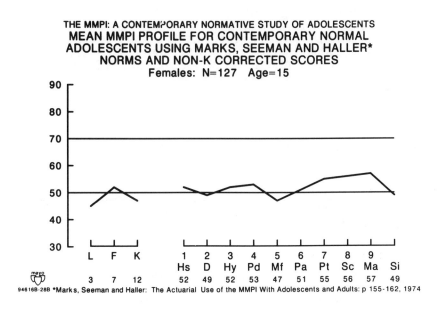

THE MMPI: A CONTEMPORARY NORMATIVE STUDY OF ADOLESCENTS
MEAN MMPI PROFILE FOR CONTEMPORARY NORMAL
ADOLESCENTS USING MARKS, SEEMAN AND HALLER*
NORMS AND NON-K CORRECTED SCORES
Females: N=127   Age=15

	L	F	K		1 Hs	2 D	3 Hy	4 Pd	5 Mf	6 Pa	7 Pt	8 Sc	9 Ma	Si
	3	7	12		52	49	52	53	47	51	55	56	57	49

946168-28B *Marks, Seeman and Haller: The Actuarial Use of the MMPI With Adolescents and Adults: p 155-162, 1974

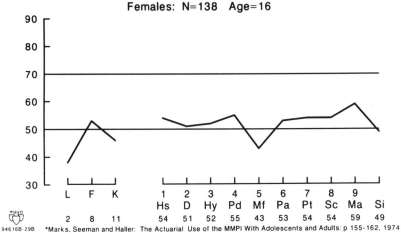

THE MMPI: A CONTEMPORARY NORMATIVE STUDY OF ADOLESCENTS
MEAN MMPI PROFILE FOR CONTEMPORARY NORMAL
ADOLESCENTS USING MARKS, SEEMAN AND HALLER*
NORMS AND NON-K CORRECTED SCORES
Females: N=138   Age=16

	L	F	K		1 Hs	2 D	3 Hy	4 Pd	5 Mf	6 Pa	7 Pt	8 Sc	9 Ma	Si
	2	8	11		54	51	52	55	43	53	54	54	59	49

946168-29B   *Marks, Seeman and Haller: The Actuarial Use of the MMPI With Adolescents and Adults: p 155-162, 1974

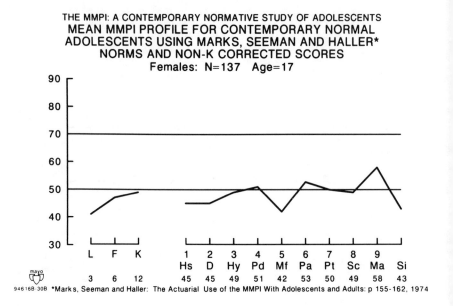

THE MMPI: A CONTEMPORARY NORMATIVE STUDY OF ADOLESCENTS
MEAN MMPI PROFILE FOR CONTEMPORARY NORMAL ADOLESCENTS USING MARKS, SEEMAN AND HALLER* NORMS AND NON-K CORRECTED SCORES
Females: N=137   Age=17

	L	F	K		1 Hs	2 D	3 Hy	4 Pd	5 Mf	6 Pa	7 Pt	8 Sc	9 Ma	Si
	3	6	12		45	45	49	51	42	53	50	49	58	43

94616B-30B *Marks, Seeman and Haller: The Actuarial Use of the MMPI With Adolescents and Adults: p 155-162, 1974

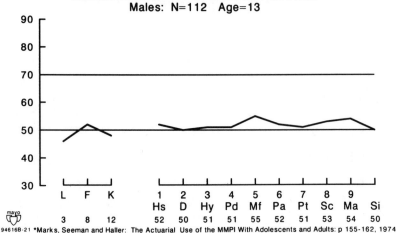

THE MMPI: A CONTEMPORARY NORMATIVE STUDY OF ADOLESCENTS
MEAN MMPI PROFILE FOR CONTEMPORARY NORMAL ADOLESCENTS USING MARKS, SEEMAN AND HALLER* NORMS AND NON-K CORRECTED SCORES
Males: N=112   Age=13

	L	F	K		1 Hs	2 D	3 Hy	4 Pd	5 Mf	6 Pa	7 Pt	8 Sc	9 Ma	Si
	3	8	12		52	50	51	51	55	52	51	53	54	50

94616B-21 *Marks, Seeman and Haller: The Actuarial Use of the MMPI With Adolescents and Adults: p 155-162, 1974

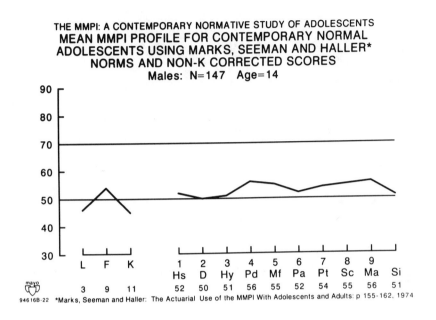

THE MMPI: A CONTEMPORARY NORMATIVE STUDY OF ADOLESCENTS
**MEAN MMPI PROFILE FOR CONTEMPORARY NORMAL
ADOLESCENTS USING MARKS, SEEMAN AND HALLER*
NORMS AND NON-K CORRECTED SCORES**
Males: N=147   Age=14

	L	F	K		Hs	D	Hy	Pd	Mf	Pa	Pt	Sc	Ma	Si
					1	2	3	4	5	6	7	8	9	
	3	9	11		52	50	51	56	55	52	54	55	56	51

94616B-22 *Marks, Seeman and Haller: The Actuarial Use of the MMPI With Adolescents and Adults: p 155-162, 1974

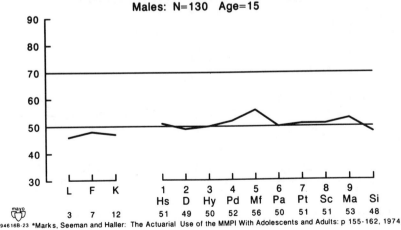

THE MMPI: A CONTEMPORARY NORMATIVE STUDY OF ADOLESCENTS
**MEAN MMPI PROFILE FOR CONTEMPORARY NORMAL
ADOLESCENTS USING MARKS, SEEMAN AND HALLER*
NORMS AND NON-K CORRECTED SCORES**
Males: N=130   Age=15

	L	F	K		Hs	D	Hy	Pd	Mf	Pa	Pt	Sc	Ma	Si
					1	2	3	4	5	6	7	8	9	
	3	7	12		51	49	50	52	56	50	51	51	53	48

94616B-23 *Marks, Seeman and Haller: The Actuarial Use of the MMPI With Adolescents and Adults: p 155-162, 1974

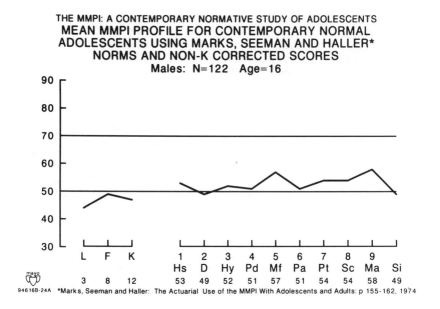

THE MMPI: A CONTEMPORARY NORMATIVE STUDY OF ADOLESCENTS
MEAN MMPI PROFILE FOR CONTEMPORARY NORMAL ADOLESCENTS USING MARKS, SEEMAN AND HALLER* NORMS AND NON-K CORRECTED SCORES
Males: N=122   Age=16

	L	F	K		1 Hs	2 D	3 Hy	4 Pd	5 Mf	6 Pa	7 Pt	8 Sc	9 Ma	Si
	3	8	12		53	49	52	51	57	51	54	54	58	49

94616B-24A *Marks, Seeman and Haller: The Actuarial Use of the MMPI With Adolescents and Adults: p 155-162, 1974

THE MMPI: A CONTEMPORARY NORMATIVE STUDY OF ADOLESCENTS
MEAN MMPI PROFILE FOR CONTEMPORARY NORMAL ADOLESCENTS USING MARKS, SEEMAN AND HALLER* NORMS AND NON-K CORRECTED SCORES
Males: N=113   Age=17

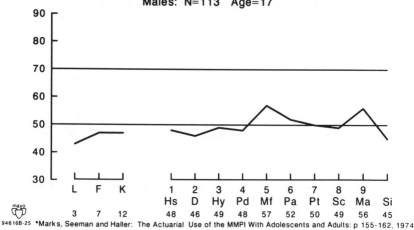

	L	F	K		1 Hs	2 D	3 Hy	4 Pd	5 Mf	6 Pa	7 Pt	8 Sc	9 Ma	Si
	3	7	12		48	46	49	48	57	52	50	49	56	45

94616B-25 *Marks, Seeman and Haller: The Actuarial Use of the MMPI With Adolescents and Adults: p 155-162, 1974

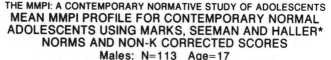

MEAN MMPI PROFILES FOR CONTEMPORARY
NORMAL ADOLESCENTS SAMPLED BY COLLIGAN
AND OFFORD USING NON-*K*-CORRECTED
CONTEMPORARY ADOLESCENT NORMS

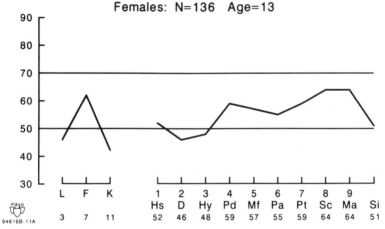

THE MMPI: A CONTEMPORARY NORMATIVE STUDY OF ADOLESCENTS
MEAN MMPI PROFILE FOR CONTEMPORARY NORMAL
ADOLESCENTS USING CONTEMPORARY ADULT NORMS
AND NON-K CORRECTED SCORES
Females: N=136   Age=13

	L	F	K		1 Hs	2 D	3 Hy	4 Pd	5 Mf	6 Pa	7 Pt	8 Sc	9 Ma	Si
	3	7	11		52	46	48	59	57	55	59	64	64	51

94616B-11A

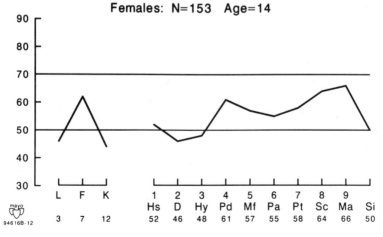

THE MMPI: A CONTEMPORARY NORMATIVE STUDY OF ADOLESCENTS
MEAN MMPI PROFILE FOR CONTEMPORARY NORMAL
ADOLESCENTS USING CONTEMPORARY ADULT NORMS
AND NON-K CORRECTED SCORES
Females: N=153   Age=14

	L	F	K		1 Hs	2 D	3 Hy	4 Pd	5 Mf	6 Pa	7 Pt	8 Sc	9 Ma	Si
	3	7	12		52	46	48	61	57	55	58	64	66	50

94616B-12

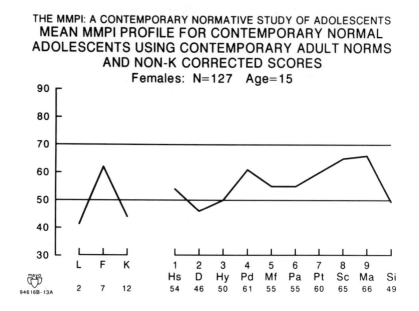

THE MMPI: A CONTEMPORARY NORMATIVE STUDY OF ADOLESCENTS
MEAN MMPI PROFILE FOR CONTEMPORARY NORMAL
ADOLESCENTS USING CONTEMPORARY ADULT NORMS
AND NON-K CORRECTED SCORES
Females: N=127   Age=15

	L	F	K		1 Hs	2 D	3 Hy	4 Pd	5 Mf	6 Pa	7 Pt	8 Sc	9 Ma	Si
	2	7	12		54	46	50	61	55	55	60	65	66	49

94616B-13A

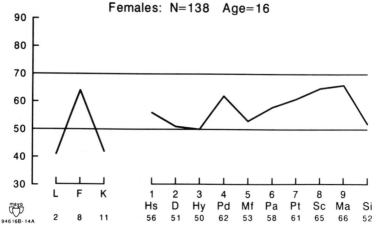

THE MMPI: A CONTEMPORARY NORMATIVE STUDY OF ADOLESCENTS
MEAN MMPI PROFILE FOR CONTEMPORARY NORMAL
ADOLESCENTS USING CONTEMPORARY ADULT NORMS
AND NON-K CORRECTED SCORES
Females: N=138   Age=16

	L	F	K		1 Hs	2 D	3 Hy	4 Pd	5 Mf	6 Pa	7 Pt	8 Sc	9 Ma	Si
	2	8	11		56	51	50	62	53	58	61	65	66	52

94616B-14A

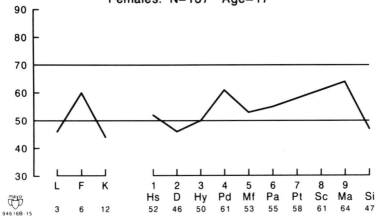

THE MMPI: A CONTEMPORARY NORMATIVE STUDY OF ADOLESCENTS
MEAN MMPI PROFILE FOR CONTEMPORARY NORMAL ADOLESCENTS USING CONTEMPORARY ADULT NORMS AND NON-K CORRECTED SCORES
Females: N=137   Age=17

	L	F	K		1 Hs	2 D	3 Hy	4 Pd	5 Mf	6 Pa	7 Pt	8 Sc	9 Ma	Si
	3	6	12		52	46	50	61	53	55	58	61	64	47

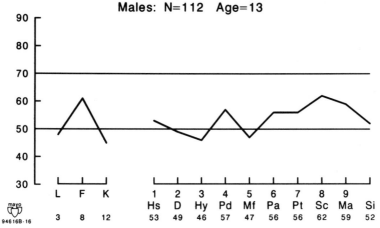

THE MMPI: A CONTEMPORARY NORMATIVE STUDY OF ADOLESCENTS
MEAN MMPI PROFILE FOR CONTEMPORARY NORMAL ADOLESCENTS USING CONTEMPORARY ADULT NORMS AND NON-K CORRECTED SCORES
Males: N=112   Age=13

	L	F	K		1 Hs	2 D	3 Hy	4 Pd	5 Mf	6 Pa	7 Pt	8 Sc	9 Ma	Si
	3	8	12		53	49	46	57	47	56	56	62	59	52

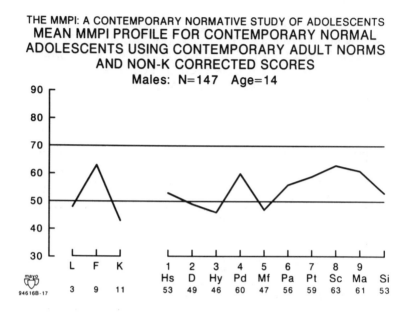

THE MMPI: A CONTEMPORARY NORMATIVE STUDY OF ADOLESCENTS
MEAN MMPI PROFILE FOR CONTEMPORARY NORMAL
ADOLESCENTS USING CONTEMPORARY ADULT NORMS
AND NON-K CORRECTED SCORES
Males: N=147 Age=14

	L	F	K		1 Hs	2 D	3 Hy	4 Pd	5 Mf	6 Pa	7 Pt	8 Sc	9 Ma	Si
	3	9	11		53	49	46	60	47	56	59	63	61	53

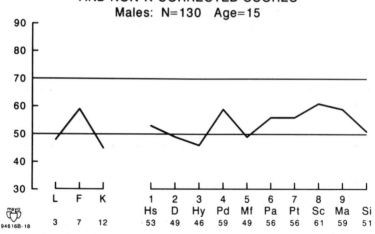

THE MMPI: A CONTEMPORARY NORMATIVE STUDY OF ADOLESCENTS
MEAN MMPI PROFILE FOR CONTEMPORARY NORMAL
ADOLESCENTS USING CONTEMPORARY ADULT NORMS
AND NON-K CORRECTED SCORES
Males: N=130 Age=15

	L	F	K		1 Hs	2 D	3 Hy	4 Pd	5 Mf	6 Pa	7 Pt	8 Sc	9 Ma	Si
	3	7	12		53	49	46	59	49	56	56	61	59	51

THE MMPI: A CONTEMPORARY NORMATIVE STUDY OF ADOLESCENTS
MEAN MMPI PROFILE FOR CONTEMPORARY NORMAL ADOLESCENTS USING CONTEMPORARY ADULT NORMS AND NON-K CORRECTED SCORES
Males: N=122 Age=16

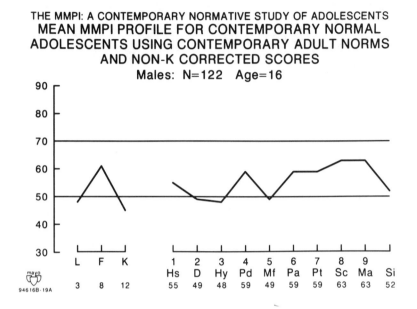

	L	F	K		1 Hs	2 D	3 Hy	4 Pd	5 Mf	6 Pa	7 Pt	8 Sc	9 Ma	Si
	3	8	12		55	49	48	59	49	59	59	63	63	52

mayo
94616B-19A

THE MMPI: A CONTEMPORARY NORMATIVE STUDY OF ADOLESCENTS
MEAN MMPI PROFILE FOR CONTEMPORARY NORMAL ADOLESCENTS USING CONTEMPORARY ADULT NORMS AND NON-K CORRECTED SCORES
Males: N=113 Age=17

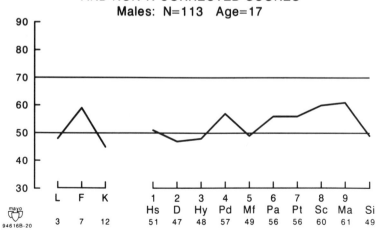

	L	F	K		1 Hs	2 D	3 Hy	4 Pd	5 Mf	6 Pa	7 Pt	8 Sc	9 Ma	Si
	3	7	12		51	47	48	57	49	56	56	60	61	49

mayo
94616B-20

NEW MMPI NORMATIVE DATA AND POWER-TRANSFORMED *T*-SCORE TABLES FOR THE HATHAWAY-MONACHESI MINNESOTA COHORT OF 14,019 15-YEAR-OLDS AND 3,674 18-YEAR-OLDS

Irving I. Gottesman
University of Virginia

Daniel R. Hanson
University of Minnesota School of Medicine

Tamara A. Kroeker
Washington University School of Medicine

Peter F. Briggs
San Diego, California

Up to the present time no truly normative and representative MMPI data exist for large samples of adolescents. At the time that Hathaway and Monachesi (1953, 1961, 1963) were conducting their research program into adolescent personality and behavior, high speed, large capacity computers were not readily available to them. From the data archives bequeathed to us (P.F.B. & I.I.G.) by Starke R. Hathaway, we have constructed new computer tapes at the item level for the combined "Minneapolis" and "statewide" samples of 15,300 ninth-grade children tested between 1948 and 1954. We also constructed a data tape for a large subset of adolescents from the statewide sample who were retested when they were in the 12th grade during the 1956–57 school year (3,856 students).

THE NEW NORMATIVE ADOLESCENT SAMPLE

The two large samples of ninth graders are essentially unselected in regard to mental health or mental illness. In the spring of 1948 the MMPI was administered to 3,971 of the 4,572 ninth graders registered in the entire Minneapolis public high school system. After scheduling to accommodate students who were ill or absent, 87% of the entire cohort had been tested. In the spring of 1954, 11,329 additional ninth graders were tested. They came from 90 public schools and 2 parochial schools distributed in 47 of Minnesota's 87 counties. The sample is composed of 36% of all public school ninth graders outside the immediate Twin Cities area of Minneapolis and St. Paul.

Tables 1 through 4 describe the sample composition by urban versus nonurban residence and by age and sex. Urban was defined as Minneapolis, St. Paul, and the suburbs within a 30-mile radius, the cities of Duluth, Rochester, St. Cloud, Austin, Mankato, and Hibbing. According to the 1950 United States census all of these areas had populations greater than 16,000. Children residing on farms or in villages with a total population less than 1,000 were classified here as farm and/or village. The remaining town sample was composed of children from communities with populations between 1,000 and 14,000. For the 18-year-olds we did not have a sufficient sample size to separate the town and farm children.

It was clear to us from studying the actual distribution of ages within the sample that many children were too old for their grade placement. Recall that Hathaway and Monachesi were sampling grades and not ages, whereas our goal is to provide the age-based normative data. We had reason to believe that a 17- or 18-year-old adolescent still in the ninth grade would not be very representative of ninth graders and did not belong in normative data characterized as "15-year-olds."

Tables 5 and 6 show the loss from the sample that led to the "clean" samples described in the first four tables and that provide the actual MMPIs analyzed for the age norms to follow. Our exclusion criteria for L or LIE ($> = 10$) and Cannot Say (?) ($> = 40$) were the same as those utilized by Hathaway and Monachesi. (We did include 41 fifteen-year-olds and 3 eighteen-year-olds who had omitted between 40 and 99 items when we observed that they had been omitted at the end of the 566-item test.) Our exclusion criterion for the F scale was less restrictive than that used (Hathaway & Monachesi, 1963) earlier ($F > = 16$). We excluded protocols where F was greater than or equal to 23 items. In work as yet unpublished involving a follow-up study of the entire cohort for adult psychopathology, we had observed that psychiatrically disturbed adults followed back to their ninth-grade MMPIs had F scores between 15 and 23 and had produced adult MMPIs often consistent with their earlier elevated profiles. We regretted having to exclude 1,066 fifteen-year-olds and 182 eighteen-year-olds from our data set but believed that we would remove more noise than signal from the normative data by doing so. Notice that the age exclusion cutoffs of 16.5 years for the 15-year-olds and 19.5 years for the 18-year-olds resulted in samples with average ages of almost exactly 15 and 18 respectively with very small standard deviations.

In Table 7 we provide the mean and standard deviation for the raw scores on the standard clinical scales and the validity scales by sex and along the rural-urban gradient. We do not have the space to provide T-score look-up tables by rural-urban status but the data in such tables provide food for thought. Notice, for example, an almost half-standard deviation difference on the Social Introversion scale as one moves from urban male to farm male. Such differences should lend themselves to clinical interpretation when evaluating adolescents who may have been reared in vastly different environments along a rural-urban gradient. In Table 7a are provided the K-corrected scores for those clinicians wishing to try out K-corrected scores for adolescents. Hathaway and Monachesi routinely used the same kind of K-correction as had been used with adults. Marks, Seeman, and Haller (1974) routinely avoid the use of any kind of K-correction with adolescent MMPIs. Empirical research on these kinds of questions has been hampered by the absence of a choice of scores to use.

Tables 8 and 8A permit a ready comparison among the raw scores for our new sample of 15-year-old adolescents by sex (6,871 boys and 7,148 girls) with those already in the literature by Marks et al. (1974) and the original Minnesota adult normative population studied by Hathaway and Briggs (1957) and reported at length in Dahlstrom, Welsh, and Dahlstrom (1972). Tables 9, 9A, 10, and 10A do the same thing for 18-year-olds.

The remaining data tables present useful means and standard deviations for some regularly used MMPI scales including Welsh's *A* and *R*, Kanun and Monachesi's (1960) Delinquency scales for males and females, and the 68-item length version of Barron's Ego-strength scale and the 49-item version of MacAndrew's Alcoholism scale plotted on contemporary profile sheets. See scales numbered 309 and 310 in Volume II of Dahlstrom et al. (1975) for the 56-item and 86-item versions of the Delinquency scales we used. We table the descriptive statistics for the scales derived by Albert Rosen (1962) in the hope that they may stimulate research on these uniquely derived scales. Rosen intended that they be used for differential diagnosis within a general *abnormal* population of psychiatric inpatients. His abnormal criterion groups were diagnosed as somatization reaction, anxiety reaction, conversion reaction, paranoid schizophrenia, and depressive reaction. The translation of these categories into DSM-III terms can be attempted in a straightforward fashion. We also table the descriptive statistics for the very useful content scales derived by Jerry Wiggins (1966, 1969). Neither the Wiggins scales nor the Rosen scales have been utilized extensively with adolescents but their availability with appropriate normative values may stimulate such research. In the look-up tables we provide, in addition to the scales already described here, *T*-scores on the Wiener-Harmon Subtle and Obvious scales (Wiener, 1948).

POWER-TRANFORMED T-SCORES
FOR ADOLESCENT MMPIs

The look-up tables that follow permit the direct and practical application of the vast amount of raw data collected on these uniquely large samples of 15- and 18-year-old adolescents. They are different in a fundamental fashion from the *T*-scores available in the Dahlstrom et al. handbooks. Following the observations and suggestions of Colligan, Osborne, Swenson, and Offord (1983) we have imposed a raw score transformation that will yield values having as normal as possible a distribution, one that permits the calculation of *T*-scores greater than 3 standard deviations above the mean of a normative population. Linear transformations that make use of percentile ranks derived from the raw scores provide an unsatisfactory solution to the problems encountered when evaluating adolescents in a clinical or psychiatric setting. Like Colligan et al. we did use a Box-Cox (1964) power transformation. However, we used a more optimal procedure for parameter estimation for which software was available. The method chosen for finding an optimum skewness-reducing power was a Fortran program called ADMIX, which has a power transform option. The program was made available to us by Jonathan Goldberg of the Department of Psychiatry at Washington University

School of Medicine in St. Louis. ADMIX is an extension of the already-documented GEMINI program (Morton, Rao, & Lalouel, 1982, pp. 236–252). The latter program optimizes a nonlinear function subject to parameter constraints using a maximum likelihood concept. Unlike the Box-Cox procedure, the GEMINI program is not constrained to integer values for the powers and therefore is an improvement over that technique.

Input for the program consists of raw scores on the MMPI scales, which have been converted to Z-scores, and values for the mean and variance of 0 and 1, respectively. During execution of the program, mean, variance, and power parameters are iterated until a "peak" is reached on the likelihood surface located within specified tolerance given differential stepsize. The power transform process "pulls" the data around a fixed point until the distribution most closely resembles a Gaussian or normal one. The sample mean and standard deviation will shift slightly during the normalization process.

The following look-up tables provide T-scores based on the optimum power transformations for our samples. Dashes represent negative values yielding negative bases raised to a power. Such raw score values are undefined given the sample and should be ignored. One important way to evaluate the success of the transformation is to compare the percentage of the population in the extreme tails of the distribution before and after the transformation has taken place. In the best of all worlds, we would expect 2.5% of the population to be above a T-score of 70 and a similar proportion to be below a T-score of 30. Looking at our 15-year-old sample of males, on the Schizophrenia scale, we found that 0% were below a T-score of 30 and 3.6% were above a T-score of 70 before the transformation process. From our tabled values using the power transformation we found 1.5% of the population under T-score 30 and 2.2% above T-score 70. Further details of the procedure and some of the findings with regard to removing skewness and getting a better fit to a normal distribution can be obtained from the authors.

Psychologists comparing our new normative data with those already available from Marks et al. should be cautioned that no exclusion criteria were applied to the Marks et al. profile collection. Furthermore, a large proportion (40%) of the adolsecent males and females for the Marks et al. norms were provided by one of us (PFB) in an unsystematic manner from the entire Hathaway-Monachesi cohort before any of the profiles were excluded for any reason including age, F, L, and omitted items.

ACKNOWLEDGMENTS

The preparation and presentation of the information in this appendix have required a tremendous expenditure of time and effort by ourselves and various computer centers. We acknowledge support from USPHS grants MH31302 and AA03539 to Washington University School of Medicine, from the John D. and Catherine T. MacArthur Foundation to the Washington University Node of the Network on Risk and Protective Factors in Major Mental Illness (Norman Garmezy, Director), from generous grants in aid from the University of Minnesota Computer Center and from the Washington University Computer Center. We owe debts of gratitude for the technical expertise of Andrew J. Pakstis, Jonathan Goldberg, and Gregory Carey. Encouragement on our long journey was received from Kevin L. Moreland and Robert P. Archer. Finally, we thank Mary Ellen Peters, Lisabeth Fisher DiLalla, David DiLalla, and Debbie Mundie for their contributions to the final product.

REFERENCES

Box, G. E. P., & Cox, D. R. (1964). An analysis of transformations. *Journal of the Royal Statistical Society, Series B, 26,* 211–243.

Colligan, R. C., Osborne, D., Swenson, W. M., & Offord, K. P. (1983). *The MMPI: A comparative study.* New York: Praeger.

Dahlstrom, W. G., Welsh, G. S., & Dahlstrom, L. E. (1972). *An MMPI handbook: Vol. I. Clinical interpretation.* Minneapolis: University of Minnesota Press.

Dahlstrom, W. G., Welsh, G. S., & Dahlstrom, L. E. (1975). *An MMPI handbook: Vol. II. Research application.* Minneapolis: University of Minnesota Press.

Hathaway, S. R., & Briggs, P. F. (1957). Some normative data on new MMPI scales. *Journal of Clinical Psychology, 13,* 364–368.

Hathaway, S. R., & Monachesi, E. D. (1953). *Analyzing and predicting juvenile delinquency with the MMPI.* Minneapolis: University of Minnesota Press.

Hathaway, S. R., & Monachesi, E. D. (1961). *An atlas of juvenile MMPI profiles.* Minneapolis: University of Minnesota Press.

Hathaway, S.R., & Monachesi, E. D. (1963). *Adolescent personality and behavior: MMPI patterns of normal, delinquent, dropout, and other outcomes.* Minneapolis: University of Minnesota Press.

Kanun, C., & Monachesi, E. D. (1960). Delinquency and the validating scales of the MMPI. *Journal of Criminal Law and Criminology, 50,* 525–534.

Marks, P.A., Seeman, W., & Haller, D. L. (1974). *The actuarial use of the MMPI with adolescents and adults.* Baltimore: Williams & Wilkins.

Morton, N. E., Rao, D. C., & Lalouel, J. M. (1982). *Methods in genetic epidemiology.* Basel: Karger.

Rosen, A. (1962). Development of the MMPI scales based on a reference group of psychiatric patients. *Psychological Monographs, 76* (8, whole no. 527).

Wiener, D. N. (1948). Subtle and obvious keys for the MMPI. *Journal of Consulting Psychology, 12,* 164–170.

Wiggins, J. S. (1966). Substantive dimensions of self-report in the MMPI item pool. *Psychological Monographs, 80* (22, whole no. 630).

Wiggins, J. S. (1969). Content dimensions in the MMPI. In J. N. Butcher (Ed.), *MMPI: Research developments and clinical applications* (pp. 127–180). New York: McGraw-Hill.

TABLES 1 THROUGH 6: LOCATION, SEX, AND
EXCLUSION TABLES FOR THE MINNESOTA SAMPLES

TABLE 1
"Fifteen" Year Old Normative Sample by Location and Place

Location	Male	Female
Urban	4010	4169
Town	1066	1108
Farm/Village	1795	1871
Total	6871	7148

TABLE 2
Mean Ages by Location and Sex

Location	Male		Female	
	M	SD	M	SD
Urban	15.12	(.60)	14.98	(.55)
Town	15.05	(.61)	14.91	(.55)
Farm/Village	15.00	(.61)	14.89	(.55)
Total	15.08	(.61)	14.94	(.55)

TABLE 3
"Eighteen" Year Old Normative Sample by Location and Sex

Location	Male	Female
Urban	745	803
Town/Farm	1065	1061
Total	1810	1864

TABLE 4
Mean Ages by Location and Sex

Location	Male		Female	
	M	SD	M	SD
Urban	18.06	(.57)	17.94	(.53)
Town/Farm	17.96	(.57)	17.87	(.53)
Total	18.00	(.57)	17.90	(.53)

TABLE 5
Samples Excluded from Norms by Reasons: Fifteen Year Olds

Reason		Urban	Town	Farm	Total
$F \geq 23$	Males	64	22	64	150
	Females	17	6	6	29
$L \geq 10$	Males	78	16	54	148
	Females	60	10	46	116
$? \geq 40$	Males	160	36	57	253
	Females	126	25	57	208
Age > 16.5	Males	112	12	16	140
	Females	53	7	6	66
Total, Any Reason	Males	394	80	186	660
	Females	246	47	113	406
	Total	640	127	299	1066

TABLE 6
Samples Excluded from Norms by Reasons: Eighteen Year Olds

Reason		Urban	Other	Total
F ≥ 23	Males	2	8	10
	Females	0	0	0
L ≥ 10	Males	4	17	21
	Females	2	8	10
? ≥ 40	Males	23	46	69
	Females	24	34	58
Age > 19.5	Males	3	7	10
	Females	1	4	5
Total, Any Reason	Males	32	77	109
	Females	27	46	73
	Total	59	123	182

TABLE 7
15 Year Olds: MMPI Clinical Scales, Raw Scores Uncorrected

	L	F	K	1	2	3	4	5	6	7	8	9	0
URBAN													
Males													
M	3.58	6.43	13.66	5.08	17.55	17.72	17.87	21.21	9.65	13.15	14.77	17.97	27.67
SD	2.01	4.38	4.57	3.29	4.16	4.30	4.51	4.45	3.42	6.97	8.25	4.83	7.68
Females													
M	3.68	5.25	13.76	5.17	18.75	19.50	17.22	35.15	9.77	14.82	14.49	16.98	27.69
SD	2.01	3.80	4.53	3.67	4.30	4.49	4.61	4.37	3.44	7.34	8.50	4.85	7.93
TOWN													
Males													
M	3.50	6.75	13.21	5.22	17.28	17.42	17.55	21.24	10.18	14.17	15.62	18.16	28.27
SD	2.06	4.58	4.70	3.39	4.19	4.31	4.38	4.57	3.43	7.29	8.72	4.87	7.79
Females													
M	3.58	5.43	13.54	5.60	18.73	19.84	17.41	35.08	10.09	15.70	15.41	16.89	28.26
SD	2.02	4.07	4.64	3.90	4.58	4.75	4.67	4.56	3.40	7.53	8.69	4.66	8.14
FARM/VILLAGE													
Males													
M	4.02	7.35	13.24	5.53	17.77	17.46	17.12	20.96	10.38	14.28	16.03	17.51	30.04
SD	2.09	4.80	4.54	3.63	4.28	4.56	4.27	4.31	3.63	7.04	8.84	4.61	7.44
Females													
M	4.03	5.93	13.30	5.73	18.76	19.33	16.65	34.41	10.16	15.42	15.58	16.28	29.80
SD	2.09	4.20	4.57	3.98	4.51	4.65	4.49	4.53	3.48	7.44	8.99	4.91	7.75

TABLES 7 THROUGH 10A: 15- AND 18-YEAR-OLDS' MMPI RAW SCORE VALUES FOR BASIC SCALES

TABLE 7A
15 Year Olds: MMPI Clinical Scales, Raw Scores *K*-Corrected

	1	4	7	8	9
URBAN					
Males					
M	12.16	23.33	26.81	28.43	20.70
SD	3.37	4.48	4.96	6.37	4.47
Females					
M	12.30	22.72	28.58	28.25	19.74
SD	3.54	4.40	5.05	6.34	4.50
TOWN					
Males					
M	12.08	22.83	27.37	28.83	20.80
SD	3.42	4.36	5.00	6.60	4.49
Females					
M	12.63	22.84	29.25	28.95	19.60
SD	3.73	4.50	5.17	6.36	4.31
FARM/VILLAGE					
Males					
M	12.40	22.41	27.52	29.27	20.15
SD	3.82	4.35	5.25	7.27	4.29
Females					
M	12.62	21.97	28.72	28.88	18.94
SD	3.86	4.42	5.17	6.85	4.56

TABLE 8
Total Sample New Norms (Age 15) Vs. Marks (Age 15) Vs. Minnesota Adults

		L	F	K	1	2	3	4	5	6	7	8	9	0
MALES														
New norms	M	3.68	6.72	13.48	5.22	17.56	17.60	17.62	21.15	9.92	13.60	15.23	17.88	28.38
(n = 6,871)	SD	2.05	4.54	4.58	3.40	4.20	4.37	4.44	4.43	3.50	7.06	8.50	4.79	7.70
Marks	M	3.9	8.1	13.4	5.7	18.3	17.8	18.3	21.3	11.0	14.5	16.9	18.4	29.2
(n = 265)	SD	2.33	5.97	4.77	4.26	4.41	4.87	4.67	4.79	4.78	7.04	10.00	5.23	7.44
Adults	M	4.05	3.88	13.45	4.53	16.63	16.49	13.99	20.44	8.06	9.86	9.57	14.51	25.00
(n = 294)	SD	2.89	4.24	5.66	4.37	4.18	5.51	3.93	5.13	3.56	7.19	7.43	4.42	9.58
FEMALES														
New norms	M	3.76	5.45	13.61	5.38	18.75	19.51	17.10	34.94	9.92	15.11	14.92	16.78	28.33
(n = 7,148)	SD	2.04	3.96	4.56	3.80	4.40	4.57	4.59	4.45	3.45	7.41	8.68	4.84	7.97
Marks	M	4.2	6.1	13.4	5.9	19.2	20.1	17.7	34.3	10.5	15.4	15.6	17.0	28.8
(n = 277)	SD	2.32	4.40	4.60	4.47	4.63	4.87	4.77	4.86	4.57	7.40	9.31	5.37	7.75
Adults	M	4.27	3.49	12.08	6.86	19.26	18.80	13.44	36.51	7.98	13.06	10.73	13.65	25.00
(n = 397)	SD	2.63	3.13	5.07	5.28	5.18	5.66	4.23	4.83	3.32	7.78	7.96	4.50	9.58

TABLE 8A
Total Sample New Norms (Age 15) Vs.
Minnesota Adults, Raw Scores K-Corrected

		1	4	7	8	9
MALES						
New Norms	M	12.21	23.01	27.08	28.71	20.57
(n = 6,871)	SD	3.50	4.44	5.05	6.66	4.43
Adults	M	11.34	19.30	22.95	22.26	17.00
(n = 294)	SD	3.90	4.11	4.88	5.21	3.87
FEMALES						
New Norms	M	12.43	22.55	28.72	28.52	19.51
(n = 7,148)	SD	3.66	4.43	5.11	6.49	4.50
Adults	M	13.14	18.41	25.21	22.65	16.12
(n = 397)	SD	4.88	4.40	6.06	6.50	4.11

TABLE 9
18 Year Olds: MMPI Clinical Scales, Raw Scores Uncorrected

	L	F	K	1	2	3	4	5	6	7	8	9	10
URBAN													
Males													
M	3.02	4.93	15.25	4.35	17.30	19.44	16.85	21.63	9.93	11.53	11.66	17.22	24.42
SD	1.86	3.56	4.52	2.96	3.71	4.09	4.24	4.60	2.76	6.49	7.16	4.55	8.16
Females													
M	3.20	4.14	15.31	4.52	18.83	20.91	16.11	35.86	10.02	13.07	11.45	16.44	25.56
SD	1.82	2.94	4.47	.06	4.13	4.05	4.19	4.13	3.11	6.72	7.22	4.41	8.32
OTHER													
Males													
M	3.40	5.39	4.90	4.33	17.13	18.45	16.64	21.24	10.02	11.85	11.86	16.63	26.12
SD	2.07	3.81	4.82	2.90	3.89	4.05	4.01	4.72	3.11	6.72	7.22	4.44	8.19
Females													
M	3.53	4.35	14.85	4.86	18.83	20.57	15.09	35.25	10.01	13.67	12.14	15.62	27.47
SD	2.04	3.11	4.61	3.55	4.28	4.45	4.17	4.28	3.17	6.99	7.31	4.45	8.65

TABLE 9A
18 Year Olds: MMPI Clinical Scales, Raw Scores K-Corrected

	1	4	7	8	9
URBAN					
Males					
M	12.23	22.94	26.78	26.91	20.26
SD	3.03	4.33	4.44	5.45	4.23
Females					
M	12.41	22.23	28.37	26.75	19.49
SD	3.07	4.08	4.69	5.29	4.14
OTHER					
Males					
M	12.05	22.59	26.74	26.75	19.62
SD	3.02	4.17	4.53	5.49	4.10
Females					
M	12.52	22.04	28.52	26.99	18.61
SD	3.38	4.16	4.79	5.43	4.18

TABLE 10
Total Sample New Norms (Age 18) Vs. Marks (Age 17) Vs. Minnesota Adults

		L	F	K	1	2	3	4	5	6	7	8	9	10
MALES														
New norms	M	3.24	5.20	15.04	4.34	17.20	18.86	16.72	21.40	9.99	11.72	11.78	16.88	25.42
(n = 1,810)	SD	2.00	3.72	4.70	2.92	3.81	4.09	4.11	4.68	2.97	6.62	7.19	4.49	8.22
Marks	M	4.80	8.2	13.5	5.9	19.1	19.3	18.9	20.8	10.4	14.9	17.8	18.1	28.9
(n = 166)	SD	2.40	4.60	4.54	3.99	5.51	5.26	4.36	4.59	3.39	6.48	9.11	4.70	6.63
Adults	M	4.05	3.88	13.45	4.53	16.63	16.49	13.99	20.44	8.06	9.86	9.57	14.51	25.00
(n = 294)	SD	2.89	4.24	5.66	4.37	4.18	5.51	3.93	5.13	3.56	7.19	7.43	4.42	9.58
FEMALES														
New norms	M	3.39	4.26	15.05	4.71	18.33	20.71	16.10	35.51	10.01	13.41	11.84	15.97	26.65
(n = 1,864)	SD	1.95	3.04	4.55	3.35	4.21	4.28	4.18	4.22	3.09	6.95	7.23	4.45	8.56
Marks	M	5.1	7.2	12.6	8.0	21.2	21.4	18.4	33.5	10.1	16.8	17.6	16.2	32.0
(n = 139)	SD	2.41	4.06	3.98	4.37	4.66	5.02	4.33	4.46	3.46	6.89	8.77	4.63	7.49
Adults	M	4.27	3.49	12.08	6.86	19.26	18.80	13.44	36.51	7.98	13.06	10.73	13.65	25.00
(n = 397)	SD	2.63	3.13	5.07	5.28	5.18	5.66	4.23	4.83	3.32	7.78	7.96	4.50	9.58

TABLE 10A
Total Sample New Norms (Age 18) Vs. Minnesota Adults, Raw Scores *K*-Corrected

		1	4	7	8	9
MALES						
New Norms	M	12.12	22.74	26.76	26.82	19.88
(*n* = 1,810)	SD	3.02	4.24	4.49	5.49	4.17
Adults	M	11.34	19.30	22.95	22.26	17.00
(*n* = 294)	SD	3.90	4.11	4.88	5.21	3.87
FEMALES						
New Norms	M	12.48	22.12	28.46	26.89	18.98
(*n* = 1,864)	SD	3.25	4.13	4.75	5.37	4.18
Adults	M	13.14	18.41	25.21	22.65	16.12
(*n* = 397)	SD	4.88	4.40	6.06	6.50	4.11

TABLES 7 THROUGH 10A: FIFTEEN AND 18-YEAR-OLDS' MMPI RAW SCORE VALUES FOR SPECIAL SCALES

TABLE 11
15-Year-Olds: Supplementary and Rosen Scales

	A	R	Es	DelM	DelF	Alc	SM	AR	CR	PZ	DR
URBAN											
Males											
M	12.27	11.63	45.92	22.99		23.63	22.75	20.12	50.98	13.52	21.79
SD	6.97	3.76	5.33	4.41		4.10	3.95	3.03	7.93	5.91	3.27
Females											
M	13.75	11.35	42.85		36.40	21.08	22.30	21.69	49.32	13.17	22.23
SD	7.26	3.45	5.47		9.84	3.66	4.09	3.13	8.26	5.64	3.11
TOWN											
Males											
M	13.05	11.46	45.25	23.23		23.79	22.79	20.34	50.15	14.56	21.98
SD	7.23	3.74	5.52	4.40		3.88	4.02	2.99	8.27	6.17	3.14
Females											
M	14.64	11.43	42.44		37.07	21.42	21.91	22.10	48.27	13.92	22.39
SD	7.31	3.30	5.54		9.66	3.62	4.14	3.12	8.43	6.02	2.98
FARM/VILLAGE											
Males											
M	13.31	12.15	44.25	22.58		22.84	23.02	20.46	49.74	15.51	22.07
SD	7.08	3.86	5.86	4.44		3.85	4.04	3.07	8.11	6.41	3.10
Females											
M	14.60	11.92	14.41		36.51	21.11	22.49	22.15	48.58	14.77	22.36
SD	7.35	3.50	5.62		9.68	3.63	4.16	3.21	8.46	6.33	3.03

TABLE 12
15-Year-Olds: Wiggins Content Scales

	SOC	DEP	FEM	MOR	REL	AUT	PSY	ORG	FAM	HOS	PHO	HYS	HEA
URBAN													
Males													
M	9.54	7.50	7.62	7.64	7.23	10.09	8.83	5.45	4.47	10.76	5.72	13.40	4.98
SD	4.45	4.59	3.22	3.96	2.49	3.92	5.56	3.84	2.75	4.50	3.31	3.80	2.76
Females													
M	8.73	8.35	19.90	8.75	7.95	7.58	9.31	5.50	4.97	9.19	8.65	13.82	4.69
SD	4.57	4.92	3.50	4.12	2.28	3.70	5.53	3.98	3.10	4.35	4.03	3.56	2.77
TOWN													
Males													
M	9.75	8.13	7.71	8.12	8.08	9.74	9.90	5.81	4.43	11.29	6.17	13.66	5.10
SD	4.42	4.87	3.44	4.06	2.19	3.79	5.74	4.11	2.62	4.68	3.44	3.80	2.92
Females													
M	9.00	8.95	19.85	9.12	8.76	7.22	10.03	5.96	4.88	9.55	9.37	14.09	4.93
SD	4.54	5.14	3.59	4.14	1.98	3.69	5.66	4.25	2.99	4.45	4.23	3.67	2.97
FARM/VILLAGE													
Males													
M	10.80	8.37	7.98	8.26	7.86	9.48	10.46	6.48	4.22	11.07	6.94	13.24	5.52
SD	4.26	4.73	3.41	3.94	2.39	3.60	5.86	4.43	2.65	4.49	3.69	3.81	3.11
Females													
M	10.17	8.86	19.70	9.29	8.65	7.45	10.66	6.32	4.50	9.52	9.81	13.72	5.11
SD	4.57	5.09	3.52	4.05	2.12	3.57	6.05	4.39	2.93	4.29	4.24	3.72	3.19

TABLE 13
18-Year-Olds: Supplementary and Rosen Scales

	A	R	Es	DelM	DelF	Alc	SM	AR	CR	PZ	DR
URBAN											
Males											
M	10.04	11.62	49.02	22.64		23.26	22.97	20.04	53.19	10.89	22.55
SD	6.77	3.70	4.94	4.08		4.02	3.62	2.92	7.53	4.93	3.16
Females											
M	11.33	11.72	46.36		33.87	20.37	22.45	21.97	51.70	10.67	23.26
SD	7.16	3.25	5.16		8.87	3.36	3.81	3.16	7.78	4.49	3.04
OTHER											
Males											
M	10.63	11.98	48.32	22.03		22.99	23.34	20.42	52.98	11.59	22.73
SD	6.99	3.68	5.28	4.02		4.01	3.80	3.01	7.63	5.18	3.10
Females											
M	12.30	12.24	44.98		33.93	20.47	22.81	22.46	50.98	11.82	23.22
SD	7.28	3.25	5.48		9.08	3.62	3.94	3.01	8.28	5.02	2.96

TABLE 14
18-Year-Olds: Wiggins Content Scales

	SOC	DEP	FEM	MOR	REL	AUT	PSY	ORG	FAM	HOS	PHO	HYS	HEA
URBAN													
Males													
M	8.08	6.31	7.08	6.37	7.04	9.26	6.74	4.29	4.06	9.19	4.57	12.56	4.23
SD	4.87	4.46	3.09	3.99	2.52	3.99	4.47	3.47	2.70	4.41	3.04	3.71	2.43
Females													
M	7.82	7.25	19.46	7.54	7.86	6.40	6.96	4.34	4.49	7.81	7.87	13.24	4.03
SD	4.76	4.70	3.32	4.09	2.22	3.40	4.42	3.35	2.87	4.05	3.90	3.56	2.55
OTHER													
Males													
M	8.97	6.65	7.30	6.69	7.84	9.02	7.55	4.32	3.67	9.53	5.22	12.43	4.19
SD	4.80	4.48	3.39	3.97	2.31	3.96	5.00	3.40	2.57	4.56	3.38	3.89	2.54
Females													
M	8.94	7.78	19.64	8.03	8.68	6.30	7.78	4.83	4.17	8.02	8.64	13.17	4.26
SD	5.16	4.82	3.37	4.25	2.00	3.44	4.88	3.70	2.75	4.15	4.20	3.75	2.80

POWER TRANSFORMED T-SCORES
HATHAWAY 15-YEAR-OLD MALES, N=6871

RAW SCORE	?	L	F	K	HS	D	HY	PD	MF	RAW SCORE
0	14	29	25	16	23	--	--	--	--	0
1	34	37	32	20	31	--	0	--	--	1
2	47	43	37	23	38	--	5	--	--	2
3	56	48	41	26	43	--	9	--	--	3
4	62	52	45	28	48	--	13	4	--	4
5	68	56	48	31	52	7	17	10	--	5
6	72	60	51	33	55	15	20	15	4	6
7	75	64	53	36	58	19	23	19	9	7
8	78	67	55	38	61	24	26	23	13	8
9	81	70	57	41	63	27	29	27	17	9
10	83	73	59	43	66	31	32	30	21	10
11	85	76	61	45	68	34	34	33	24	11
12	86	79	62	47	69	37	37	36	27	12
13	88	82	64	49	71	39	40	39	30	13
14	89	85	65	51	73	42	42	42	33	14
15	90	87	67	53	74	44	44	45	36	15
16	92		68	56	75	47	47	47	38	16
17	93		69	58	77	49	49	49	41	17
18	93		70	60	78	52	51	52	43	18
19	94		71	62	79	54	54	54	46	19
20	95		72	63	80	56	56	56	48	20
21	96		73	65	81	58	58	58	50	21
22	96		74	67	82	60	60	60	52	22
23	97		75	69	83	62	62	62	55	23
24	98		76	71	84	64	64	64	57	24
25	98		77	73	85	66	66	66	59	25
26	99		78	75	86	68	68	67	61	26
27	99		79	77	86	70	70	69	63	27
28	100		79	78	87	72	72	71	65	28
29	100		80	80	88	74	74	72	67	29
30	101		81	82	88	76	76	74	68	30
31	101		82		89	77	77	76	70	31
32	101		82		90	79	79	77	72	32
33	102		83		90	81	81	79	74	33
34	102		84			83	83	80	76	34
35	102		84			84	85	82	77	35
36	103		85			86	86	83	79	36
37	103		85			88	88	84	81	37
38	103		86			89	90	86	82	38
39	103		87			91	92	87	84	39
40	104		87			93	93	88	86	40
41	104		88			94	95	90	87	41
42	104		88			96	97	91	89	42
43	104		89			97	98	92	90	43
44	105		89			99	100	93	92	44
45	105		90			100	102	95	93	45
46	105		90			102	103	96	95	46
47	105		91			103	105	97	96	47
48	105		91			105	107	98	98	48
49	106		92			106	108	99	99	49
50	106		92			108	110	100	101	50

15-Year-Old Males (*continued*)

RAW SCORE	?	L	F	K	HS	D	HY	PD	MF	RAW SCORE
51	106		93			109	111		102	51
52	106		93			111	113		104	52
53	106		94			112	114		105	53
54	107		94			113	116		107	54
55	107		94			115	117		108	55
56	107		95			116	119		109	56
57	107		95			118	120		111	57
58	107		96			119	122		112	58
59	107		96			120	123		113	59
60	107		96			122	125		115	60
61	108		97							61
62	108		97							62
63	108		98							63
64	108		98							64
65	108									65
66	108									66
67	108									67
68	108									68
69	108									69
70	109									70
71	109									71
72	109									72
73	109									73
74	109									74
75	109									75
76	109									76
77	109									77
78	109									78
79	109									79
80	109									80
81	110									81
82	110									82
83	110									83
84	110									84
85	110									85
86	110									86
87	110									87
88	110									88
89	110									89
90	110									90
91	110									91
92	110									92
93	110									93
94	110									94
95	110									95
96	111									96
97	111									97
98	111									98
99	111									99

POWER TRANSFORMED T-SCORES
HATHAWAY 15-YEAR-OLD MALES, N=6871

RAW SCORE	PA	PT	SC	MA	SI	HS5K	PD4K	PTK	SCK	MA2K	RAW SCORE
0	3	25	21	--	--	--	--	--	--	--	0
1	13	28	24	--	--	--	--	--	--	--	1
2	20	30	27	--	--	--	--	--	--	--	2
3	26	33	30	--	--	10	--	--	--	1	3
4	30	35	33	16	--	18	--	--	--	6	4
5	35	37	35	20	--	24	--	--	--	9	5
6	38	39	37	23	17	29	--	--	--	13	6
7	42	41	39	26	19	33	--	--	--	16	7
8	45	43	41	28	21	37	--	--	--	19	8
9	48	44	43	31	23	41	--	--	--	22	9
10	51	46	44	33	24	44	14	--	--	25	10
11	54	47	46	36	26	47	18	2	--	27	11
12	56	49	48	38	28	50	22	7	1	30	12
13	59	50	49	40	29	53	25	12	8	33	13
14	61	52	50	42	31	56	28	16	13	35	14
15	64	53	52	44	32	58	31	20	18	37	15
16	66	54	53	47	34	61	34	23	22	40	16
17	68	56	54	49	35	63	36	26	25	42	17
18	70	57	55	51	37	65	39	29	28	44	18
19	72	58	56	53	38	68	41	32	31	47	19
20	74	59	57	55	39	70	44	35	34	49	20
21	76	60	58	57	41	72	46	37	36	51	21
22	78	61	59	58	42	74	48	40	39	53	22
23	80	63	60	60	43	76	50	42	41	56	23
24	82	64	61	62	45	78	53	44	43	58	24
25	83	65	62	64	46	80	55	47	45	60	25
26	85	66	63	66	47	81	57	49	47	62	26
27	87	67	64	68	49	83	59	51	49	64	27
28	89	68	65	70	50	85	61	53	50	66	28
29	90	68	65	71	51	87	63	54	52	68	29
30	92	69	66	73	52	88	65	56	53	70	30
31	93	70	67	75	54	90	67	58	55	72	31
32	95	71	68	77	55	92	69	60	56	74	32
33	96	72	68	78	56	93	70	62	58	76	33
34	98	73	69	80	57	95	72	63	59	78	34
35	99	74	70	82	58	96	74	65	60	80	35
36	101	75	70	84	60	98	76	66	62	82	36
37	102	75	71	85	61	99	78	68	63	84	37
38	104	76	72	87	62	101	80	69	64	86	38
39	105	77	72	89	63	102	81	71	65	88	39
40	106	78	73	90	64	103	83	72	66	89	40
41		79	73	92	65	105	85	74	67	91	41
42		79	74	94	67	106	87	75	68	93	42
43		80	74	95	68	108	88	77	69	95	43
44		81	75	97	69	109	90	78	70	97	44
45		81	75	99	70	110	92	79	71	99	45
46		82	76	100	71	112	93	80	72	100	46
47		83	76		72	113	95	82	73	102	47
48		84	77		73	114	97	83	74	104	48
49			77		74		98	84	75	106	49
50			78		76		100	85	76	108	50
51			78		77		102	87	77	109	51
52			79		78		103	88	78	111	52
53			79		79		105	89	79		53

15-Year-Old Males (*continued*)

RAW SCORE	PA	PT	SC	MA	SI	HS5K	PD4K	PTK	SCK	MA2K	RAW SCORE
54			80		80		107	90	79		54
55			80		81		108	91	80		55
56			81		82		110	92	81		56
57			81		83		111	93	82		57
58			81		84		113	95	82		58
59			82		85		114	96	83		59
60			82		86		116	97	84		60
61			83		87		117	98	85		61
62			83		89		119	99	85		62
63			83		90			100	86		63
64			84		91			101	87		64
65			84		92			102	87		65
66			85		93			103	88		66
67			85		94			104	89		67
68			85		95			105	89		68
69			86		96			106	90		69
70			86		97			107	91		70
71			86					108	91		71
72			87					108	92		72
73			87					109	92		73
74			87					110	93		74
75			88					111	94		75
76			88					112	94		76
77			88					113	95		77
78			89					114	95		78
79									96		79
80									96		80
81									97		81
82									98		82
83									98		83
84									99		84
85									99		85
86									100		86
87									100		87
88									101		88
89									101		89
90									102		90
91									102		91
92									103		92
93									103		93
94									104		94
95									104		95
96									104		96
97									105		97
98									105		98
99									106		99
100									106		100
101									107		101
102									107		102
103									108		103
104									108		104
105									108		105
106									109		106
107									109		107
108									110		108

POWER TRANSFORMED T-SCORES
HATHAWAY 15 YEAR OLD MALES, N=6871

RAW SCORE	D-O	D-S	HY-O	HY-S	PD-O	PD-S	PA-O	PA-S	MA-O	MA-S	RAW SCORE
0	19	13	27	13	23	--	32	18	24	--	0
1	25	17	34	17	29	12	41	24	29	13	1
2	30	21	40	20	34	16	47	29	33	17	2
3	35	25	45	24	38	20	52	34	37	21	3
4	39	29	49	27	42	24	56	39	41	25	4
5	43	32	53	30	45	28	59	43	44	28	5
6	47	36	56	33	48	32	62	48	47	32	6
7	50	40	59	35	51	36	64	52	50	36	7
8	53	43	62	38	54	40	66	56	53	40	8
9	55	47	64	41	56	44	68	60	55	44	9
10	58	50	66	43	59	48	70	64	58	48	10
11	60	54	68	46	61	52	71	68	61	52	11
12	62	58	70	49	63	56	73	72	63	55	12
13	64	61	72	51	65	60	74	76	65	59	13
14	66	65	74	53	67	64	75	80	68	63	14
15	68	68	75	56	69	67	76	84	70	67	15
16	70	72	76	58	70	71	78	88	72	71	16
17	71	75	78	61	72	75	79	91	74	75	17
18	73	79	79	63	73	79	79		76	79	18
19	74	82	80	65	75	83	80		78	82	19
20	76	86	81	67	76	87	81		80	86	20
21	77		82	70	78	91	82		82	90	21
22	79		83	72	79	94	83		84	94	22
23	80		84	74	80		84		86	98	23
24	81		85	76	81						24
25	82		85	78	82						25
26	83		86	80	83						26
27	84		87	82	85						27
28	85		88	84	86						28
29	86		88								29
30	87		89								30
31	88		90								31
32	89		90								32
33	90										33
34	91										34
35	92										35
36	92										36
37	93										37
38	94										38
39	95										39
40	95										40

POWER TRANSFORMED T-SCORES
HATHAWAY 15 YEAR OLD MALES, N=6871

RAW SCORE	A	R	MAC	ES	DELM	SM	AR	CR	PZ	DR	RAW SCORE
0	29	14	--	--	--	--	--	--	7	--	0
1	31	18	--	--	--	--	--	--	12	--	1
2	33	22	--	--	--	--	--	--	17	--	2
3	35	25	--	--	--	--	--	--	21	--	3
4	37	28	--	--	--	--	--	--	25	--	4
5	39	31	--	--	--	--	--	--	29	--	5
6	41	35	--	--	--	--	--	--	32	13	6
7	42	37	--	--	--	18	--	--	35	13	7
8	44	40	9	--	3	19	--	--	38	15	8
9	46	43	12	--	9	20	11	--	41	16	9
10	47	46	15	--	13	21	15	--	43	18	10
11	49	48	18	--	17	23	18	17	45	20	11
12	50	51	21	--	21	24	22	17	48	22	12
13	52	54	23	--	24	26	26	17	50	24	13
14	53	56	26	--	27	28	29	18	51	26	14
15	54	59	29	--	30	30	33	18	53	29	15
16	56	61	31	--	33	32	36	18	55	32	16
17	57	63	34	--	36	34	39	18	57	34	17
18	58	66	37	--	39	37	43	19	58	37	18
19	59	68	39	--	41	39	46	19	60	40	19
20	60	70	42	--	44	42	49	19	61	43	20
21	62	72	44	--	46	44	53	20	62	47	21
22	63	75	47	--	49	47	56	20	64	50	22
23	64	77	49	--	51	50	59	21	65	53	23
24	65	79	51	19	53	53	62	21	66	57	24
25	66	81	54	19	55	56	65	22	67	60	25
26	67	83	56	20	57	59	69	23	68	64	26
27	68	85	59	21	59	62	72	23	69	68	27
28	69	87	61	22	61	65	75	24	70	71	28
29	70	90	63	23	63	68	78	25	71	75	29
30	71	92	66	24	65	71	81	26	72	79	30
31	72	94	68	25	67	75	84	26	73	83	31
32	73		70	26	69	78	87	27	74	87	32
33	73		73	28	71	82	90	28	75	92	33
34	74		75	29	72	85	93	29	76	96	34
35	75		77	31	74	89	96	30	76	100	35
36	76		80	32	76	92	99	31	77	104	36
37			82	34	77	96	102	32	78	109	37
38			84	35	79	100	105	33	79	113	38
39			86	37	81	104	108	34	79	118	39
40			89	39	82	108	111	35	80		40
41			91	41	84	112		36	81		41
42			93	43	85	116		38	81		42
43			95	45	87	120		39	82		43
44			98	47	88	124		40	82		44
45			100	49	90			41	83		45
46			102	51	91			43	84		46
47			104	53	93			44	84		47
48			106	55	94			45	85		48
49			109	57	96			47	85		49
50				59	97			48	86		50

15-Year-Old Males (*continued*)

RAW SCORE	A	R	MAC	ES	DELM	SM	AR	CR	PZ	DR	RAW SCORE
51				61	99			50	86		51
52				64	100			51	87		52
53				66	101			53	87		53
54				68	103			54	87		54
55				71	104			56	88		55
56				73	105			57	88		56
57				76				59	89		57
58				78				61	89		58
59				81				62	90		59
60				83				64	90		60
61				86				66	90		61
62				89				68	91		62
63				91				70			63
64				94				71			64
65				97				73			65
66				99				75			66
67				102				77			67
68				105				79			68
69								81			69
70								83			70
71								85			71
72								87			72

POWER TRANSFORMED T-SCORES
HATHAWAY 15 YEAR OLD MALES, N=6871

RAW SCORE	SOC	DEP	FEM	MOR	REL	AUT	RAW SCORE
0	25	27	18	28	22	23	0
1	28	31	24	31	24	26	1
2	31	35	29	35	27	29	2
3	34	39	34	38	30	32	3
4	36	42	38	40	34	35	4
5	39	45	42	43	37	37	5
6	41	47	45	46	42	40	6
7	44	50	49	49	46	43	7
8	46	52	52	51	51	45	8
9	49	54	55	53	57	48	9
10	51	56	58	56	62	50	10
11	53	58	60	58	68	53	11
12	55	60	63	60	75	56	12
13	57	62	65	62		58	13
14	59	63	68	64		61	14
15	61	65	70	66		63	15
16	63	66	72	68		66	16
17	65	68	74	70		68	17
18	67	69	76	72		71	18
19	69	70	78	74		73	19
20	71	72	80	76		75	20
21	72	73	81				21
22	74	74	83				22
23	76	75	85				23
24	78	76	86				24
25	79	77	88				25
26	81	78	90				26
27		79	91				27
28		80	93				28
29		81	94				29
30		82	95				30
31		83					31
32		84					32
33		85					33

POWER TRANSFORMED T-SCORES
HATHAWAY 15 YEAR OLD MALES, N=6871

RAW SCORE	PSY	ORG	FAM	HOS	PHO	HYP	HEA	RAW SCORE
0	26	26	29	25	27	15	23	0
1	30	33	35	27	32	18	30	1
2	33	38	41	30	37	20	37	2
3	37	43	46	32	41	23	42	3
4	40	47	50	35	45	25	47	4
5	42	50	54	37	48	28	51	5
6	45	53	57	39	51	31	55	6
7	47	56	60	42	54	33	58	7
8	49	58	63	44	57	36	61	8
9	51	61	65	46	59	38	64	9
10	53	63	68	48	61	41	67	10
11	55	64	70	50	63	44	69	11
12	56	66	72	53	65	46	71	12
13	58	68	74	55	67	49	73	13
14	59	69	76	57	69	52	75	14
15	61	71	78	59	71	54	77	15
16	62	72	80	61	73	57	78	16
17	63	73		63	74	60	80	17
18	65	74		65	76	62	81	18
19	66	75		67	78	65	83	19
20	67	76		69	79	68	84	20
21	68	77		71	80	70	85	21
22	69	78		73	82	73	87	22
23	70	79		75	83	76	88	23
24	71	80		77	84	78	89	24
25	72	81		79	86	81	90	25
26	73	82		81	87		91	26
27	74	82					92	27
28	74	83						28
29	75	84						29
30	76	84						30
31	77	85						31
32	78	86						32
33	78	86						33
34	79	87						34
35	80	87						35
36	80	88						36
37	81							37
38	82							38
39	82							39
40	83							40
41	84							41
42	84							42
43	85							43
44	85							44
45	86							45
46	86							46
47	87							47

POWER TRANSFORMED T-SCORES
HATHAWAY 15-YEAR-OLD FEMALES, N=7148

RAW SCORE	?	L	F	K	HS	D	HY	PD	MF	RAW SCORE
0	5	29	24	13	24	--	--	--	--	0
1	23	37	33	18	32	--	--	--	--	1
2	38	42	39	22	38	--	--	--	--	2
3	51	47	44	25	43	--	--	--	--	3
4	61	52	48	28	48	--	3	--	--	4
5	70	56	51	30	52	--	8	6	--	5
6	78	60	54	33	55	5	13	12	--	6
7	84	63	57	35	58	13	16	18	--	7
8	89	67	59	38	61	18	20	22	--	8
9	94	70	62	40	63	23	23	27	--	9
10	98	73	64	43	65	27	27	31	--	10
11	101	77	65	45	67	30	30	34	--	11
12	104	80	67	47	69	33	32	37	--	12
13	106	82	68	49	71	36	35	41	8	13
14	108	85	70	51	72	39	38	43	9	14
15	110	88	71	53	73	42	40	46	11	15
16	112		73	55	75	44	43	49	12	16
17	113		74	57	76	47	45	51	14	17
18	115		75	59	77	49	47	53	15	18
19	116		76	61	78	51	49	55	17	19
20	117		77	63	79	53	52	57	19	20
21	118		78	65	80	56	54	59	20	21
22	118		79	67	81	58	56	61	22	22
23	119		80	69	82	60	58	63	24	23
24	120		81	71	83	62	60	65	26	24
25	120		82	73	84	63	62	67	28	25
26	121		82	74	84	65	64	68	30	26
27	121		83	76	85	67	65	70	32	27
28	121		84	78	86	69	67	71	34	28
29	122		85	80	86	71	69	73	36	29
30	122		85	81	87	72	71	74	39	30
31	122		86		88	74	73	75	41	31
32	123		87		88	76	74	77	43	32
33	123		87		89	77	76	78	45	33
34	123		88			79	78	79	48	34
35	123		88			80	79	80	50	35
36	123		89			82	81	82	52	36
37	124		90			83	82	83	55	37
38	124		90			85	84	84	57	38
39	124		91			86	86	85	59	39
40	124		91			88	87	86	62	40
41	124		92			89	89	87	64	41
42	124		92			91	90	88	67	42
43	124		93			92	92	89	69	43
44	124		93			93	93	90	72	44
45	124		94			95	94	91	74	45
46	125		94			96	96	92	77	46
47	125		95			97	97	93	79	47
48	125		95			99	99	94	82	48
49	125		95			100	100	95	84	49
50	125		96			101	101	95	87	50

15-Year-Old Females (*continued*)

RAW SCORE	?	L	F	K	HS	D	HY	PD	MF	RAW SCORE
51	125		96			103	103		90	51
52	125		97			104	104		92	52
53	125		97			105	105		95	53
54	125		97			106	107		97	54
55	125		98			107	108		100	55
56	125		98			109	109		103	56
57	125		99			110	111		106	57
58	125		99			111	112		108	58
59	125		99			112	113		111	59
60	125		100			113	114		114	60
61	125		100							61
62	125		100							62
63	125		101							63
64	125		101							64
65	125									65
66	125									66
67	125									67
68	125									68
69	125									69
70	125									70
71	125									71
72	125									72
73	125									73
74	125									74
75	125									75
76	125									76
77	125									77
78	125									78
79	125									79
80	125									80
81	125									81
82	125									82
83	125									83
84	125									84
85	125									85
86	125									86
87	125									87
88	125									88
89	126									89
90	126									90
91	126									91
92	126									92
93	126									93
94	126									94
95	126									95
96	126									96
97	126									97
98	126									98
99	126									99

POWER TRANSFORMED T-SCORES
HATHAWAY 15-YEAR-OLD FEMALES, N=7148

RAW SCORE	PA	PT	SC	MA	SI	HS5K	PD4K	PTK	SCK	MA2K	RAW SCORE
0	0	24	21	5	3	--	--	--	--	--	0
1	12	27	25	9	5	--	--	--	--	--	1
2	19	29	28	13	8	--	--	--	--	--	2
3	25	31	30	16	10	7	--	--	--	1	3
4	30	33	33	19	13	15	--	--	--	6	4
5	34	35	35	22	15	21	--	--	--	10	5
6	38	37	38	25	17	26	--	--	--	14	6
7	42	39	40	28	19	31	--	--	--	18	7
8	45	41	42	31	21	36	2	--	--	21	8
9	48	42	43	33	23	40	7	--	--	24	9
10	51	44	45	36	24	43	12	--	--	27	10
11	54	45	47	38	26	47	17	--	--	30	11
12	57	47	48	40	28	50	21	--	--	33	12
13	59	48	50	43	29	53	24	5	6	35	13
14	62	50	51	45	31	56	28	10	12	38	14
15	64	51	52	47	32	58	31	14	17	40	15
16	66	52	53	49	34	61	34	18	21	43	16
17	68	53	55	51	35	63	37	21	25	45	17
18	71	55	56	53	37	65	40	25	28	47	18
19	73	56	57	55	38	67	42	28	31	49	19
20	75	57	58	57	40	69	45	31	34	52	20
21	77	58	59	59	41	71	47	33	36	54	21
22	79	59	60	61	42	73	49	36	39	56	22
23	80	60	61	62	44	75	52	38	41	58	23
24	82	61	62	64	45	77	54	41	43	60	24
25	84	62	63	66	46	78	56	43	45	62	25
26	86	63	63	68	48	80	58	45	47	64	26
27	88	65	64	69	49	81	60	47	49	66	27
28	89	66	65	71	50	83	62	49	51	68	28
29	91	66	66	73	51	84	64	51	52	69	29
30	92	67	67	74	53	86	66	53	54	71	30
31	94	68	67	76	54	87	68	55	55	73	31
32	96	69	68	78	55	88	69	57	57	75	32
33	97	70	69	79	56	90	71	59	58	77	33
34	99	71	69	81	57	91	73	60	60	78	34
35	100	72	70	82	58	92	75	62	61	80	35
36	102	73	71	84	59	93	76	64	62	82	36
37	103	74	71	85	61	94	78	65	63	84	37
38	104	75	72	87	62	96	79	67	65	85	38
39	106	75	72	88	63	97	81	68	66	87	39
40	107	76	73	90	64	98	82	70	67	89	40
41		77	73	91	65	99	84	71	68	90	41
42		78	74	93	66	100	85	73	69	92	42
43		79	75	94	67	101	87	74	70	93	43
44		79	75	95	68	102	88	75	71	95	44
45		80	76	97	69	103	90	77	72	97	45
46		81	76	98	70	104	91	78	73	98	46
47		82	77		71	105	93	79	74	100	47
48		83	77		72	105	94	81	75	101	48
49			77		73		95	82	76	103	49
50			78		74		97	83	77	104	50
51			78		75		98	84	77	106	51
52			79		76		99	86	78	107	52
53			79		77		100	87	79		53

15-Year-Old Females (*continued*)

RAW SCORE	PA	PT	SC	MA	SI	HS5K	PD4K	PTK	SCK	MA2K	RAW SCORE
54			80		78		102	88	80		54
55			80		79		103	89	81		55
56			80		80		104	90	82		56
57			81		81		105	91	82		57
58			81		82		107	92	83		58
59			82		83		108	94	84		59
60			82		84		109	95	85		60
61			82		85		110	96	85		61
62			83		86		111	97	86		62
63			83		87			98	87		63
64			83		87			99	87		64
65			84		88			100	88		65
66			84		89			101	89		66
67			84		90			102	89		67
68			85		91			103	90		68
69			85		92			104	91		69
70			85		93			105	91		70
71			86					106	92		71
72			86					107	92		72
73			86					108	93		73
74			87					108	94		74
75			87					109	94		75
76			87					110	95		76
77			88					111	95		77
78			88					112	96		78
79									97		79
80									97		80
81									98		81
82									98		82
83									99		83
84									99		84
85									100		85
86									100		86
87									101		87
88									101		88
89									102		89
90									102		90
91									103		91
92									103		92
93									104		93
94									104		94
95									105		95
96									105		96
97									106		97
98									106		98
99									106		99
100									107		100
101									107		101
102									108		102
103									108		103
104									109		104
105									109		105
106									110		106
107									110		107
108									110		108

POWER TRANSFORMED T-SCORES
HATHAWAY 15 YEAR OLD FEMALES, N=7148

RAW SCORE	D-O	D-S	HY-O	HY-S	PD-O	PD-S	PA-O	PA-S	MA-O	MA-S	RAW SCORE
0	17	12	25	12	22	--	31	20	26	9	0
1	23	16	32	15	29	11	40	25	31	13	1
2	28	20	38	18	34	15	47	29	36	17	2
3	33	23	43	21	39	19	52	34	40	22	3
4	37	27	47	24	44	23	56	39	43	26	4
5	41	31	51	27	47	27	59	43	47	30	5
6	44	34	54	29	51	31	62	47	50	34	6
7	47	38	57	32	54	35	65	52	53	37	7
8	50	42	60	35	57	39	67	56	55	41	8
9	53	46	62	37	59	43	69	61	58	45	9
10	55	49	64	40	62	47	70	65	60	49	10
11	58	53	66	43	64	51	72	69	63	53	11
12	60	57	68	45	66	55	73	73	65	56	12
13	62	60	70	48	68	59	75	78	67	60	13
14	64	64	72	50	69	63	76	82	69	64	14
15	66	68	73	53	71	67	77	86	71	67	15
16	67	72	74	55	72	71	78	90	73	71	16
17	69	75	76	58	74	75	79	95	75	75	17
18	71	79	77	60	75	79	80		77	78	18
19	72	83	78	63	76	84	81		78	82	19
20	74	86	79	65	77	88	82		80	85	20
21	75		80	68	78	92	83		82	89	21
22	77		81	70	79	96	83		83	92	22
23	78		82	73	80		84		85	96	23
24	79		83	75	81						24
25	80		83	78	82						25
26	81		84	80	83						26
27	83		85	82	84						27
28	84		86	85	85						28
29	85		86								29
30	86		87								30
31	87		87								31
32	88		88								32
33	89										33
34	89										34
35	90										35
36	91										36
37	92										37
38	93										38
39	94										39
40	94										40

POWER TRANSFORMED T-SCORES
HATHAWAY 15-YEAR-OLD FEMALES, N=7148

RAW SCORE	A	R	MAC	ES	DELF	SM	AR	CR	PZ	DR	RAW SCORE
0	28	12	--	--	--	--	--	--	1	--	0
1	30	16	--	--	--	--	--	--	8	--	1
2	32	20	--	--	--	--	--	--	14	--	2
3	34	24	--	--	1	--	--	--	19	--	3
4	35	27	--	--	3	--	--	--	24	--	4
5	37	30	--	--	5	--	--	--	28	--	5
6	39	34	--	--	8	18	--	--	32	--	6
7	40	37	2	--	10	19	--	--	35	13	7
8	42	40	7	--	12	20	--	--	38	14	8
9	44	43	12	--	14	21	--	--	41	15	9
10	45	46	16	--	15	23	12	--	44	16	10
11	46	49	19	--	17	24	15	--	46	18	11
12	48	52	23	--	19	26	18	--	49	20	12
13	49	54	26	--	21	28	22	--	51	22	13
14	51	57	30	--	22	30	25	--	53	25	14
15	52	60	33	14	24	32	28	--	55	27	15
16	53	63	36	14	25	34	31	20	56	30	16
17	55	65	39	15	27	36	35	20	58	33	17
18	56	68	42	15	28	39	38	20	60	36	18
19	57	70	44	16	30	41	41	20	61	39	19
20	58	73	47	17	31	43	44	21	62	42	20
21	59	76	50	18	33	46	47	21	64	45	21
22	61	78	53	19	34	49	50	22	65	48	22
23	62	80	55	20	35	51	54	22	66	52	23
24	63	83	58	21	37	54	57	23	68	56	24
25	64	85	60	22	38	57	60	23	69	59	25
26	65	88	63	23	39	60	63	24	70	63	26
27	66	90	65	24	40	63	66	25	71	67	27
28	67	92	68	25	41	66	69	25	72	71	28
29	68	95	70	27	43	69	72	26	73	75	29
30	69	97	73	28	44	72	75	27	74	79	30
31	70	99	75	30	45	75	79	28	74	84	31
32	71		77	31	46	78	82	29	75	88	32
33	72		80	33	47	82	85	30	76	92	33
34	73		82	34	48	85	88	31	77	97	34
35	74		84	36	49	88	91	32	78	102	35
36	75		87	38	50	92	94	33	78	106	36
37			89	39	51	95	97	34	79	111	37
38			91	41	52	99	100	35	80	116	38
39			93	43	53	102	103	36	80	121	39
40			95	45	54	106	106	37	81		40
41			98	47	55	110		38	82		41
42			100	49	56	113		40	82		42
43			102	51	57	117		41	83		43
44			104	53	58	121		42	83		44
45			106	55	59			44	84		45
46			108	57	60			45	85		46
47			110	59	61			46	85		47
48			112	61	62			48	86		48
49			114	63	62			49	86		49
50				65	63			51	87		50

15-Year-Old Females (*continued*)

RAW SCORE	A	R	MAC	ES	DELF	SM	AR	CR	PZ	DR	RAW SCORE
51				68	64			52	87		51
52				70	65			54	88		52
53				72	66			55	88		53
54				74	67			57	88		54
55				77	67			58	89		55
56				79	68			60	89		56
57				82	69			61	90		57
58				84	70			63	90		58
59				87	71			65	91		59
60				89	71			67	91		60
61				92	72			68	91		61
62				94	73			70	92		62
63				97	74			72			63
64				99	74			74			64
65				102	75			76			65
66				105	76			77			66
67				107	76			79			67
68				110	77			81			68
69					78			83			69
70					79			85			70
71					79			87			71
72					80			89			72
73					81						73
74					81						74
75					82						75
76					83						76
77					83						77
78					84						78
79					84						79
80					85						80
81					86						81
82					86						82
83					87						83
84					88						84
85					88						85
86					89						86

POWER TRANSFORMED T-SCORES
HATHAWAY 15-YEAR-OLD FEMALES, N=7148

RAW SCORE	SOC	DEP	FEM	MOR	REL	AUT	RAW SCORE
0	25	27	--	27	19	27	0
1	29	31	--	30	21	31	1
2	32	34	--	33	23	34	2
3	35	37	15	35	26	38	3
4	38	40	16	38	29	41	4
5	41	43	17	41	32	44	5
6	44	46	18	43	37	47	6
7	46	48	19	46	42	49	7
8	48	50	20	48	47	52	8
9	51	52	22	50	53	54	9
10	53	54	23	53	60	57	10
11	55	56	25	55	67	59	11
12	57	58	27	57	75	62	12
13	59	60	30	60		64	13
14	61	61	32	62		66	14
15	62	63	35	64		68	15
16	64	65	37	66		70	16
17	66	66	40	68		72	17
18	67	67	43	70		74	18
19	69	69	46	73		76	19
20	70	70	50	75		78	20
21	72	71	53				21
22	73	72	57				22
23	75	74	60				23
24	76	75	64				24
25	77	76	68				25
26	78	77	72				26
27		78	77				27
28		79	81				28
29		80	85				29
30		81	90				30
31		82					31
32		82					32
33		83					33

POWER TRANSFORMED T-SCORES
HATHAWAY 15-YEAR-OLD FEMALES, N=7148

RAW SCORE	PSY	ORG	FAM	HOS	PHO	HYP	HEA	RAW SCORE
0	25	25	29	25	25	15	25	0
1	29	32	35	29	29	17	32	1
2	33	37	40	32	32	19	38	2
3	36	42	45	35	35	22	44	3
4	39	47	49	38	38	24	48	4
5	41	50	52	40	41	26	52	5
6	44	54	55	43	43	29	56	6
7	46	56	58	45	46	31	59	7
8	48	59	61	48	48	34	62	8
9	50	61	63	50	50	36	65	9
10	52	64	66	52	53	39	67	10
11	54	66	68	54	55	42	70	11
12	56	67	70	56	57	45	72	12
13	57	69	71	58	59	47	74	13
14	59	71	73	60	61	50	76	14
15	60	72	75	62	63	53	77	15
16	61	73	76	64	65	56	79	16
17	63	74		66	67	59	80	17
18	64	76		68	69	62	82	18
19	65	77		69	71	65	83	19
20	66	78		71	73	68	85	20
21	68	79		73	75	71	86	21
22	69	79		75	76	74	87	22
23	70	80		76	78	77	88	23
24	71	81		78	80	80	89	24
25	72	82		79	82	83	90	25
26	73	83		81	83		91	26
27	74	83					92	27
28	75	84						28
29	75	84						29
30	76	85						30
31	77	86						31
32	78	86						32
33	79	87						33
34	80	87						34
35	80	88						35
36	81	88						36
37	82							37
38	82							38
39	83							39
40	84							40
41	85							41
42	85							42
43	86							43
44	86							44
45	87							45
46	88							46
47	88							47

POWER TRANSFORMED T-SCORES
HATHAWAY 18-YEAR-OLD MALES, N=1810

RAW SCORE	?	L	F	K	HS	D	HY	PD	MF	RAW SCORE
0	0	30	23	--	25	--	--	--	--	0
1	23	39	32	20	34	--	--	--	--	1
2	42	45	39	22	41	--	--	--	--	2
3	57	50	44	24	46	--	--	--	--	3
4	69	55	49	27	51	--	--	--	--	4
5	79	59	52	29	55	--	--	10	--	5
6	87	62	55	31	59	8	--	17	--	6
7	94	65	58	33	62	16	19	21	--	7
8	100	69	61	35	64	21	22	26	12	8
9	105	71	63	37	67	25	25	29	17	9
10	109	74	65	39	69	29	28	32	21	10
11	112	77	67	41	71	33	31	36	25	11
12	115	79	69	43	73	36	33	39	28	12
13	117	82	70	46	75	39	36	41	31	13
14	120	84	72	48	76	42	38	44	33	14
15	121	86	73	50	78	45	41	46	36	15
16	123		75	52	79	48	43	49	39	16
17	124		76	54	80	50	46	51	41	17
18	126		77	56	82	53	48	54	43	18
19	127		78	58	83	55	51	56	45	19
20	127		79	61	84	57	53	58	48	20
21	128		80	63	85	60	55	60	50	21
22	129		81	65	86	62	58	62	52	22
23	130		82	67	87	64	60	64	54	23
24	130		83	69	88	66	62	66	56	24
25	131		84	71	88	68	65	68	58	25
26	131		85	74	89	71	67	70	60	26
27	131		86	76	90	73	69	72	61	27
28	132		87	78	91	75	71	74	63	28
29	132		87	80	91	77	74	76	65	29
30	132		88	82	92	78	76	77	67	30
31	133		89		93	80	78	79	68	31
32	133		89		93	82	80	81	70	32
33	133		90		94	84	83	82	72	33
34	133		91			86	85	84	73	34
35	133		91			88	87	86	75	35
36	133		92			89	89	87	77	36
37	134		93			91	91	89	78	37
38	134		93			93	94	91	80	38
39	134		94			95	96	92	81	39
40	134		94			96	98	94	83	40
41	134		95			98	100	95	84	41
42	134		95			100	102	97	86	42
43	134		96			101	104	98	87	43
44	134		96			103	107	100	89	44
45	134		97			105	109	101	90	45
46	134		97			106	111	103	92	46
47	134		98			108	113	104	93	47
48	134		98			109	115	106	95	48
49	134		99			111	117	107	96	49
50	135		99			112	119	108	97	50

18-Year-Old Males (*continued*)

RAW SCORE	?	L	F	K	HS	D	HY	PD	MF	RAW SCORE
51	135		100			114	121		99	51
52	135		100			115	124		100	52
53	135		101			117	126		101	53
54	135		101			118	128		103	54
55	135		101			120	130		104	55
56	135		102			121	132		105	56
57	135		102			123	134		107	57
58	135		103			124	136		108	58
59	135		103			126	138		109	59
60	135		103			127	140		111	60
61	135		104							61
62	135		104							62
63	135		104							63
64	135		105							64
65	135									65
66	135									66
67	135									67
68	135									68
69	135									69
70	135									70
71	135									71
72	135									72
73	135									73
74	135									74
75	135									75
76	135									76
77	135									77
78	135									78
79	135									79
80	135									80
81	135									81
82	135									82
83	135									83
84	135									84
85	135									85
86	135									86
87	135									87
88	135									88
89	135									89
90	135									90
91	135									91
92	135									92
93	135									93
94	135									94
95	135									95
96	135									96
97	135									97
98	135									98
99	135									99

POWER TRANSFORMED T-SCORES
HATHAWAY 18 YEAR OLD MALES, N=1810

RAW SCORE	PA	PT	SC	MA	SI	HS5K	PD4K	PTK	SCK	MA2K	RAW SCORE
0	--	23	16	2	5	--	--	--	--	--	0
1	--	27	22	6	8	--	--	--	--	--	1
2	16	30	26	10	11	7	--	--	--	--	2
3	22	33	30	14	13	13	--	--	--	--	3
4	28	36	34	17	16	18	--	--	--	5	4
5	32	39	37	21	18	23	--	--	--	9	5
6	36	41	40	23	20	28	4	--	--	13	6
7	40	43	43	26	23	32	8	--	--	16	7
8	44	45	45	29	25	36	12	--	--	19	8
9	47	47	47	32	27	40	15	--	--	22	9
10	51	49	50	34	28	43	18	--	--	25	10
11	54	51	51	37	30	47	21	--	--	28	11
12	57	52	53	39	32	50	23	2	4	31	12
13	60	54	55	42	34	53	26	7	11	33	13
14	63	55	56	44	35	56	29	12	16	36	14
15	66	57	58	46	37	59	31	17	20	38	15
16	68	58	59	48	38	62	34	20	24	41	16
17	71	59	61	51	40	65	36	24	28	43	17
18	74	60	62	53	41	68	39	27	31	46	18
19	76	62	63	55	43	71	41	31	34	48	19
20	79	63	64	57	44	74	44	34	36	51	20
21	81	64	65	59	45	76	46	36	39	53	21
22	84	65	66	61	47	79	48	39	41	55	22
23	86	66	67	63	48	81	51	42	43	57	23
24	89	67	68	65	49	84	53	44	45	60	24
25	91	68	69	67	50	86	55	47	48	62	25
26	93	69	70	69	52	89	58	49	49	64	26
27	96	69	70	71	53	91	60	51	51	66	27
28	98	70	71	73	54	93	62	53	53	69	28
29	100	71	72	75	55	96	64	56	55	71	29
30	102	72	73	77	56	98	67	58	57	73	30
31	104	73	73	78	57	100	69	60	58	75	31
32	107	74	74	80	58	102	71	62	60	77	32
33	109	74	75	82	59	105	73	63	61	79	33
34	111	75	75	84	60	107	75	65	63	81	34
35	113	76	76	85	61	109	77	67	64	84	35
36	115	76	76	87	62	111	80	69	66	86	36
37	117	77	77	89	63	113	82	71	67	88	37
38	119	78	78	91	64	115	84	72	69	90	38
39	121	78	78	92	65	117	86	74	70	92	39
40	123	79	79	94	66	119	88	76	71	94	40
41		80	79	96	67	121	90	77	73	96	41
42		80	80	97	68	123	92	79	74	98	42
43		81	80	99	69	125	94	80	75	100	43
44		81	80	101	70	127	96	82	76	102	44
45		82	81	102	71	129	98	83	78	104	45
46		82	81	104	72	131	100	85	79	106	46
47		83	82		73	133	102	86	80	108	47
48		84	82		73	135	104	88	81	110	48
49			82		74		106	89	82	112	49
50			83		75		108	91	83	113	50
51			83		76		110	92	84	115	51
52			84		77		112	93	85	117	52
53			84		78		114	95	86		53

RAW SCORE	PA	PT	SC	MA	SI	HS5K	PD4K	PTK	SCK	MA2K	RAW SCORE
54			84		78		116	96	87		54
55			85		79		118	97	88		55
56			85		80		120	99	90		56
57			85		81		122	100	90		57
58			86		81		124	101	91		58
59			86		82		126	103	92		59
60			86		83		128	104	93		60
61			86		84		130	105	94		61
62			87		84		132	106	95		62
63			87		85			107	96		63
64			87		86			109	97		64
65			88		87			110	98		65
66			88		87			111	99		66
67			88		88			112	100		67
68			88		89			113	101		68
69			89		89			114	102		69
70			89		90			115	102		70
71			89					117	103		71
72			89					118	104		72
73			90					119	105		73
74			90					120	106		74
75			90					121	107		75
76			90					122	107		76
77			90					123	108		77
78			91					124	109		78
79									110		79
80									111		80
81									111		81
82									112		82
83									113		83
84									114		84
85									114		85
86									115		86
87									116		87
88									117		88
89									117		89
90									118		90
91									119		91
92									119		92
93									120		93
94									121		94
95									122		95
96									122		96
97									123		97
98									124		98
99									124		99
100									125		100
101									126		101
102									126		102
103									127		103
104									128		104
105									128		105
106									129		106
107									129		107
108									130		108

POWER TRANSFORMED T-SCORES
HATHAWAY 18-YEAR-OLD MALES, N=1810

RAW SCORE	D-O	D-S	HY-O	HY-S	PD-O	PD-S	PA-O	PA-S	MA-O	MA-S	RAW SCORE
0	16	13	26	17	22	--	31	--	22	11	0
1	23	17	34	19	29	15	43	22	29	15	1
2	30	20	41	21	34	18	51	26	34	18	2
3	35	24	46	23	39	22	57	31	38	22	3
4	40	27	51	25	43	25	61	35	43	26	4
5	44	31	55	27	47	29	65	39	46	29	5
6	48	35	58	29	50	33	67	44	50	33	6
7	51	38	61	32	54	37	70	48	53	37	7
8	55	42	64	34	56	41	72	52	56	40	8
9	57	46	67	36	59	44	74	57	59	44	9
10	60	50	69	39	62	48	76	61	62	48	10
11	62	54	71	41	64	52	77	65	64	52	11
12	65	57	73	44	66	56	78	70	67	56	12
13	67	61	74	46	68	61	80	74	69	59	13
14	69	65	76	49	70	65	81	78	71	63	14
15	71	69	77	51	72	69	82	82	74	67	15
16	72	73	79	54	73	73	83	87	76	71	16
17	74	77	80	56	75	77	83	91	78	75	17
18	75	81	81	59	76	81	84		80	79	18
19	77	85	82	61	78	85	85		82	83	19
20	78	89	83	64	79	89	86		84	86	20
21	80		84	67	81	94	86		86	90	21
22	81		85	69	82	98	87		87	94	22
23	82		86	72	83		88		89	98	23
24	83		87	75	84						24
25	84		88	77	85						25
26	85		88	80	86						26
27	86		89	83	87						27
28	87		90	85	88						28
29	88		90								29
30	89		91								30
31	90		92								31
32	91		92								32
33	92										33
34	92										34
35	93										35
36	94										36
37	95										37
38	95										38
39	96										39
40	97										40

POWER TRANSFORMED T-SCORES
HATHAWAY 18-YEAR-OLD MALES, N=1810

RAW SCORE	A	R	MAC	ES	DELM	SM	AR	CR	PZ	DR	RAW SCORE
0	28	13	--	--	--	--	--	--	0	--	0
1	31	17	--	--	--	--	--	--	8	--	1
2	34	21	--	--	--	--	--	--	15	--	2
3	37	24	--	--	--	--	--	--	21	--	3
4	39	28	--	--	--	--	--	--	26	--	4
5	42	31	--	--	--	--	--	--	31	--	5
6	44	34	--	--	--	--	--	--	35	--	6
7	46	37	--	--	--	--	--	--	39	--	7
8	48	40	10	--	--	--	--	--	43	13	8
9	50	43	13	--	4	19	10	--	46	14	9
10	51	45	16	--	10	20	14	--	49	16	10
11	53	48	19	--	15	21	18	--	52	18	11
12	55	51	22	--	19	22	21	--	54	20	12
13	56	53	24	--	23	24	25	--	56	22	13
14	57	56	27	--	27	26	29	--	58	24	14
15	59	59	30	--	30	28	32	--	60	27	15
16	60	61	32	--	33	30	36	17	62	29	16
17	61	63	35	--	36	32	39	17	64	32	17
18	62	66	37	--	39	35	42	17	66	35	18
19	63	68	40	--	42	37	46	18	67	38	19
20	64	71	42	--	45	40	49	18	68	41	20
21	65	73	45	--	47	43	53	18	70	44	21
22	66	75	47	--	50	46	56	18	71	47	22
23	67	78	50	--	52	49	59	18	72	51	23
24	68	80	52	--	55	52	62	19	73	54	24
25	69	82	55	--	57	55	66	19	74	58	25
26	70	84	57	--	59	58	69	19	75	61	26
27	71	87	60	--	61	62	72	20	76	65	27
28	71	89	62	19	63	65	75	20	77	69	28
29	72	91	65	19	65	69	79	21	78	73	29
30	73	93	67	20	67	73	82	21	79	77	30
31	73	95	69	20	69	77	85	22	80	81	31
32	74		72	21	71	80	88	23	80	85	32
33	75		74	22	73	84	91	23	81	89	33
34	75		76	23	75	89	95	24	82	94	34
35	76		79	24	77	93	98	25	83	98	35
36	77		81	25	79	97	101	26	83	102	36
37			84	27	80	101	104	27	84	107	37
38			86	28	82	106	107	28	84	111	38
39			88	30	84	110	110	29	85	116	39
40			91	31	85	115	113	30	85		40
41			93	33	87	119		31	86		41
42			95	35	88	124		32	86		42
43			98	37	90	129		33	87		43
44			100	39	92	133		34	87		44
45			102	41	93			36	88		45
46			105	43	95			37	88		46
47			107	45	96			39	89		47
48			109	48	98			40	89		48
49			112	50	99			42	89		49
50				52	100			43	90		50

18-Year-Old Males (*continued*)

RAW SCORE	A	R	MAC	ES	DELM	SM	AR	CR	PZ	DR	RAW SCORE
51				55	102			45	90		51
52				58	103			47	91		52
53				60	105			48	91		53
54				63	106			50	91		54
55				66	107			52	92		55
56				69	109			54	92		56
57				72				56	92		57
58				75				58	92		58
59				78				60	93		59
60				81				62	93		60
61				84				64	93		61
62				87				67	94		62
63				90				69			63
64				94				72			64
65				97				74			65
66				101				76			66
67				104				79			67
68				108				82			68
69								84			69
70								87			70
71								90			71
72								93			72

POWER TRANSFORMED T-SCORES
HATHAWAY 18-YEAR-OLD MALES, N=1810

RAW SCORE	SOC	DEP	FEM	MOR	REL	AUT	RAW SCORE
0	27	26	17	29	22	25	0
1	31	32	23	33	24	28	1
2	34	37	29	37	26	31	2
3	37	41	35	41	29	34	3
4	40	45	39	44	33	37	4
5	43	48	43	47	37	40	5
6	45	51	47	50	41	43	6
7	48	54	51	53	46	45	7
8	50	56	54	55	51	48	8
9	52	59	57	57	57	50	9
10	54	61	60	59	63	53	10
11	56	63	62	61	69	55	11
12	58	64	65	63	76	57	12
13	60	66	67	65		59	13
14	61	67	69	67		62	14
15	63	69	71	68		64	15
16	64	70	73	70		66	16
17	66	71	75	71		68	17
18	67	73	77	73		70	18
19	69	74	78	74		72	19
20	70	75	80	75		74	20
21	71	76	82				21
22	73	77	83				22
23	74	78	84				23
24	75	78	86				24
25	76	79	87				25
26	77	80	89				26
27		81	90				27
28		81	91				28
29		82	92				29
30		83	93				30
31		83					31
32		84					32
33		84					33

POWER TRANSFORMED T-SCORES
HATHAWAY 18-YEAR-OLD MALES, N=1810

RAW SCORE	PSY	ORG	FAM	HOS	PHO	HYP	HEA	RAW SCORE
0	23	25	29	25	26	--	25	0
1	30	35	37	29	34	--	34	1
2	35	42	43	32	39	21	41	2
3	39	47	48	35	44	24	46	3
4	43	52	53	38	49	27	51	4
5	46	56	57	41	52	30	55	5
6	49	60	60	43	56	33	59	6
7	52	63	63	45	58	36	62	7
8	55	65	65	48	61	38	65	8
9	57	68	68	50	63	41	68	9
10	59	70	70	52	66	44	70	10
11	61	72	72	54	68	46	72	11
12	62	73	74	56	69	49	75	12
13	64	75	75	58	71	52	77	13
14	65	76	77	60	73	54	79	14
15	67	77	78	62	74	57	80	15
16	68	79	80	63	76	59	82	16
17	69	80		65	77	61	84	17
18	71	81		67	78	64	85	18
19	72	82		69	79	66	87	19
20	73	83		70	81	69	88	20
21	74	84		72	82	71	90	21
22	75	84		73	83	73	91	22
23	76	85		75	84	76	92	23
24	76	86		76	85	78	93	24
25	77	86		78	86	81	95	25
26	78	87		79	86		96	26
27	79	88					97	27
28	80	88						28
29	80	89						29
30	81	89						30
31	81	90						31
32	82	90						32
33	83	91						33
34	83	91						34
35	84	92						35
36	84	92						36
37	85							37
38	85							38
39	86							39
40	86							40
41	87							41
42	87							42
43	88							43
44	88							44
45	88							45
46	89							46
47	89							47

POWER TRANSFORMED T-SCORES
HATHAWAY 18-YEAR-OLD FEMALES, N=1864

RAW SCORE	?	L	F	K	HS	D	HY	PD	MF	RAW SCORE
0	4	29	23	--	24	--	--	--	--	0
1	27	38	34	--	32	--	--	--	--	1
2	44	44	41	21	39	--	--	--	--	2
3	58	49	47	23	45	--	--	--	--	3
4	69	54	52	25	50	--	1	4	--	4
5	78	58	56	28	54	--	6	11	--	5
6	85	62	59	30	57	--	10	16	--	6
7	91	65	62	32	61	5	14	21	--	7
8	96	69	65	35	63	13	17	25	--	8
9	100	72	67	37	66	19	20	29	--	9
10	104	75	69	39	68	24	23	33	--	10
11	106	78	71	41	70	28	26	37	--	11
12	109	81	73	43	72	32	29	40	--	12
13	111	83	75	46	74	35	31	43	--	13
14	113	86	76	48	75	38	34	46	--	14
15	114	89	78	50	77	41	37	48	--	15
16	115		79	52	78	44	39	51	--	16
17	116		81	54	80	46	42	53	--	17
18	117		82	56	81	49	44	55	--	18
19	118		83	59	82	51	46	58	13	19
20	119		84	61	83	54	49	60	15	20
21	120		86	63	84	56	51	62	17	21
22	120		87	65	85	58	53	64	19	22
23	121		88	67	86	60	55	66	21	23
24	121		89	69	87	62	58	68	23	24
25	121		90	71	88	64	60	69	26	25
26	122		91	74	88	66	62	71	28	26
27	122		91	76	89	67	64	73	30	27
28	122		92	78	90	69	66	74	32	28
29	123		93	80	91	71	68	76	35	29
30	123		94	82	91	73	70	77	37	30
31	123		95		92	74	72	79	39	31
32	123		95		92	76	75	80	42	32
33	123		96		93	77	77	82	44	33
34	123		97			79	79	83	46	34
35	124		98			80	81	85	49	35
36	124		98			82	82	86	51	36
37	124		99			83	84	87	53	37
38	124		100			85	86	89	56	38
39	124		100			86	88	90	58	39
40	124		101			88	90	91	61	40
41	124		101			89	92	92	63	41
42	124		102			90	94	93	66	42
43	124		102			92	96	95	68	43
44	124		103			93	98	96	71	44
45	124		104			94	100	97	73	45
46	124		104			95	101	98	76	46
47	124		105			97	103	99	78	47
48	125		105			98	105	100	81	48
49	125		106			99	107	101	83	49
50	125		106			100	109	102	86	50

18-Year-Old Females (*continued*)

RAW SCORE	?	L	F	K	HS	D	HY	PD	MF	RAW SCORE
51	125		107			102	110		88	51
52	125		107			103	112		91	52
53	125		108			104	114		94	53
54	125		108			105	116		96	54
55	125		108			106	117		99	55
56	125		109			107	119		101	56
57	125		109			108	121		104	57
58	125		110			109	123		107	58
59	125		110			111	124		109	59
60	125		111			112	126		112	60
61	125		111							61
62	125		111							62
63	125		112							63
64	125		112							64
65	125									65
66	125									66
67	125									67
68	125									68
69	125									69
70	125									70
71	125									71
72	125									72
73	125									73
74	125									74
75	125									75
76	125									76
77	125									77
78	125									78
79	125									79
80	125									80
81	125									81
82	125									82
83	125									83
84	125									84
85	125									85
86	125									86
87	125									87
88	125									88
89	125									89
90	125									90
91	125									91
92	125									92
93	125									93
94	125									94
95	125									95
96	125									96
97	125									97
98	125									98
99	125									99

POWER TRANSFORMED T-SCORES
HATHAWAY 18-YEAR-OLD FEMALES, N=1864

RAW SCORE	PA	PT	SC	MA	SI	HS5K	PD4K	PTK	SCK	MA2K	RAW SCORE
0	--	24	17	--	--	--	--	--	--	--	0
1	5	27	22	--	--	--	--	--	--	--	1
2	15	29	27	--	--	--	--	--	--	--	2
3	22	32	30	14	5	--	--	--	--	1	3
4	27	34	34	18	9	10	--	--	--	6	4
5	32	37	37	22	13	18	--	--	--	11	5
6	36	39	40	25	16	25	--	--	--	14	6
7	40	41	43	28	19	30	--	--	--	18	7
8	44	43	45	31	22	35	--	--	--	21	8
9	47	44	47	34	24	39	--	--	--	24	9
10	51	46	49	37	26	43	13	--	--	27	10
11	54	48	51	39	28	46	18	--	--	30	11
12	57	49	53	41	30	49	22	--	1	33	12
13	60	51	55	44	32	53	26	--	8	35	13
14	62	52	56	46	34	56	29	2	14	38	14
15	65	54	58	48	35	58	32	8	19	41	15
16	68	55	59	51	37	61	35	13	23	43	16
17	70	56	60	53	38	64	38	17	26	46	17
18	73	57	62	55	40	66	40	21	29	48	18
19	75	59	63	57	41	68	43	25	32	50	19
20	77	60	64	59	43	71	45	29	35	53	20
21	80	61	65	61	44	73	48	32	38	55	21
22	82	62	66	63	45	75	50	35	40	57	22
23	84	63	67	65	47	77	52	38	43	59	23
24	86	64	68	67	48	79	55	40	45	62	24
25	88	65	69	69	49	81	57	43	47	64	25
26	90	66	70	70	50	83	59	45	49	66	26
27	92	67	71	72	51	85	61	48	51	68	27
28	94	68	72	74	52	87	63	50	53	70	28
29	96	69	72	76	54	89	66	52	55	72	29
30	98	70	73	78	55	90	68	54	57	74	30
31	100	71	74	79	56	92	70	56	59	76	31
32	102	72	74	81	57	94	72	58	60	78	32
33	104	73	75	83	58	95	74	60	62	80	33
34	106	74	76	85	59	97	76	62	64	82	34
35	107	74	76	86	60	99	78	64	65	84	35
36	109	75	77	88	61	100	79	65	67	86	36
37	111	76	78	90	62	102	81	67	68	88	37
38	113	77	78	91	62	103	83	69	70	90	38
39	114	78	79	93	63	105	85	70	71	92	39
40	116	78	79	95	64	106	87	72	73	94	40
41		79	80	96	65	108	89	73	74	95	41
42		80	80	98	66	109	91	75	75	97	42
43		81	81	99	67	110	92	76	77	99	43
44		81	81	101	68	112	94	78	78	101	44
45		82	82	103	69	113	96	79	79	103	45
46		83	82	104	69	114	98	80	81	104	46
47		84	83		70	116	100	82	82	106	47
48		84	83		71	117	101	83	83	108	48
49			84		72		103	84	84	110	49
50			84		73		105	85	85	111	50
51			84		73		106	87	87	113	51
52			85		74		108	88	88	115	52
53			85		75		110	89	89		53

RAW SCORE	PA	PT	SC	MA	SI	HS5K	PD4K	PTK	SCK	MA2K	RAW SCORE
54			86		76		111	90	90		54
55			86		76		113	91	91		55
56			86		77		115	93	92		56
57			87		78		116	94	93		57
58			87		78		118	95	94		58
59			87		79		120	96	95		59
60			88		80		121	97	96		60
61			88		81		123	98	98		61
62			88		81		124	99	99		62
63			89		82			100	100		63
64			89		83			101	101		64
65			89		83			102	102		65
66			90		84			103	102		66
67			90		85			104	103		67
68			90		85			105	104		68
69			90		86			106	105		69
70			91		87			107	106		70
71			91					108	107		71
72			91					109	108		72
73			91					110	109		73
74			92					110	110		74
75			92					111	111		75
76			92					112	112		76
77			92					113	113		77
78			93					114	114		78
79									114		79
80									115		80
81									116		81
82									117		82
83									118		83
84									119		84
85									119		85
86									120		86
87									121		87
88									122		88
89									123		89
90									123		90
91									124		91
92									125		92
93									126		93
94									127		94
95									127		95
96									128		96
97									129		97
98									130		98
99									130		99
100									131		100
101									132		101
102									133		102
103									133		103
104									134		104
105									135		105
106									135		106
107									136		107
108									137		108

POWER TRANSFORMED T-SCORES
HATHAWAY 18 YEAR OLD FEMALES, N=1864

RAW SCORE	D-O	D-S	HY-O	HY-S	PD-O	PD-S	PA-O	PA-S	MA-O	MA-S	RAW SCORE
0	16	--	24	14	20	--	32	20	26	13	0
1	23	13	31	16	29	11	43	23	31	16	1
2	28	16	38	18	35	15	51	27	36	19	2
3	33	20	43	20	41	19	56	30	41	23	3
4	37	24	48	22	46	23	60	34	45	26	4
5	41	28	52	24	50	27	64	39	49	30	5
6	45	32	56	26	54	31	67	43	52	34	6
7	48	36	59	28	58	35	70	48	55	37	7
8	51	40	62	31	61	39	72	53	58	41	8
9	54	44	64	33	63	43	74	57	61	45	9
10	56	48	66	36	66	47	76	62	64	49	10
11	59	52	69	38	68	52	77	68	66	53	11
12	61	56	70	41	70	56	79	73	69	57	12
13	63	60	72	43	72	60	80	78	71	61	13
14	65	64	74	46	74	64	81	84	73	65	14
15	67	69	75	48	75	68	82	89	75	69	15
16	68	73	77	51	77	72	83	95	77	73	16
17	70	77	78	54	78	76	84	100	79	77	17
18	72	81	79	56	79	80	85		80	81	18
19	73	86	81	59	80	84	86		82	85	19
20	74	90	82	62	82	88	87		84	89	20
21	76		83	65	83	92	88		85	93	21
22	77		84	67	84	96	89		87	97	22
23	78		84	70	85		89		88	101	23
24	80		85	73	86						24
25	81		86	76	86						25
26	82		87	79	87						26
27	83		88	82	88						27
28	84		88	85	89						28
29	85		89								29
30	86		90								30
31	87		90								31
32	88		91								32
33	89										33
34	89										34
35	90										35
36	91										36
37	92										37
38	93										38
39	93										39
40	94										40

POWER TRANSFORMED T-SCORES
HATHAWAY 18 YEAR OLD FEMALES, N=1864

RAW SCORE	A	R	MAC	ES	DELM	SM	AR	CR	PZ	DR	RAW SCORE
0	28	5	--	--	--	--	--	--	--	--	0
1	30	11	--	--	--	--	--	--	3	--	1
2	33	15	--	--	--	--	--	--	11	--	2
3	35	19	--	--	--	--	--	--	17	--	3
4	38	23	--	--	--	16	--	--	24	--	4
5	40	27	--	--	--	17	--	--	29	--	5
6	42	31	--	--	--	17	--	--	34	--	6
7	44	34	5	--	3	18	--	--	38	--	7
8	45	38	10	--	6	19	1	--	42	--	8
9	47	41	14	--	9	20	5	--	45	12	9
10	49	44	18	--	12	21	9	--	49	13	10
11	50	47	21	--	14	22	12	17	52	15	11
12	52	50	25	--	17	24	16	17	54	17	12
13	53	53	28	--	19	25	19	17	57	19	13
14	55	56	31	--	21	27	23	17	59	21	14
15	56	59	34	--	23	29	26	17	61	24	15
16	57	62	38	--	25	31	30	17	63	27	16
17	58	65	40	--	27	33	33	17	65	29	17
18	59	67	43	--	29	36	36	18	67	32	18
19	61	70	46	--	31	38	39	18	68	35	19
20	62	73	49	--	32	41	43	18	70	39	20
21	63	75	52	--	34	44	46	18	71	42	21
22	64	78	55	--	35	47	49	19	72	45	22
23	65	81	57	--	37	50	52	19	74	49	23
24	66	83	60	18	38	53	56	20	75	52	24
25	67	86	63	19	40	57	59	20	76	56	25
26	67	88	65	19	41	60	62	21	77	60	26
27	68	91	68	20	43	64	65	21	78	63	27
28	69	93	70	21	44	68	68	22	79	67	28
29	70	96	73	22	45	72	72	22	80	71	29
30	71	98	75	23	46	76	75	23	81	75	30
31	71	100	78	24	48	80	78	24	81	79	31
32	72		80	25	49	85	81	25	82	84	32
33	73		83	27	50	89	84	25	83	88	33
34	74		85	28	51	94	87	26	84	92	34
35	74		87	30	52	98	90	27	84	96	35
36	75		90	31	53	103	93	28	85	101	36
37			92	33	54	108	97	29	85	105	37
38			95	34	55	114	100	30	86	110	38
39			97	36	56	119	103	31	87	114	39
40			99	38	57	124	106	32	87		40
41			101	40	58	130		34	88		41
42			104	42	59	136		35	88		42
43			106	44	60	142		36	89		43
44			108	46	61	148		37	89		44
45			111	48	62			39	90		45
46			113	50	63			40	90		46
47			115	52	64			42	90		47
48			117	55	65			43	91		48
49			119	57	66			45	91		49
50				59	66			46	92		50

18-Year-Old Females (*continued*)

RAW SCORE	A	R	MAC	ES	DELM	SM	AR	CR	PZ	DR	RAW SCORE
51				62	67			48	92		51
52				64	68			50	92		52
53				67	69			51	93		53
54				69	70			53	93		54
55				72	70			55	93		55
56				74	71			57	94		56
57				77	72			59	94		57
58				80	73			61	94		58
59				82	73			63	95		59
60				85	74			65	95		60
61				88	75			67	95		61
62				91	76			69	95		62
63				94	76			71			63
64				97	77			74			64
65				100	78			76			65
66				103	78			78			66
67				106	79			81			67
68				109	80			83			68
69					80			86			69
70					81			88			70
71					82			91			71
72					82			94			72
73					83						73
74					83						74
75					84						75
76					85						76
77					85						77
78					86						78
79					86						79
80					87						80
81					88						81
82					88						82
83					89						83
84					89						84
85					90						85
86					90						86

POWER TRANSFORMED T-SCORES
HATHAWAY 18 YEAR OLD FEMALES, N=1864

RAW SCORE	SOC	DEP	FEM	MOR	REL	AUT	RAW SCORE
0	27	25	--	29	18	27	0
1	31	30	--	32	19	33	1
2	34	35	--	35	21	38	2
3	38	38	--	38	23	41	3
4	41	42	--	41	26	44	4
5	43	45	--	44	30	47	5
6	46	48	--	46	35	50	6
7	48	51	18	49	41	53	7
8	51	53	19	51	46	55	8
9	53	55	21	54	53	57	9
10	55	58	23	56	60	60	10
11	57	60	25	58	68	62	11
12	58	61	28	60	76	64	12
13	60	63	30	62		66	13
14	62	65	33	64		68	14
15	63	66	36	66		70	15
16	65	68	39	67		72	16
17	66	69	42	69		73	17
18	67	70	45	71		75	18
19	69	72	48	73		77	19
20	70	73	51	74		78	20
21	71	74	54				21
22	72	75	58				22
23	73	76	61				23
24	74	77	65				24
25	75	78	68				25
26	76	79	72				26
27		80	76				27
28		81	79				28
29		81	83				29
30		82	87				30
31		83					31
32		84					32
33		84					33

POWER TRANSFORMED T-SCORES
HATHAWAY 18 YEAR OLD FEMALES, N=1864

RAW SCORE	PSY	ORG	FAM	HOS	PHO	HYP	HEA	RAW SCORE
0	25	26	29	27	27	14	25	0
1	31	35	37	32	30	17	34	1
2	36	41	42	35	34	20	41	2
3	40	47	47	39	37	22	47	3
4	43	51	51	41	40	25	51	4
5	46	54	54	44	42	28	56	5
6	49	57	57	47	45	30	59	6
7	51	60	60	49	48	33	63	7
8	53	63	62	51	50	36	66	8
9	55	65	64	53	52	38	68	9
10	57	67	67	55	55	41	71	10
11	59	69	69	57	57	44	73	11
12	60	70	71	59	59	47	75	12
13	62	72	73	61	61	49	76	13
14	63	73	74	63	63	52	78	14
15	65	75	76	64	65	55	80	15
16	66	76	78	66	67	58	81	16
17	67	77		68	69	60	83	17
18	69	78		69	70	63	84	18
19	70	79		71	72	66	85	19
20	71	80		73	74	69	86	20
21	72	81		74	76	71	87	21
22	73	82		76	77	74	88	22
23	74	83		77	79	77	89	23
24	75	84		79	81	80	90	24
25	76	85		80	82	83	91	25
26	77	86		82	84		92	26
27	78	86					92	27
28	79	87						28
29	80	88						29
30	81	88						30
31	81	89						31
32	82	90						32
33	83	90						33
34	84	91						34
35	85	91						35
36	85	92						36
37	86							37
38	87							38
39	87							39
40	88							40
41	89							41
42	90							42
43	90							43
44	91							44
45	91							45
46	92							46
47	93							47

ITEM COMPOSITION OF THE HARRIS-LINGOES SUBSCALES

COMPOSITION OF HARRIS SUBSCALES*

Scale 2 — Depression

D₁ — Subjective Depression
True: 32, 41, 43, 52, 67, 86, 104, 138, 142, 158, 159, 182, 189, 236, 259
False: 2, 8, 46, 57, 88, 107, 122, 131, 152, 160, 191, 207, 208, 242, 272, 285, 296

D₂ — Psychomotor Retardation
True: 41, 52, 182, 259
False: 8, 30, 39, 57, 64, 89, 95, 145, 207, 208, 233

D₃ — Physical Malfunctioning
True: 130, 189, 193, 288
False: 2, 18, 51, 153, 154, 155, 160

D₄ — Mental Dullness
True: 32, 41, 86, 104, 159, 182, 259, 290
False: 8, 9, 46, 88, 122, 178, 207

D₅ — Brooding
True: 41, 67, 104, 138, 142, 158, 182, 236
False: 88, 107

Scale 3 — Hysteria

Hy₁ — Denial of Social Anxiety
True: None
False: 141, 172, 180, 201, 267, 292

Hy₂ — Need for Affection
True: 253
False: 26, 71, 89, 93, 109, 124, 136, 162, 234, 265, 289

Hy₃ — Lassitude-Malaise
True: 32, 43, 76, 189, 238
False: 2, 3, 8, 9, 51, 107, 137, 153, 160, 163

Hy₄ — Somatic Complaints
True: 10, 23, 44, 47, 114, 186
False: 7, 55, 103, 174, 175, 188, 190, 192, 230, 243, 274

Hy₅ — Inhibition of Aggression
True: None
False: 6, 12, 30, 128, 129, 147, 170

Scale 4 — Psychopathic Deviate

Pd₁ — Familial Discord
True: 21, 42, 212, 216, 224, 245
False: 96, 137, 235, 237, 527

Pd₂ — Authority Problems
True: 38, 59, 118, 520
False: 37, 82, 141, 173, 289, 294, 429

Pd₃ — Social Imperturbability
True: 64, 479, 520, 521
False: 82, 141, 171, 180, 201, 267, 304, 352

Pd₄ₐ — Social Alienation
True: 16, 24, 35, 64, 67, 94, 110, 127, 146, 239, 244, 284, 305, 368, 520
False: 20, 141, 170

Pd₄ᵦ — Self-Alienation
True: 32, 33, 61, 67, 76, 84, 94, 102, 106, 127, 146, 215, 368
False: 8, 107

Scale 6 — Paranoia

Pa₁ — Personality Ideas
True: 16, 24, 35, 10, 121, 123, 127, 151, 157, 202, 275, 284, 291, 293, 338, 364
False: 347

Pa₂ — Poignancy
True: 24, 158, 299, 305, 317, 341, 365
False: 111, 268

Pa₃ — Naiveté
True: 314
False: 93, 109, 117, 124, 313, 316, 319, 348

Scale 8 — Schizophrenia

Sc₁ₐ — Social Alienation
True: 16, 21, 24, 35, 52, 121, 157, 212, 241, 282, 305, 312, 324, 325, 352, 364
False: 65, 220, 276, 306, 309

Sc_{1B} — Emotional Alienation
  True: 76, 104, 202, 301, 339, 355, 360, 363
  False: 8, 196, 322
Sc_{2A} — Lack of Ego Mastery, Cognitive
  True: 32, 33, 159, 168, 182, 335, 345, 349, 356
  False: 178
Sc_{2B} — Lack of Ego Mastery, Conative
  True: 32, 40, 41, 76, 104, 202, 259, 301, 335, 339, 356
  False: 8, 196, 322
Sc_{2C} — Lack of Ego Mastery, Defective Inhibition
  True: 22, 97, 156, 194, 238, 266, 291, 303, 352, 354, 360
  False: None
Sc_3 — Bizarre Sensory Experiences
  True: 22, 33, 47, 156, 194, 210, 251, 273, 291, 332, 334, 341, 345, 350
  False: 103, 119, 187, 192, 281, 330

Scale 9 — Hypomania

Ma_1 — Amorality
  True: 143, 250, 271, 277, 298
  False: 289
Ma_2 — Psychomotor Acceleration
  True: 13, 97, 100, 134, 181, 228, 238, 266, 268
  False: 111, 119
Ma_3 — Imperturbability
  True: 167, 222, 240
  False: 105, 148, 171, 180, 267
Ma_4 — Ego Inflation
  True: 11, 59, 64, 73, 109, 157, 212, 232, 233
  False: None

MMPI ADOLESCENT PROFILE FORMS FOR MALES AND FEMALES

MMPI PROFILE FORM
ADOLESCENT NORMS: MALE

NAME _____   AGE _____   DATE TESTED _____

ADDITIONAL INFORMATION _____

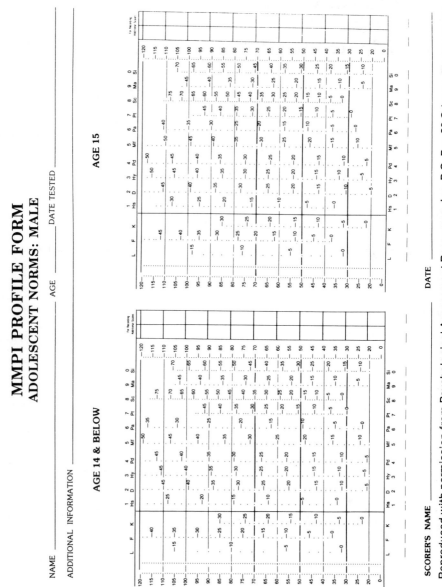

AGE 14 & BELOW

AGE 15

SCORER'S NAME _____   DATE _____

MMPI PROFILE FORM
ADOLESCENT NORMS: FEMALE

NAME _____ AGE _____ DATE TESTED _____

ADDITIONAL INFORMATION _____

AGE 14

AGE 15

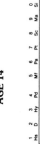

SCORER'S NAME _____   DATE _____

Reproduced with permission from Psychological Assessment Resources, Inc. P.O. Box 98 Odessa, Florida 33556

FORM #404-PF

MMPI PROFILE FORM
ADOLESCENT NORMS: MALE

NAME _____ AGE _____ DATE TESTED _____

ADDITIONAL INFORMATION _____

AGE 16

AGE 17 & 18

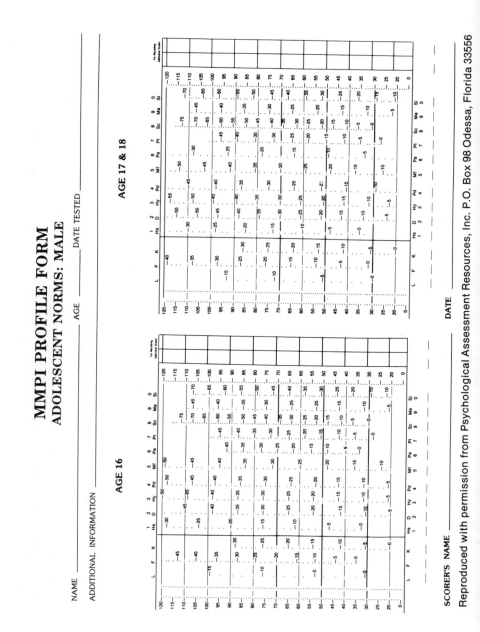

SCORER'S NAME _____ DATE _____

Reproduced with permission from Psychological Assessment Resources, Inc. P.O. Box 98 Odessa, Florida 33556

MMPI PROFILE FORM
ADOLESCENT NORMS: FEMALE

NAME _____ AGE _____ DATE TESTED _____

ADDITIONAL INFORMATION _____

AGE 16

AGE 17 & 18

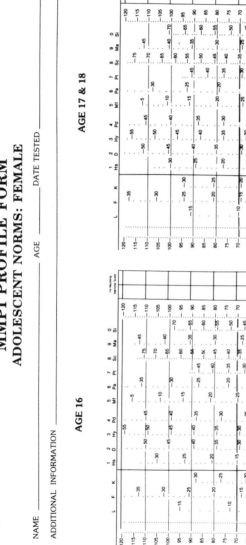

SCORER'S NAME _____   DATE _____

Reproduced with permission from Psychological Assessment Resources, Inc. P.O. Box 98 Odessa, Florida 33556

FORM #406-PF

REFERENCES

Adrian, R. J., Vacchiano, R. B., & Gilbart, T. E. (1966). Linear discriminant function classification of accepted and rejected adoptive applicants. *Journal of Clinical Psychology, 22,* 251–254.

Anthony, E. J. (1975). *Explorations in child psychiatry.* New York: Plenum.

Archer, R. P. (1984). Use of the MMPI with adolescents: A review of salient issues. *Clinical Psychology Review, 4,* 241–251.

Archer, R. P. (In press). Using the MMPI with adolescents: Overview and recommendations. In C. D. Spielberger & J. N. Butcher (Eds.), *Advances in personality assessment* (Vol. 7). Hillsdale, NJ: Lawrence Erlbaum Associates.

Archer, R. P., Ball, J. D., & Hunter, J. A. (1985). MMPI characteristics of borderline psychopathology in adolescent inpatients. *Journal of Personality Assessment, 49,* 47–55.

Archer, R. P., Gordon, R. A., & Kircher, F. H. (1986). [MMPI response set characteristics of adolescents.] Unpublished raw data.

Archer, R. P., Stolberg, A. L., Gordon, R. A., & Goldman, W. R. (1986). Parent and child MMPI responses: Characteristics among families with adolescents in inpatient and outpatient settings. *Journal of Abnormal Child Psychology, 14,* 181–190.

Archer, R. P., Sutker, P. B., White, J. L., & Orvin, G. H. (1978). Personality relationships among parents and adolescent offspring in inpatient treatment. *Psychological Reports, 42,* 207–214.

Archer, R. P., White, J. L., & Orvin, G. H. (1979). MMPI characteristics and correlates among adolescent psychiatric inpatients. *Journal of Clinical Psychology, 35,* 498–504.

Ball, J. C. (1960). Comparison of MMPI profile differences among Negro-white adolescents. *Journal of Clinical Psychology, 16,* 304–307.

Ball, J. C., & Carroll, D. (1960). Analysis of MMPI cannot say scores in an adolescent population. *Journal of Clinical Psychology, 16,* 30–31.

Ball, J. D., Archer, R. P., Struve, F. A., Hunter, J. A., & Gordon, R. A. (in press). *MMPI correlates of a controversial EEG pattern among adolescent inpatients.* Journal of Clinical Psychology.

Balswick, J. O., & Macrides, C. (1975). Parental stimulus for adolescent rebellion. *Adolescence, 10,* 253–266.

Bandura, A. (1964). The stormy decade: Fact or fiction? *Psychology in the School, 1,* 224–231.

Barron, F. (1953). An ego strength scale which predicts response to psychotherapy. *Journal of Consulting Psychology, 17,* 327–333.

Baughman, E. E., & Dahlstrom, W. G. (1968). *Negro and white children: A psychological study in the rural south.* New York: Academic Press.

Bell, R. Q. (1979). Parent, child and reciprocal influences. *American Psychologist, 34,* 821–826.

Bertelson, A. D., Marks, P. A., & May, G. D. (1982). MMPI and race: A controlled study. *Journal of Consulting and Clinical Psychology, 50,* 316–318.

Block, J. (1965). *The challenge of response sets: Unconfounding meaning, acquiescence and social desirability in the MMPI.* New York: Appleton-Century-Crofts.

Bloom, W. (1977). Relevant MMPI norms for young adult Air Force trainees. *Journal of Personality Assessment, 41,* 505–510.

Blos, P. (1962). *On adolescence: A psychoanalytic interpretation.* New York: Free Press.

Blos, P. (1967). The second individuation process of adolescence. *The Psychoanalytic Study of the Child, 22,* 162–186.

Blotcky, M. J., & Looney, J. G. (1980). Normal female and male adolescent psychological development: An overview of theory and research. *Adolescent Psychiatry, 8,* 184–199.

Bonfilio, S. A., & Lyman, R. D. (1981). Ability to simulate normalcy as a function of differential psychopathology. *Psychological Reports, 49,* 15–21.

Bowen, M. (1961). Family psychotherapy. *American Journal of Orthopsychiatry, 30,* 40–60.

Briggs, P. F., Wirt, R. D., & Johnson, R. (1961). An application of prediction tables to the study of delinquency. *Journal of Consulting Psychology, 25,* 46–50.

Burke, E. L., & Eichberg, M. A. (1972). Personality characteristics of adolescent users of dangerous drugs as indicated by the Minnesota Multiphasic Personality Inventory. *Journal of Nervous and Mental Disease, 154,* 291–298.

Buros, O. K. (1974). *Tests in print II.* Highland Park, NJ: Gryphon Press.

Butcher, J. N. (Ed.). (1972). *Objective personality assessment: Changing perspectives.* New York: Academic Press.

Butcher, J. N. (1985a). Why use the MMPI? In J. N. Butcher & J. R. Graham (Eds.), *Clinical applications of the MMPI:* 1 (pp. 1–2). Minneapolis: University of Minnesota Department of Conferences.

Butcher, J. N. (1985b). Why MMPI short forms should not be used for clinical predictions. In J. N. Butcher & J. R. Graham (Eds.), *Clinical applications of the MMPI* (pp. 10–11). Minneapolis: University of Minnesota Department of Conferences.

Butcher, J. N., & Messick, D. M. (1966). Parent-child profile similarity and aggression: A preliminary study. *Psychological Reports, 18,* 440–442.

Butcher, J. N., & Owen, P. L. (1978). Objective personality inventories: Recent research and some contemporary issues. In B. B. Wolman (Eds.), *Clinical diagnosis of mental disorders: A handbook* (pp. 475–545). New York: Plenum.

Butcher, J. N., & Pancheri, P. (1976). *Handbook of cross-national MMPI research.* Minneapolis: University of Minnesota Press.

Butcher, J. N., & Tellegen, A. (1978). Common methodological problems in MMPI research. *Journal of Consulting and Clinical Psychology, 46,* 620–628.

Caldwell, A. B. (1969). *MMPI critical items.* (Available from Caldwell Reports, 3122 Santa Monica Boulevard, Penthouse West, Los Angeles, California 90404).

Capwell, D. F. (1945). Personality patterns of adolescent girls: Delinquents and nondelinquents. *Journal of Applied Psychology, 29,* 284–297.

Carson, R. C. (1969). Interpretative manual to the MMPI. In J. N. Butcher (Ed.), *MMPI: Research development and clinical applications* New York: McGraw.

Cattell, R. B., & Cattell, M. D. L. (1969). *Handbook for the Jr.-Sr. High School Personality Questionnaire.* Champaign, IL: Institute for Personality and Ability Testing.

Cattell, R. B., Eber, H. W., & Tatsuoka, M. (1970). *Handbook for the Sixteen Personality Factor Questionnaire.* Champaign, IL: Institute for Personality and Ability Testing.

Chase, T. V., Chaffin, S., & Morrison, S. D. (1975). False positive adolescent MMPI profiles. *Adolescence, 40,* 507–519.

Clopton, J. R. (1978). A note on the MMPI as a suicide predictor. *Journal of Consulting and Clinical Psychology, 46,* 335–336.

Clopton, J. R. (1979). The MMPI and suicide. In C. S. Newmark (Ed.), *MMPI: Clinical and research trends* (pp. 149–166). New York: Praeger.

Coleman, J. C. (1978). Current contradictions in adolescent theory. *Journal of Youth and Adolescence, 7,* 1–11.

Colligan, R. C., & Offord, K. P. (1986, March). *Today's adolescent and the MMPI: Patterns of MMPI responses from normal teenagers of the 80's.* Paper presented at the 32nd Annual Meeting of the Southeastern Psychological Association, Orlando, Florida.

Colligan, R. C., Osborne, D., & Offord, K. P. (1984). Normalized transformations and the interpretation of MMPI T scores: A reply to Hsu. *Journal of Consulting and Clinical Psychology, 52,* 824–826.

Colligan, R. C., Osborne, D., Swenson, W. M., & Offord, K. P. (1983). *The MMPI: A contemporary normative study.* New York: Praeger.

Colligan, R. C., Osborne, D., Swenson, W. M., & Offord, K. P. (1984). The MMPI: Development of contemporary norms. *Journal of Clinical Psychology, 40,* 100–107.

Dahlstrom, W. G., & Welsh, G. S. (1960). *An MMPI handbook: A guide to use in clinical practice and research.* Minneapolis: University of Minnesota Press.

Dahlstrom, W. G., Welsh, G. S., & Dahlstrom, L. E. (1972). *An MMPI handbook: Vol. 1. Clinical interpretation.* Minneapolis: University of Minnesota Press.

Dahlstrom, W. G., Welsh, G. S., & Dahlstrom, L. E. (1975). *An MMPI handbook: Vol. 2. Research Applications.* Minneapolis: University of Minnesota Press.

Douvan, E., & Adelson, J. (1966). *The adolescent experience.* New York: Wiley.

Drake, L. E., & Oetting, E. R. (1959). *An MMPI handbook for counselors.* Minneapolis: University of Minnesota Press.

Duckworth, J. C., & Duckworth, E. (1975). *An MMPI interpretation manual for clinicians and counselors.* Muncie, IN: Accelerated Development, Inc.

Dudley, H. K., Mason, M., & Hughes, R. (1972). The MMPI and adolescent patients in a state hospital. *Journal of Youth and Adolescence, 1,* 165–178.

Dworkin, R. H., Burke, B. W., Maher, B. A., & Gottesman, I. I. (1976). A longitudinal study of the genetics of personality. *Journal of Personality and Social Psychology, 34,* 510–518.

Dworkin, R. H., Burke, B. W., Maher, B. A., & Gottesman, I. I. (1977). Genetic influences on the organization and development of personality. *Developmental Psychology, 13,* 164–165.

Ehrenworth, N. V. (1984). *A comparison of the utility of interpretive approaches with adolescent MMPI profiles.* Unpublished doctoral dissertation, Virginia Consortium for Professional Psychology, Norfolk, VA.

Ehrenworth, N. V., & Archer, R. P. (1985). A comparison of clinical accuracy ratings of interpretive approaches for adolescent MMPI responses. *Journal of Personality Assessment, 49,* 413–421.

Eme, R., Maisiak, R., & Goodale, W. (1979). Seriousness of adolescent problems. *Adolecence, 14,* 93–99.

Erikson, E. H. (1956). The concept of ego identity. *The Journal of the American Psychoanalytic Association, 4,* 56–121.

Erickson, M. T. (1968). MMPI profiles of parents of young retarded children. *American Journal of Mental Deficiency, 73,* 728–732.

Evans, R. G. (1984). Normative data for two MMPI critical item sets. *Journal of Clinical Psychology, 40,* 512–515.

Exner, J. E. (1978). *The Rorschach, a comprehensive system: Current research and advanced interpretation* (Vol. 2). New York: Wiley.

Fowler, R. D. (1966). *The MMPI notebook: A guide to the clinical use of the automated MMPI.* Nutley, NJ: Roche Psychiatric Service Institute.

Fox, D. D., Sunlight, C., & Permanente, K. (1985, March). *The validity of MMPI critical items in different ethnic groups.* Paper presented at the 20th Annual Symposium on Recent Developments in the Use of the MMPI, Honolulu, HI.

Freud, A. (1958). Adolescence. *Psychoanalytic study of the child, 13,* 255–278.

Fuller, J. L., & Thompson, W. R. (1960). *Behavior genetics.* New York: Wiley.

Gilberstadt. H., & Duker, J. (1965). *A handbook for clinical and actuarial MMPI interpretation.* Philadelphia: Saunders.

Gjerde, C. M. (1949). *Parent-child resemblances in vocational interests and personality traits.* Unpublished doctoral dissertation, University of Minnesota, Minneapolis.

Goodstein, L. D. (1960a). MMPI differences between parents of children with cleft palates and parents of physically normal children. *Journal of Speech and Hearing Research, 3,* 31–38.

Goodstein, L. D. (1960b). Personality test differences in parents of children with cleft palates. *Journal of Speech and Hearing Research, 3,* 39–43.

Goodstein, L. D., & Dahlstrom, W. G. (1956). MMPI difference between the parents of stuttering and nonstuttering children. *Journal of Consulting Psychology, 20,* 365–70.

Goodstein, L. D., & Rowley, V. N. (1961). A further study of MMPI differences between parents of disturbed and nondisturbed children. *Journal of Consulting Psychology, 25,* 460.

Gottesman, I. I. (1963). Heritability of personality: A demonstration. *Psychological Monographs, 77* (9, Whole No. 572).

Gottesman, I. I., & Fishman, D. B. (1961). *Adolescent psychometric personality: A phenotypic psychosis.* Paper presented at the meeting of the American Psychological Association.

Gough, H. B. (1964). *California Personality Inventory Manual.* Palo Alto, CA: Consulting Psychologists Press.

Graham, J. R. (1977). *The MMPI: A practical guide.* New York: Oxford University Press.

Graham, J. R. (1985). Interpreting the MacAndrew Alcoholism Scale. In J. N. Butcher & J. R. Graham (Eds.), *Clinical applications of the MMPI* (pp. 27–28). Minneapolis: University of Minnesota Department of Conferences.

Graham, J. R., & Mayo M. A. (1985, March). *A comparison of MMPI strategies for identifying black and white male alcoholics.* Paper presented at the 20th Annual Symposium on recent developments in the use of the MMPI, Honolulu, HI.

Grayson, H. M. (1951). *Psychological admissions testing program and manual.* Los Angeles: Veterans Administration Center, Neuropsychiatric Hospital.

Grayson, H. M., & Olinger, L. B. (1957). Simulation of "normalcy" by psychiatric patients on the MMPI. *Journal of Consulting Psychology, 21,* 73–77.

Greene, R. L. (1980). *The MMPI: An interpretive manual.* New York: Grune and Stratton.

Greene, R. L. (in press). Ethnicity and MMPI performance: A review. *Journal of Consulting and Clinical Psychology.*

Group for the Advancement of Psychiatry. (1968). *Normal adolescence: Its dynamics and impact.* New York: Charles Scribner's Sons.

Guerin, P. J. (1976). *Family therapy: Theory and practice.* New York: Gardner.

Gynther, M. D. (1961). The clinical utility of "invalid" MMPI F scores. *Journal of Consulting Psychology, 25,* 540–542.

Gynther, M. D. (1972). White norms and black MMPIs: A prescription for discrimination? *Psychological Bulletin, 78,* 386–402.

Gynther, M. D., Altman, H., & Warbin, R. (1972). Interpretation of uninterpretable Minnesota Multiphasic Personality Inventory profiles. *Journal of Consulting and Clinical Psychology, 40,* 78–83.

Gynther, M. D., Altman, H., & Sletten, I. W. (1975). Replicated correlates of MMPI 2-point types: The Missouri actuarial system. *Journal of Clinical Psychology,* Monograph supplement No. 39.

Gynther, M. D., & Shimkunas, A. M. (1966). Age and MMPI performance. *Journal of Consulting Psychology, 30,* 118–121.

Hafner, A. J., Butcher, J. N., Hall, M. D., & Quast, W. (1969). Parent personality and childhood disorders: A review of MMPI findings. In J. N. Butcher (Ed.), *MMPI: Research developments and clinical applications* (pp. 181–189). New York: McGraw-Hill.

Hall, G. S. (1904). *Adolescence: Its psychology and its relationship to physiology, anthropology, sociology, sex, crime, religion and education.* New York: Appleton.

Harris, R. E., & Lingoes, J. C. (1955). *Subscales for the MMPI: An aid to profile interpretation.* Unpublished manuscript, University of California.

Hathaway, S. R., & Dahlstrom, W. G. (1974). Foreword to the revised edition. In P. A. Marks, W. Seeman, & D. L. Haller, *The actuarial use of the MMPI with adolescents and adults* (pp. vii–x). New York: Oxford University Press.

Hathaway, S. R., & McKinley, J. C. (1942). A multiphasic personality schedule (Minnesota): III. The measurement of symptomatic depression. *Journal of Psychology, 14,* 73–84.

Hathaway, S. R., & Monachesi, E. D. (Eds.) (1953). *Analyzing and predicting juvenile delinquency with the MMPI.* Minneapolis: University of Minnesota Press.

Hathaway, S. R., & Monachesi, E. D. (1961). *An atlas of juvenile MMPI profiles.* Minneapolis: University of Minnesota Press.

Hathaway, S. R., & Monachesi, E. D. (1963). *Adolescent personality and behavior.* Minneapolis: University of Minnesota Press.

Hathaway, S. R., Monachesi, E., & Salasin, S. (1970). A follow-up study of MMPI high 8, schizoid children. In M. Róff and D. F. Ricks, (eds.). *Life history research in psychopathology.* Minneapolis: University of Minnesota Press (pp. 171–188).

Heilbrun, A. B. (1963). Revision of the MMPI *K* correction procedure for improved detection of maladjustment in a normal college population. *Journal of Consulting Psychology, 27,* 161–165.

Hill, M. S., & Hill, R. N. (1973). Hereditary influences on the normal personality using the MMPI. Age-corrected parent-offspring resemblances. *Behavior Genetics, 3,* 133–144.

Hoffman, N. G., & Butcher, J. N. (1975). Clinical limitations of MMPI short forms. *Journal of Consulting and Clinical Psychology, 43,* 32–39.

Hoffman, H., Loper, R. F., & Kammeier, M. L. (1974). Identifying future alcoholics with MMPI alcoholism scales. *Quarterly Journal of Studies on Alcohol, 35,* 1230–1237.

Horn, J. M., Loehlin, J. C., & Willerman, L. (1979). Intellectual resemblance among adoptive and biological relatives: The Texas Adoption Project. *Behavior Genetics, 9,* 177–207.

Hsu, L. M. (1984). MMPI T scores: Linear versus normalized. *Journal of Consulting and Clinical Psychology, 52,* 821–823.

Huber, N. A., & Danahy, S. (1975). Use of the MMPI in predicting completion and evaluating changes in a long-term alcoholism treatment program. *Journal of Studies on Alcohol, 36,* 1230–1237.

Huesmann, L. R., Lefkowitz, M. M., & Eron, L. D. (1978). Sum of MMPI scales, F, 4, and 9 as a measure of aggression. *Journal of Consulting and Clinical Psychology, 46,* 1071–1078.

Kanun, C., & Monachesi, E. D. (1960). Delinquency and the validating scales of the MMPI. *Journal of Criminal Law, Criminology and Police Science, 50,* 525–534.

Kimmel, D. C., & Weiner, I. B. (1985). *Adolescence: A developmental transition.* Hillsdale, NJ: Lawrence Erlbaum Associates.

King, G. D., & Kelley, C. K. (1977). MMPI behavioral correlates of spike-5 and 2-point code types with scale 5 as one elevation. *Journal of Clinical Psychology, 33,* 180–185.

Klinge, V. (1983). A comparison of parental and adolescent MMPIs as related to substance use. *The International Journal of the Addictions, 18,* 1179–1185.

Klinge, V., Lachar, D., Grissell, J., & Berman, W. (1978). Effects of scoring norms on adolescent psychiatric drug users' and nonusers' MMPI profiles. *Adolescence, 13,* 1–11.

Klinge, V., & Strauss, M. E. (1976). Effects of scoring norms on adolescent psychiatric patients' MMPI profiles. *Journal of Personality Assessment, 40,* 13–17.

Kranitz, L. (1972). Alcoholics, heroin addicts, and nonaddicts: Comparisons on the MacAndrew Alcoholism Scale of the MMPI. *Quarterly Journal of Studies on Alcohol, 33,* 807–809.

L'Abate, L. (1960). The effect of paternal failure to participate during the referral of child psychiatric patients. *Journal of Clinical Psychology, 16*, 407–408.

Lachar, D. (1974). *The MMPI: Clinical assessment and automated interpretation.* Los Angeles, CA: Western Psychological Services.

Lachar, D., Berman, W., Grissell, J., & Schoof, K. (1976). The MacAndrew Alcoholism Scale as a general measure of substance abuse. *Journal of Studies on Alcohol, 87*, 1609–1615.

Lachar, D., Godowski, C. L., & Keegan, J. F. (1979). MMPI profiles of men alcoholics, drug addicts and psychiatric patients. *Journal of Studies on Alcohol, 40*, 45–56.

Lachar, D., Klinge, V., & Grissell, J. L. (1976). Relative accuracy of automated MMPI narratives generated from adult norm and adolescent norm profiles. *Journal of Consulting and Clinical Psychology, 44*, 20–24.

Lachar, D., & Sharp, J. R. (1979). Use of parents' MMPI in the research and evaluation of children. In J. N. Butcher (Ed.), *New development in the use of the MMPI* (pp. 203–240). Minneapolis: University of Minnesota Press.

Lachar, D., & Wrobel, T. A. (1979). Validating clinicians' hunches: Construction of a new MMPI critical item set. *Journal of Consulting and Clinical Psychology, 47*, 781–782.

Larzelere, R. E., & Mulaik, S. A. (1977). Single-sample tests for many correlations. *Psychological Bulletin, 84*, 557–569.

Lauterbach, C. G., London, P., & Bryan, J. (1961). MMPIs of parents of child guidance cases. *Journal of Clinical Psychology, 17*, 151–154.

Lauterbach, C. G., Vogel, W., & Hart, J. (1962). Comparison of the MMPI's of male problem adolescents and their parents. *Journal of Clinical Psychology, 18*, 485–487.

Lewandowski, D., & Graham, J. R. (1972). Empirical correlates of frequently occurring 2-point code types: A replicated study. *Journal of Consulting and Clinical Psychology, 39*, 467–472.

Liverant, S. (1959). MMPI differences between parents of disturbed and nondisturbed children. *Journal of Consulting Psychology, 23*, 256–260.

Loehlin, J. C., Horn, J. M., & Willerman, L. (1981). Personality resemblance in adoptive families. *Behavior Genetics, 11*, 309–330.

Loehlin, J. C., Willerman, L., & Horn, J. M. (1982). Personality resemblances between unwed mothers and their adopted-away offspring. *Journal of Personality and Social Psychology, 42*, 1089–1099.

Loehlin, J. C., Willerman, L., & Horn, J. M. (1985). Personality resemblances in adoptive families when the children are late-adolescent or adult. *Journal of Personality and Social Psychology, 48*, 376–392.

Looney, J. G. (1985). Research priorities in adolescent psychiatry: Report of the Committee on Research of the American Society for Adolescent Psychiatry. In S. C. Feinstein, M. Sugar, A. H. Esman, J. G. Looney, A. Z. Schwartzberg, & A. D. Sorasky (Eds.), *Adolescent psychiatry: Developmental and clinical studies* (Vol. 12, pp. 104–116). Chicago, IL: University of Chicago Press.

Looney, J. G., & Gunderson, E. K. E. (1978). Transient situation disorders: A longitudinal study in young men. *American Journal of Psychiatry, 135*, 660–663.

Lueger, R. J. (1983). The use of the MMPI-168 with delinquent adolescents. *Journal of Clinical Psychology, 39*, 139–141.

MacAndrew, C. (1965). The differentiation of male alcoholic outpatients from nonalcoholic psychiatric outpatients by means of the MMPI. *Quarterly Journal of Studies on Alcohol, 26*, 238–246.

MacAndrew, C. (1979). On the possibility of psychometric detection of persons prone to the abuse of alcohol and other substances. *Addictive Behaviors, 4*, 11–20.

Macbeth, L., & Cadow, B. (1984). Utility of the MMPI–168 with adolescents. *Journal of Clinical Psychology, 40*, 142–148.

Marks, P. A. (1961). An assessment of the diagnostic process in a child guidance setting. *Psy-

chology Monographs, 73 (3, Whole No. 507).

Marks, P. A., & Seeman, W. (1963). *The actuarial description of abnormal personality: An atlas for use with the MMPI.* Baltimore, MD: Williams & Wilkins.

Marks, P. A., Seeman, W., & Haller, D. (1974). *The actuarial use of the MMPI with adolescents and adults.* Baltimore, MD: William & Wilkins.

Masterson, J. F. (1968). The psychiatric significance of adolescent turmoil. *American Journal of Psychiatry, 124,* 107–112.

McAdoo, W. G., & Connolly, F. J. (1975). MMPIs of parents in dysfunctional families. *Journal of Consulting and Clinical Psychology, 43,* 270.

McAdoo, W. G., & DeMeyer, M. K. (1978). Personality characteristics of parents. In M. Rutter & E. Schopler (Eds.), *Autism: A reappraisal of concepts and treatment.* New York: Plenum.

McDonald, R. L., & Gynther, M. D. (1962). MMPI norms for southern adolescent Negroes. *Journal of Social Psychology, 58,* 277–282.

Mead, M. (1928), *Coming of age in Samoa.* New York: Morrow.

Mead, M. (1930). Adolescence in primitive and modern society. In F. V. Calverton & S. D. Schmalhausen, (Eds.), *The new generation: A symposium.* New York: Macauley.

Meehl, P. E. (1945). The dynamics of structured personality tests. *Journal of Clinical Psychology, 1,* 296–304.

Meehl, P. E. (1951). *Research results for counselors.* St. Paul, MN: State Department of Education.

Meehl, P. E. (1966a). Profile analysis of the MMPI in differential diagnosis. In G. S. Welsh & W. G. Dahlstrom (Eds.), *Basic reading on the MMPI in psychology and medicine* (pp. 292–297). Minneapolis: University of Minnesota Press.

Meehl, P. E. (1956b). Wanted—a good cookbook. *American Psychologist, 11,* 263–272.

Meehl, P. E., & Dahlstrom, W. G. (1960). Objective configural rules for discriminating psychotic from neurotic MMPI profiles. *Journal of Consulting Psychology, 24,* 375–387.

Meltzoff, J., & Kornreich, M. (1970). *Research in psychotherapy.* New York: Atherton Press.

Miller, W. H., & Keirn, W. C. (1978). Personality measurement in parents of retarded and emotionally disturbed children: A replication. *Journal of Clinical Psychology, 34,* 686–90.

Millon, T., Green, C. J., & Meagher, R. B. (1977). *Millon Adolescent Personality Inventory.* Minneapolis, MN: National Computer Systems.

Minuchin, S., & Fishman, C. H. (1981). *Family therapy techniques.* Cambridge, MA: Harvard University Press.

Mlott, S. R. (1972). Some significant relationships between adolescents and their parents as revealed by the Minnesota Multiphasic Personality Inventory. *Adolescence, 7,* 169–182.

Mlott, S. R. (1973). The Mini-Mult and its use with adolescents. *Journal of Clinical Psychology, 29,* 376–377.

Monachesi, E. D., & Hathaway, S. R. (1969). The personality of delinquents. In J. N. Butcher (Ed.), *MMPI: Research developments and clinical applications* (pp. 207–219). Minneapolis: University of Minnesota Press.

Monge, R. H. (1973). Developmental trends in factors of adolescent self-concept. *Developmental Psychology, 8,* 382–393.

Moore, C. D., & Handal, P. J. (1980). Adolescents' MMPI performance, cynicism, estrangement, and personal adjustment as a function of race and sex. *Journal of Clinical Psychology, 36,* 932–936.

Newmark, C. S., Gentry, L., & Whitt, J. K. (1983). Utility of MMPI indices of schizophrenia with adolescents. *Journal of Clinical Psychology, 39,* 170–172.

Newmark, C. S., Gentry, L., Whitt, J. K., McKee, D. C., & Wicker, C. (1983). Simulating normal MMPI profiles as a favorable prognostic sign in schizophrenia. *Australian Journal of Psychology, 35,* 433–444.

Newmark, C. S., & Thibodeau, J. R. (1979). Interpretive accuracy and empirical validity of abbreviated forms of the MMPI with hospitalized adolescents. In C. S. Newmark (Ed.), *MMPI: Clinical and research trends.* (pp. 248–275). New York, NY: Praeger.

Offer, D. (1969). *The psychological world of the teenager.* New York: Basic Books.

Offer, D., & Offer, J. B. (1975). *From teenager to young manhood.* New York: Basic Books.

Osborne, D. (1979). Use of the MMPI with medical patients. In J. N. Butcher (Ed.), *New developments in the use of the MMPI.* (pp. 141–164). Minneapolis: University of Minnesota Press.

Pancoast, D., Archer, R. P., & Gordon, R. A. (in press). *Clinical diagnosis and the MMPI: A comparison of MMPI diagnostic classification systems with clinical diagnoses.* Journal of Personality Assessment.

Piaget, J. (1969). The intellectual development of the adolescent. In G. Caplan & S. Lebovici (Eds.), *Adolescence: Psychosocial perspectives.* New York: Basic Books.

Pinneau, S. R., & Hopper, H. E. (1958). The relationship between incidence of specific gastro-intestinal reactions in the infant and psychological characteristics of the mother. *Journal of Genetic Psychology, 93,* 3–13.

Post, R. D., & Gasparikova-Krasnec, M. (1979). MMPI validity scales and behavioral disturbance in psychiatric inpatients. *Journal of Personality Assessment, 43,* 155–159.

Rathus, S. A. (1978). Factor structure of the MMPI-168 with and without regression weights. *Psychological Reports, 42,* 643–646.

Rathus, S. A., Fox, J. A., & Ortins, J. B. (1980). The MacAndrew scale as a measure of substance abuse and delinquency among adolescents. *Journal of Clinical Psychology, 36,* 579–583.

Rempel, P. P. (1958). The use of multivariate statistical analysis of Minnesota Multiphasic Personality Inventory scores in the classification of delinquent and nondelinquent high school boys. *Journal of Consulting Psychology, 22,* 17–23.

Rice, D. G. (1968). Rorschach responses and aggressive characteristics of MMPI F > 16 scorers. *Journal of Projective Techniques, 32,* 253–261.

Routh, D. K. (1970). MMPI responses of mothers and fathers as a function of mental retardation of the child. *American Journal of Mental Deficiency, 75,* 376–377.

Scarr, S., Webber, P. L., Weinberg, R. A., & Wittig, M. A. (1981). Personality resemblance among adolescents and their parents in biologically related and adoptive families. *Journal of Personality and Social Psychology, 40,* 885–898.

Schenkenberg, T., Gottfredson, D. K., & Christensen, P. (1984). Age differences in MMPI scales scores from 1,189 psychiatric patients. *Journal of Clinical Psychology, 40,* 1420–1426.

Sharp, V. (1980). Adolescence. In J. R. Bemporad (Ed.), *Child development in normality and psychopathology* (pp. 174–220). New York: Brunner/Mazel.

Smith, P. E., Burleigh, R. L., Sewell, W. R., & Krisak, J. (1984). Correlation between the Minnesota Multiphasic Personality Inventory profiles of emotionally disturbed adolescents and their mothers. *Adolescence, 19,* 31–38.

Sopchak, A. L. (1958). Spearman correlations between MMPI scores of college students and their parents. *Journal of Consulting Psychology, 22,* 207–209.

Sperling, M. (1970). The clinical effects of parental neurosis on the child. In E. J. Anthony & T. Benedek (Eds.), *Parenthood: Its psychology and psychopathology* (pp. 639–569). Boston, MA: Little, Brown.

Spielberger, C. D. (1966). Theory and research on anxiety. In C. D. Spielberger (Ed.), *Anxiety and behavior* (pp. 3–22). New York: Academic Press.

Spitz, R. A. (1970). The effects of personality disturbances in the mother on the well-being of her infant. In E. J. Anthony & T. Benedek (Eds.), *Parenthood: Its psychology and psychopathology* (pp. 501–524). Boston, MA: Little, Brown.

Stehbens, J. A. (1970). Comparison of MMPI scores of mothers of enuretic and control children. *Journal of Clinical Psychology, 26,* 496.

Stone, L. J., & Church, J. (1957a). Pubescence, puberty, and physical development. In A. H.

Essman (Ed.), *The Psychology of Adolescence: Essential Readings* (pp. 75–85). New York: International Universities Press.

Stone, L. J., & Church, J. (1957b). Adolescence as a cultural invention. In A. H. Essman (Ed.), *The Psychology of Adolescence: Essential Readings* (pp. 7–11). New York: International Universities Press.

Sutker, P. B., Allain, A. N., & Geyer, S. (1980). Female criminal violence and differential MMPI characteristics. *Journal of Consulting and Clinical Psychology, 46*, 1141–1143.

Sutker, P. B., & Archer, R. P. (1979). MMPI characteristics of opiate addicts, alcoholics, and other drug abusers. In C. S. Newmark (Ed.), *MMPI clinical and research trends* (pp. 105–148). New York: Praeger.

Sutker, P. B., Archer, R. P., & Kilpatrick, D. G. (1981). Sociopathy and antisocial behavior: Theory and treatment. In S. M. Turner, K. S. Calhoun, & H. E. Adams (Eds.), *Handbook of clinical behavior therapy* (pp. 665–712). New York: Wiley.

Sutker, P. B., Moan, C. E., Goist, K. C., & Allain, A. N. (1984). MMPI subtypes and antisocial behaviors in adolescent alcohol and drug abusers. *Drug and Alcohol Dependence, 13*, 235–244.

Thurstone, L. L. (1953). *Examiner manual for the Thurstone Temperament Schedule.* Chicago, IL: Science Research Associates.

Watson, N., Harris, W. G., Johnson, J. H., & LaBeck, L. (1983). MMPI clinical and content norms for a mixed psychiatric adolescent population. *Journal of Clinical Psychology, 39*, 696–709.

Weiner, I. B., & Del Gaudio, A. C. (1976). Psychopathology in adolescence: An epidemiological study. *Archives of General Psychiatry, 33*, 187–193.

Welsh, G. S. (1956). Factor dimensions A and R. In G. S. Welsh & W. G. Dahlstrom (Eds.), *Basic reading on the MMPI in Psychology and Medicine.* Minneapolis: University of Minnesota.

Westendorp, M. D., & Kirk, L. B. (1982). Characteristics of adolescents treated at six different treatment settings. *Adolescence, 18*, 19–35.

Williams, C. L. (1985). Use of the MMPI with adolescents. In J. N. Butcher & J. R. Graham (Eds.), *Clinical applications of the MMPI* (pp. 37–39). Minneapolis: University of Minnesota Department of Conferences.

Williams, C. L., Butcher, J. N., & Graham, J. R. (1986, March). *Appropriate MMPI norms for adolescents: An old problem revisited.* Paper presented at the 21st Annual Symposium on Recent Developments in the Use of the MMPI, Clearwater, FL.

Wimbish, L. G. (1984). *The importance of appropriate norms for the computerized interpretation of adolescent MMPI profiles.* Unpublished doctoral dissertation, Ohio State University. Columbus, Ohio.

Wirt, R. D., & Briggs, P. F. (1959). Personality and environmental factors in the development of delinquency. *Psychological Monographs: General and Applied*, Whole No. 485, 1–47.

Wirt, R. D., Lachar, D., Klinedinst, J. E., Seat, P. D., & Broen, W. E. (1982). *The Personality Inventory for Children (PIC), Revised Format.* Los Angeles Western Psychological Services.

Wisniewski, N. M., Glenwick, D. S., & Graham, J. R. (1985). MacAndrew Scale and sociodemographic correlates of adolescent alcohol and drug use. *Addictive Behaviors, 10*, 55–67.

Wolfson, K. P., & Erbaugh, S. E. (1984). Adolescent responses to the MacAndrew Alcoholism Scale. *Journal of Consulting and Clinical Psychology, 52*, 625–630.

Wolking, W. D., Dunteman, G. H., & Bailey, J. P. (1967). Multivariate analysis of parents' MMPIs based on the psychiatric diagnosis of their children. *Journal of Consulting Psychology, 31*, 521–24.

Wolking, W. D., Quast, W., & Lawton, J. J. (1966). MMPI profiles of the parents of behaviorally disturbed children and parents from the general population. *Journal of Clinical Psychology, 22*, 39–48.

AUTHOR INDEX

SUBJECT INDEX